RELIGIOUS AND SECULAR REFORM IN AMERICA

European Papers in American History
SERIES EDITOR: DAVID K. ADAMS

1. REFLECTIONS ON AMERICAN EXCEPTIONALISM
   Edited by David K. Adams and Cornelis A. van Minnen

2. FROM THEODORE ROOSEVELT TO FDR: INTERNATIONALISM AND ISOLATIONISM IN AMERICAN FOREIGN POLICY
   Edited by Daniela Rossini

3. TOWARDS A NEW AMERICAN NATION? REDEFINITIONS AND RECONSTRUCTION
   Edited by Anna Maria Martellone

4. AMERICAN AND EUROPEAN NATIONAL IDENTITIES: FACES IN THE MIRROR
   Edited by Stephen Fender

5. ASPECTS OF WAR IN AMERICAN HISTORY
   Edited by David K. Adams and Cornelis A. van Minnen

6. RELIGIOUS AND SECULAR REFORM IN AMERICA: IDEAS, BELIEFS AND SOCIAL CHANGE
   Edited by David K. Adams and Cornelis A. van Minnen

7. THE ROOSEVELT YEARS: NEW PERSPECTIVES ON AMERICAN HISTORY, 1933–1945
   Edited by Robert A. Garson and Stuart Kidd

Religious and Secular Reform in America

Ideas, Beliefs and Social Change

Edited by David K. Adams
and Cornelis A. van Minnen

SERIES EDITOR: DAVID K. ADAMS

Edinburgh University Press

© in this edition Edinburgh University Press, 1999
Copyright in the individual contributions is retained by the authors.

Edinburgh University Press
22 George Square, Edinburgh

Typeset in Janson Text by
Carnegie Publishing, Chatsworth Rd, Lancaster, and
printed and bound in Great Britain by
Cambridge University Press

A CIP catalogue record for this book is available from the British Library

ISBN 1 85331 247 9 (cased)
ISBN 1 85331 249 5 (limp)

The right of the contributors to be identified
as authors of this work has been asserted
in accordance with the Copyright, Designs
and Patents Act 1988

Contents

    Notes on Contributors   vii

    Introduction   xi
    David K. Adams and Cornelis A. van Minnen

1. Reform, Authority and Conflict in the Churches of the Middle Colonies, 1700–1770   1
   Mark Häberlein

2. 'The Perfect Law of Liberty': Radical Religion and the Democratization of New England, 1780–1840   29
   Louis Billington

3. Unitarian Voluntary Societies and the Revision of Elite Authority in Boston, 1780–1820   51
   Anthony Mann

4. Orestes Brownson and the Relationship between Reform and Democracy   77
   Naomi Wulf

5. Sectarian Perfectionism and Universal Reform: The Radical Social and Political Thought of William Lloyd Garrison   91
   Louis J. Kern

6. 'Rational Recreation': Reforming Leisure in Antebellum America   121
   Robert Lewis

7. Sabbatarianism: The Intersection of Church and State in the Orchestration of Everyday Life in Nineteenth-Century America   133
   Alexis McCrossen

8. The Woman's Christian Temperance Union Reform Movement in the South in the Late Nineteenth Century   159
   Valeria Gennaro Lerda

9. War in the Social Order: The Great War and the
   Liberalization of American Quakerism   179
   Howell John Harris

10. Progressivism, Poststructuralism and the Writing of
    American History   205
    Melvyn Stokes

11. The Cultural Foundations of Democracy: The Struggle
    between a Religious and a Secular Intellectual Reform
    Movement in the American Age of Conformity   231
    Jan C. C. Rupp

12. Evangelicalism, Social Reform and the US Welfare State,
    1970–1996   249
    Axel R. Schaefer

Notes on Contributors

David K. Adams is Professor Emeritus of American Studies at Keele University, Staffordshire, United Kingdom, chair of the David Bruce Centre and series editor of 'European Papers in American History'. He has published on many aspects of twentieth-century American affairs.

Louis Billington is Senior Research Fellow in the American Studies Department at the University of Hull, United Kingdom. He is the author of many articles on eighteenth- and nineteenth-century British and American history, and has a particular interest in the social history of religion. Currently, he is working on a study of South Kingstown, Rhode Island, from the Revolution to the 1840s, focusing on its Quaker community.

Mark Häberlein teaches American and early modern history at the University of Freiburg, Germany. His research focuses on long-distance trade and merchant communities in early modern Europe as well as on colonial American social and religious history. His publications include *Von Oberrhein zum Susquehanna. Studien zur badischen Auswanderung nach Pennsylvania im 18. Jahrhundert* (1993).

Howell John Harris is Reader in History at the University of Durham, United Kingdom. He is the author of *The Right to Manage: Industrial Relations Policies of American Business in the 1940s* (1982) and co-editor of *Industrial Democracy in America: The Ambiguous Promise* (1993). His book *The Rise and Fall of the Open Shop Order: Masters, Unions, and Men in the Philadelphia Medal Trades, 1890–1940* is scheduled for publication in 1999.

Louis J. Kern is Professor of History at Hofstra University, Hempstead, New York where he teaches American Studies, cultural history, film and popular culture. He is the author of *An Ordered Love: Sex Roles and Sexuality in Victorian Utopias* (1981), and co-editor of *Women in Spiritual and Communitarian Societies in the US* (1993). His current research interests centre on sexuality and gender, free love, and the encultured body.

Valeria Gennaro Lerda is Professor of North American History at the University of Genoa, Italy, and director of its Center for Euro-

Atlantic Studies. Her research interests focus on the United States South (Populism and Progressivism, women's history, and reform movements), and western Canada. Her books include *Dall' Arcadia alle Riforme: Studi sul Sud degli Stati Uniti* (1992) and *'Il suono delle nostre voci': Il riformismo sociale delle donne nel Sud degli Stati Uniti* (1992).

Robert Lewis is Lecturer in American history and American and Canadian Studies at the University of Birmingham, United Kingdom. His major teaching and research interests include US nineteenth-century popular culture, middle-class culture, and slavery in the antebellum American South.

Anthony Mann is currently completing a doctoral thesis in the Department of American Studies at Keele University and taught at the Universities of Hull, Manchester and Keele, United Kingdom. His work focuses upon the nature of social and economic elites in post-Revolutionary Boston, Massachusetts.

Alexis McCrossen is Assistant Professor of American social and cultural history at Southern Methodist University in Dallas, Texas. Her research interests include consumer culture, the Great Depression, time-consciousness and lived religion. She is the author of *Holy Day, Holiday: The American Sunday* (1998).

Cornelis A. van Minnen is Executive Director of the Roosevelt Study Center in Middelburg, The Netherlands. He is the author of *American Diplomats in the Netherlands, 1815–1850* (1993) and the co-editor of *FDR and His Contemporaries: Foreign Perceptions of an American President* (1992), *Reflections on American Exceptionalism* (1994), and *Aspects of War in American History* (1997).

Jan C. C. Rupp is Senior Fellow at the Amsterdam School for Social Science Research of the University of Amsterdam, The Netherlands. In 1997 he published *Van oude en nieuwe universiteiten* (*The Transformation of the University: The Superseding of German by American Influences on Scholarship and Higher Learning in the Netherlands, 1945–1995*). His research interests include religious-political reform movements, and the political economy of public and private academic exchange programmes.

Axel R. Schaefer is Assistant Professor at the Center for US Studies at Martin Luther University Halle-Wittenberg, Germany. He has published articles on nineteenth- and twentieth-century US social and intellectual history. His book *Social Ethics and Police Power: American Progressives and German Reform, 1890–1920* is scheduled for publication in 1998. His current research project focuses on the relationship between Evangelicalism and the modern US welfare state.

Melvyn Stokes teaches in the Department of History of University College London. He is the editor of *Race and Class in the American South Since 1890* (1994), *The Market Revolution in America* (1996), and *The United States and the European Alliance Since 1945* (forthcoming). His research interests are the intellectual and discursive history of Progressivism in the United States and American film history.

Naomi Wulf is Assistant Professor of American history at the Anglo-American Studies Department of the University of Paris XII-Val de Marne. She co-edited *Vie privée, bien public. Histoire de la sociabilité américaine* (1997) and is currently preparing for publication her PhD. dissertation on the idea of democracy in the early American Republic. Her main research interest is political thought in antebellum America.

Introduction

David K. Adams
Cornelis A. van Minnen

At its creation the United States, beguiled by the Enlightenment and enthused by a sense of destiny as the embodiment of liberty, believed that by its successful revolution from Britain it had launched a *novus ordo seclorum*. Change was the midwife of this new nation and reform its characteristic, despite a continuing tory presence. The well-springs of reform lay deep in the religious and ideological traditions of colonial America. Apart from Native Americans and, later, blacks brought in as slaves, the land had been settled by two main groups: those seeking religious freedom for the worship of God and the salvation of souls, and those aspiring to material improvement in their condition through the pursuit of individual economic gain. The availability of land, and perceptions of a greater degree of political and social democracy in the distant colonies, lured Europeans across the Atlantic. The result of one hundred and fifty years of development was the Declaration of Independence of 1776 and, after years of war, recognition by Britain of American independence in the treaty of peace of 1783.

The Founding Fathers generally subscribed to eighteenth-century philosophical beliefs in progress, and their republican ideals and achievements re-invigorated an older sense of the 'newness' of the New World and of its destiny that had been carried by the Pilgrim Fathers to New England. The Puritan Edward Johnson saw it as 'the place where the Lord will create a new Heaven, and a new faith, new Churches, and a new Commonwealth together,' and John Winthrop referred to the 'city upon a hill, the eyes of all people upon us.' This sense of destiny, of being what Herman Melville in the nineteenth century termed a 'peculiar, chosen people, the Israel of our times; we bear the ark of the liberties of the world,' was to permeate the American experience from colonial to modern times. The journalist John Louis O'Sullivan in the 1840s called it 'manifest destiny,' a phrase that was to reverberate through the decades and provide a justification for imperialism. It is not surprising that the nation state vigorously asserted its identity. A Yankee-Protestant tradition lived uncertainly at times with the Church of Rome, Mormonism and innumerable sects of varied persuasion, but all existed within a socio-political culture that emphasized liberty and democracy. Of course, definitions changed from time to time, and there were the inevitable conflicts that differing interests prescribed, but at all times society and its *mores* were rigorously reviewed by some, and reform movements flourished.

It is the agendas and interactions of a number of reform movements that are addressed in this volume. The chapters do not necessarily constitute a history of secular and religious reform movements in American history. Such a project would, in any case, require many volumes. Each essay approaches a particular phenomenon and is based on original research. The volume is organized in a roughly chronological sequence and illuminates a number of the sacerdotal and secular phases of a reform impulse that is the counterpoint to national consensus in American history.

Conflict is inherent in reform, and the opening chapter by Mark Häberlein reviews the historiography of the Great Awakening in the eighteenth century through analysis of four sects in the middle colonies. He examines their institutional development, and also the internal conflicts within these churches. His conclusion is that the Great Awakening should be considered in a wider time frame and that the highly competitive colonial environment, with its variety of religious groups and mixed ethnic stock, led to a heightened sense of denominational identity rather than contributing to a developing sense of national consciousness. Louis Billington then analyzes radical Evangelicalism in New England in the half-century or so that straddles the American Revolution and the establishment of American independence. He places the movement in a wider context of rapid socio-economic change and the growth of the market economy. In Chapter 3, Anthony Mann extends this analysis by exploring the involvement of Boston Unitarians in voluntary associations for civic and personal improvement in the early national period.

Within the general context of religion and reform, Chapter 4 by Naomi Wulf addresses the role of Orestes Brownson, a triumphal figure in the ferment of ideas in the 1830s. He left Congregationalism for Unitarianism and became active in most contemporary reform movements, with a particular concern for the relationship between the liberty of the individual and the needs of the wider social community. Community rights led him to accept a positive role for government in a democratic state. This was to be a recurring theme for reformers thereafter.

In antebellum America, socio-political debates came to be dominated by the conflict between abolitionists and those who defended the institution of slavery. Chapter 5 by Louis Kern presents a discussion of the perfectionist vision of William Lloyd Garrison, founder of the anti-slavery journal *The Liberator* and one of the leading publicists for the abolitionist movement in the decades before the eventual outbreak of the Civil War. Garrison enlarged the debate by appealing to a higher, or natural, law that justified resistence to the authority of the state 'and spirited opposition to the law of society'.

Society, of course, was both expansionist and complex, and despite the pressures of enforced work and labour it was not without leisure. In a highly individual research exercise, Robert Lewis examines the development of commercially motivated leisure activities and amusements that were some of the harbingers of later social change. He shows how by 1854 Edward Everett Hale could believe that 'recreation or amusement are but other names for rest,' a considerable change in outlook from that of Samuel Rodman, a New Bedford Quaker merchant twenty years before, who believed the mainstream theatre to be immoral and 'fashionable gaiety' and 'fancy balls' unacceptable.

Within the tumult of American society during its developing years Sabbatarianism gathered renewed momentum and managed 'to inscribe its meanings for Sunday onto American life and into statute law'. Its methods, as revealed by Alexis McCrossen, were both persuasive and coercive; and they were successful. Vociferous from 1810, and active throughout the nineteenth century, its influence can still be traced in the late twentieth century when, despite secularization, the state is still in many ways prepared to regard the Sabbath as different from the traditional working week.

Amongst the many reform movements that flourished in the great melting pot of late nineteenth-century America, characterized by massive population movements, the rise of great cities, corporate industry and the increasing mechanization of agriculture, was temperance. Its roots lay deep in the puritan past, and churches and temperance organizations increasingly looked to the states for legislation to control the supply and sale of liquor. Valeria Gennaro Lerda combines in her research the concerns of present-day scholarship with regionalism and gender in her chapter on the Women's Christian Temperance Union in the South in the late nineteenth century.

The movement away from national generalizations that necessarily simplify history also finds expression in the growth of local studies, witnessed by Anthony Mann's earlier essay on Boston Unitarians and civic improvements. This tradition is upheld by the award-winning historian Howell John Harris in his chapter on 'War in the Social Order', exploring the particular responses of Philadelphia Quakers to the ethical and philosophical challenges presented by the Great War. In it are questioned the nature of millennianism, capitalism and the contemporary socio-economic order.

The Progressive Movement of the early twentieth century, and also Progressivism more generally, has exercised many historians to the extent that it has come to be regarded not as a movement for fundamental reform but rather one for the defence of capitalism – as if the two are mutually exclusive! In his innovative philosophical and semantic analysis, Melvyn Stokes considers Progressivism in the light of postmodern and poststructuralist theories, particularly those of Foucault and Derrida. His interest in the interaction of language, power and the conceptualization of political ideas suggests that Progressivism merits being placed once again at the forefront of the historians' intellectual agenda.

Jan Rupp perhaps would not dissent from this. He questions the periodicity customarily given to twentieth-century American history, beginning with the Progressive period. Primarily concerned with the 'so-called consensus driven Forties and Fifties,' he suggests that in fact they embrace a great number of national discourses that were often mutually antagonistic. In its sociological and linguistic concerns and questioning of received wisdom, his essay, like that of Melvyn Stokes, moves the debate about reform from the empirical to a discourse about the nature of knowledge, the self and society.

The final essay in this volume, by Axel Schaefer, draws together the secular with the well established tradition of reform movements based in religious groups. Schaefer considers Evangelicalism, social reform and the welfare state in the United States from 1970 to 1996. His conclusion is that the classic conflict between 'scientific charity' and 'religious philanthropy' still infuses the system of social provision in the United States.

This volume is based on the idea that the interaction of comparative views helps to break down national preoccupations, and it therefore contains several chapters from European contributors as well as Americans. Together, the published papers illuminate the reform tradition in America. The publication of this volume was made possible by the generous sponsorship of the Roosevelt Study Center, Middelburg, The Netherlands; the Franklin and Eleanor Roosevelt Institute, Hyde Park, New York; USIS, The Hague; and the David Bruce Centre for American Studies at Keele University. And last, but certainly not least, we acknowledge with gratitude the indispensable and most efficient secretarial services of Leontien Joosse of the Roosevelt Study Center and Tracy Chesworth of Keele University throughout the project.

1

Reform, Authority and Conflict in the Churches of the Middle Colonies, 1700–1770

Mark Häberlein

Introduction

The religious revivals of the 1740s known as the Great Awakening have long been recognized as the first major intercolonial movement in eighteenth-century America. During the past two decades, however, this movement has been subject to considerable scholarly debate and reinterpretation. Whereas the revivals have been long been regarded as a sudden and momentous outburst of religious renewal after a long period of spiritual decline, recent studies note the persistent vitality and steady growth of churches in the eighteenth-century American colonies.[1] While some scholars have emphasized the Awakening's challenge to traditional sources of authority and the emancipation of the laity from clerical leadership,[2] others have pointed to organizational efforts and pro-authoritarian attitudes of leading revivalist ministers.[3] In 1982, Jon Butler even challenged the whole concept of a Great Awakening. For Butler, the Great Awakening was essentially a nineteenth-century construct, an 'interpretative fiction' that 'distorts the character of eighteenth-century American religious life and misinterprets its relationship to pre-revolutionary American society and politics.' He views the revivals as disconnected local and regional events that produced few lasting social or political changes.[4]

While most recent scholars have not followed Butler's advice and retain the label 'Great Awakening',[5] there is a growing consensus that the mid-eighteenth-century revivals should be analyzed in a long-term perspective that ties them to patterns of migration, settlement, cultural transfer and the organizational development of churches in the New World. Much recent scholarship on eighteenth-century religion has focused on the 'middle colonies,' the ethnically and culturally heterogeneous group of provinces including New York, New Jersey, Pennsylvania and Delaware. Historians have thus begun to move away from the long-held notion that social and cultural developments in puritan New England provided an appropriate model for British

America as a whole; instead, there is a growing awareness that the middle colonies in fact constituted America's first plural societies and thus a particularly fruitful field for studying the interaction of diverse ethnic and religious groups.[6]

Most recent studies of religious and social life in the middle colonies can be divided into three groups. First, a number of scholars have traced the development of individual ethnic or religious groups – Scottish and Scotch-Irish Presbyterians, British Quakers, Dutch Reformed, or German Lutherans – and examined their adaptation to their New World environment.[7] Second, several studies have focused on the interaction of people from diverse ethnic and religious backgrounds in specific localities or provinces in order to show how concepts of religious toleration and pluralistic societies were worked out in practice.[8] Third, several recent works have treated ethno-religious distinctions as secondary to issues of social class.[9]

In this paper, I adopt a comparative approach. By looking at the institutional development and internal conflicts in four colonial churches – the Dutch Reformed, Presbyterian, German Lutheran and German Reformed – and placing their experiences within the larger context of colonial developments, I attempt to show how patterns of migration and settlement were related to issues of religious reform and institutional authority, and what solutions were found to intradenominational conflicts over matters of doctrine, ministerial qualifications, and the proper distribution of power. The four denominations studied here accounted for well over half the congregations in mid-eighteenth century New York, New Jersey and Pennsylvania.[10] In addition, certain common features of these churches such as their reliance on a trained, ordained ministry, their emergence from a state church tradition in the Old World and the impact of religious reform movements such as pietism and Evangelicalism upon all of them, make comparative examination possible.[11]

It seems useful to analyze the development of these four churches in three chronological steps. First, I will examine the dynamics of settlement and migration and the organizational efforts among the various colonial denominations up to 1740. A series of bitter conflicts among clergymen as well as between ministers and laymen during that period highlight the peculiar problems of religious reform and the strong position of the laity well before the coming of the Great Awakening. The second part will attempt to show how the Great Awakening of the 1740s influenced the patterns of lay participation, while Evangelical ministers simultaneously emphasized religious renewal, clerical authority and doctrinal integrity. Religious revival and institutional growth emerge as parallel processes during the peak years of the awakening. The third part, covering the 1750s and 1760s, deals with the complex legacy of the Great Awakening and examines how the movement encouraged both interdenominational cooperation and increased denominational consciousness. In addition, this last section will examine the churches' efforts to meet the organizational problems caused by continuing immigration, population growth and the inability of European church bodies to meet the growing demand for qualified ministers. The central argument is that movements for reform and renewal within the colonial churches involved complex negotiations – and sometimes intense conflicts – over the distribution of authority among ministers and laymen.

Migration Patterns, Organizational Problems, and Intradenominational Conflict Before 1740

During the first decades of the eighteenth century, the dynamics of migration and settlement confronted each of the four churches considered here with strong challenges. As large numbers of German and Scotch-Irish settlers arrived in the middle colonies and Dutch, Scottish and English settlers fanned out from older areas of settlement, the Reformed, Presbyterian and Lutheran churches struggled to meet the colonists' demand for spiritual solace.

About 9,000 people were living in New Netherland when the English took over the colony in 1664. Many were recent immigrants who had arrived during a large wave of migration that had brought 3,000 to 4,000 settlers to the Dutch colony between 1657 and 1664. While the Dutch Reformed Church had been the established church during the New Netherland period, the presence of English and Scottish dissenters, German Lutherans, French-speaking Walloons and other non-Dutch groups of settlers had prevented the formation of a culturally homogeneous society in the province from the beginning. Despite the English conquest and the fact that migration from the Netherlands to North America between 1664 and the end of colonial period was insignificant, the Dutch retained a strong presence due to natural increase and the inability of New York to attract large numbers of English settlers.[12]

The Classis of Amsterdam, which had supervised the Dutch Reformed clergy of the colony since the New Netherland period, continued to send ministers to New York, but the supply did not meet the demand created by demographic growth and internal migration. By 1700, declining economic opportunities, growing pressure for anglicization and political discontent that had erupted in the insurrection known as Leisler's Rebellion in 1689, caused significant numbers of Dutch farmers and artisans to leave the older areas of settlement in New York and on Long Island and move to the upper Hudson and Mohawk Valleys and into northern New Jersey. New York's orthodox Dutch Reformed ministers, who had allied with the colony's English ruling class since the conquest of 1664 and later opposed Leisler's Rebellion, left the settlers on the frontier to pietistic preachers who lacked formal training for the ministry. Since the early 1690s, Guiliam Bertholf, a cooper by trade and former parishioner of the influential Dutch pietist Jacob Koelman, ministered to the Dutch Reformed in New Jersey and organized a number of congregations there. In 1694, he was ordained by the pietist-oriented Classis of Walcheren.[13] In the first decade of the eighteenth century, the activities of the pietist minister Bernardus Freeman, whose ordination at Lingen was not considered valid by the orthodox New York *Dominies*, caused a schism in the Dutch Reformed congregations on Long Island.[14]

From 1720 onwards, Dutch Reformed pietism found its strongest and most controversial advocate in Theodorus Jacobus Frelinghuysen, a native of Westphalia who had served as pastor in East Friesland and ministered to the Dutch settlers in the Raritan Valley of New Jersey after his arrival in America. Frelinghuysen's pietism and his insistence on judging the spiritual state of others quickly offended both the orthodox New York ministers and a number of his parishioners. By restricting access to the communion table to those who had experienced spiritual rebirth, by exercising strict ecclesiastical discipline and forming conventicles, Frelinghuysen built up a loyal following particularly among his younger and poorer parishioners, while his assertion of ministerial leadership and his inclination to censor others alienated many wealthier members of his congregations. In 1725, his opponents filed a lengthy complaint against Frelinghuysen which started 'one of the longest and most bitter ecclesiastical disputes in colonial history.'[15]

Frelinghuysen's controversial ministry highlights the ambiguous effects of the pietists' efforts at religious renewal on the relations between ministers and laymen. On one hand, Frelinghuysen appealed to rural settlers who were alienated from traditional religious and political authorities, and assigned prominent roles to lay leaders. Thus Hendrik Visscher, a schoolmaster who had accompanied Frelinghuysen to the New World, became lay preacher in the Raritan congregation and translated Frelinghuysen's sermons for publication in English. On the other hand, the minister's behaviour was resented by those economically successful laymen who had played a prominent role in their communities' affairs before Frelinghuysen's arrival and now resisted his attempts to censor and control them.[16] Pietistic ministers like Frelinghuysen, it appears, did not encourage greater lay participation *per se*, but tried to alter the power structure within the congregation by promoting those laymen who were their most loyal supporters.[17]

Presbyterianism in the middle colonies originated from two distinct sources. While Puritan settlers from New England established Presbyterian congregations on Long Island and in New Jersey since the late seventeenth century, Scottish and Scotch-Irish settlers transplanted Presbyterianism directly from the Old World. Scottish immigrants began arriving in significant numbers in the 1680s when the efforts to colonize east New Jersey attracted several hundred settlers from diverse religious backgrounds. Migration from Scotland to America probably remained well below 1,000 in each of the first three decades of the eighteenth century and may have ranged around 2,000 in the 1730s. Immigration from northern as well as southern Ireland, however, steadily increased during the first half of the eighteenth century. High rents, bad harvests, rising grain prices and economic depression led to a rise in emigration figures from Ireland since the late 1720s. According to recent estimates, 4,400 northern and 7,400 southern Irish reached the colonies in the 1730s. Most of these immigrants were Presbyterian, and many settled in the middle colonies.[18]

The Presbyterian church was better prepared than either the Dutch or German churches to meet the challenges of demographic growth. Never dependent on European church authorities, Presbyterian ministers established a presbytery in Philadelphia with power to examine and ordain ministerial candidates as early as 1706 and organized a synod in 1716. In the latter year, twenty-seven Presbyterian ministers served thirty congregations, nearly all of them in the middle colonies. By 1740, the number of presbyteries had grown to six, the number of ministers to fifty. Although lay elders were permitted to attend synodical conferences, ministers clearly controlled them.[19] Despite these organizational achievements, the influx of ministers from Scotland, Ireland and New England did not keep pace with the growth of congregations – a situation which ministers like William Tennent Sr sought to remedy by establishing their own private training schools for ministers.[20]

Recent studies have emphasized the fact that the rise of revivalism among colonial Presbyterians and the controversies within the Synod during the 1720s and 1730s were closely linked to developments in the Old World. As Marilyn Westerkamp and Leigh Eric Schmidt have shown, religious revivalism with its emotional forms of worship and its emphasis on conversion and spiritual renewal flourished in Scotland and Northern Ireland since the 1620s and survived even under the difficult circumstances of the Restoration period. Of central importance in Scottish and Scotch-Irish religion were the communion feasts – highly ritualized mass gatherings that lasted several days and featured multiple sermons exhorting the audience to confession of their sins and acceptance of God's saving grace. When thousands of Scottish and Scotch-Irish migrants resettled in the New World, they transferred the tradition of the communion feast to America. 'The sacramental occasion,' Schmidt has argued, 'was ideally suited to this colonal situation, to holding an immigrant group together in the face of the fragmenting effects of having been uprooted ... For colonial Presbyterians they were an opportunity to come together, to heal breaches between neighbors, and to invigorate a camaraderie that made their dispersed, regional communities work.'[21]

But not only Scotch-Irish piety and sacramental rituals found their way to the middle colonies: theological debates that divided the Old World clergy reached the New World Presbyterians as well. In the 1720s, the Synod of Ulster had split over the question of subscription to the Westminster Confession of Faith. This conflict illustrates the differences that had developed between Scottish and Irish Presbyterianism by the early eighteenth century. While subscription to the document was readily accepted in Scotland where Presbyterianism was the established national church since 1689, Irish Presbyterians were a dissenting minority whose ministers depended on the voluntary support of their congregations. While the Irish non-subscribers, who represented the progressive elite of Ulster's ministers, argued that the church had no authority to enforce adherence to a written doctrinal statement, a majority of ministers and laymen thought subscription necessary in order to maintain the purity of the church and prevent the spread of heresy.[22] When the issue of subscription was raised at the synodical meetings of American Presbyterians in 1722 and 1727, the clergy divided over essentially the same arguments as the Ulster ministers. The subscription controversy in the colonies pitted a majority of the Scottish and Scotch-Irish ministers, who emphasized the authority of the synod and the importance of doctrinal integrity, against the New England ministers, who argued for local congregational autonomy, the sole authority of the Bible in doctrinal matters, and the freedom of individual conscience. The leader of the New England group, Jonathan Dickinson, was well aware of the fact that his position in the controversy exactly mirrored that of the Irish non-subscribers.[23]

While the Adopting Act of 1729 represented a compromise between the two factions, the controversy over subscription merged with the issues of ministerial qualifications, itinerancy and revivalism to create a deepening rift in the synod in the 1730s. Several ministers who had received their training in William Tennent's so-called 'Log College' started local revivals in New Jersey and Pennsylvania from the late 1720s. In the agrarian community of Freehold, New Jersey, for example, the arrival of the Evangelical ministers Theodorus Jacobus Frelinghuysen and Gilbert Tennent caused a split within the ethnically mixed community which forced the Presbyterian minister Joseph Morgan, a native of New England who had served the congregation for two decades, to withdraw. In 1730, a leading lay member of the congregation, the Scot Walter Ker, recruited the Log College graduate John Tennent for the vacant congregation. During the early 1730s, John Tennent and his brother William, Jr led a revival among the community's Scottish and Scotch-Irish settlers.[24] The conservative majority of Scotch-Irish ministers responded to the revivalist activities of the Log College men by tightening the subscription requirements in 1736, demanding synodical examination of ministerial candidates and censoring the 'intrusions' of itinerant ministers into vacant congregations. The laity, which had largely stayed out of the subscription controversy, meanwhile demonstrated its sympathies by supporting the revivals led by the Evangelical Tennent group.[25]

The situation among colonial Presbyterians by the late 1730s was thus characterized by growing divisions among a unified, highly organized body of ministers. Among the German Lutheran and Reformed settlers in the middle colonies, by contrast, clerical leadership was virtually non-existent before the 1740s. The few men who ministered to the thousands of Lutheran and Reformed immigrants in the first decades of the eighteenth century worked largely on their own and frequently clashed with their parishioners. While radical Pietists and sectarian groups had predominated among the early German settlers who came to Pennsylvania in the 1680s and 1690s, Lutheran and Reformed migrants outnumbered the sectarians after 1700. While several thousand southwest Germans were transported to New York during a first mass exodus in 1709–1710, German migration to Pennsylvania started on a larger scale in the late 1720s and gradually increased in size during the following decades. An estimated 13,000 Germans reached the American colonies during the 1730s, the majority settling in the Delaware valley.[26]

Before the 1740s, European church authorities made only weak efforts to supply the rapidly increasing number of German colonists with pastors. From 1733 to 1742, the only ordained Lutheran pastor in Pennsylvania was Johann Caspar Stoever, and his ordination was of dubious validity by European standards. Stoever's ministry ranged over a wide area, and although he performed more than 1,400 baptisms and close to 400 marriages during that period, he could visit most Lutheran congregations in Pennsylvania only infrequently. Swedish Lutheran pastors and irregular ministers, mostly former schoolteachers, could not fill this vacuum effectively. The German Reformed fared only slightly better: the few ordained pastors who came to Pennsylvania since the mid-1720s worked independently of each other; they had to share the field with a number of untrained, unordained ministers, and one of their most capable men, Johann Peter Miller, left the Reformed ministry in 1735 to join the radical pietist community at Ephrata.[27] In 1740, three Reformed pastors had to serve twenty-six congregations, and the only Lutheran pastor – Johann Caspar Stoever – twenty-seven congregations in Pennsylvania.[28]

Moreover, conflicts between the few Lutheran and Reformed clergymen and their parishioners were endemic in the 1730s. Caspar Stoever reportedly was engaged in a salary dispute with one of his congregations in late 1734, and the following year a number of the Lutherans at Tulpehocken (Berks County, Pennsylvania) left his congregation, complaining later about the minister's abusive and devious behaviour. Wilhelm Berkenmeyer, an orthodox Lutheran minister in New York, called Stoever a deceiver and vagabond preacher.[29] In New Jersey's Raritan Valley, the Lutheran congregation was locked in a bitter dispute with their pastor, Johann August Wolf, within a year of his being sent to the colonies by the consistory of Hamburg in 1734. While the parishioners charged their pastor with neglecting his ministerial duties and leading a dissolute life, Wolf accused the congregation of not paying him the salary they had promised him in their call. The conflict dragged on until 1745, when Wolf obtained financial compensation for withdrawing from the community.[30]

Given the small number and often dubious qualifications of Lutheran and German Reformed pastors and the conflicts which racked the Pennsylvania and New Jersey congregations, it is not surprising that pastors writing to Europe described the colonies as a spiritual wilderness and German church people as a confused multitude who lost their faith and fell prey to radical sects.[31] While the religious diversity of the middle colonies, the shortage of regular ministers and the lack of support from state authorities were certainly unsettling to pastors coming from a state church background, their bleak descriptions should not be accepted at face value. A crucial factor in the early development of Lutheran and Reformed congregations in the middle colonies was the initiative of laymen. In the absence of religious institutions and resident ministers, Lutheran and Reformed settlers assembled voluntarily for prayer, the singing of hymns and the reading of sermons. Under the direction of pious elders, Lutheran and Reformed laymen built churches, often under difficult financial conditions, and invited unordained men to conduct religious services in order to maintain their confessional identity and reconstitute community life in a religiously diverse, intensely competitive environment. In addition to providing scattered immigrant communities with a religious focus, laymen who organized congregational life on their own initiative learned important lessons about self-government in the New World.[32]

By the late 1730s, therefore, far from declining all four churches considered here had experienced several decades of expansion and some measure of consolidation. The Presbyterians were most successful in building up institutions for governing church affairs and asserting ministerial authority. Lay support was crucial, however, in determining the success of locally trained Evangelical ministers. Among the Dutch Reformed, internal migration had opened a wide field for pietist ministers who closely collaborated with groups of like-minded laymen. Within both the Presbyterian and Dutch Reformed churches, religious reformers' efforts at spiritual rebirth and moral renewal met with strong opposition from orthodox ministers and some influential laymen. The German Lutherans and Reformed suffered most severely from a shortage of trained ministers and a lack of organizational unity, but pious laymen had gone to great lengths to form congregations and reconstitute local religious communities. In the future, these laymen would often hesitate to yield control to newly-arrived ministers who held their own notions of authority.

Ministerial Authority, Lay Participation, and Institutional Development During the Great Awakening

By the late 1730s,[33] local revivals were well under way among Presbyterians, Dutch Reformed and German Sectarians in the middle colonies, and the Moravian missionary Augustus Gottlieb Spangenberg even perceived 'signs of a waking-up' among German church people in Pennsylvania.[34] Nevertheless, nearly all scholars agree that George Whitefield's arrival in 1739 changed the scope and character of revivalism in the middle colonies. According to Ned Landsman, the revivals among the Scottish settlers of New Jersey were of a distinctly Presbyterian and 'nativistic' character until Whitefield's preaching tour broke down ethnic and denominational boundaries and brought diverse ethnic and religious groups together in a unified intercolonial movement in which Scottish ministers and elders, however, retained positions of leadership.[35] While revivalists like Gilbert Tennent had published a number of sermons since the 1730s, thereby appealing to readers beyond the boundaries of individual congregations,[36] Whitefield's innovative use of the print media and his aggressive marketing strategies (including advance publicity through newspaper advertising) were directed at a much larger audience. In fact, recent studies have suggested that Whitefield's adaptation of commercial strategies to religious purposes and his willingness to cross traditional denominational and territorial boundaries pioneered new ways of bringing religious messages to a mass public and creating a transatlantic Evangelical community.[37] Through his alliances with revivalist Presbyterian and Dutch Reformed ministers, Whitefield became a 'catalyst' who deepened the divisions that had troubled these churches for years.

The most prominent example of intradenominational conflict at the height of the Great Awakening was the schism that split the Presbyterian Church in 1741. The preaching tours of George Whitefield, Gilbert Tennent and other Evangelical ministers, the spread of revivals, and several sharp attacks by revivalist ministers on their 'unconverted' conservative colleagues highlighted the controversial issues of itinerancy, ministerial qualifications and revivalism and split the synod into a New Side and Old Side faction in 1741.[38] While the social outlook of the two groups was much more similar than contemporary polemics and some later historians suggest, there were differences nonetheless. Old Side ministers were mostly mature men who were already advanced in their careers, and many had received their education in Scotland and gathered some professional experience there or in Ulster; the New Side men were younger and had either been born in the colonies or had migrated there in their youth. Patricia Bonomi has suggested that these differences may account for the 'respect for discipline and ecclesiastical order' of the Old Side and the 'anti-institutionalism' of the New Side men.[39] The importance of ethnic origins in the schism is not clear. While Elizabeth Nybakken has noted the 'Irish' character of the Old Side men who refused to compromise on the question of ministerial education, but – in her view – were liberal in matters of creed and ecclesiastical hierarchy,[40] Marilyn Westerkamp found the Scotch-Irish ministers about evenly divided between Old and New Sides.[41] Finally, Ned Landsman has argued that in New Jersey the revivals received greatest support in the oldest Scottish and Scotch-Irish congregations, and that the movement, which had begun among small farmers and artisans, drew more and more people from commercial backgrounds into its orbit as it progressed.[42]

The fact that Evangelical New Side ministers repeatedly sought the support of an awakened laity in their confrontations with their Old Side colleagues, and Gilbert Tennent's famous sermon *The Danger of an Unconverted Ministry* (1740), in which he exhorted the laity to reject ministers who neglected the experiential dimension of religion, are often cited to demonstrate that the Great Awakening led to a break with traditional patterns of ministerial authority and an emancipation of the laity.[43] It is important to note, however, that Gilbert Tennent and other Evangelicals affirmed the necessity of ministerial education, ordination, clerical discipline and leadership just as much as their opponents.[44] In fact, Tennent himself expected his advice to choose converted ministers to be followed by no more than a minority of laymen: 'And as for Breaking of Congregations to Pieces,' he argued in his controversial sermon, 'upon the Account of People's Going from Place to Place, to hear the Word, with a View to get greater Good; that spiritual Blindness and Death, that so generally prevails, will put this out of Danger. It is but a very few, that have got any spiritual Relish; the most will venture their Souls with any Formalist, and be well satisfied with the sapless Discourses of such dead Drones.' He also admonished his audience not to leave their pastors without prior application for ministerial consent.[45] Descriptions of local revivals such as Samuel Blair's account of the awakening at Fagg's Manor, Pennsylvania, emphasize the importance of ministerial direction and guidance of their parishioners' quest for spiritual rebirth. Evangelical ministers sought to bolster the revivals by sending assistants to pastors in whose congregations an awakening was underway. Thus Jonathan Dickinson, pastor at Elizabethtown, New Jersey, came to Aaron Burr's assistance during the revival at Newark, which had started in August 1739. Both pastors tried to lead the congregation to conversion and rebirth while seeking to prevent emotional excesses.[46] According to Ned Landsman and Jon Butler, Gilbert Tennent, his brothers and other New Side Presbyterians 'cultivated community, Christianity and Presbyterian adherence through long-term residential ministries' in their New Jersey and Pennsylvania parishes, and emphasized doctrinal instruction, catechization and regeneration in their pastoral work. The Tennents, moreover, styled themselves as 'holy men' who experienced supernatural intervention, apparitions and miracles.[47] Lay support, therefore, was of vital importance for the success of the New Side ministers in their struggle with the Old Side, but the Evangelicals were not prepared to give up their ministerial standards or their claims to clerical leadership.

George Whitefield's evangelizing tours also drew the Dutch Reformed revivalists into the larger movement and gave the work of ministers like Theodorus Jacobus Frelinghuysen prominence and larger significance. In 1740, Frelinghuysen and New York City's Reformed minister Gualtherus DuBois appeared on the same stage with Whitefield, and Bernardus Freeman invited the English evangelist to preach in his church at Flatbush, New York.[48] More than Whitefield's endorsement of revivalism among the Dutch Reformed, however, the controversial ministry of John Henry Goetschius rekindled the lingering conflict between the pietist and orthodox factions within the colonial Dutch church. Goetschius, the son of a Swiss Reformed pastor, had come to America at age seventeen in 1735; almost immediately after his arrival in the colonies, he had begun to minister to German and Dutch Reformed settlers in New York and Pennsylvania, arousing complaints about intrusions into settled congregations, inadequate ministerial qualifications and offensive personal behaviour. After receiving some private education from the Dutch Reformed pastor Peter Henry Dorsius, Goetschius was ordained by Dorsius, Frelinghuysen and Gilbert Tennent in 1741 and installed in several Dutch Reformed congregations on Long Island. Like earlier Dutch Reformed pietists,

Goetschius emphasized the importance of personal religious experience and the necessity of conversion. In his introduction to Goetschius' only published sermon, *The Unknown God* (1743), Frelinghuysen described his young colleague as one of 'those faithful teachers who stress inward Christianity, the necessity of rebirth of water and spirit, and godly life and conversation in and through the Spirit'. Like Frelinghuysen, Goetschius railed against the 'mocking, contemptuous, skimping Epicureans, who never stop, day or night, to reject those who experience the knowledge and worship of God, and ... who impose on many people, against their will, their old, rotten, and stinking routine of religion.' Goetschius also followed Frelinghuysen's lead when he extended his preaching beyond the bounds of his own parish and denomination and disobeyed the authority of the Classis of Amsterdam, which had declared his ordination invalid. Moreover, he attempted to consolidate his ministerial authority in his congregations by dismissing the church consistories and appointing elders loyal to him. In 1748, Goetschius finally consented to a reordination and accepted a call as associate pastor to the Dutch Reformed at Hackensack, New Jersey. His disagreements with his orthodox colleagues, however, continued in his new congregation.[49]

During his tours through the middle colonies, George Whitefield preached to German settlers as well. He drew large audiences in such centres of German settlement in Pennsylvania as Germantown and Skippack, and the Moravian Peter Boehler served as his assistant and interpreter.[50] Of crucial significance for the development of the German Lutheran and Reformed Churches during the 1740s, however, was the American tour of Count Nikolaus von Zinzendorf, the leader of the Moravian Brethren, in 1741–1742. Zinzendorf responded to the bewildering religious diversity in the middle colonies with a broad interdenominational approach: between January and July 1742, he and his followers organized seven ecumenical synods at which members of all denominations were invited to attend and discuss the possibilities for uniting behind those beliefs they all held in common. The ecumenical effort failed, as Zinzendorf's dominance of the meetings drove members of other denominations away, but the 'Congregation of God in the Spirit', as the undertaking was called, nevertheless confronted the churches of the middle colonies with the challenge to clarify their doctrinal positions and demonstrate that the mysticism, perfectionism and syncretism of the Moravians were incompatible with their own principles.[51] Accordingly, members of all denominations reacted strongly against the perceived Moravian threat. The Dutch Reformed *dominies* Fryenmoet and DuBois reported to Amsterdam that they had to deal with Moravian proselytizing in their congregations, and the Presbyterian Gilbert Tennent published a lengthy critique of Moravianism under the title *The Necessity of Holding Fast to the Truth* in 1743.[52] The German Reformed ministers Samuel Güldin and Johann Philipp Boehm also authored anti-Moravian tracts.[53]

For the German Lutherans and Reformed in the middle colonies, the Moravian challenge added to the problems of ministerial scarcity and denominational competition that had troubled them from the beginning. Heinrich Melchior Mühlenberg, who was sent from Halle to Pennsylvania in 1741 and became the dominant figure among the Lutheran pastors in the colonies, was a pietist who strove for religious renewal and sought to 'awaken' his hearers. The presence of Moravians, German sectarians and irregular ministers, however, induced Mühlenberg to take a confessionalist position and emphasize Lutheran doctrine. For Mühlenberg, therefore, pietism and orthodoxy were not mutually exclusive.[54] Mühlenberg proved to be very successful in establishing his authority in southeastern Pennsylvania's German congregations against the claims of irregular preachers and Moravian itinerants. Within weeks of his arrival in Pennsylvania, he had secured written calls from the three congregations of Philadelphia, New Hanover, and Providence, although both Nikolaus von Zinzendorf and Valentine Kraft, a minister who had been dismissed from office in Germany, challenged his authority there. During the next years, he extended his ministry to major German settlements in the middle colonies such as Germantown, Lancaster and Tulpehocken. Mühlenberg's perseverance, his willingness to itinerate between congregations spread over a wide area, and his ability to adapt to an environment in which the Lutheran church could not rely on state support and where pastors had to collaborate with groups of dedicated laymen were decisive factors in his success.[55] Mühlenberg's organizational efforts were matched by those of Michael Schlatter, a native of Switzerland, among the German Reformed. Schlatter came to Pennsylvania in 1746 with explicit instructions from the Synods of North and South Holland to bring order to the affairs of the scattered Reformed people in the colony. Within months after his arrival, Schlatter had achieved remarkable successes in securing the cooperation of other Reformed pastors and organizing a colonial coetus. For Schlatter as for Mühlenberg, itinerancy became a fact of life: between 1746 and 1750s, the Swiss pastor travelled several thousand miles to visit about fifty Reformed congregations and communities in four colonies.[56]

The consolidation of German Lutheran and Reformed congregations in the middle colonies during the Great Awakening can be measured by the number of church buildings erected. While Lutheran and Reformed congregations had built seven churches in Pennsylvania before 1738, another forty-five churches were constructed in Pennsylvania and Maryland between 1739 and 1748, thus giving the commitment of German settlers to their churches visible shape. Henry Melchior Mühlenberg had recognized the importance of church building for community development and confessional identity early in his American career, but most church buildings continued to be undertaken on lay initiative in rural areas without settled pastors.[57]

The church building boom among the Lutheran and Reformed settlers in Pennsylvania highlights the fact that the processes of religious renewal and institutional consolidation were closely linked during the 1740s. Indeed, all four denominations considered here undertook major steps toward organizational unity and stabilization during the 1740s. The New Side Presbyterians formed their own governing body, the Synod of New York, in 1745 and founded the College of New Jersey in 1746 in order to secure an adequate supply of native-trained ministers committed to experiential religion.[58] Both the Dutch and German Reformed formed their coetus in 1747, and Mühlenberg organized a Lutheran Ministerium in 1748.[59] Thus all four denominations had formed bodies for governing church affairs, exercising discipline and examining and ordaining ministerial candidates by the late 1740s. The effectiveness of these bodies in meeting the challenges of demographic and social change would be tested during the following two decades.

The Legacy of the Great Awakening

The development of the colonial Dutch Reformed Church after the Great Awakening was marked by continuing growth as well as by persistent conflicts. While the number of Dutch Reformed congregations in the colony of New York grew from forty-eight in 1750 to seventy-six in 1775, the questions of a native-trained ministry and the process of assimilation to the English language and culture continued to divide the Dutch clergy. During the 1750s and 1760s, Evangelical ministers emerged as the leading proponents of ecclesiastical self-sufficiency and ministerial training in America. John Henry Goetschius privately tutored at least fourteen ministerial candidates up to 1774, and Theodorus Frelinghuysen, Reformed pastor at Albany and son of the pietist pastor in the Raritan valley, travelled to the Netherlands in 1759 to obtain support for the establishment of a Reformed college in the colonies. Five years earlier, the plans of the coetus to establish itself as a Classis and the projected college had split the governing body of the colonial Dutch church. While the Evangelical ministers saw ecclesiastical independence as the only way to secure the survival of Dutch religion in a predominantly English environment, their conservative opponents, who organized themselves as the Conferentie Party in 1754, declared: 'Our object is that the tie between us and the churches of the Fatherland, instead of being broken, may become stronger and stronger.' The establishment of Queen's College in 1772 and the constitution of the Dutch Reformed coetus as a classis in the same year effectively decided the question of ecclesiastical independence. By 1776, more than half of the forty-one ministers active in the Dutch Reformed Church had been born and trained in America.[60]

In places such as New York City, where anglicizing tendencies among the Dutch inhabitants had been apparent since the first decades of the eighteenth century, the language question became enmeshed with the debate over revivalism when the church consistory called an English-speaking Evangelical minister whose use of the English language during services offended Dutch traditionalists as much as his insistence on religious renewal. Randall Balmer portrays the Dutch of New York City during the late colonial period as a people torn between the 'excesses of revivalism' and 'conservative reaction.' In this conflict, the orthodox Dutch Reformed lost members to both the pietists and the Anglican Church. The Dutch settlers in New Jersey, on the other hand, were drawn into the mainstream of colonial evangelical culture during the Great Awakening. In rural New Jersey, Evangelicalism provided a common language for diverse ethnic and religious groups, and inter-group contacts served to assimilate the Dutch to the larger colonial culture.[61]

David G. Hackett's portrait of religion and society in colonial Albany, however, differs markedly from Balmer's analysis of developments among the Dutch in New York City and New Jersey. According to Hackett, Albany remained a predominantly Dutch town up to the 1760s and retained a communal way of life which relied on extended family networks, hierarchical social organization, adherence to the local Dutch Reformed Church and the mediating role of the leading local merchants between the community and the outside world. The hierarchical structure of the community visibly manifested itself in the arrangement of church seats and in the fact that the social and political leaders of the community were often identical with the elders of the Reformed congregation: 'As members of the Dutch church, nearly all of the town's people submitted themselves to the leadership of this hereditary hierarchy of merchant-elders who, in turn, committed themselves to oversee the congregation's spiritual welfare in obedience to God.' Significantly, the impact of Evangelical religion on colonial Albany was relatively small, and the Dutch inhabitants successfully retained their cultural norms within an English legal system. It took the combined effects of the French and Indian War, the Revolution, the massive immigration of New Englanders since the 1790s and the socio-economic changes of the early industrial revolution to alter the Dutch communal character of Albany decisively.[62]

Within the Presbyterian, Lutheran, and German Reformed Churches, the issue of assimilation that troubled the Dutch Reformed was secondary to the central problem of reaching out to the thousands of immigrants who continued to come to the middle colonies. After fewer than 30,000 Scots had migrated to the American colonies between 1700 and 1760, about 40,000 more went to America during the 1760–1775 period. Meanwhile, Ulster migration to the American colonies rose from 9,200 during the 1740s to 14,200 in the 1750s and peaked at 21,200 during the 1760s and 13,200 during the first half of the 1770s. The total number of Ulster immigrants to the Delaware Valley for the period from 1729 to 1774 has been estimated at 52,700.[63] Such large-scale Scottish and Irish immigration confronted the colonial Presbyterian Church with grave organizational problems despite the reunification of the Old Side and New Side synods in 1758 and the fact that the College of New Jersey had trained dozens of ministers since the late 1740s. Presbyterian communities on the expanding colonial frontier suffered a constant shortage of ministers; the difficulties of organizing frontier congregations were aggravated by high rates of geographical mobility.[64] The Presbyterian clergy, which was overwhelmingly American-trained by the late 1750s, also faced a more assertive laity during the last two decades of the colonial period. The reluctance of Scotch-Irish settlers to pay for their ministers created a consistent problem of salary arrears, and more and more congregations demanded that church elders be nominated by laymen instead of ministers, and that the whole congregation elect the elders.[65] During the final years of his ministry, even the leading Evangelical Presbyterian minister of the Great Awakening, Gilbert Tennent, began to feel the disaffection of the laity with the apparent loss of his Evangelical fervour. Tennent, who had adopted a more decorous appearance during his ministry in Philadelphia, initiated the construction of an ornate new church in the city, tenaciously worked for the reunification of the two synods and redirected his attention to political affairs during the Seven Years' War, found that his congregation sought to call a young Evangelical minister, George Duffield, as his assistant and thereby check the older minister's influence in the early 1760s.[66] This case suggests that the increasing assertiveness of the Presbyterian laity at the end of the colonial period was less a direct result of the message of the Great Awakening than a response to the decline of Evangelical leadership after the leading New Side ministers had either died early (like Samuel Blair or Samuel Finley) or became more conservative (like Gilbert Tennent).

German immigration to the American colonies, mostly through the port of Philadelphia, peaked in the years 1749–1754, when more than 30,000 people – over one third of all eighteenth century German immigrants to America – crossed the Atlantic. After the Seven Years' War interrupted the flow of migration, it resumed on a smaller scale and ebbed during the last years before American independence. The overall volume of German migration to the American colonies between 1740 and 1775 has recently been estimated at more than 65,000.[67] German Lutheran and Reformed pastors in the middle colonies were acutely aware of the problems which this massive influx of immigrants created for them. In 1744, the Reformed minister Johann Philipp Boehm identified most of his parishioners as poor immigrants. 'Although our congregations are now increasing,' he wrote to the Synods of North and South Holland, 'they consist almost entirely of poor people, who arrive ever[y] year from all sorts of countries and of whom many are seen going about the country begging for their passage money'.[68] Three years later Henry Melchior Mühlenberg wrote that '[o]ur German Evangelical settlers in Pennsylvania are, for the most part, the most recent immigrants to this province' and noted high geographical mobility among his parishioners, who migrated westward to acquire cheaper land. When German immigration to Pennsylvania reached its peak at mid-century, Mühlenberg repeatedly expressed his extreme concern over the problem of organizing these migrants into congregations and providing for their spiritual welfare.[69]

The problems of reaching out to these immigrant multitudes were exacerbated by the failure of the Lutheran and Reformed authorities in Halle and Amsterdam to send an adequate number of ministers to America. Between 1754 and 1764, for example, no ministers from Halle reached the middle colonies. The consequence was a continuing shortage of regularly ordained ministers. In 1776, 82 Lutheran and Reformed pastors had to serve 348 congregations in the Pennsylvania field, and only a minority of those pastors had been trained and ordained in Europe. According to Charles Glatfelter, '[n]o colonial American church with the tradition of a learned clergy encountered irregular ministers to the extent experienced by the German Lutheran and Reformed in the Pennsylvania field.'[70] By the 1760s, this ministerial shortage led to growing friction between the German Reformed Coetus in Pennsylvania and the Classis of Amsterdam over the question of Classis approval for American ordinations and the training of ministerial candidates in the colonies. While the Classis denied the Coetus' independent power of ordination, the colonial body in fact began to ordain ministers on its own authority.[71]

In contrast to the Classis of Amsterdam, the Lutheran authorities in Halle and London had never effectively exercised control over the Lutheran ministerium in Pennsylvania; Gotthilf August Francke in

Halle and Friedrich Michael Ziegenhagen in London had in fact declined Mühlenberg's proposal that they formally assume responsibility for the Lutheran church in the colonies. As a recent study has shown, this reluctance of Francke and Ziegenhagen reflected the fact that they distrusted Mühlenberg's intentions and abilities and misconceived the colonial situation to a much greater extent than had hitherto been assumed.[72] Although Mühlenberg continued to regard the Halle and London authorities as spiritual leaders of the colonial Lutheran Church, the Pennsylvania ministerium performed ordinations and governed its affairs largely independently from Europe.[73]

On the local level, the conflicting claims of ministerial authority and lay participation led to a number of salary disputes, dismissals of pastors and, in the case of Germantown, Pennsylvania, to a schism in one of the oldest German Lutheran congregations that lasted for thirteen years. The larger part of the Germantown congregation, which severed its ties with the ministerium in 1753, showed its supreme disregard for the Halle pastors' claims to leadership and a traditional church hierarchy when they called a layman as their pastor. While Mühlenberg explained the opposition's acts in the Germantown dispute as the disorderly behaviour of recent immigrants, the leaders of the opposition were in fact well-established older residents of the community who had long been active in church affairs, but had been alienated when the Halle pastors tried to impose their own conceptions of authority and thus upset the balance of power within the congregation.[74] The Reformed minister Michael Schlatter similarly aroused strong lay opposition when he introduced changes in the liturgy, highhandedly installed new consistory members, vigorously pushed the completion of a new church building and through these and other measures gave the impression that he desired to rule the congregation in an authoritarian manner. By 1749, Schlatter also faced charges of embezzlement of church funds, neglect of his pastoral duties and adultery, and the church elders, who had resisted Schlatter's demand for an indefinite pastoral call all along, called the newly-arrived Johann Conrad Steiner as their minister. Although a committee of arbitrators completely vindicated Schlatter from charges of misconduct in 1750, only a minority of the Philadelphia congregation eventually stayed with him. Like the Germantown Lutherans, the majority of Philadelphia's Reformed laypeople had asserted their understanding of liberty and lay participation against ministerial claims of authority. The New Side Presbyterian minister Gilbert Tennent, who came to Schlatter's defence in the dispute, commented that, in Pennsylvania, 'the elders arrogate to themselves all the power over the church, and want to rule the ministers with an iron rod'.[75]

Such conflicts, however, should not obscure the fact that the overall tendency of church development among the German Lutheran and Reformed was towards stability and consolidation. A good example of the growth and stabilization of German congregations in the middle colonies is Lancaster, Pennsylvania, founded as a county seat in 1729 and the largest inland town of British North America at the end of the colonial period.[76] The Lutheran congregation, in the founding of which the ubiquitous Johann Caspar Stoever had played an important role in the early 1730s, was in uproar by the mid-1740s when the Moravian sympathies of its pastor, the Swedish-born Laurentius Nyberg, became publicly known. The attempt of Nyberg's opponents to lock him out of the church was followed by fistfights and a lawsuit. The attempts of Henry Melchior Mühlenberg and his father-in-law, the prominent justice of the peace and Indian interpreter Conrad Weiser, to arbitrate the dispute in 1746 produced no results, but Nyberg relented and formed his own congregation after the consistory of Uppsala, which had sent him to America, condemned his Moravian tendencies.[77] Nyberg's successor Friedrich Handschuh, a Halle pietist who served the Lancaster congregation since 1748, had to resign after three years because his congregation objected to his marriage to a poor woman and withheld his salary. The Lancaster Lutherans then appealed to the Württemberg consistory, which sent Johann Siegfried Gerock to Pennsylvania in 1753. Gerock's ministry at Lancaster was also overshadowed by divisions, however, and part of the congregation called an irregular pastor whom Heinrich Melchior Mühlenberg described as a very godless man ('*ein Ausbund an Gottlosigkeit*'). Considering these conflicts, it is not surprising that Mühlenberg referred to the Lancaster Lutherans as a wild, raw, undisciplined rabble.[78]

In the 1760s and 1770s, however, the development of the Lutheran congregation in Lancaster was marked by consolidation and signs of religious renewal. During Gerock's tenure, a new stone church was erected between 1761 and 1766. In October, 1767, almost 400 people took communion in the new church, and in April, 1768, 380 communicants were registered, 82 of them communing for the first time. The congregation reportedly had 1,300 members in 1772. The pew rent lists, started in 1766, show that a stable core of wealthy members now supported the church consistently for a number of years. The pastorate of the Halle pietist Johann Heinrich Helmuth at Lancaster, which lasted from 1769 to 1779, is generally regarded to have been the most successful since the congregation's founding.[79] According to a historian of Lancaster, the religious awakening among the town's Lutheran inhabitants thus did not reach its climax until the late 1760s and early 1770s.[80] The Reformed congregation at Lancaster, which like the Lutheran congregation was organized in the early 1730s, showed a similar development. In 1740, Johann Philipp Boehm told the Classis of Amsterdam that up to that time the Lancaster Reformed 'have acted according to their own pleasure. They have never cared for church order, but thus far have allowed themselves to be served by irregular men.'[81] While the congregation had as many as 225 communicants in 1747, a succession of mostly unordained preachers served only brief terms there until the early 1750s. The congregation entered a period of stablization in 1752, when the pietist Philipp Wilhelm Otterbein became the first of several coetus members to hold successful pastorates in Lancaster. During Otterbein's tenure, the congregation erected a new stone church in 1753–1754.[82]

Congregational development in places such as Lancaster, Pennsylvania, demonstrates that religious renewal and institutional growth in the churches of the middle colonies were not confined to the period from 1739 to 1745, commonly called the Great Awakening, but often lasted for several decades.[83] Indeed, the pastor–people relationship constantly had to be renegotiated, and the balance of power between pastors and congregations adjusted under the influence of social change and religious reform. Pastors' attempts to harness their local authority and institute religious reforms often met with vigorous resistance from laymen who saw their traditional position in the community threatened.

Conclusion

Religious reform in the eighteenth-century middle colonies had complex results. Evangelical ministers encouraged the laity to make a conscious decision for spiritual renewal, but they insisted on maintaining clerical authority, controlling the progress of awakenings and building up a loyal following in their congregations. Consequently, the shape of denominations on the eve of the American Revolution was usually the result of a compromise between the demands of ministers and laymen. In addition, the struggles over religious reform and authority in the competitive, religiously and ethnically diverse environment of the middle colonies led to a heightened sense of denominational identity. While it is true that Evangelicals frequently cooperated with each other and in the process discovered 'that they could accept Protestant pluralism as congruent with their basic understanding of Christianity',[84] toleration and cooperation did not diminish doctrinal differences. Significantly, Nikolaus von Zinzendorf's ecumenical initiative and the proposed merger of the German Reformed and the (Old Side) Presbyterians in 1744 were unsuccessful.[85] Ministers like Heinrich Melchior Mühlenberg may easily have preached in several languages and cultivated friendly relationships with clergymen of other denominations, but in the end they concentrated on furthering the institutional growth and confessional identity of their own church.[86] The confrontation with people from a variety of cultural backgrounds thus ultimately had a unifying effect on Dutch, German, Scottish and Irish settlers in the middle colonies, and this sense of common identity often had its institutional and spiritual focus in the colonial churches.[87]

Notes

1. Patricia U. Bonomi and Peter R. Eisenstadt, 'Church Adherence in the Eighteenth-Century British American Colonies,' *William and Mary Quarterly*, 3d ser., 39 (1982): 245–87; Richard W. Pointer, *Protestant Pluralism and the New York Experience. A Study of Eighteenth-Century Religious Diversity* (Bloomington: Indiana University Press, 1988), 30–1; Jon Butler, *Awash in a Sea of Faith: Christianizing the American People* (Cambridge, MA and London: Harvard University Press, 1990), Chapter 4. For the decline argument, see Charles Hartshorn Maxson, *The Great Awakening in the Middle Colonies* (Chicago: University of Chicago Press, 1920); Martin Lodge, 'The Crisis of the Churches in the Middle Colonies', *Pennsylvania Magazine of History and Biography* 95 (1971): 196–221; John B. Frantz, 'The Awakening of Religion among the German Settlers in the Middle Colonies', *William and Mary Quarterly*, 3d ser., 33 (1976): 266–288.
2. Dietmar Rothermund, *The Layman's Progress: Religious and Political Experience in Pennsylvania, 1740–1775* (Philadelphia: University of Pennsylvania Press, 1961); Patricia U. Bonomi, *Under the Cope of Heaven: Religion, Society, and Politics in Colonial America* (New York and Oxford: Oxford University Press, 1986), 132–3, 157 and *passim*; Marilyn J. Westerkamp, *Triumph of the Laity: Scots-Irish Piety and the Great Awakening, 1625–1760* (New York and Oxford: Oxford University Press, 1988), 184, 189–91, 194 and *passim*.
3. Butler, *Awash in a Sea of Faith*, 180–182; Jon Butler, 'Whitefield in America: A Two Hundred Fiftieth Commemoration,' *Pennsylvania Magazine of History and Biography* 113 (1989): 515–26, esp. 522–3.
4. Jon Butler, 'Enthusiasm Described and Decried: The Great Awakening as Interpretative Fiction,' *Journal of American History* 69 (1982): 305–25 (quote on 322).
5. See, for example, Bonomi, *Under the Cope of Heaven*; Westerkamp, *Triumph of the Laity*, 4; Timothy D. Hall, *Contested Boundaries: Itinerancy and the Reshaping of the Colonial American Religious World* (Durham, NC and London: Duke University Press, 1994), 3–12.
6. For critiques of the 'New England-paradigm' in colonial American historiography, see Michael Zuckerman, 'Puritans, Cavaliers, and the Motley Middle,' in Michael Zuckerman, ed., *Friends and Neighbors: Group Life in America's First Plural Society* (Philadelphia: University of Pennsylvania

Press, 1982), 3–25; Jack P. Greene, *Pursuits of Happiness: The Social Development of Early Modern British Colonies and the Formation of American Culture* (Chapel Hill: University of North Carolina Press, 1988). For a review of recent scholarship on the middle colonies, see Wayne Bodle, 'Themes and Directions in Middle Colonies Historiography, 1980–1994,' *William and Mary Quarterly*, 3d ser., 51 (1994): 355–88.

7. These studies include Ned Landsman, *Scotland and its First American Colony, 1683–1765* (Princeton, NJ: Princeton University Press, 1985); Westerkamp, *Triumph of the Laity*; Barry Levy, *Quakers and the American Family: British Settlement in the Delaware Valley, 1650–1765* (New York: Oxford University Press, 1988); Randall Balmer, *A Perfect Babel of Confusion: Dutch Religion and English Culture in the Middle Colonies* (New York and Oxford: Oxford University Press, 1989); A. G. Roeber, *Palatines, Liberty, and Property: German Lutherans in Colonial British America* (Baltimore: John Hopkins University Press, 1993); Mark Häberlein, *Vom Oberrhein zum Susquehanna. Studien zur badischen Auswanderung nach Pennsylvania im 18. Jahrhundert* (Stuttgart: Kohlhammer, 1993); Thomas J. Müller, *Kirche zwischen zwei Welten. Die Obrigkeitsproblematik bei Heinrich Melchior Mühlenberg und die Kirchengründung der deutschen Lutheraner in Pennsylvania*, Transatlantische historische Studien 2 (Stuttgart: Franz Steiner, 1994).

8. Joyce D. Goodfriend, *Before the Melting Pot: Society and Culture in Colonial New York City, 1664–1730* (Princeton, NJ: Princeton University Press, 1992); David G. Hackett, *The Rude Hand of Innovation: Religion and Social Order in Albany, New York, 1652–1836* (New York and Oxford: Oxford University Press, 1991); Stephanie Grauman Wolf, *Urban Village: Population, Community, and Family Structure in Germantown, Pennsylvania, 1683–1800* (Princeton, NJ: Princeton University Press, 1976); Pointer, *Protestant Pluralism*; Douglas C. Jacobsen, *An Unprov'd Experiment: Religious Pluralism in Colonial New Jersey*, Chicago Studies in the History of American Religion 9 (Brooklyn, NY: Carlson, 1991); Sally Schwartz, *'A Mixed Multitude': The Struggle for Toleration in Colonial Pennsylvania* (New York: New York University Press, 1988); J. William Frost, *A Perfect Freedom: Religious Liberty in Pennsylvania* (New York and Oxford: Oxford University Press, 1991); Alan W. Tully, 'Englishmen and Germans: National-Group Contact in Colonial Pennsylvania, 1700–1755', *Pennsylvania History*, 45 (1978): 237–56.

9. Billy G. Smith, *The 'Lower Sort:' Philadelphia's Laboring People, 1750–1800* (Ithaca, NY and London: Cornell University Press, 1988); Ronald Schultz, *The Republic of Labor: Philadelphia Artisans and the Politics of Class, 1720–1830* (Cambridge et al.: Cambridge University Press, 1993).

10. Charles H. Glatfelter, *Pastors and People: German Lutheran and Reformed Churches in the Pennsylvania Field, 1717–1793*, 2 vols (Breinigsville, PA: Pennsylvania German Society, 1979–1981), 2: 137–49; Pointer, *Protestant Pluralism*, 4; Lester J. Cappon et al., eds, *Atlas of Early American History: The Revolutionary Era, 1760–1790* (Princeton, NJ: Princeton University Press, 1976), 38.

11. For a comparative view that is not limited to religious issues, see

A. G. Roeber, '"The Origin of Whatever Is Not English Among Us:"' The Dutch-Speaking and the German-Speaking Peoples of Colonial British America', in Bernard Bailyn and Philip D. Morgan, eds, *Strangers Within the Realm: Cultural Margins of the First British Empire* (Chapel Hill: University of North Carolina Press, 1991), 220–283.
12. Oliver Rink, *Holland on the Hudson. An Economic and Social History of Dutch New York* (Ithaca and London: Cornell University Press, 1986), 139–171; Jan Lucassen, 'The Netherlands, the Dutch, and Long-Distance Migration, in the Late Sixteenth to Early Nineteenth Centuries,' in Nicholas Canny, ed., *Europeans on the Move: Studies on European Migration, 1500–1800* (Oxford: Clarendon Press, 1994), 154–91, esp. 178–80.
13. Balmer, *A Perfect Babel*, 36–68; Randall Balmer, 'The Social Roots of Dutch Pietism in the Middle Colonies,' *Church History* 53 (1984): 187–199. Cf. James Tanis, 'Reformed Pietism in Colonial America,' in F. Ernest Stoeffler, ed., *Continental Pietism and Early American Christianity* (Grand Rapids, MI: Eerdmans, 1976), 34–73, esp. 43–5; Jacobsen, *An Unprov'd Experiment*, 92–101.
14. Balmer, *A Perfect Babel*, 73–78; Tanis, 'Reformed Pietism', 45–6.
15. J. M. Bumsted and John E. Van de Wetering, *What Must I Do To Be Saved? The Great Awakening in Colonial America* (Hinsdale, IL: Dryden Press, 1976), 47–9 (quote on 48). Cf. James Tanis, *Dutch Calvinistic Pietism in the Middle Colonies: A Study in the Life and Theology of Theodorus Jacobus Frelinghuysen* (The Hague: Martinus Nijhoff, 1967), 46–64; Tanis, 'Reformed Pietism', 47–53; Balmer, *A Perfect Babel*, 103–13; Herman Harmelink III, 'Another Look at Frelinghuysen and his "Awakening",' *Church History*, 37 (1968): 423–38 finds little objective evidence for a revival in Frelinghuysen's congregations, but a lot of evidence for strife and disaffection.
16. Tanis, 'Reformed Pietism', 56–7; Tanis, *Dutch Calvinistic Pietism*, 46, 54.
17. Cf. Jacobsen, *An Unprov'd Experiment*, 75–83; Balmer, *A Perfect Babel*, 103–4.
18. Landsman, *Scotland and its First American Colony*, 48–72; T. C. Smout, N. C. Landsman, and T. M. Devine, 'Scottish Emigration in the Seventeenth and Eighteenth Centuries', in Canny, ed., *Europeans on the Move*, 76–112, esp. 86–7, 91, 97–8; L. M. Cullen, 'The Irish Diaspora of the Seventeenth and Eighteenth Centuries,' in *ibid.*, 113–49, esp. 128–30; Aaron Fogleman, 'Migrations to the Thirteen British North American Colonies, 1700–1775: New Estimates,' *Journal of Interdisciplinary History* 22 (1992): 691–709, esp. 698, 704–8.
19. Leonard J. Trinterud, *The Forming of an American Tradition: A Re-examination of Colonial Presbyterianism* (Philadelphia: Westminster Press, 1949), 30–5; Westerkamp, *Triumph of the Laity*, 142–4; Butler, *Awash in a Sea of Faith*, 124–5.
20. Lodge, 'Crisis,' 199–200; Schwartz, 'A Mixed Multitude,' 110.
21. Leigh Eric Schmidt, *Holy Fairs: Scottish Communions and American Revivals in the Early Modern Period* (Princeton, NJ: Princeton University Press, 1989), Chapter 1 (quote on 58); Westerkamp, *Triumph of the Laity*, Chapters 1–2. For the role of Scotch-Irish sacramental piety in the

ministry of a leading Presbyterian revivalist, see Janet F. Fishburn, 'Gilbert Tennent, Established "Dissenter,"' *Church History* 63 (1994): 31–49.
22. Westerkamp, *Triumph of the Laity*, Chapter 4.
23. Trinterud, *Forming of an American Tradition*, 39–50; Coalter, *Gilbert Tennent*, 29–38; Westerkamp, *Triumph of the Laity*, 145–56; Maldwyn A. Jones, 'The Scotch-Irish in British America', in Bailyn and Morgan, eds, *Strangers Within the Realm*, 284–313, esp. 289–90, 302–3.
24. Bumsted/Van de Wetering, *What Must I Do To Be Saved?*, 63–6; Ned Landsman, 'Revivalism and Nativism in the Middle Colonies: The Great Awakening and the Scots Community in East New Jersey', *American Quarterly* 34 (1982): 149–64, esp. 155–7.
25. Trinterud, *Forming of an American Tradition*, 58–69; Westerkamp, *Triumph of the Laity*, 169–84.
26. Fogleman, 'Migrations,' 698. Cf. Marianne S. Wokeck, 'The Flow and Composition of German Immigration to Philadelphia, 1727–1775,' *Pennsylvania Magazine of History and Biography* 105 (1981): 249–78.
27. Glatfelter, *Pastors and People*, 1: 139–43 (on Stoever); 2: 19–51.
28. Lodge, 'Crisis,' 199; Häberlein, *Vom Oberrhein zum Susquehanna*, 196.
29. Glatfelter, *Pastors and People*, 2:30, 77–8.
30. Müller, *Kirche zwischen zwei Welten*, 104–18. For Wilhelm Berkenmeyer, see David J. Webber, 'Berkenmeyer and Lutheran Orthodoxy in Colonial New York', *Concordia Historical Institute Quarterly* 60 (1987): 19–31.
31. Frantz, 'Awakening of Religion', 265–73; Schwartz, '*A Mixed Multitude*', 112–3, 143–4, 146.
32. Bonomi, *Under the Cope of Heaven*, 72–9; Glatfelter, *Pastors and People*, 2: 152–7, 185–6.
33. For revivals among German sectarian groups during the 1720s and 1730s, see Stephen L. Longenecker, *Piety and Tolerance: Pennsylvania German Religion, 1700–1850*, Pietist and Wesleyan Studies 6 (Metuchen, NJ and London: Scarecrow Press 1994), 48–9.
34. Spangenberg quoted in Glatfelter, *Pastors and People*, 2:68.
35. Landsman, 'Revivalism and Nativism'; Landsman, *Scotland and its First American Colony*, 228–9; cf. Westerkamp, *Triumph of the Laity*, 185–7; Schwartz, '*A Mixed Multitude*', 125.
36. For a bibliography of Tennent's published works, see Coalter, *Gilbert Tennent*, 205–10.
37. Frank Lambert,'*Pedlar in Divinity*': *George Whitefield and the Transatlantic Revivals, 1737–1770* (Princeton, NJ: Princeton University Press, 1994), esp. Chapters 2–4; Hall, *Contested Boundaries*, 29–39, 75–84; Harry S. Stout, 'George Whitefield in Three Countries,' in Mark A. Noll, David W. Bebbington and George A. Rawlyk, eds, *Evangelicalism. Comparative Studies of Popular Protestantism in North America, the British Isles, and Beyond, 1700–1990* (New York and Oxford: Oxford University Press, 1994), 58–72. Cf. also Susan O'Brien, 'Eighteenth-Century Publishing Networks in the First Years of Transatlantic Evangelicalism', in *ibid.*, 38–57.
38. Trinterud, *Forming of an American Tradition*, 86–108; Alan Heimert and Perry Miller, eds, *The Great Awakening. Documents Illustrating the Crisis*

and Its Consequences (Indianapolis and New York: Bobbs-Merrill 1967), xxix–xxxv.
39. Bonomi, *Under the Cope of Heaven*, 145–7.
40. Elizabeth I. Nybakken, 'New Light on the Old Side: Irish Influences on Colonial Presbyterianism,' *Journal of American History* 68 (1992): 813–32.
41. Westerkamp, *Triumph of the Laity*, 204.
42. Landsman, *Scotland and its First American Colony*, 231–2, 243–50.
43. Cf. Bonomi, *Under the Cope of Heaven*, 139–45; Westerkamp, *Triumph of the Laity*, 172–3, 189–94; Coalter, *Gilbert Tennent*, 64–7; Hall, *Contested Boundaries*, 49–50.
44. Trinterud, *Forming of an American Tradition*, 90–1; Butler, *Awash in a Sea of Faith*, 180–1.
45. Gilbert Tennent, 'The Danger of an Unconverted Ministry', in Heimert and Miller, eds, *The Great Awakening*, 71–99 (quote on 95).
46. Trinterud, *Forming of an American Tradition*, 77–80; Maxson, *Great Awakening*, 54–5, 63.
47. Landsman, 'Revivalism and Nativism', 157–61; Butler, *Awash in a Sea of Faith*, 183–5 (quote on 183). Cf. also Fishburn, 'Gilbert Tennent', 39–42.
48. Maxson, *Great Awakening*, 19, 59–60; Tanis, *Dutch Calvinistic Pietism*, 82–5.
49. Randall Balmer, 'John Henry Goetschius and The Unknown God: Eighteenth-Century Pietism in the Middle Colonies', *Pennsylvania Magazine of History and Biography* 113 (1989): 575–608 (quotes on 586, 599). Cf. also Balmer, *A Perfect Babel of Confusion*, 123–7; Tanis, *Dutch Calvinistic Pietism*, 72–3; Glatfelter, *Pastors and People*, 1:46–7.
50. Maxson, *Great Awakening*, 59; Frantz, 'Awakening of Religion', 283; Glatfelter, *Pastors and People*, 2: 60; Schwartz, '*A Mixed Multitude*', 127; Longenecker, *Piety and Tolerance*, 71–2.
51. See Glatfelter, *Pastors and People*, 2: 68–87; Schwartz, '*A Mixed Multitude*', 135–42.
52. Balmer, *A Perfect Babel*, 122–3; Trinterud, *Forming of an American Tradition*, 114–5, 132–3; Coalter, *Gilbert Tennent*, 96–112; Schwartz, '*A Mixed Multitude*', 128–30; Westerkamp, *Triumph of the Laity*, 207–8.
53. William J. Hinke, *Life and Letters of the Rev. John Philip Boehm, Founder of the Reformed Church in Pennsylvania, 1683–1749* (New York: Arno Press, 1972; first published 1916), 82–108, 348–65, 373–84; Tanis, 'Reformed Pietism,' 60–2, 65; Glatfelter, *Pastors and People*, 2: 91–4; Longenecker, *Piety and Tolerance*, 79–81.
54. Karl-Otto Strohmidel, 'Turning Confessionalist: Heinrich Melchior Mühlenberg und das Luthertum im pluralistischen Pensyvlania,' *Amerikastudien/American Studies* 38 (1993): 383–98, esp. 387–8; Müller, *Kirche zwischen zwei Welten*, 87–94; Longenecker, *Piety and Tolerance*, 84–5; Theodore G. Tappert, 'The Influence of Pietism in Colonial American Lutheranism,' in Stoeffler, ed, *Continental Pietism*, 13–33, esp. 18–22.
55. Glatfelter, *Pastors and People*, 1: 95–7; 2: 96–112; Frantz, 'Awakening of Religion,' 280–1; Müller, *Kirche zwischen zwei Welten*, 96–101.
56. Glatfelter, *Pastors and People*, 1: 117–9; 2: 112–22; Marthi Pritzker-Ehrlich, 'Michael Schlatter von St. Gallen (1716–1790). Eine biographische Unter-

suchung zur schweizerischen Amerika-Auswanderung des 18. Jahrhunderts' (Ph.D. diss., Universität Zürich, 1981), 46–60, 71–94.
57. Glatfelter, *Pastors and People*, 2: 102–4, 154–5.
58. Trinterud, *Forming of an American Tradition*, 120–7.
59. Pointer, *Protestant Pluralism*, 22; Glatfelter, *Pastors and People*, 2: 122–6; Butler, *Awash in a Sea of Faith*, 126.
60. Pointer, *Protestant Pluralism*, 4, 16–17, 24 (quote on 24); Balmer, *A Perfect Babel*, 128–32; Tanis, *Dutch Calvinistic Pietism*, 91; Maxson, *Great Awakening*, 120–2.
61. Balmer, *A Perfect Babel*, 132–40. For anglicization in New York city, see also Goodfriend, *Before the Melting Pot*, esp. Chapters 8–9.
62. Hackett, *The Rude Hand of Innovation*, 9–35 (quote on 20).
63. Smout, Landsman and Devine, 'Scottish Emigration', 97–8; Cullen, 'Irish Diaspora,' 128; Fogleman, 'Migrations,' 698.
64. Trinterud, *Forming of an American Tradition*, 129, 137, 199. Cf. Glatfelter, *Pastors and People*, 2: 148, according to whose estimate 45–50 Presbyterian ministers served at least 112 congregations in Pennsylvania in 1776.
65. Trinterud, *Forming of an American Tradition*, 131, 152, 203–6, 210.
66. Coalter, *Gilbert Tennent*, 121–62.
67. Wokeck, 'Flow and Ebb'; Fogleman, 'Migrations', 698.
68. Hinke, *Life and Letters*, 389; cf. Glatfelter, *Pastors and People*, 2:49.
69. Theodore G. Tappert and John W. Doberstein, eds, *The Journals of Henry Melchior Mühlenberg*, 3 vols (Philadelphia, 1942–1957), 1:142, 260. Cf. Glatfelter, *Pastors and People*, 2:140, 224–5.
70. Glatfelter, *Pastors and People*, 2:144–6, 189–201 (quote on 195), 226.
71. *Ibid.*, 207–16.
72. Müller, *Kirche zwischen zwei Welten*, 33, 178–200.
73. *Ibid.*, 96; Glatfelter, *Pastors and People*, 2:226–36.
74. Müller, *Kirche zwischen zwei Welten*, 129–77.
75. Glatfelter, *Pastors and People*, 2:217–20; Pritzker-Ehrlich, 'Michael Schlatter,' 96–127. Although Schlatter obtained substantial funds for the colonial Reformed Church and recruited six new ministerial candidates during a tour to Europe in 1751–1752, he was unable to heal the breach in his Philadelphia congregation, and, amidst continuing controversy, ceased to be a member of the Reformed coetus by 1756. Pritzker-Ehrlich, 'Michael Schlatter', 127–72.
76. For the social development of the town, see Jerome S. Wood, *Conestoga Crossroads: Lancaster, Pennsylvania, 1730–1790* (Harrisburg: Pennsylvania Historical and Museum Commission, 1979).
77. For a detailed examination of this controversy, see Müller, *Kirche zwischen zwei Welten*, 118–29. Cf. also Schwartz, '*A Mixed Multitude*', 140–1.
78. Kurt Aland *et al.*, eds, *Die Korrespondenz Heinrich Melchior Mühlenbergs aus der Frühzeit des deutschen Luthertums in Nordamerika*, 4 vols (Berlin: De Gruyter, 1986–1993), 1:408, 448–9; 2:15, 117, 144, 182; Häberlein, *Vom Oberrhein zum Susquehanna*, 198–9.
79. Glatfelter, *Pastors and People*, 1: 316–7; Debra D. Smith and Frederick S. Weiser, eds, *Trinity Lutheran Church Records, Lancaster, Pennsylvania. Volume 2: 1767–1782* (Apollo, PA: Closson Press, 1995), 208–16, 303–465.

80. Wood, *Conestoga Crossroads*, 198–9.
81. Hinke, *Life and Letters*, 276.
82. Glatfelter, *Pastors and People*, 1:101–3, 317–18.
83. Similarly, Pointer, *Protestant Pluralism*, 43–5, argues that 'the progressive dissemination of an Evangelical witness into virtually every part of the colony' continued well beyond the 1740s.
84. Pointer, *Protestant Pluralism*, 50–1.
85. Cf. Trinterud, *Forming of an American Tradition*, 136–7; Glatfelter, *Pastors and People*, 2: 273–4; Schwartz, 'A Mixed Multitude', 149–50.
86. Schwartz, 'A Mixed Multitude', 142–9; Strohmidel, 'Turning Confessionalist,' 290–8.
87. Cf. Landsman, *Scotland and its First American Colony*, 258–9.

2

'The Perfect Law of Liberty': Radical Religion and the Democratization of New England, 1780–1840

Louis Billington

Introduction

There is now a growing literature exploring the development of radical Evangelicalism in post-revolutionary New England. This movement broke with Calvinism to create a popular Arminian religious culture which offered the hope of salvation to all. While differing in detail, scholars offer a broadly similar account of the origins and early history of this radical movement, and agree on what most characterized its culture.[1] Some consensus may also be found in the literature on the geographical location of the movement, and its areas of greatest strength.[2] More problematic are questions concerning the changing socio-economic status of radical Evangelicals, the relationship between the sects and the 'market revolution' and their association with party politics. These problems will be addressed in later sections of this paper. First, a profile of the early movement will be presented.

A Profile of the Early Movement

Radical Evangelicalism emerged in a region where, except for Rhode Island, the Puritan ideal of a single church community, the Congregationalist Standing Order, survived the Revolution and was embodied in law. Tax-supported, college-educated ministers represented a religious establishment which resented any challenge to its monopoly. In New Hampshire, for example, nearly forty years after effective disestablishment, Congregationalists still seethed with indignation at the intrusion of radical Evangelicals into their parishes.[3] The radical Evangelicals were in continual conflict with the Standing Order, a conflict exacerbated by sharp political and social differences. Congregationalism itself, of course was divided into different theological factions, but it is debatable how far these divisions weakened efforts to meet the radical challenge. The predominant party was heir to a New

Light Calvinism pioneered by Jonathan Edwards, but in Massachusetts especially, Calvinists faced a challenge from proto-Unitarians, who increasingly criticized the orthodox doctrine of the Trinity, predestination, election and substitutionary atonement. Yet these liberals shared with their Calvinist brethren a firm belief in a religious establishment and a vision of a unified, hierarchic and godly society. Liberals and Calvinists were equally arrogant and dismissive in the face of 'unlettered preachers'. It was in this context that radical Evangelicalism gained support, especially on the rapidly expanding northern frontiers of the region.[4]

Often perfectionist and fervently millenarian, radical Evangelicalism was pioneered by a plethora of sects, which together fashioned a noisy, experiential religion fostering a sense of community and shared equality. It was a syncretic religion which drew upon popular traditions going back to the Great Awakening and before; traditions which were revitalized and democratized in the New Light 'stir' of the 1780s. In this milieu, denominational boundaries were lightly regarded, and elements of Congregationalist, Baptist, Methodist and Quaker practice were found in worship and church government. Government itself was often viewed with suspicion and challenged by enthusiasts, who saw it as impeding the work of the Holy Spirit. Individual conscience was exalted over formal organizations, and many questioned the need for, and the validity of, all existing religious institutions, and sought to restore 'primitive' Christianity on a New Testament basis. From the 1780s to the War of 1812 and beyond, these radical sects, Freewill Baptists, Christians, Methodists and others shared much in common, while disagreeing vigorously over aspects of faith, worship and religious practice. The more unstructured Freewill Baptists and Christians, for example, were long wary of the Methodists because of the latter's stronger system of regional and national episcopal church government.[5]

Threatened by the Congregationalist clergy, and in some localities by a more professional and better educated Baptist ministry, the radical sects resolutely opposed the development of a separate clerical order, which they saw as contrary to scripture. Clerical and academic titles, as well as distinct forms of clerical dress were anathema to them and fiercely ridiculed. Many questioned the need for any separate order of paid clergy, and insisted that their preachers earn a living as farmers or artisans. Some allowed preachers out-of-pocket expenses, but even when more regular payments were made, these were often low and uncertain. Some women and a few African-Americans found new roles and importance as preachers and church organizers. The strong current of anticlericalism among the radicals became deep-rooted, and opposition to theological schools and professional training for the ministry was long divisive. The radicals were by no means anti-intellectual, however, and many leaders sought avidly to improve their own education, and bemoaned the limited schooling available to them when growing up in frontier New England.[6]

Most preachers worked more as itinerants than settled ministers, and all believers played a part in the work of spreading the gospel, a work made urgent by the widespread expectation of Christ's second coming. These were like-minded, nonconformist men and women, determined to reject the world's customs and fashions. Religion was at the core of home and work, and preaching and worship took place in houses, barns and the open air rather than in churches, which were few and of the simplest kind. Despising the formal, written sermons of many Congregationalist clergy, the radicals preached extempore, and brought sinners to repentance with vivid, colloquial language. Conversions were often accompanied by shouting, weeping and violent physical movements, and among the most enthusiastic, worship sometimes incorporated forms of 'gospel dance'.[7]

Since the Great Awakening of the mid-1700s, New Light revivalists had developed a tradition of spiritual songs very different in their words and music from the classic hymnody of Isaac Watts venerated by Evangelical Congregationalists. Sung to folk tunes and well known popular airs, the spiritual songs were published in a succession of cheap collections which were borrowed without acknowledgement from each other. Sometimes close to doggerel, the songs embodied the actual language, experiences and hopes of farmers and artisans, and presented in a succinct form the core of the evangelists' message. Although most New Englanders were functionally literate, popular religious songs became part of a predominantly oral culture. They flourished at a time when New England was experiencing a Golden Age of popular music as self-taught rural singing teachers developed an indigenous style based on familiar tunes and simple choral effects. The spiritual songs fitted easily into this popular musical tradition, but there was less consensus among the radicals over the legitimacy of musical instruments. Church organs were still uncommon in New England, but many Calvinist congregations made use of flute, bassoon and bass viol, and radical preachers generally opposed the use of these 'dumb idols'.[8]

Although popular Evangelicalism was rooted in an oral culture, reading was rapidly becoming 'a necessity of life' for more and more New Englanders. As early as 1780, many subsistence farm families already possessed a Bible and a few classic texts of Protestant Christianity, and in succeeding decades, the radical Evangelicals gradually provided a new style of cheap magazines, tracts and a popular biographical and autobiographical literature which, while extending the horizons of many an isolated farmer, also rooted some even more securely in what was still essentially a sacred world view. The format, content and tone of this literature differed sharply from that of the established Congregationalists, who in their missionary work were too inclined to patronize their audiences and too anxious to improve by imposing their own cultural standards. The radical Evangelical magazines were written by and for people of little formal education, and they provide invaluable insights into the beliefs and values of radical Evangelicalism. The autobiographies, journals and biographies of pioneer preachers, male and female which began to be published with growing frequency after 1800, also helped to familiarize second-generation New Lights with the early history and struggles of their movement.[9] In general, this literature reveals the survival of a magical world view, where witches and cunning men still held sway, and visions and trances were commonplace. Accidents, illness and death were frequently reported, and holy dying was a common theme. Many of the preachers were experienced healers, using both herbal and regular medical means. Radical Evangelical literature is rich in reports of this work, as well as accounts of spiritual healing and miraculous cures.[10] It also depicts a world where heavy drinking was commonplace, and dances, frolics and huskings offered lively alternatives to the worship and religious sociability of the Lord's people. The challenge mounted by the Evangelicals to these popular customs including Sabbath hunting and fishing was a major cause of the verbal abuse and casual violence shown to radical preachers.[11]

The radical Evangelicals enjoyed their greatest success on New England's northern frontiers. The Congregationalists responded to this challenge in the 1790s with home missionary societies based in Connecticut and Massachusetts, and within a decade similar agencies had been founded in the two northern states and the District of Maine. These societies offered a neo-Edwardsian Calvinism which emphasized the sovereignty of God, but left room for the ability of man. The conversion experience was central to their message, but this was conversion defined and regulated by an educated elite, and transformed into an orderly, manageable process. While insisting on human depravity and predestination, they stressed the need for activism through prayer meetings, pastoral visits and Evangelical missions. Such missions were undertaken by carefully chosen itinerant preachers. The societies also subsidized struggling frontier congregations, and provided them with ministers. Ministers and missionaries struggled to adjust to the physical hardships and cultural standards of the frontier.[12] Nathan Perkins' classic missionary report of a tour through western Vermont in 1789 repeatedly decries the 'lack of politeness' and 'an abundance of profanity' among a people generally described as 'nasty, poor and low-lived,' but some later missionaries like Jotham Sewell in Maine were physically tough and socially adaptable. Yet they made comparatively few converts, and the ground was not held for the Standing Order.[13] Missionaries and settled ministers were always in short supply, and widespread migration from New England meant that much missionary effort was directed towards Yankees in western New York, and the territory north of the Ohio River. While striving for flexibility, the Congregationalists still retained a vision of an ordered, covenanted community led by a dominant minister, who defined theology, administered discipline and controlled admissions to the church.[14]

By 1820, such covenanted communities were no longer dominant across northern New England. In Maine, the combined churches of the Baptists, both Calvinist and Freewill, Methodists, Christians and other sects outnumbered Congregationalist parishes four to one. In New Hampshire, the Congregationalists were similarly threatened. In the Connecticut river valley of Vermont, it proved impossible to stem the anti-Calvinist tide, with the Congregationalists rapidly losing ground to the Methodist, Freewill Baptist, Christian and Universalist onslaught. Elsewhere in the state, radical Evangelicalism grew rapidly, especially in upland hill districts away from the major population centres and communication routes. The radicals also had some success in outlying areas of towns, where small-scale industries developed. In every state, local conditions moulded particular radical success, even in areas of general growth.[15]

In Maine, for example in 1820, the radical Freewill sects did much better in the more recently settled and rapidly growing Kennebec valley than they did in the older southeastern counties of the new state. Similarly in the more economically advanced and accessible region of the Lake Champlain valley in Vermont, between Burlington and Middlebury, Congregationalism remained strong, although the Calvinist Baptists made some inroads. Only a few miles away in more isolated towns, Methodists, Freewill Baptists and other radicals made much more headway. The Lake Champlain fringe, like the marketing and manufacturing towns of the Connecticut river valley to the east, also supported proto-Unitarian and Episcopal congregations among the wealthier and better educated, who found both Evangelical Calvinism and popular Arminianism intellectually crude and narrowly judgemental. These genteel Christians rejected revivalism, and stressed a spirit of civility, enlightenment and tolerance. Modern studies and local histories also underline the problems faced by all Evangelical groups including the radicals in sustaining their work in isolated, poorly populated districts, where congregations drifted in and out of existence, changed denominational loyalties or tried to develop 'Union' churches in the face of lack of numbers, funds or interest.[16]

In southern New England, the radical Evangelicals generally had more limited success. While proto-Unitarianism found support in eastern Massachusetts, Evangelical Congregationalism was strong throughout that state, and it dominated Connecticut, where Unitarianism made no headway. Many towns in both states saw Evangelical Congregationalism maintain a religious monopoly into the nineteenth century, and the main challenge came from a variety of separatist groups created by the Great Awakening, which evolved into a network of Calvinist Baptist churches. In Connecticut, for example, there were sixty Baptist churches by 1795 and the number was even larger in Massachusetts. These Baptists represented the largest body of dissenters in many towns, and offered the only alternative to the Standing Order. Although weakened by divisions, the Universalists also slowly made some headway in southern New England by providing a radical alternative to the predominant Calvinism, but one that was more intellectually accessible and less socially elitist than that offered by the Unitarians.[17] With their national system of church government and better focused resources, the Methodists also made some headway across southern New England. Populist preaching and emotional camp meetings produced converts who were able to develop their spiritual gifts in class meetings and social prayer meetings. Though long derided by Congregationalists and Calvinist Baptists, the Methodists found support among small farmers and artisans and had some success among country people drawn into mill villages and the later factory towns. The growth of such towns also provided openings for Freewill Baptists and Christians as their members migrated from the countryside to Lowell and other industrial centres seeking work. Young women especially found the radical sects supportive in the new world of industrial work.[18]

Compared with their successes in northern New England, however, indigenous sects like the Christians and Freewill Baptists gained only limited support in the south. Success seems to have been greatest in neighbourhoods, which offered special opportunities. Perhaps the best documented case study is of the hilltowns of northwestern Rhode Island, where, in a series of sweeping revivals from 1812 onwards, Christian and then Freewill Baptist preachers made numerous converts and organized a network of successful churches. The message and the methods of the preachers were identical to those employed in the north, even to the popularity of women evangelists and trouble with ultra-enthusiasts, who hugged, kissed, rolled on the floor, and confessed 'obscene things' in public. The socio-religious context of this radical success is significant.[19]

While long rejecting a religious establishment, post-Revolutionary Rhode Island was dominated by Calvinist Baptists, Quakers and Congregationalists who lived in the commercial east of the state. Leaders of these denominations were successful merchants and pioneer industrialists. By comparison, the northwest was a relatively isolated region characterized economically by semi-subsistence agriculture and culturally by adherence to the old Six-Principle Baptists, who by the early nineteenth century were in marked decline. As the century progressed, back-country farmers increasingly clashed with the Providence-based elite over the latter's attempts to commercialize and industrialize the northwest's economy, leading to conflict over internal improvements, water rights and access to cash and credit. Like their counterparts in other states, Congregationalists and Calvinist Baptists felt they had a mission to civilize the hilltowns, and set up societies which focused their energies on the 'wilds of western Rhode Island.' The reports of these missionaries echo those of their colleagues in frontier Maine or Vermont. According to the Congregationalists, the people of the northwest were ignorant, illiterate and indifferent to religion. The Baptists were somewhat more cautious in their judgement of what were technically their co-religionists, but representing an urban, educated elite, the Calvinist Baptists were seriously alarmed by the 'irreligion,' anti-clericalism, and general opposition to progress evident in the northwest.[20]

Not surprisingly, struggling western farmers and artisans showed marked resentment at being criticized and patronized by 'hireling priests' of Congregationalism, whose Standing Order, as good Rhode Islanders they had long loathed. Scarcely less objectionable were the urban Baptists who had become too 'Congregational' for rural sensibilities. Given the economic issues which had long divided easterners and westerners, and their political ramifications, it is not surprising that the radicals gained the ground. They provided a new style of popular religion, indifferent to the narrow sectarian concerns of the Old Six-Principle Baptists, but retaining elements of the Baptist tradition. Christians and Freewillers brought spiritual enthusiasm, which they combined with the provisions of a new moral order for localistic rural communities under threat. The Christians enjoyed the earliest successes, but by mixing a vigorous, simple faith with a stronger institutional framework, the Freewill Baptists overtook them and became an important presence in antebellum northwestern Rhode Island, playing a major role in that region's adjustment to a market economy.[21]

The relative success of the radical Evangelicals in southern Maine and coastal New Hampshire also spilled over into northeastern Massachusetts, where Essex county became the home of a growing number of radical congregations. Between 1780 and 1840, Essex witnessed economic transformation as farmers and fishermen were drawn into a market economy, and while men remained attached to older ideas of landed independence, more and more young people became wage labourers, or toiled at outwork, especially in the shoe industry. A detailed study of the relationship between socio-economic change and religious affiliation has not yet been attempted for Essex and its northern hinterland, but many communities proved excellent recruiting grounds for the radical sects.[22] The Universalists found some of their earliest supporters in the area, and Benjamin Randall, the founder of the Freewill Baptists, and Elias Smith, the Christian leader, both gained a strong following in Essex and the Merrimac river valley. Methodist preachers made converts too, and from 1784 to 1819, the diary of the patrician William Bentley of Salem charts the passage through Essex county of a stream of radical preachers, 'men without education' who nonetheless met with a degree of success among those whom Bentley viewed as lacking knowledge and cultivation.[23] The outcome was evident by Bentley's death. Statistics are not always reliable, but by the 1820s, the Freewill sects plus the Calvinist Baptists in Essex almost equalled the number of Evangelical Standing Order churches – a pattern very similar to that prevailing in the adjacent area of south-eastern Maine.[24]

The autobiographies and biographies of the early radical preachers are replete with stories of hardship and poverty in southern New England, migration to the northern frontier, and the isolation and great physical privations endured there. Some found these experiences so traumatic that they turned their backs on farming as a livelihood. Such men had little opportunity for formal education, as is confirmed by a study which shows that before 1830 more than 90 percent of Freewill Baptist preachers had a common school education, or less. A similar situation almost certainly prevailed among the Christians and Methodists.[25]

The radicals' early literature was consciously aimed at 'the lower classes of society', and there is ample evidence that their preachers had a profound understanding of the experiences, hopes and aspirations of frontier pioneers, semi-subsistence farmers in older settled regions and artisans across New England. Literary evidence can sometimes be supplemented by other sources, such as church records including membership lists. Attempts have been made to collate such material with local tax and personal inventories to identify the occupations, wealth and social standing of early sect members. Such research has thrown light on the social composition of some congregations, but further work is made difficult by the fact that comparatively few congregational records for the period before 1820 have survived. Many congregations were shortlived and left little trace, and even well established churches and their records disappeared with the great shifts in New England's rural population in the second half of the nineteenth century.

Some of the surviving records emphasize the fluidity of the

early days, with congregations shifting between Calvinist and Freewill Baptist, or Christian and Universalist loyalties with bewildering frequency; the same rough notebook sometimes containing the surviving records of a congregation's shift between two or three different sects. However, church membership lists need to be supplemented by minute books if the causes of withdrawals and expulsions from congregations are to be identified, and such surviving minute books are scarce. In addition, membership lists and minute books do not record the many who are known to have attended meetings and provided financial support without ever giving that testimony of a conversion experience which formal membership required. Evidence for assessing the social standing of sect members is scarcer for women than for men, and yet, perhaps not surprisingly, the best documented of the women preachers seem to come from much wealthier backgrounds than average.[26] Much remains impressionistic, but some useful generalizations about the socio-economic composition of the early radical sects can now be made. Of course, definitions and perceptions of class in this period are problematic, and class or occupation alone provides no more than a clue as to why an individual joined a particular church. Ties of family and broader social networks were important, as well as the idiosyncrasies of person and place already touched on in exploring the geography of the sects.

From the beginning, the radical preachers were able to convert individuals who were moderately wealthy by the standards of their particular community. In New Durham, New Hampshire in 1784, Benjamin Randall's pioneer Freewill Baptist congregation included farmers who were selectmen, militia officers, a state legislator and the town clerk, and their average wealth was slightly higher than that of other property owners in the town. Similar substantial farmers can be found among the membership of other early churches, and the sects had some success among men of property in urban areas.[27] Elias Smith's Christian congregation in early nineteenth-century Portsmouth, New Hampshire, contained a number of wealthier members, though in this seaport community they were overwhelmingly ship-owners or highly skilled artisans such as a goldsmith, a painting contractor and the owner of a carriage and sign-painting business. Such men were also active in local government and trade associations. Sect members who were labourers, artisans or mentioned as 'coloured' can sometimes be identified, though they owned no taxable property, but all too often such people remain socially anonymous, absent from local directories and tax records.[28]

Fewer women church members have proved traceable through probate and tax lists or other secular records, although they made up a majority in many congregations. Those identified were rarely of any financial or social prominence, though a few widows were substantial property-owners. Single women generally left very modest estates, and many were related to other church members. When identifiable single women married, their partners were typically less prosperous artisans and small farmers. Women of similar background are also found among female sect members who sought employment in mill villages and later factory towns. One or two can be more fully identified because they became female preachers. Salome Lincoln was the daughter of a poor Massachusetts farmer, and combined female preaching with factory work, including the leadership of a textile strike in 1829. Almira Prescott of Gorham, Maine, married a local farmer, Jeremiah Bullock, and both became Freewill Baptist preachers.[29] A few very well documented female activists came from much wealthier social backgrounds. Harriet Livermore was the granddaughter of a Federalist US senator from New Hampshire, and the daughter of a justice of the state supreme court. She attended two superior schools before taking up a career as an evangelist: Byfield Seminary and Atkinson, New Hampshire, Academy. Livermore was sometimes seen as eccentric, but this could not be said of Clarissa Danforth, a woman of good education and family, whose controlled and dignified style of preaching impressed even Congregationalists. Danforth converted Nancy Towle, who was born in Hampton, New Hampshire, in 1796, the daughter of Colonel Philip Towle, scion of one of the oldest and most prominent families in an old coastal community. She attended Hampton Academy until she was twenty, and enjoyed considerable academic success there. For a time, she worked as a schoolteacher before becoming an evangelist on both sides of the Atlantic.[30]

Women such as Livermore, Danforth and Towle were clearly exceptional in background, talent and education, as were the comparatively wealthy sect members in New Durham, Portsmouth and other communities. What is evident from existing studies, however, is that while the radical sects did recruit among the poor, they constituted much more than a religious movement of the dispossessed or marginal. In Rhode Island and adjacent rural areas of Massachusetts and Connecticut, for example, the Christian and Freewill Baptist congregations included a few individuals who were wealthy by the standards of their communities, and many who represented a cross-section of local rural society. Recruiting was particularly strong among farmers, skilled artisans and shopkeepers.[31] In the Connecticut valley towns of Vermont, Randolph Roth suggests that the radical sects contained a good cross-section of craftsmen, journeymen, and middling and subsistence farmers plus some labourers. Agriculture was still the predominant source of income, but only a few were larger, commercial farmers.[32] Given the predominance of the sects in geographic localities where elite members of society were lacking, it is not surprising that some members and supporters became selectmen, sheriffs and justices of the peace.

Great Socio-Economic Changes in New England

The evidence so far cited largely covers the period from 1780 through the 1820s, years which saw great socio-economic changes in New England. These changes obviously affected the sects. Many members migrated away from the region, while others undoubtedly suffered great hardship in the countryside and in the emerging industrial towns; but by the late 1830s it is difficult to escape the general conclusion that the sects as a whole were experiencing a process of 'embourgeoisement.'[33] Sect leaders became better educated and pressed for the creation of academies, seminaries and ultimately colleges. Some were short lived and all had financial problems, but by the 1840s, the Freewill Baptists, Christians and Methodists possessed institutions providing a good secondary education, and the Methodists had created Wesleyan University in Connecticut. Freewill Baptist leaders graduated from the Calvinist Baptist-controlled Brown University and Colby College, and in turn pressed for their own denominational institutions. Ministers were paid more regular salaries and developed a new professionalism which allowed them to challenge the Calvinist Baptists and even the Congregationalists in their commitment to institutional structures and greater respectability. Conventional religious and academic titles like 'reverend' or 'doctor' replaced the more familiar 'elder' or 'brother'. Women preachers disappeared, and new-style denominational weekly newspapers introduced ladies' columns.[34] Women and men were urged to support new missionary societies, and the shift from piety to moralism evident among the major neo-Calvinist denominations was also reflected among the radicals in a growing commitment to the temperance and anti-slavery movements.[35]

Of course, these changes met with fierce opposition and were one factor in drawing off the dissatisfied into a succession of antinomian and millenarian movements, including the Mormons and the Millerites. Old-fashioned Methodists loathed the new-style 'minister factories', whose graduates read sermons and aspired to higher salaries and more costly churches. The Freewill Baptists and Christians lost members to localized sects, which in their opposition to a more professionalized clergy, missionary and temperance societies, and similar 'modern' improvements, reflected an outlook similar to that of the more familiar anti-mission Baptists of the South and Midwest.[36]

Perhaps the growth of bourgeois values, especially among the prosperous laity is best reflected in a painting by the folk artist, Joseph

H. Davis of the Thomas Lord family of Lee, New Hampshire, completed in 1837. Davis is famous for his concern with symbols of middle-class respectability, and Lord, like so many of Davis's sitters, is dressed in black with his top hat on the table. His wife is holding their child and is given a bouquet of flowers, a formal hairdo and the usual apron. The table displays a Bible and smaller untitled books, standard Davis props, and in the background, a framed painting of the sitters' elegant home. In the foreground is another Davis trademark, the brightly painted carpet or floor covering. As in other Davis portraits, Lord demonstrates his loyalties by reading a newspaper with a quite legible logo, *The Morning Star*, the Freewill Baptist weekly.[37]

The Market Revolution

In his sweeping account of early nineteenth-century America, Charles Sellers places the radical sects at the core of resistance to the 'market revolution'. He labels the sects 'antinomian', a misleading and very odd use of that term. Sellers is also prone to reductionism, attaching significance to religion only insofar as it operates as a function of economic change, but he does raise an important question. Were the sects, as he claims, rooted in a traditionalist, agrarian culture, which centred relationships on love, community and equality, and did this culture make them opposed and resistant to the 'market revolution'?[38]

Much in the early part of this paper might seem to support Sellers' thesis, but the most convincing evidence for his view comes from the early years, well before the date at which he begins his study of Jacksonian America. There is no doubt that early sect members were predominantly farmers and artisans who created egalitarian, supportive communities which rejected the world. They wore simple dress and preached repeatedly against frills, ruffles and all unnecessary adornments. Even certain hairstyles were deemed too worldly. Sect leaders showed disgust at skimped or imperfect work, and often condemned professionals like lawyers and doctors who monopolized knowledge and exploited honest handworkers. In business, they condemned the customs of the world, teaching that God's people should do as they would be done by. Such attitudes, combined with a fervent millenarianism, led some to 'come out' of a corrupt world altogether and retreat into communitarian sects.[39] By the 1820s, as the 'market revolution' forged ahead, there is also evidence that some radical Evangelicals felt threatened and feared the loss of economic independence. In Maine, the radicals resisted absentee landlords and pressed successfully for statehood, but they could not maintain their world of equal small producers.⁴⁰ Some became victims of the new economic order which forced them to work on other mens' land or drove them into the 'slavery' of the factories.⁴¹

Sellers, however, makes too little of the process of 'embourgeoisement' which had transformed the sects by the 1840s. The differences between their world view and that of the middle-class moderate Calvinists whom Sellers labels 'pro-marketeers' were becoming few. Growing numbers of Freewill Baptists, for example, were now commercial farmers, not backwoods pioneers, and a new generation of leaders seldom recalled childhood poverty. Their parents were rarely rich, but some were substantial farmers, or small-scale industrialists. They represented an ambitious, well connected middle class very different from the mass of immigrant workers or their own pioneering grandparents. Of course, many struggled or failed on isolated farms or in factory towns, and a few may have remained in a sectarian and economic timewarp, but the forces of the market were all-pervasive. Research on the Shakers, for example, now questions their popular depiction as simple agrarian people, and shows that by the 1830s they were unremitting in their search for markets for a growing range of manufactured products.⁴²

Party Politics

Sellers rightly identifies the radical sects with the Jeffersonian Republican-Democratic tradition. Yet while the links between religious affiliation and political party loyalty are generally clear, problems remain. The radicals, whether struggling frontier settlers, prosperous farmers or successful artisans and tradesmen, had little time for claims to deference based on supposed superior breeding, college education or inherited wealth. In religion, they claimed the inalienable right to search the Scriptures for themselves and organize their churches accordingly. A religious establishment defended by a Congregationalist clergy claiming special authority and status was nothing more than a remnant of a 'Popish, Anti-Christian' tradition. From the 1790s onwards, it is not surprising that members of all the non-establishment sects in New England were likely to have Democratic-Republican sympathies, if only because of their fervent desire to erect 'a wall of separation' between church and state, as they could no longer be oppressed by a government-supported ecclesiastical establishment.⁴³ Freewill Baptists, Methodists and Christians all provided ministers who served as Jeffersonian legislators in the New England state assemblies, and some took a key part in the struggle for disestablishment. In New Hampshire, for example, the final battle was led by a Methodist preacher, Dan Young, who, according to his own account, entered politics solely for the purpose of ending the Standing Order.[44]

Differences between the radical sects and their political opponents involved much more than disestablishment, and, indeed by the early nineteenth century some Congregationalists saw the advantages or the inevitability, of a voluntary system. Apart from fundamental differences over gospel liberty and inalienable rights, complex disagreements over local and regional issues were important. We have already seen how in Rhode Island, where disestablishment was never an issue, the Federalist east clashed with the northwest over economic development, while in Maine, conflict over disestablishment became bound up with the movement for Maine's separation from Massachusetts, as well as a bitter struggle between absentee Federalist landlords and frontier squatters and farmers. In Vermont, while most of the radical sects supported the Democratic-Republicans, local circumstances could also make for atypical party loyalties.[45]

It is also important to remember that many radicals had doubts about any involvement in the political process, or any recognition of state authority. They were God's people who kept separate from the world. There was much disagreement over the legitimacy of taking advantage of the right provided by more and more New England states for the dissenting sects to incorporate their churches – that is, have them recognized by acts of the legislatures as bodies eligible for tax exemption. While many Calvinist Baptists and some radical congregations accepted the practice, others vigorously opposed it as unscriptural and an unacceptable recognition of state authority.[46] Elias Smith's *Herald of Gospel Liberty* was overtly political, and radical preachers did serve in state legislatures, but other radical magazines largely ignored politics and some evangelists proudly boasted that they had never voted in years. Even those voting or holding office were constantly torn between defending 'justice, truth, equality and liberty' in the political arena and dedicating themselves to religious witness.[47] Elias Smith could support the War of 1812, justifying it in terms of a necessary resistance to the reimposition of a tyrant's yoke, but other radicals were pacifists who bore testimony against the use of 'carnal weapons'.[48]

After 1815, the radical sects generally continued loyal to the Democratic-Republican tradition through the shifting politics of the 'era of good feelings'. In some areas, the continuing struggle for the separation of church and state bound the sects to the Jeffersonian cause, and even when that separation had been achieved, conflict continued with the Congregationalists over control of local funds, meeting houses and schools.

In emerging industrial communities, the radicals often empowered their members to resist wage reductions, deteriorating conditions, excessive profits and abuses of employers' power. Evangelical religion in this context was certainly not a manufacturer's tool to tame the turbulent hand of labour. Indeed, labour activists raised in the traditions of the radical sects drew on those traditions to condemn not only greed and injustice, but the way they found expression in ostentatious urban churches and the inflated salaries of clergy who lived like princes while preaching resignation to the poor. Such activists, like the radical preachers a generation before, 'had no faith in a clergyman who cannot live as cheaply as a Carpenter, Blacksmith or Tailor'.[49]

Although the Universalists sometimes supported freemasonry, it was more often associated with the 'genteel Christianity' of Unitarians and Episcopalians. The radical Evangelical sects had long condemned freemasonry as elitist, secular and a threat to their tightly knit communities, and Methodists, Freewill Baptists and Christians all took a prominent part in the antimasonry movement of the late 1820s and early 1830s. Though the links between antimasonry and the ballot box are sometimes unclear, as a moral reform, the antimasonic crusade received widespread sect support. The crusade was never a movement of the marginal or dispossessed, and a profile of its supporters fits typical patterns of sect membership by the 1830s.[50]

Anti-slavery proved divisive for New England Methodism as the Church's national leaders struggled to placate slave-owning members, but the other radical sects had no such southern links and abolitionism quickly gained support. The total abstinence movement created more conflict, largely because traditionalists saw it as unscriptural, divisive and an unnecessary rival to the church community. For some, the temperance movement also had echoes of the old Standing Order's attempts at legislating morality. Such opposition soon faded, however, or became embodied in small schismatic sects, and by the late 1830s support for the anti-slavery and temperance movements was firmly rooted among many New England Methodists and the great majority of Freewill Baptists and Christians. These changes, along with others already considered, gave the radical Evangelicals a social outlook and denominational agencies not dissimilar to those of the revival-orientated Congregationalists and Calvinist Baptists.[51]

By the 1840s, many members of Arminian churches were able to join Congregationalists and Baptists, their Calvinism by now much 'arminianized' in the emerging Whig Party. The Whigs were supported not only as the party of economic and social improvement, but also as the guardians of Protestant integrity. Although the Democrats stressed their opponents' Federalist roots and their threat to the separation of church and state, New England Evangelicals of many traditions now saw a much greater threat in growing Irish and German Catholic communities, which the Democrats embraced. For Methodists, Freewill Baptists and others who followed this route into Whiggery, the move was from being cultural 'outsiders' to 'insiders'.[52] Not all, however, could or would go down that road. In the Connecticut valley of Vermont, for example, Randolph Roth reports that between 1835 and 1850 Methodist, Freewill Baptist and Christian party activists were almost equally divided between the Democrats and the Whigs, but the Whigs were more likely to be drawn from the valley's centres of wealth and power. The Democrats did best among outsiders in the poorer towns and the countryside, who were worst placed to capitalize on economic growth.[53] A few outsiders clung to an ultra-sectarianism, damning all parties but especially the Whigs, and embodying their views in doggerel hymns which attacked lawyers, doctors, clergymen, colleges, railroads and abolitionism. Many more rejected or drifted away from the respectability represented by all the churches and social reform movements. These woodsmen and -women struggled to find some relief from hard, physical work in activities which had characterized the backwoods prior to 1815, drinking, hunting, dancing and casually socializing in a manner which had appalled the early pioneer preachers and now shocked their college-educated successors.[54]

The radical sects had become respectable denominations, with New England Methodism part of the nation's largest church. After the Civil War, northern New England went through a long winter of rural depopulation and change, and in many communities denominational boundaries further blurred as Protestant churches struggled to maintain a presence in town after town. The way was open for the evolution of a social and ideological consensus where radical enthusiasms had once flourished. Republican and temperately respectable, these townsfolk came to view their ancestors' religious eccentricities as quaint or forgettable. Protestantism became a shared faith as Mormons and Adventists faded from the scene and theological divisions lost importance. In the 1850s, however, something of an earlier world survived in those Republican virtues of competence and modest independence still endorsed by so many northern New England farmers, small entrepreneurs and craftsmen.[55]

Notes

1. Nathan O. Hatch, *The Democratization of American Christianity* (New Haven, CT, 1989); Stephen A. Marini, *Radical Sects of Revolutionary New England* (Cambridge, MA, 1982); Michael G. Kenny, *The Perfect Law of Liberty: Elias Smith and the Providential History of America* (Washington, DC, 1994).

2. See, for example, Stephen Marini, 'Religious Revolution in the District of Maine', in Charles E. Clark, James S. Leamon, Karen Bowen, eds, *Maine in the Early Republic: From Revolution to Statehood* (Hanover, NH, 1988), 118–45; Daniel P. Jones, *The Economic and Social Transformation of Rural Rhode Island* (Boston, 1992), 131–71.
3. Thomas Curry, *The First Freedoms: Church and State in America to the Passage of the First Amendment* (New York, 1986), 163–92; Robert F. Lawrence, *The New Hampshire Churches* (Claremont, NH, 1856).
4. Hatch, *Democratization of American Christianity*, 170–89; Marini, 'Religious Revolution,' 125–8; James R. Rohrer, *Keepers of the Covenant: Frontier Missions and the Decline of Congregationalism* (New York, 1995), 15–29.
5. Marini, *Radical Sects*, 11–24; Hatch, *Democratization of American Christianity*, 68–93; Louis Billington, 'Northern New England Sectarianism in the Early Nineteenth Century,' *Bulletin of the John Rylands University Library of Manchester* 70 (Autumn, 1988): 124–5; Albert C. Outler, '"Biblical Primitivism" in Early American Methodism', in Richard T. Hughes, ed., *The American Quest for the Primitive Church* (Urbana, IL, 1988), 131–43.
6. Hatch, *Democratization of American Christianity*, 174–5; William G. McLoughlin, *Soul Liberty: The Baptist Struggle in New England, 1630–1833* (Hanover, NH, 1991), 270–6; Hiram Munger, *The Life and Religious Experiences of Hiram Munger* (Boston, 1885), 10–30; Ephraim Stinchfield, *Some Memoirs of the Life, Experiences and Travels of Elder Ephraim Stinchfield* (Portland, ME, 1819), 5; Elias Smith, *The Life, Conversion, Preaching, Travels and Sufferings of Elias Smith* (Portsmouth, NH, 1816), 60–276.
7. This is based on numerous preachers' memoirs and reports. For example, Peter Young, *A Brief Account of the Life and Experiences of Peter Young* (Portsmouth, NH, 1817); Mark Fernald, *Life of Mark Fernald Written by Himself* (Newburyport, MA, 1852).
8. Marini, *Radical Sects*, 156–71; Billington, 'New England Sectarianism,' 126–7; Fernald, *Life*, 144, 216–17.
9. William J. Gilmore, *Reading Becomes a Necessity of Life: Material and Cultural Life in Rural New England, 1790–1835* (Knoxville, TN, 1989), 344–74. Magazines examined include *Herald of Gospel Liberty* and *Christian Herald* (Portsmouth, NH), 1808–1825; John Buzzell, ed., *A Religious Magazine* (Portland, ME), 1811–1812 and (Kennebunk, ME), 1820–1822; Ebenezer Chase, ed., *The Religious Informer* (Andover, NH), 1819–1821; *Freewill Baptist Magazine* (Providence, RI), 1826–1830.
10. Fernald, *Life*, 139; A. D. Jones, *Memoir of Elder Abner Jones* (Boston, 1842), 38–101; Kenny, *Perfect Law of Liberty*, 194–220; Marini, *Radical Sects*, 66. See also John L. Brooke, *The Refiner's Fire: The Making of Mormon Cosmology, 1644–1844* (Cambridge, MA, 1994), 71–2, 112–17.
11. The preachers' memoirs are replete with reports on popular culture. For example, Fernald, *Life*, 115; D. M. Graham, *The Life of Clement Phinney* (Dover, NH, 1851), 15–17.
12. Rohrer, *Keepers of the Covenant*, 15–143; Calvin M. Clark, *History of the Congregational Church in Maine* (Portland, ME, 1926), vol. 1; Paul Jeffrey Potash, 'Welfare of the Region Beyond,' *Vermont History* 46 (1978): 109–28.

13. Nathan Perkins, *A Narrative of a Tour in the State of Vermont* (Rutland, VT, 1964); Jotham Sewall, *A Memoir of Jotham Sewall* (Boston, 1853); Alan Taylor, *Liberty Men and Great Proprietors: The Revolutionary Settlement on the Maine Frontier, 1760–1820* (Chapel Hill, NC, 1990), 139–140.
14. Rohrer, *Keepers of the Covenant*, 143–52.
15. Marini, 'Religious Revolution'; Lynn Warren Turner, *The Ninth State: New Hampshire's Formative Years* (Chapel Hill, NC, 1983), 202–8; Randolph A. Roth, *Democratic Dilemma: Religion, Reform and the Social Order in the Connecticut River Valley of Vermont, 1791–1850* (Cambridge, MA, 1987), 41–79.
16. Marini, 'Religious Revolution,' 136; P. Jeffrey Potash, *Vermont's Burned Over District: Patterns of Community Development and Religious Activity, 1761–1850* (Brooklyn, NY, 1991), 123–87; Roth, *Democratic Dilemma*, 55–60, 82. For a typical union church see Town History Committee, *History of Corinth, Vermont* (Corinth, VT, 1964), 121–3.
17. John L. Brooke, *The Heart of the Commonwealth: Society and Political Culture in Worcester County, Massachusetts, 1713–1861* (Cambridge, MA, 1989), 155–88, 269–72; Charles R. Keller, *The Second Great Awakening in Connecticut* (New Haven, CT, 1942), 188–220; C. C. Goen, *Revivalism and Separatism in New England, 1740–1800* (New Haven, CT, 1962), 258–95; Russell E. Miller, *The Larger Hope: The First Century of the Universalist Church in America, 1770–1870* (Boston, MA, 1979), 159–61.
18. George C. Baker, *Introduction to the History of Early New Methodism* (New York, 1969) provides the basics. For an excellent case study of Methodism in an early industrial town, see David Richard Kasserman, *Fall River Outrage: Life, Murder, and Justice in Early Industrial New England* (Philadelphia, 1986). See also Jonathan Prude, *The Coming of Industrial Order: Town and Factory Life in Rural Massachusetts* (Cambridge, MA, 1983), 125–6, 193–254; Thomas Dublin, ed., *From Farm to Factory: Women's Letters, 1830–60* (New York: 1983), 45, 176.
19. *The Christian Herald* (Portsmouth, NH) provides contemporary coverage. See especially the issue for March 1819; Richard Cecil Stone, *Life Incidents of Home School and Church* (St. Louis, MO, 1874), 56–9. Stone grew up in Rhode Island. A good picture of the origins and growth of the Freewill Baptists in Rhode Island can be built up from the entries in Works Projects Administration, *Inventory of the Church Archives of Rhode Island: Baptist* (Providence, RI, 1941), 154–83.
20. Jones, *Economic and Rural Transformation*, 133–7.
21. *Freewill Baptist Magazine* (Providence, RI), August 1826–May 1830, provides reports of quarterly meetings and evangelistic work. See also Jones, *Economic and Rural Transformation*.
22. Daniel Vickers, *Farmers and Fishermen: Two Centuries of Work in Essex County, Massachusetts, 1630–1850* (Chapel Hill, NC, 1994), 294–327.
23. Miller, *The Larger Hope*, 3–49; Marini, *Radical Sects*, 64–88; Kenny, *Perfect Law of Liberty*, 105–7, 145–9; William Bentley, *The Diary of William Bentley D.D.*, 4 vols (reprint, Gloucester, MA, 1962). The diary covers the years 1784 to Bentley's death in 1819. The quotation comes from volume 2, page 260, 6 March 1789.

24. *Contributions to The Ecclesiastical History of Essex County* (Boston, 1865), 234–7. This is a Congregationalist publication, but it gives details of other denominations and is frank on the shortcomings of some post-Revolutionary Standing Order clergy.
25. Smith, *Life*, 14–43; Jones, *Memoir of Abner Jones*, 9–17; E. G. Holland, *Memoir of Joseph Badger* (New York, 1854), 25–31; Ruth D. Bordin, 'The Sect to Denomination Process in America: The Freewill Baptist Experience', *Church History* 34 (1965): 77–94.
26. Ronald P. Formisano, *The Transformation of Political Culture: Massachusetts Parties, 1790s–1840* (New York, 1983), page 369, outlines the problems. Erik Barnouw, *House with a Past* (Montpelier, VT, 1992), 25–47. Barnouw uses 'minnet' books to trace a church in Benson, Vermont which was in turn Calvinist Baptist, Freewill Baptist and Mormon. Church and town histories indicate similar progressions. For example, R. G. Johnson, *Historical Sketch of the North Springfield Baptist Church* (Ludlow, VT, 1880), 3–24; Henry Hobart Vail, *Pomfret, Vermont* (Boston, 1930), 234–5.
27. Marini, *Radical Sects*, 96–8.
28. Kenny, *Perfect Law of Liberty*, 139–47.
29. Billington, '"Female Laborers in the Church:" Women Preachers in the Northeastern United States, 1790–1840,' *Journal of American Studies* 19 (1985): 370–4; Kenny, *Perfect Law of Liberty*, 148–9, 168–9.
30. Billington, 'Female Laborers in the Church,' 380–6 and autobiographies cited there. More detailed family information on Towle can be found in John Dow, *History of the Town of Hampton, New Hampshire* (Salem, MA, 1893), 1011–12. A Congregationalist comment on Danforth can be found in *Ecclesiastical History of Essex County*, 154.
31. Jones, *Economic and Social Transformation*, 154.
32. Roth, *Democratic Dilemma*, 57.
33. Bordin, 'The Sect to Denomination Process,' 81–95; Billington, 'Female Laborers in the Church,' 392–4; Norman A. Baxter, *History of the Freewill Baptists* (Rochester, NY, 1957) offers a traditional denominational account.
34. Jones, *Economic and Social Transformation*, 150–2; Fernald, *Life*, 285–90; Kenny, *Perfect Law of Liberty*, 152; Emeline Burlingame-Cheney, *The Story of the Life and Work of Oren B. Cheney: Founder and First President of Bates College* (Boston, 1907), 15–21; David D. Friend, *Centennial Address* (Middletown, CT, 1853), 180–3, 223–4; Works Projects Administration, *Inventory*, 157–8.
35. Jones, *Economic and Social Transformation*, 154–60; *The Morning Star* (Limerick, ME) reflects support for temperance and anti-slavery through the 1830s, as do the memoirs of the preachers. For example, Fernald, *Life*, 265–352.
36. Billington, 'New England Sectarianism', 133–4; Stephen Allen and W. H. Pillsbury, *History of Methodism in Maine* (Augusta, ME, 1887), 235–272, show numerous local schisms over 'traditional' practices. The expression 'minister factory' is from Munger, *Life*, 28.
37. The painting is in the Abbey Aldrich Rockefeller Folk Art Centre, Williamsburg, Virginia. For Davis see Esther Sparks, 'Joseph H. Davis active c. 1832–1838,' in Jean Lipman, Tom Armstrong, eds, *American Folk*

Painters of Three Centuries (New York, 1980), 66–9. For such itinerant painters as part of a market culture, see David Jaffee, 'Peddlers of Progress and the Transformation of the Rural North, 1760–1860,' *Journal of American History* 78 (1991): 511–35.

38. Charles Sellers, *The Market Revolution: Jacksonian America 1815–1846* (New York, 1991), 30–3, 157–61.
39. Louis Billington, 'Different Paths to Perfection: The Shakers and Radical Sects in New England, 1780–1850', in Mick Gidley, ed., *Locating the Shakers: Cultural Origins and Legacies of an American Religious Movement* (Exeter, 1990), 26; Hatch, *The Democratization of American Christianity*, 26–9; Kenny, *The Perfect Law of Liberty*, 194–214; Leigh Eric Schmidt, '"A Church-going People are a Dress-Loving People": Clothes, Communication, and Religious Culture in Early America', *Church History* 58 (1989): 36–51.
40. Taylor, *Liberty Men and Great Proprietors*, 246–7.
41. Munger, *Life*, page 11, for the 'slavery' of the factories. William L. Camp, *The Green Mountain Preacher or the Travels and Labors of William L. Camp* (Fitchburg, MA, 1853), pages 23–5 and 137–8, for an account of a migratory farm worker and marginal preacher.
42. Sellers, *Market Revolution*, 215–36; Burlingame-Cheney, *Oren P. Cheney*, 1–19; Billington, 'Female Laborers in the Church,' 393–4. Jacob Osgood, *The Life and Christian Experiences of Jacob Osgood* (Warner, NH, 1867 and 1873) for a rigid group which comes close to being a caricature of Sellers' 'antinomian sect'. For the Shakers, see Stephen J. Stein, *The Shaker Experience in America* (New Haven, CT, 1992), 140.
43. William G. McLoughlin, *New England Dissent: The Baptists and the Separation of Church and State, 1633–1833* (Cambridge, MA, 1971). Volume 2 covers the question in great detail for the Calvinist Baptists. See also Taylor, *Liberty Man and Great Proprietors*, 131–53. Kenny, *The Perfect Law of Liberty*, 67–97; Turner, *The Ninth State*, 352–6.
44. W. P. Strickland, ed., *Autobiography of Dan Young* (New York, 1860), 279–81.
45. Jones, *Economic and Social Transformation*, 179–80; Taylor, *Liberty Men and Great Proprietors*, 209–42; Roth, *Democratic Dilemma*, 72–3.
46. William G. McLoughlin, ed., *The Diary of Isaac Backus* (Providence, RI, 1979), 3:1317–18; Smith, *Life*, 234.
47. This is based on a comparison of *Herald of Gospel Liberty* and early Freewill Baptist magazines. Fernald, *Life*, page 311, for a preacher not voting, and Timothy Morse, *Collection of Letters Written by Elder Timothy Morse: With a Brief Sketch of His Life* (Newport, NH, 1831), page 4, for his doubts about holding office.
48. Kenny, *The Perfect Law of Liberty*, 183–6; Fernald, *Life*, 64; John Colby, *The Life, Experiences and Travels of John Colby* (Newport, NH, 1831), 163–4.
49. Taylor, *Liberty Men and Great Proprietors*, 242; Teresa Anne Murphy, *Ten Hours' Labor: Religion, Reform and Gender in Early New England* (Ithaca, NY, 1991) is sensitive to the complexities of the relations between popular Evangelicalism and industrialization. The quotation is from Jama Lazerow, *Religion and the Working Class in Antebellum America* (Washington, DC,

1995), 95. See also Lazerow's generally important analysis of radical Evangelicalism and labour reform in New England, pages 71–91.
50. Paul Goodman, *Towards a Christian Republic: Antimasonry and the Great Transition in New England, 1826–36* (New York, 1988), 116–17; Formisano, *The Transformation of Political Culture*, 219–20.
51. Two contemporary works provide excellent accounts of radical Methodism and anti-slavery. See Lucius C. Matlack, *The Life of Orange Scott* (New York, 1847); idem, *History of American Slavery and Methodism and History of the Wesleyan Methodist Connection of America* (New York, 1849). The Freewill Baptist and Christian press document the rise of anti-slavery and temperance in detail.
52. Richard Carwardine, *Evangelicals and Politics in Antebellum America* (New Haven, CT, 1993), 109–10, 125–7. Carwardine's excellent study shows the complexity of the relationships between party loyalty and particular religious groups, but he broadly supports the interpretations offered here. See also his '"Antinomians" and "Arminians": Methodists and the Market Revolution', unpublished paper given at the Commonwealth Fund Colloquium, University College, London, 1992. Richard Carwardine was focusing on Methodists, but his arguments apply equally well to the Freewill Baptists and Christians.
53. Roth, *Democratic Dilemma*, 251–9; Carwardine, *Evangelicals and Politics*, 109–12, 306–7; Osgood, *Life*; Edward D. Ives, *George Magoon and the Down East Game War* (Urbana, IL, 1988) for post-Civil-War 'traditionalists' in Maine, who fought for their hunting and shooting rights.
54. Harold Fisher Wilson, *The Hill Country of Northern New England: Its Social and Economic History 1790–1930* (New York, 1936), 97–213; Hal Barron, *Those Who Stayed Behind: Rural Society in Nineteenth-Century New England* (Cambridge, MA, 1984), 112–32.
55. Eric Foner, *Free Soil, Free Labor, Free Men: The Ideology of the Republican Party before the Civil War* (New York, 1970), 316.

3

Unitarian Voluntary Societies and the Revision of Elite Authority in Boston, 1780–1820

Anthony Mann

Introduction

Historians of Boston, Massachusetts, are in substantial agreement that at some stage during the nineteenth century the collection of diverse social and economic elites coalesced into the Boston Brahmins: a coherent, distinctive and powerful urban upper class. Scholars have differed as to when this process occurred, but there is broad unanimity that during the period 1830 to 1870 'something akin to a true patriciate, a hereditary class ... emerged'. From the work of Edward Pessen and Frederic Cople Jaher in the 1960s and 1970s to Betty Farrell's recent analysis of elite families, however, the focus of research has been on demonstrating the manner by which an industrial and commercial elite combined economic power with cultural and political dominance. This body of work has provided a detailed understanding of the social and institutional ties which bound one of the most influential social groups the United States has known. Yet, although an enormous amount is now known concerning elite society during the Jacksonian era, there has been a comparative neglect of the era between the Declaration of Independence and the presidency of John Quincy Adams.[1]

The importance of this period in terms of class formation is acute. Many, if not most, of the diverse institutions which operated to support the cohesion and authority of the Brahmin class were founded during the generation which followed the American Revolution. In the economic sphere, the Massachusetts Bank, Boston's first such financial institution, was chartered in 1784, the first incorporated insurance company emerged in 1795, and the Boston Manufacturing Company, the founding corporation of the Waltham-Lowell textile industrial empire, was established in 1813. Other important financial institutions followed: the Provident Institution for Savings (1816), the Massachusetts Hospital Life Insurance Company (1818) and the Suffolk Bank (1818), each playing significant roles in the economic infrastructure which supported the Brahmin class. Elsewhere, in medicine for example, this era saw the foundation of many elite-sponsored institutions, most notably: Harvard Medical School (1781), Massachusetts Medical Society (1782), Boston Dispensary (1795), Massachusetts General Hospital (1811) and the McLean Asylum (1816). Culturally, the Boston Athenæum (1807) and the *North American Review* (1815) are lasting legacies of the creative impulse of the Early Republic. Moreover, it was during this era that many of families who would later occupy important roles within the Brahmin upper class relocated to Boston from provincial New England. The Appletons, Cabots, Lawrences, Lowells and Sturgises were just a few of the clans who moved to the Massachusetts capital after 1776.[2]

By the Jacksonian era the basis of Brahmin cohesion and power had been laid. Within a generation of the Revolution a multitude of important institutions had been founded, exhibiting a high degree of cooperation amongst elites of wealth and status. The aim of this essay is to examine the creation of a number of such post-Revolutionary institutions, in the hope that an understanding of the dynamics which surrounded their origins will allow greater insight into the adjustment of New England elites to the new world order of Republican America. In so doing, it assesses the diverse motivations among secular and religious elites which coincided in the establishment of organizational structures which were later to play important roles in the formation of a coherent and distinct upper class. Finally, the essay will reflect upon the origins of the class authority claimed by nineteenth-century Brahmins.

Fundamental Characteristics of Four New Institutions

Four institutions of the Early Republic are the subject of this essay: the American Academy of Arts and Sciences, established in 1780, which in spite of its name was essentially a Boston organization; the Humane Society of Massachusetts (1787); the Massachusetts Historical Society (founded in 1791 and incorporated in 1794); and the Massachusetts Society for Promoting Agriculture (1792).[3] These organizational forms were new. Whereas the great majority of private societies founded before 1780 were either masonic lodges or church-inspired charitable bodies, mixing the opportunity for social interaction with fundraising to relieve poverty, the post-1780 institutions were more complex in their aspirations.

In addition to a shared reputation for elite patronage, the four new institutions held much in common. They shared the same basic structure, in that each was incorporated by vote of the Massachusetts legislature. As such, each bore an ambiguous relationship towards the state government. In a standard fashion they were permitted to establish regulations for internal self-government and to function in law 'as a body politic and corporate', with the right to sue and be sued, and so protect institutional property. In the case of the American Academy and also of the Historical Society, legislators were guaranteed access to libraries and collections, but ultimately all four institutions, although validated by their relation to the state, were independent of it.[4]

These private societies shared more than an equal legal status. Indeed, it is possible to sketch their fundamental characteristics as follows:

1. The prime instigators were predominantly men of Unitarian affiliation.

The work of Conrad Wright has shown that it was Unitarians who predominated as the founders and early organizers of these four and similar post-Revolutionary private societies. Routinely, a majority of first members were Unitarian ministers or laymen. Equally, Wright has shown that Unitarian men of wealth and status were disproportionately inclined to join such organizations. This is perhaps unsurprising for, by the late eighteenth century, Unitarianism had become the dominant form of Protestantism within Boston. Rationalistic and antagonistic to emotional Christianity, the creed appealed to a conservative Patriot elite which had done so much to lead the nation into home rule and then aspired to maintain social order within political independence. One study suggests that 70 percent of Boston's wealthiest 255 men of known church affiliation in 1798 belonged to Unitarian congregations. It was these lay and clerical elites, frequently holding multiple memberships, who dominated the establishment of the four institutions explored here. A number of active individuals such as the Unitarian ministers Joseph Stevens Buckminster, William Emerson and John Kirkland Thornton belonged to all four, as did their co-religionists the physician Aaron Dexter, the lawyer John Lowell and Federalist politician Josiah Quincy. In all, the distinctive pattern of early membership allows Wright to assert that 'a closely-knit clique' of Unitarians, operating in and around Boston, was brought into frequent social contact through their involvement in this wave of newly created private societies.[5]

2. The prime instigators were men of status, but rarely merchants.

As might be expected, the institutions were established by, and then attracted as members, men of standing in post-Revolutionary Boston. However, one major social group appears underrepresented. Investigations into the occupations of the founders of four societies demonstrates that there were no merchants among the four prime instigators of the Humane Society of Massachusetts (HSM), nor among the ten men who established the Massachusetts Historical Society (MHS). Of the sixty-two incorporators of the American Academy of Arts and Sciences (AAAS) only five were merchants or men of independent means, whilst one-third of the officers of the Massachusetts Society for Promoting Agriculture (MSPA) during its first twenty years were commercial men involved in overseas trade. Rather, in terms of profession, it was ministers, lawyers, jurists, physicians, public officials and Harvard educators who predominated. In their initial establishment these institutions are best seen as being, typically, the products of elites of status, rather than as resulting from the efforts of men occupying positions of the greatest economic importance.[6]

However, although disproportionately absent as founders, men of substantial economic power did join these institutions. One way to measure this growing involvement is to compare the activities of the thirty-five officers of the three Boston banks in 1796 against the membership patterns of forty-one men who instigated three of the most important economic institutions of the antebellum era: the founding shareholders of the Boston Manufacturing Company (1813); the first officers of the Suffolk Bank (1818); and those of the Massachusetts Hospital Life Insurance Company (1823). All six institutions were the result of cooperative endeavours by men of wealth who predominantly secured from seaborne trade the capital they would pool for financial institutions. They can therefore be seen as representative of the merchant economic elite. *Table 3.1* demonstrates a substantial and growing engagement in the four voluntary societies by men of the greatest economic importance.

Table 3.1: Membership in four voluntary societies of Boston bankers in 1796 and men of economic power (1813–1823).[7]

Group	Number	AAAS	HSM	MHS	MSPA
Boston Bankers 1796	35	14%	69%	17%	29%
Manufacturers/ Financiers 1813–1823	41	29%	51%	24%	39%

3. In membership, the societies were exclusive, yet inclusive of elites of wealth and of status.

The membership of these four societies was socially distinctive. Unitarian congregations during this era did include artisans, but their presence within the membership of the four voluntary societies was negligible. All the institutions maintained a degree of social exclusivity. The American Academy of Arts and Sciences and the Historical Society both limited numbers to some 60 resident members with the election of new entrants subject to veto by a majority of existing members. The other organizations were larger. Some 150 belonged to the Humane Society in 1788, whilst the Agricultural Society expanded from some 28 incorporators to 365 members by 1817. With the HSM and MSPA, exclusivity was maintained by the informality with which prospective members were approached. Thus, whilst the labouring classes were excluded, in occupational terms, as suggested earlier, a broad cross-section of elites, wealth and status was included. Although each of the societies was dominated by advocates of Federalism and Unitarianism, political and religious dissenters of sufficient standing were welcome. Governor James Sullivan, for example, was a leading Jeffersonian Republican, but also president of the Historical Society between 1791 and 1806 and the Reverend Jedidiah Morse, who was among the most vocal critics of Unitarianism, belonged to both the Historical Society and the Academy of Arts and Sciences.[8]

4. The societies encompassed a claim to public utility based upon a diffusion of empirically derived Enlightenment knowledge.[9]

Although privately constructed and exclusive in membership, the societies aimed to support the public good in a manner which went beyond the relief of poverty. According to its charter, the American Academy of Arts and Sciences was established to cultivate 'every art and science which may tend to advance the interest, honor, dignity, and happiness of a free, independent and virtuous people'. James Bowdoin's founding oration confirmed that the society, formed as it was 'on the plan of the philosophical societies of Europe', would follow 'the fundamental principle' in basing all of its enquiries upon 'fact and observation'. The purpose of the Humane Society was to diffuse knowledge concerning how best to revive people feared drowned, emphasizing in its first publication that 'the acquisition of one deserving member of society [is not] an object unworthy [of] public attention'. Such an attempt to improve the human condition was based, equally, upon scientific discoveries. 'From a variety of faithful experiments and incontestable facts,' began the society's founding notice reprinted in local newspapers, 'it is now considered an established truth, that the total suspension of the vital function in the animal body, is by no means incompatible with life; and consequently, the marks of apparent death may subsist without any implication of an absolute extinction of the animating principle.' The extrinsic integrity of the endeavour was further supported by accompanying quantified details of the successes of the British Humane Society.[10]

The members of the Historical Society also saw something noble in their enterprise, as they sought to rescue, improve and promote 'the true history of this country from the ravages of time and the effects of ignorance and neglect'. Elsewhere, utility was asserted in that the Society would protect documents from the 'ravages of unprincipled men' in the hope that 'a faithful record of various events of time, leads to a probable prediction of the future'. That the historians shared in the basic assumptions of their more obviously scientific peers is revealed in an early publication exploring the nature of the so-called Dark Day of 19 May 1780. In a revealing aside, the anonymous author argued that, as 'it was supernatural was never supposed but by the ignorant and superstitious, it must then admit of a rational and philosophical explanation.'[11]

Finally, the Agricultural Society affirmed in its *Rules and Regulations* of 1793 that the 'members of the Society have no other interest, than the benefit of the human species at large'. To achieve such a goal, the members of the Society encouraged rational experimentation in farming and diffused material concerning similar endeavours in Europe. The agriculturists' first publication, in 1793, offered prizes for successful indigenous experiment, and included advice, extracted from foreign publications, on cattle breeding and cheese making. A Boston reviewer of the Society's 1804 *Papers* reminded readers that the MSPA's members were 'convinced that Agriculture derives aid from the discoveries and labours of the philosopher, the naturalist and the chemist,' and 'that inquiry is the road to improvement'. By 1820, the Society had found a label for its agrarian vision. That year's presidential address was given by the future mayor of Boston Josiah Quincy. He urged the farmers of the state to adopt the principles of 'systematic agriculture'.[12]

5. The societies maintained high public profiles.

A degree of social prominence must be expected of voluntary organizations seeking to diffuse useful knowledge, but in their public excursions the societies frequently went beyond what might be seen as the purely practical. In addition to newspaper reports of meetings and publications, the wider public would have been aware of institutional activity in a variety of civic ceremonies and spectacles. The organized presence of the societies was witnessed at the funerals of the leading men of post-Revolutionary Boston, such as that of the Unitarian Minister Simeon Howard in 1804, and Federalist leader Fisher Ames in 1808. In 1810, the long procession which preceded the inauguration of John Thornton Kirkland, another Unitarian minister, as president of Harvard College included representatives of the Academy of Arts and Sciences and the Humane Society marching just before 'Gentlemen [sic] particularly invited' and 'Judges of the Supreme Judicial Court'. The activities of the Humane Society were even more visually striking. From the start, the Society adopted the British habit of an annual anniversary day wherein, amid 'a great deal of pomp and circumstance', officers and members paraded from a suitably dignified venue such as the Massachusetts State House, to a respectable church where they heard sermons and orations delivered by ministers, physicians and public officials. Throughout the day those fortunate individuals who had been saved from drowning by the innovations of the Society were presented to the public. In a similar fashion, from 1816 the MSPA sponsored an annual agricultural show. On the principal day, the members of the Society with invited guests formed in front of a specially constructed hall, before marching, in step to drums, fifes, clarinets and cymbals, to a local meeting house where they commenced their annual meeting.[13]

The four institutions, therefore, were distinctive in the character of their founders and early membership. They maintained high public profiles and self-consciously aspired to improve the human condition through the adaptation of empirical, scientific knowledge. Although the societies engaged in diverse areas of interest, the similarities between them are striking. Exploration of the context which surrounded the birth of these institutions offers ways of accounting for the apparently consistent patterns which shaped the formative years of their institutional growth.

Explanations for the Emergence of the Four Institutions

Established within twenty years of the Declaration of Independence, each of the four societies can be seen as embodying a patriotic desire to create the cultural infrastructure of a new nation. However, the manner in which this objective was undertaken was derivative. Three of the four were modelled explicitly on European institutions, with the exception, the Historical Society, reflecting the widespread desire among the aristocracy and urban gentry of Georgian Britain for institutionalizing its interest in antiquarian pursuits.[14] An initial interpretation of these institutions is to see them emerging from an aspirational legacy retained from the late colonial era, when American elites took from Britain definitions of what it was to be a true gentleman. The cultivated individual, learned in science and classical literature, interested in antiquarian pursuits, benevolent and polished in polite society, was an ideal of the late eighteenth century shared by many Americans. A desire for inclusion within a transatlantic cultural world continued after the Revolution, when this desire for distinction was now also expressed within indigenous private societies.[15]

An examination of the demography of post-Revolutionary Boston elites reveals strong reasons why cultural aspirations might take institutional forms. The Revolution produced a significant change among the personnel who constituted the social and economic elites of Massachusetts. A substantial number of Loyalist merchants and public officials were replaced by new men, many of whom would fail and in turn be replaced during the unprecedentedly unstable trading conditions of the 1780s. When James Bowdoin wrote to a friend of Boston, in 1783, he may have been exaggerating the scale, but not the substance of the events he had experienced: 'When you come, you will scarcely see any other than new faces ..., the change which in that respect has happened within the few years since the revolution is as remarkable as the revolution itself.'[16]

Earlier, in 1779, General James Warren wrote to John Adams, lamenting that 'fellows who would have cleaned my shoes five years ago, have amassed fortunes, and are riding in chariots. Were you to be set down here you could not realize what you would see. You would think you was upon enchanted ground in a world turned topsy turvy.' The following year, both men, alongside James Bowdoin, would become founding members of the American Academy of Arts and Science. The foundation, exclusivity and membership of the four institutions, therefore, may be seen as reflective of a desire to clarify social identities. Certainly, decisions made in the foundation of the four societies emphasized a structured exclusivity regulating the inclusion of men enjoying status and wealth. They were organized as subscriber democracies. The key distinction would be between those within the society, and those outside who were unwilling or unable to join. As with the subscription dances of the eighteenth-century Anglo-American world, insiders met on terms of equality, holding the same voting rights and office-holding potential.

Moreover, the institutions visibly associated their members with the most powerful of colonial vertical ties in continuing transatlantic connections to the British ruling class. Cultural deference was maintained in both the choice of institutional focus and in the structures within which their activities took place. Early in their histories, the societies sought to align themselves with symbols of Anglocentric gentility. The Historical Society, between 1794 and 1833, occupied rooms in Charles Bulfinch's neoclassical and London-inspired Tontine Crescent; whilst the American Academy, having met at a number of locations, from 1817 established permanent residence within the elegant Boston Athenæum. The Humane Society, from the start, held functions at the homes of its wealthiest supporters.[17]

In part, therefore, the emergence of these societies can be attributed to a desire for social codification expressing itself through the cultural parameters of late colonial society, yet such an explanation is, in itself, insufficient. It does not account for the peculiar founding roles of Unitarian ministers and laymen, nor the initial absence of economic elites. Moreover, a number of unincorporated, yet still formal, societies appeared during the same era, offering alternative means of social codification. Alongside the highly regulated Assembly dances and subscription balls, from 1777 serious conversationalists had the opportunity of attending the Wednesday Evening Club's weekly dinner. Men with a strong amateur interest in science could, from 1801, apply for membership of the Society for the Study of Natural Philosophy. This group met once a week through the winter months to study texts on electricity, metallurgy, chemistry and other scientific works. As ten of the twelve founders, none of whom could be labelled a professional scientist, were also members of the American Academy of Arts and Sciences, the implication must be that the latter institution cannot have sufficiently fulfilled the desire for empirical knowledge among the collection of Unitarian ministers, physicians and lawyers who established the new society. Post-Revolutionary elites might have followed the same interests and engaged in diverse processes of social codification without the need for incorporated, exclusive, public institutions.[18]

A second and related possible explanation for the emergence of these institutions is in terms of the maintenance of authority. Frederic Cople Jaher has argued that the voluntary societies of nineteenth-century Boston 'functioned expressively and instrumentally to perpetuate patrician hegemony'. Clearly, in addition to offering a mechanism for cultural and institutional cohesion, the high public profiles, explicitly altruistic aims, and shared emphasis on Enlightenment thought suggest an engagement in contemporary debates concerning the development appropriate to post-Revolutionary New England. The idea for the American Academy of Arts and Sciences was first generated by John Adams, after he witnessed a Baptist meeting in Philadelphia where the preacher unnervingly spoke in a manner 'violent to a degree bordering on fury'. As such societies were established and supported by religious, professional and economic elites, the question of social control must be addressed.

Social control, defined by F. M. L. Thompson from the context of Victorian Britain as the imposition of opinions and habits by one class upon another, does appear to have been at least one of the motivations of the members of the Agricultural Society. The MSPA was founded five years after Shays's Rebellion and addressed an issue of central importance to the Massachusetts' farmers who took up arms on that occasion. Whereas the Rebels had explained their parlous economic state in terms of excessive taxation and avarice on the part of powerful east coast merchants and lawyers, the Boston society sought to persuade agrarians that their problems stemmed from an insufficient understanding of the principles of scientific agriculture. The approach of the MSPA clearly acted to de-legitimize the claims of the insurgents and alter popular interpretations of rural decline.[19]

However, as Thompson asserts, while elites might seek to impose social control, the success of any such endeavour is by no means assured. The case of the MSPA is illustrative. Farmers occupying smallholdings, excluded from membership, refused to become involved in the activities of the Society. Indeed, in his presidential address of 1800, the Boston jurist and financier John Lowell acknowledged that many doubted the utility of the organization. He recognized that many had asked: 'Why do [these trustees] pretend to be instructors of the farmers of our Country? Are they not a number of gentlemen, who live in or near the Metropolis, and have little knowledge of the subject, except some theoretical notions derived from books?' Lowell's response was to reposition the role of the Society. 'We do not pretend to much knowledge,' he affirmed, 'and that not of the best; but we do profess to be lovers of the best interest of our Country, and are willing to take some trouble to promote it.' President Lowell recognized that the information diffused by the MSPA was not always of universal and incontestable value, but this was, to him, of secondary importance. It was rather the inherent benevolence motivating the members of the Society that Lowell sought to emphasize. The point was not what they were doing, but why they were doing it. In drawing such a distinction, the president engaged in a debate concerning private intentions and public roles which flourished through the Early Republic and provides, perhaps, the most useful context for explaining the rise of the MSPA and its less obviously authoritarian institutional cousins.[20]

The Leadership Ideal: Ability and Integrity

Private motivations were important in New England during the late eighteenth century. The remnants of Puritan theology and of Republican theory combined to envisage a society dependent for its stability upon individual and collective virtue. The *Essex Result* of 1778 is illustrative. The document contributed to an ongoing debate concerning the post-Revolutionary constitutional settlement appropriate to Massachusetts, expressing the collective opinion of the professional and merchant elites of the port towns of Essex County, Massachusetts. The writers argued:

> That among gentlemen of education, fortune and leisure, we shall find the largest number of men, possessed of wisdom, learning, and

a firmness of character. That among the bulk of the people, we shall find the greatest share of honesty, probity, and a regard to the interest of the whole, of which they compose the majority. That wisdom and firmness are not sufficient without good intentions, nor the latter without the former. The conclusion is, let the legislative body unite them all. The former are called the excellencies that result from an aristocracy; the latter, those that result from a democracy.[21]

The Essex Result held that elites were legitimate if they combined personal altruism with ability, and such thinking influenced the final Massachusetts Constitution of 1780. That document, largely the work of Patriot elites, enshrined a graduated link between property qualifications and elected state office and advised voters to elect men who adhered to the private virtues of 'piety, moderation, temperance, industry and frugality'.

Within this leadership ideal deference was given to the man of ability and integrity, not to the advocate of political measures. The responsible, active leader would be governed by his own conscience, rather than by the whim of popular opinion. 'Human nature has its weaknesses,' the Massachusetts jurist Theophilus Parsons wrote in 1783, 'but it [is] our duty not to indulge, but correct them.' The special obligation of the gentleman of fortune, education and leisure was to secure social stability through virtuous example. 'The bulk of the people know but little of the government under which they live', wrote the Boston merchant Stephen Higginson in 1789, 'their opinions are formed, principally at least, from the character and conduct of the magistrates and other executive officers, who live near them.' John Adams was thinking in the same fashion in 1786 when he located the popular virtue of New England in its towns, militias, schools and churches. These were the traditional vertical institutions of closest social proximity wherein the private character of elites would be most readily witnessed.[22]

Any hopes, however, which post-Revolutionary elites might have maintained about the continuation of popular deference after Independence were to be disappointed. In addition to the agrarian discontent which culminated in Shays's Rebellion, the considered opinion of the self-regarding aristocracy of virtue and talent was challenged during the campaign to ratify the Federal Constitution and, more permanently, by the rise of Jeffersonian Republicanism. In the national election of 1800, Massachusetts was retained by the Adams's slate, but still 43 percent of voters ignored the advice of the reconstituted 'Standing Order' of Federalist social and economic elites. Hence, the reaction of the conservative activist Theodore Sedgwick to Jefferson's triumph: 'The aristocracy of virtue is destroyed; personal influence is at an end'.[23]

Due to the nature of their concept of authority, post-Revolutionary New England elites were deeply concerned by these continual challenges to their leadership. Republics were widely perceived as fragile creatures whose stability was dependent upon the disinterested willingness of inhabitants to place the public good before private desires. Elites felt a heavy obligation to serve wisely. If the natural aristocracy abdicated its responsibilities to lead in an active, virtuous manner, then an 'honest, but deluded' people would quickly find themselves the dupes of 'designing men'.[24] Jonathan Jackson, Boston merchant and an early Federalist leader, delicately criticized his peers for such a dangerous failure to fulfil their obligations in an 1788 essay: 'Men of merit, and of the best understandings,' he lamented, 'are too much inclined to seek the shade of retirement.'[25]

Others were more forthcoming than Jackson in criticizing the actions of the rich and powerful. The Boston press of the 1780s continually returned to a theme of elites engaging in behaviour which was decidedly unvirtuous. In a series of pseudonymous and unsigned articles the excesses of polite society were exposed. The immediate background to the formation of the Humane Society was one of frequent and bitter attacks upon the social activities of the town's rich and fashionable classes. An attempt to establish the Boston Orchestra as a venue for Italian opera in 1785 was assaulted as a threat to industry and frugality, with the subscribers condemned as intimates of Loyalists. The same year saw newspapers record a bitter debate over the Sans Souci Club, a gathering of the young members of wealthy families for dancing and card playing. An article signed by 'Observer' in the *Massachusetts Centinel* of January 1785 was typical, viewing the club as representative of a society 'exchanging prudence, virtue and economy for the glaring spectres of luxury, prodigality and profligacy. We are prostituting all our glory as a people, for new modes of pleasure, ruinous in their expenses, injurious to virtue, and totally detrimental to the well being of society.' In their private actions it appeared that the most excessively genteel sections of the economic elite were placing themselves in opposition to the public good. A writer in the *Boston Gazette* charged: '... Are not our mushroom gentry, in conjunction with those on the other side of the atlantic [sic], introducing every species of foreign luxuries, not only in dress, but at their tables? How is the course of nature changed ... is it not *Bon Ton* to rise at 10 – breakfast at 11 – and dine at 4 o'clock or later, rattling through our paved streets in their carriages to the great annoyance of the peaceful inhabitants; especially the *sick and the dying*?'[26]

Furthermore, just as the personal morality of elites was challenged, so too their private motives were suspected. An attempt to incorporate the town of Boston in November 1785 was denounced by 'Publicola' in the *Massachusetts Centinel*; the writer claiming that 'the offices of Mayor and alderman will become in a degree hereditary among the families of the rich and increase their power and insolence'. 'Crito' in March 1786 portrayed attempts to cut the funding of Boston's public schools as the duplicitous work of 'men of narrow, contracted, arbitrary principles ... artful and ambitious whose object is power, and whose Deity is mammon.'[27]

To an extent the criticisms of the 1780s can be read as popular challenges to elite authority. The economic background was one of slump, as from 1783 British merchants and imported goods returned to Boston, threatening the livelihoods of artisans and small traders. Simultaneously, controversies developed surrounding the return of suspected Loyalists, many of whom, such as John Temple, son-in-law of Governor James Bowdoin, were linked to prominent members of the Boston elite. The critics reflected these developments in intertwining themes of Loyalism, British commercial ties and the excessive consumption of European luxury goods. However, when the censors of elite irresponsibility and extravagance can be identified, it emerges that they were members of the same broad social and economic 'Standing Order'. In addition to later leading Jeffersonians, such as Samuel Adams and Benjamin Austin Jr, other less likely individuals are distinguished, most notably: General James Warren, Harvard tutor, physician Benjamin Waterhouse, the Unitarian Minister John Eliot and the merchant Jonathan Jackson.[28]

Such evidence suggests that shortly after Independence, the broad Massachusetts elite was undergoing a crisis of identity as well as of legitimacy. Unstable in terms of personnel, differentiated in origins and attitudes, social and economic elites failed to agree on the behaviour appropriate to a Republican aristocracy. Herein lie multiple reasons why individuals, including those critics above named, might seek to establish institutions which would serve to engage economic elites in more acceptable social pursuits. They also reminded the public of the innate benevolence of society's 'higher orders'. The four voluntary societies reacted to particular historical circumstances: they hoped to collectivize private virtue, and make institutional affiliation itself a token of the patriotic and disinterested intent to serve the public good. Hence, the high public profile of the societies; the need for exclusivity; and the willingness of diverse political elites to become involved. Clearly, men such as Samuel Adams, in acting to encourage the agricultural pursuits of the MSPA, hoped for a reformation of elites themselves. Others, acutely aware of the damaging public image of fashionable living, hoped for a change in the popular understanding of elites. Either way, the context out of which the four institutions emerged was one where conservatives aspired to alter the public perception of the 'Standing Order', and particularly economic elites, and strengthen and defend the existing social order.

Debates over the inadequacies of elite virtue intensified with the development of the first party system in 1793. The Federalist coalition of men of wealth and status was accused, in the representative words of Republican farmer William Manning, of 'ever hankering & striving after Monerca [sic] or Aristocracy whare [sic] the people have nothing to do in matters of government but to seport [sic] the few in luxury & idleness.' Faced with a more severe crisis of authority, the overwhelmingly Federalist Unitarian activists responded by refining their arguments and redoubling their missionary work among the less responsible sections of elite society. In so doing, an insight emerges into two final questions concerning the essential characteristics of these institutions of the Early Republic: why it was that Unitarians played such central creative roles; and why their societies predicated public utility so fully upon the adaptation of Enlightenment knowledge.[29]

Unitarian Actions to Secure a Deferential and Stable Social Order

The deepest roots of New England Unitarianism are to be found in the eighteenth-century Congregational Church. Although increasingly theological differences made for distinct denominations, the Unitarian ministers of the Early Republic retained the commitment of their forbears to a social order secured through virtuous hierarchy. The Reverend John Thornton Kirkland envisaged in 1798 'an equality which secures the rich from rapacity, no less than the poor from oppression; an equality, which claims peace alike to the mansions of the affluent, and the humble dwellings of the poor.' Within this structured social order, ministers shared the early Federalist view that stability depended in great part upon the deportment of men of status and power. The Reverend Peter Thacher, for example, in an 1793 sermon idealized a paternalistic role for secular elites, acting to restrain vice by making men 'ashamed of doing base and unworthy actions'.[30]

It is then to be expected that the Unitarian ministers, who did so much to establish the four institutions which are the subject of this essay, were deeply concerned by the behaviour of elites. They feared it would undermine the harmonious community they idealized. In a similar manner to the critics of the 1780s, John Thornton Kirkland saw profound dangers arising from the private actions of men of wealth. 'We are becoming familiar with wealth,' he wrote in 1807. 'Out of wealth grows luxury. If those enjoyments that flow from literature and taste are not emulated, we shall be exposed to that enervating and debasing luxury, the object of which is sensual indulgence, its immediate effect, vice, and its ultimate issue, publick [*sic*] degradation.' Kirkland was writing in the *Monthly Anthology and Boston Review*, a journal dominated by Unitarian ministers including Joseph Stevens Buckminster, William Emerson and Samuel Cooper Thacher, together with lay members of their congregations. These were men who shared Kirkland's views. 'Thoughts on Dress', published in 1804, for example, criticized a readership of social and economic elites: 'We have imported the worst of French corruptions, the want of female delicacy, exposing the chaste bosom to the gaze of wantonness.' The 'fluttering fop' and others were reminded that: 'Utility is the basis of ornament.'[31]

It was the desire for reform that stimulated the movement to establish the Boston Athenæum. The Unitarian recognition of the need to appeal to local families of wealth is seen most explicitly in an 1807 document supporting its proposed establishment. The memorandum, drawn up by Kirkland on behalf of his fellow Anthologists, was circulated among those men of wealth thought to be able and willing to invest the considerable sum of $300 demanded for one of 150 hereditary shares in the proprietorial library. Explicitly addressing merchants, professionals and 'men of leisure', Kirkland presented the Athenæum as a place of intellectual improvement; a 'fountain, at which all, who choose, may gratify their thirst for knowledge.'

In encouraging the application of wealth 'to some of its noblest uses', Kirkland drew a connection between the private behaviour of elites and their social roles. 'It concerns the public interest, as well as honor,' he maintained, 'that the higher classes of society, and possessors of superfluous wealth, should prefer elegant and innoxious luxuries to those of a different character.' Furthermore:

> It is obvious to all, who attend ... the history of human society, and it is verified by observing the state of manners in our own country, that affluence and prosperity are ever attended by a correspondent passion for amusement and pleasures ... It is equally obvious, that whatever serves to correct and regulate this passion is an additional security to public and private morals. In this view it must be acknowledged important, not only to check that dissipation which enervates and depraves, but also to moderate and qualify a propensity to what are deemed the less exceptionable modes of pleasure, – to show and equipage, convivable entertainments, festive assemblies, and theatrical exhibitions. One effectual method of accomplishing this purpose is to promote a relish for the pleasures of knowledge ... In these respects therefore, as tending to substitute mental occupation for sensual indulgence, and to create a fund of rational and salutary enjoyments in a place and state of society, where

the love of pleasure and the means of it are continually augmenting, and where expense is not grudged to amusements of a different nature, it is presumed this institution will be thought to deserve the countenance of the wise and patriotic.[32]

The Athenæum would be a logical expression of Unitarian thought. The library would act as a repository for the most advanced knowledge available within the transatlantic world. Access to this cultural realm would provide a legitimate arena for elites to engage in an acceptable use of their leisure time. As with the societies of the 1780s and 1790s, the Athenæum would be of public utility, not because the public could use the facilities, but because it would improve the quality of those best suited to govern.

The Unitarian clerical and lay elite were motivated, in part, by a desire to secure a deferential, stable social order through a reformation of the private behaviour of secular economic elites. Their actions, however, cannot be seen as wholly selfless. Unitarians had theological reasons to be drawn to Enlightenment thought. Faced with the dual threat of the dangerous emotionalism of Baptists and Methodists, and the 'infidel philosopher, equally subversive of freedom, as of morals', associated with Jacobin France and Paineite Deism, the Boston ministers looked to empirical knowledge for proof of a creative divine being. The mysteries of the universe were being uncovered by scholars throughout the western world and ultimately institutions devoted to the study and diffusion of ideas connected to history, science, agriculture and human physical capabilities sustained a religious faith predicated upon reason and enquiry.[33]

'An Essay on Civilization', published in the *Monthly Anthology* in May 1804, had defined savagery in terms of ignorance of the revealed truths of the gospel, but also as an unwillingness to acknowledge the verity of the progress discovered by Enlightenment thought:

> In civilized life ... we are to look for the enjoyments of refined science, and here only can we find a proficiency of useful knowledge. Savage indeed, and beyond question barbarous must be that man who situated on the beauteous mount of science, does not rejoice in his elevated station, and sensibly regret the fate of his bewildered brethren, who grope below in the vales of darkness and errour [sic].[34]

In drawing upon 'incontestable facts' to support the work of the Humane Society and in establishing the Historical Society to rescue the 'true history' of their nation, Unitarian elites were engaged in a broader attempt to buttress the claims of Christianity with the evidence of scientific investigation. The Reverend William Emerson reminded the supporters of the Humane Society that they were 'both friends of science and lovers of mercy'. In so doing, Unitarianism and its associated institutions successfully appealed to many social and economic secular elites anxious for certainty in an unstable and troubled world. The Athenæum was to be one of the most successful of nineteenth-century private institutions.[35]

Conclusion

As Henry Adams wrote, the colonial world ruled Boston long after 1776.[36] The creation by elites of voluntary societies during the Early Republic confirms this. Post-Revolutionary elites retained aspirations to social legitimacy through maintenance of transatlantic cultural identities. Yet, this position was fraught with dangers. Their excesses threatened to undermine the civic authority of social and economic elites by associating them with the private vices of vanity and luxury and so rendering them unfit to lead an independent New England. Unitarian ministers and laymen agreed with Republican theorists in emphasizing the peculiar importance of personal character in legitimating deference to governance by the few. In sponsoring the construction of cultural and philanthropic private societies, Unitarian activists offered an acceptable level of genteel behaviour and a responsible use of leisure. Private virtue, thereafter, would be demonstrated in collective form.

In terms of class formation, the institutions offered mechanisms wherein social ties and loyalties would be strengthened. More than this, the societies encouraged a revision of the relationship between elites and masses.[37] Whereas, during the pre-Revolutionary era, benevolence was chiefly a private characteristic and institutionalized only to relieve the worst extremes of poverty, after Independence benevolence became a matter of active leadership. Drawing on the application of Enlightenment knowledge to improve the human condition, elites would act as interested amateurs occupying crucial institutional roles as the sponsors, importers and diffusers of external and incontestable knowledge.

It would be churlish to suggest that many involved in these institutions were not motivated by a sincere desire to improve the lives of New Englanders through collective effort and the application of reason. As Daniel Walker Howe has stated, nineteenth-century Boston Unitarians 'were probably the most convinced believers in progress the world has ever known'. Moreover, Conrad Wright reminds us that 'a sense of responsibility for the community as a whole served to temper the temptation to be guided purely by narrow class interest'. However, the nature of the social obligations felt, and the character of the progress envisaged, were shaped by the interests of secular and religious elites as they sought to adjust to a post-Revolutionary world marked by a deep and unsettling instability. Adapting the ideological legacy of colonial theories of legitimate authority, the elites of the Early Republic inadvertently constructed institutions which would act to consolidate their transformation into arguably the most powerful and important urban upper class of nineteenth-century America.[38]

Notes

1. As with any essay investigating the 'higher levels' of nineteenth-century America, it is necessary to offer a definition of terms to be used. It is the assumption of this work that a number of broadly coherent 'elites' were identifiable in post-Revolutionary Boston. Of these, the most important for this essay were: a commercial elite, largely comprised of merchants and financiers, occupying the highest positions of economic power; a political elite, which was largely unified in opposition to Shays's Rebellion and in support of the Federal Constitution and then strongly Federalist after 1793; and a religious elite of active ministers and laymen within the Unitarian wing of the Congregational Church, the dominant Protestant denomination in late eighteenth-century Boston. Unless otherwise prefixed, 'elite' or 'natural aristocracy' is used to describe the collective of all 'elites'; i.e. following F. C. Jaher, 'all groups that wield power or possess high status and large fortune'. As the post-Revolutionary 'elite' was strongly characterized by a religiously derived attachment to social stability and hierarchy, the term 'Standing Order', adapted from late colonial usage, will be used to identify this broad 'elite' when united by political attitudes. Lacking institutional mechanisms for reproducing their family status and economic position across generations, the post-Revolutionary 'elite' cannot be seen as an upper class. Ultimately, the 'elite' of the Early Republic owed their positions to a combination of personal talent, good fortune and family background. The upper class of the nineteenth century, supported by trust funds and dividends, enjoyed an unprecedented degree of stability, allowing for a perpetuation of social status across generations. This understanding of the difference between 'elite' and 'upper class' is particularly informed by Frederic Cople Jaher, ed., *The Rich, the Well Born and the Powerful, Elites and Upper Classes in History* (Secaucus, NJ: Citadel Press, 1975), Introduction; E. Digby Baltzell, *Puritan Boston and Quaker Philadelphia: Two Protestant Ethics and the Spirit of Class Authority and Leadership* (New York: Free Press, 1979), 19–34; Conrad Wright, 'Ministers, Churches, and the Boston Elite, 1791–1815', in Conrad Edick Wright, ed., *Massachusetts and the New Nation* (Boston: Massachusetts Historical Society, 1992), 118.
2. The historiography of the nineteenth-century Boston elite is rich. Works which focus strongly upon the Jacksonian era include Betty G. Farrell,

Elite Families: Class and Power in Nineteenth Century Boston (Albany: State University of New York Press, 1993); Paul Goodman, 'Ethics and Enterprise: The Values of the Boston Elite, 1800–1860', *American Quarterly* 18 (1966): 437–51; Frederic Cople Jaher, 'The Boston Brahmins in the Age of Industrial Capitalism', in Frederic Cople Jaher, ed., *The Age of Industrialism in America: Essays in Social Structure and Cultural Values* (New York: Free Press, 1968); Frederic Cople Jaher, 'Nineteenth Century Elites in Boston and New York', *Journal of Social History* 6 (1972), 33–66; William H. Pease and Jane H. Pease, *The Web of Progress: Private Values and Public Styles in Boston and Charleston, 1828–1843* (New York: Oxford University Press, 1985); Edward Pessen, *Riches, Class and Power before the Civil War* (Lexington, MA: D. C. Heath, 1973); Robert Rich, '"A Wilderness of Whigs": The Wealthy Men of Boston,' *Journal of Social History* 4 (1970–1971): 264–76. Works which spend some time on the Early Republic include Robert F. Dalzell, *Enterprising Elite: The Boston Associates and the World They Made* (New York: W. W. Norton and Company, 1993); Peter Dobkin Hall, *The Organisation of American Culture, 1700–1900: Private Institutions, Elites, and the Origins of American Nationality* (New York: New York University Press, 1982); Ronald Story, *The Forging of an Aristocracy: Harvard and the Boston Upper Class, 1800–1870* (Middletown, CT: Wesleyan University Press, 1980); Tamara Plakins Thornton, *Cultivating Gentlemen: The Meaning of Country Life among the Boston Elite, 1785–1860* (New Haven, CT: Yale University Press, 1989), 15 n.1 for 'patriciate' quote. Two works follow the fortunes of Boston elites from the early colonial era to the twentieth century: E. Digby Baltzell, *Puritan Boston and Quaker Philadelphia*; Frederic Cople Jaher, *The Urban Establishment: Upper Strata in Boston, New York, Charleston, Chicago and Los Angeles* (Chicago: University of Illinois Press, 1982).

3. The four institutions discussed in this paper can be seen as representative of a number of societies which emerged during the same era such as the Massachusetts Charitable Fire Society (1786), the Society for the Propagation of the Gospel among the Indians (1787), the Massachusetts Society for the Aid of Immigrants (1794) and the Association for Town Improvement (1801). For the historical context of such organisations, see Conrad Edick Wright, *The Transformation of Charity in Post-revolutionary New England* (Boston: Northeastern University Press, 1992). For details of the four institutions, see for the American Academy of Arts and Sciences: 'The Centennial Celebration of the Academy'*, *Memoirs of the American Academy of Arts and Sciences* 11 (1888): 1–103; Brooke Hindell, *The Pursuit of Science in Revolutionary America* (Chapel Hill: University of North Carolina Press, 1956), 263–8; for the Massachusetts Historical Society, see Stephen T. Riley, *The Massachusetts Historical Society, 1791–1959** (Boston: Massachusetts Historical Society, 1959); for the Humane Society of Massachusetts, see M. A. DeWolfe Howe, *The Humane Society of the Commonwealth of Massachusetts. An Historical Review, 1785–1916** (Boston: The Humane Society, 1918); for the Massachusetts Society for Promoting Agriculture: *An Outline of the History of the Massachusetts Society for Promoting Agriculture** (Boston: Meador Publishing, 1942); *Centennial Year*

(*1792–1892*) *of the Massachusetts Society for Promoting Agriculture* (Boston: Massachusetts Society for Promoting Agriculture, 1892); Thornton, *Cultivating Gentlemen*.

(*Note*: The institutional histories which are starred contain membership lists and details of founding charters and regulations. The starred MSPA publication lists members for the period 1792 to 1816, covering the greater part of the period of interest in this essay. Membership after that date is drawn from the three texts noted above concerning the activities of the Agricultural Society.)

4. Pauline Maier, 'The Debate over Incorporation in Massachusetts,' in Conrad Edick Wright, ed., *Massachusetts and the New Nation* (Boston: Massachusetts Historical Society, 1992), 75.

5. Conrad Wright finds that 7 of the 10 founding officers of the MHS were Unitarians, as were 11 of 15 officers in 1804, in which year 6 out of 7 AAAS officers were of the same faith. Comparisons of founding officers with Unitarians identified by Wright, shows that 7 of the 12 founding officers of the HSM were Unitarian, as were at least 4 of the 13 men who first ran the MSPA. Conrad Wright, *The Beginnings of Unitarianism in America* (Boston: Beacon Press, 1955), 260–5; Wright, 'Ministers, Churches, and the Boston Elite, 1791–1815' in Wright, *Massachusetts and the New Nation*, 118–51; see page 120 for details of 1798 affiliation of rich. On the elite composition of Unitarian congregations, see Anne C. Rose, 'Social Sources of Denominationalism Reconsidered: Post-Revolutionary Boston as a Case Study', *American Quarterly* 38 (1986): 242–64.

6. Walter Muir Whitehill, 'Early Learned Societies in Boston and Vicinity', in Alexandra Oleson and Sanborn C. Brown, eds, *The Pursuit of Knowledge in the Early American Republic: American Scientific and Learned Societies from Colonial Times to the Civil War* (Baltimore: John Hopkins University Press, 1976), 156–63; Thornton, *Cultivating Gentlemen*, 57–60.

7. Details of bankers holding office in the Massachusetts Bank, the Union Bank and the Boston branch of the Bank of the United States, can be found in John West, *Boston Directory Containing the Names of the Inhabitants, their Occupations, Places of Business, and Dwelling Houses* (Boston: John West, 1796), 117. For founders of the Boston Manufacturing Company and Suffolk Bank, see Vera Shlakman, *Economic History of a Factory Town: A Study of Chicopee, Massachusetts* (1934; reprint, New York: Octagon Books, 1969), 39, 244; for founding officers of Massachusetts Hospital Life Insurance Company, see Gerald T. White, *A History of the Massachusetts Hospital Life Insurance Company* (Cambridge, MA: Harvard University Press, 1955), appendix 1. See note 3 for details of institutional membership lists. Membership is noted for any stage of an individual's life. It should be remembered that given the inadequacies of the MSPA list, figures for this institution must be treated as a minimum level of participation. On the economic significance of these institutions and the merchant status of those involved in their founding, see Dalzell, *Enterprising Elite*, 27–30, 94–8, 100.

8. Very few members of even the most prestigious of artisanal organizations, the Massachusetts Charitable Mechanics Society (established 1795) joined

these four societies, whilst very few of a selected sample of Boston's 'men of affairs' 1791–1815 did not belong to at least one of the societies. See Wright, 'Ministers, Churches and the Boston Elite', 133, 137, 149–51; Rose, 'Social Sources of Denominationalism Reconsidered', 247–9. On membership numbers and institutional structures, for AAAS, MHS and MSPA see note 3; for HMS, see J. P. Brissot de Warville, *New Travels in the United States of America, 1788*, ed. Durand Echeverria (Cambridge, MA: Belknap Press of Harvard University Press, 1964), 99. See also Wright, *Beginnings of Unitarianism in America*, 260–5.

9. Henry May has identified two coherent wings of Enlightenment thought influential in eighteenth-century America. The Revolutionary Enlightenment, drawn from Rousseau is associated with Deists such as Thomas Paine within the United States. May finds that Boston Unitarianism was strongly influenced by the Moderate Enlightenment of John Locke, Samuel Clarke and the Scottish Common Sense school of philosophy. Until the mid-1790s, the divisions within Enlightenment philosophy were ill-formed. This essay uses 'Enlightenment' to refer to the eighteenth-century intellectual movement which sought truth through observation and empirical research. This rational approach stressed that experience was the 'foundation of all knowledge'. Henry F. May, *The Enlightenment in America* (New York: Oxford University Press, 1976), 54–9, 184, 337–8.

10. 'Charter of Incorporation,' Bowdoin quoted in 'Address by the Hon. Robert C. Winthrop', *Memoirs of AAAS* 9 (1880): 78–9; Howe, *Humane Society*, 11; *Massachusetts Centinel*, 8 March 1786.

11. 'Introductory Address from the Historical Society to the Public', *Collections of the Massachusetts Historical Society, for the Year 1792*, vol. 1, 3; *The American Apollo, Containing Essays, Moral, Political, and Poetical, and the Daily Occurrence in the Natural, Civil and Commercial World*, no. 1, part 2, vol. 1 (1792); 'Dr Tenney's letter on the Dark Day, May 19, 1780,' *The American Apollo*, part 1, vol. 1 (1792), 95.

12. *Centennial Year of the MSPA*, 6; 'Papers on Agriculture,' *Monthly Anthology and Boston Review* 1 (August 1804): 465; *Outline of the History of the MSPA*, 14. See also Thornton, *Cultivating Gentlemen*, 61–4 on the early importance of scientific, experimental agriculture within the MSPA.

13. Winifred Bernard, *Fisher Ames: Federalist and Statesman, 1758–1808* (Chapel Hill: University of North Carolina Press, 1965), 349–50; 'Necrology', *Monthly Anthology and Boston Review* 1 (August 1804): 477; Andrews Norton, 'The Inauguration of President Kirkland,' in Lewis P. Simpson, ed., *The Federalist Literary Mind: Selections from the Monthly Anthology and Boston Review, 1803–1811, Including Documents Relating to the Boston Athenæum* (Baton Rouge: Louisiana State University Press, 1962), 123; Edward Warren, *The Life of John Warren MD* (Boston: Noyes, Holmes and Company, 1874), 234; Howe, *Humane Society*, 234; *Outline of the History of the MSPA*, 17.

14. On the importance of European models, see Thornton, *Cultivating Gentlemen*, 21–6, 61; Whitehill, 'Early Learned Societies in Boston', 152; Brooke Hindell, *The Pursuit of Science in Revolutionary America, 1735–1789* (Chapel Hill: University of North Carolina Press, 1956), 264, 284–5. On

the British amateur interest in history, see Paul Langford, *A Polite and Commercial People, England 1727–1783* (Oxford: Clarendon Press, 1989), 96–9. On the nature and development of comparable British institutions and elite behaviour, see Morris Berman, '"Hegemony" and the Amateur Tradition in British Science,' *Journal of Social History* 8 (1974–1975): 30–50.

15. Richard L. Bushman, *The Refinement of America: Persons, Houses, Cities* (New York: Alfred A. Knopf, 1992), part 1; Colin Bonwick, 'The American Revolution as a Social Movement Revisited', *Journal of American Studies* 20 (1986): 361–3. On comparable social aspirations within British urban culture, see Paul Langford, *A Polite and Commercial People*, 94–101; John Seed, 'Theologies of Power: Unitarianism and the Social Relation of Religious Discourse, 1800–1850', in R. J. Morris, ed., *Class, Power and Social Structure in British Nineteenth Century Towns* (Leicester: Leicester University Press, 1986), 110, 118.

16. On the impact of Loyalism, see John W. Tyler, *Smugglers and Patriots: Boston Merchants and the Advent of the American Revolution* (Boston: Northeastern University Press, 1986). Bowdoin quote – Richard D. Brown, 'The Confiscation and Disposition of Loyalists' estates in Suffolk County, Massachusetts', *William and Mary Quarterly* 21 (1964): 548. For quantitative details of the instability of elite personnel, see Allan Kulikoff, 'The Progress of Inequality in Revolutionary Boston', *William and Mary Quarterly* 28 (1971): 375–411. The twenty-eight incorporators of the Agricultural Society in 1792, for example, embodied disparate origins and allegiances. They included: the old Republican Samuel Adams; future Federalist Governor Christopher Gore, a lawyer who was the son of a Boston Loyalist; John Lowell, who had moved his successful legal practice from Newburyport, Essex County, Massachusetts to Boston in 1776; and three successful merchants, Stephen Higginson (originally from Salem), the Episcopalian David Sears (originally from Cape Cod), and the Orthodox Congregationalist Samuel Phillips (originally of Andover, Massachusetts).

17. Warren quoted in Richard D. Brown, 'The Confiscation and Disposition of Loyalists' estates in Suffolk County, Massachusetts', *William and Mary Quarterly* 21 (1964): 548; *Here We Have Lived: The Houses of the Massachusetts Historical Society* (Boston: Massachusetts Historical Society, 1967); Josiah Quincy, *A History of the Boston Athenæum, with Biographical Notices of its Deceased Founders* (Cambridge, MA: Metcalf and Company, 1851), 65; Warren, *Life of John Warren*, 235. On the importance of the institutional form of subscriber democracies, see R. J. Morris, 'Voluntary Societies and British Urban Elites, 1780–1850,' *Historical Journal* 26 (1983): 95–118. On the increasing importance of institutional identities during the eighteenth century, see Richard D. Brown, *Modernization: The Transformation of American Life, 1600–1865* (New York: Hill and Wang, 1976), 53–5; James Henretta, *The Evolution of American Society, 1700–1815: An Interdisciplinary Analysis* (Lexington, MA: D. C. Heath and Company, 1973), 212.

18. For membership and activities of the Wednesday Evening Club, see

Wright, *Beginnings of Unitarianism in America*, 261; Records of the *Society for the Study of Natural Philosophy*, 1801–1807, Boston Athenæum, MSS S42; Linda K. Kerber, 'Science in the Early Republic: The Society for the Study of Natural Philosophy', *William and Mary Quarterly* 29 (1972): 263–80.

19. Jaher, *Urban Establishment*, 57; John Adams – Abigail Adams, 4 August 1776 in L. H. Butterfield, Marc Friedlaender, Mary-Jo Kline, eds, *The Book of Abigail and John: Selected Letters of the Adams Family, 1762–1784* (Cambridge, MA: Harvard University Press, 1975), 149; F. M. L. Thompson, 'Social Control in Victorian Britain', *Economic History Review* 34 (1981): 190; Thornton, *Cultivating Gentlemen*, 60–1, 67–8. The empirical approach of the AAAS and the HSM can be seen, in a similar fashion, as seeking to achieve human progress through the adaptation of scientific principles. Shays's Rebellion was the subject of one of the first indigenous history books of post-Revolutionary New England. George Richards Minot, a founder of the MHS, published his *History of the Insurrections* in 1788, shaping the final product to concur with the assumptions of the Boston elite, whilst appealing to a British audience that the Rebellion did not preclude the success of the republican experiment, see Robert A. Peer, 'George Richards Minot's *History of the Insurrections*: History, Propaganda, and Autobiography,' *New England Quarterly* 35 (1962): 203–28.

20. Thompson, 'Social Control in Victorian Britain', 190; Lowell cited in *Outline of the History of the MSPA*, 10–11. Thornton, *Cultivating Gentlemen*, 57–77, discusses the role of the MSPA in providing elites with an opportunity for 'a public stance of virtue'.

21. 'From the Essex Result, 1778' in Robert J. Taylor, ed., *Massachusetts, Colony to Commonwealth: Documents on the Formation of its Constitution, 1775–1780* (Chapel Hill: University of North Carolina Press, 1961), 77–8.

22. On the complexities surrounding the concept of 'virtue' during the Early Republic, see J. G. A. Pocock, *Virtue, Commerce and History: Essays on Political Thought and History, Chiefly in the Eighteenth Century* (Cambridge: Cambridge University Press, 1985); Daniel T. Rogers, 'Republicanism: the Career of a Concept', *Journal of American History* 79 (1982): 11–30; Myron F. Wehtje, 'The Ideal of Virtue in Post-Revolutionary Boston', *Historical Journal of Massachusetts* 17 (1989): 67–83; Ronald M. Peters, Jr, *The Massachusetts Constitution of 1780: A Social Compact* (Amherst: University of Massachusetts Press, 1978), appendix, 200. Quotations from David H. Fischer, 'The Myth of the Essex Junto', *William and Mary Quarterly* 21 (1968): 204, 209; L. H. Butterfield, ed., *Diary and Autobiography of John Adams, Volume Three, Diary 1782–1804, Autobiography Part One to October 1776* (Cambridge, MA: Harvard University Press, 1961), 195 – entry for 21 July 1786. Such thought concerning the social importance of elite example was firmly rooted in the region's religious past, see Richard L. Bushman, *From Puritan to Yankee: Character and Social Order in Connecticut, 1690–1760* (Cambridge, MA: Harvard University Press, 1967), esp. Chapter 1.

23. Sedgwick, a Federalist grandee based in Springfield, Massachusetts saw Shays's Rebellion as a war 'on virtue, property and distinctions in the

community'. See David H. Fischer, *The Revolution of American Conservatism: The Federalist Party in the Era of Jeffersonian Democracy* (New York: Harper and Row, 1969), 13, 26; see also, on the broad support given to the Federalist Party by elites of wealth and status, James M. Banner Jr, *To the Hartford Convention: The Federalists and the Origins of Party Politics in Massachusetts, 1789–1815* (New York: Alfred A. Knopf, 1970), esp. Chapter 5.

24. Samuel Adams (1786) cited in William Pencak, 'Samuel Adams and Shays's Rebellion', *New England Quarterly* 62 (1989): 65, 71. Adams called on 'men of principle who love their country' to unite with 'men of property, of wisdom, of influence' in response to agrarian insurrection, page 71. See also Robert H. Gardiner, 'The Multiplicity of Our Literary Institutions', (1807) in Simpson, *The Federalist Literary Mind*, 71.

25. Fischer, 'Myth of the Essex Junto,' 208. For a fine insight into the dominant ideology of the Early Republic, see John R. Rowe, Jr, 'Republican Thought and the Political Violence of the 1790s', *American Quarterly* 19 (1967): 147–65.

26. Charles Warren, 'Samuel Adams and the Sans Souci Club in 1785', *Proceedings of the Massachusetts Historical Society* 60 (1926): 321; Wehtje, 'Ideal of Virtue in Post-Revolutionary Boston', 68–82; Bushman, *Refinement of America*, 191–203; Kenneth Silverman, *A Cultural History of the American Revolution: Painting, Music, Literature, and the Theatre in the Colonies and the United States of America from the Treaty of Paris to the Inauguration of George Washington* (New York: Thomas Y. Crowell, 1976), 505–13. See also 'The Lady of the Ton' in the *Massachusetts Centinel*, 30 December 1786, page 3; an article which satirized the self-importance of polite society, describing the late arrival at a formal dance of 'a certain Lady of the *Ton*', who entered to the 'rustlings of silks, gauze and other foreign frippery' and was surrounded immediately by gentlemen 'ambitious to display their gallantry and incredible proficiency in the Chesterfieldian science of politeness, dress and address.'

27. *Massachusetts Centinel*, 9 November 1785, page 2, and 15 March 1786, page 3. See also, *American Apollo*, no. 3, part 2, vol. 1 (1792), page 28, when a further attempt to incorporate Boston was met with similar suspicions of motives.

28. Critics are identified in Warren, 'Samuel Adams and the Sans Souci', 319, 324, 331, 343; Fischer, 'Myth of the Essex Junto', 206–7.

29. William Manning, 'The Key of Libberty [sic]', (1798) in Theodore R. Crance, ed., *The Colleges and the Public, 1787–1862* (New York: Columbia University Publications, 1963). The institutional allegiances of the six male identified critics of polite society are as follows:

Institutional affiliation of identified critics of elite behaviour during the 1780s. Earliest known date of membership is given for AAAS and MHS. For HSM membership is over period 1786–1836; for MSPA for period 1792–1816. See note 3 for institutional sources.

Critic	AAAS	HSM	MHS	MSPA
Samuel Adams	1780	Yes	No	Yes
Benjamin Austin, Jr.	No	Yes	No	No
John Eliot	1805	Yes	1791	No
Jonathan Jackson	1780	Yes	No	Yes
James Warren	1780	No	No	Yes
Benjamin Waterhouse	1795	Yes	No	Yes

30. Kirkland cited in Wright, *Beginnings of American Unitarianism*, 250; Peter Thacher, 'A Sermon preached before the Ancient and Honorable Artillery Company', (1793) in Ellis Sandoz, ed., *Political Sermons of the American Founding Era, 1730–1805* (Indianapolis: Liberty Fund, 1990), 1142.
31. Thirteen of the fourteen founders of the Anthology Society, publishers of the *Monthly Anthology*, were Unitarians. Many were active in the other societies discussed here, although none was a founder. Ministers Joseph Stevens Buckminster and William Emerson belonged to all four, as did Kirkland who joined the Anthologists in 1806. Daniel Walker Howe, *The Unitarian Conscience: Harvard Moral Philosophy, 1805–1861* (Cambridge, MA: Harvard University Press, 1970), 176; Wright, 'Ministers, Churches and the Boston Elite', 120; Wright, *Beginnings of American Unitarianism*, 245–250; J. T. Kirkland, 'The Anthology: Objects and Principles,' in Simpson, *The Federalist Literary Mind*, 144; 'Cato,' 'Thoughts on Dress,' *Monthly Anthology and Boston Review* 1 (January 1804): 100–2.
32. The document can be read in its entirety in Josiah Quincy, *The History of the Boston Athenæum, with Biographical Notices of its Deceased Founders* (Cambridge, MA: Metcalf and Company, 1851), 24–43; long quotation, page 36. On the significance of the institution in socially integrating the antebellum Boston elite, see Ronald Story, 'Class and Culture in Boston: The Athenæum, 1807–1860,' *American Quarterly* 27 (1975): 178–99.
33. On the importance of Enlightenment knowledge to Unitarian theology, see Howe, *The Unitarian Conscience*, esp. 1–11, 27–38. Howe describes Unitarianism as 'a confluence of Protestantism with the Enlightenment,' page 5; May, *Enlightenment in America*, 350–7; Conrad Wright, *A Stream of Light: A Sesquicentennial History of American Unitarianism* (Boston: Unitarian Universalist Association, 1975), xi–xiv. The essays from the *Monthly Anthology* reprinted in Simpson, *Federalist Literary Mind*, are representative of the search for rational, empirical knowledge. See these sources on fear of emotional Christianity and Deism; quoted is William Emerson, 'An Oration in Commemoration of the Anniversary of American Independence,' in Sandoz, *Political Sermons of the American Founding Era*, 1156.
34. 'An Essay on Civilization,' *Monthly Anthology and Boston Review* 7 (1804): 291–3.

35. Emerson's oration before the Humane Society (1809), cited in Howe, *Humane Society*, 123. On the success of the Athenæum, see Story, 'Class and Culture in Boston'.
36. Henry Adams, *The Education of Henry Adams: An Autobiography* (1918; reprint, Boston: Houghton Mifflin Company, 1971), 19–20.
37. For similarities with Britain in the nineteenth century, see Alan J. Kidd, 'Philanthropy and the "Social History Paradigm"', *Social History* 21 (1996): 189.
38. Daniel Walker Howe, '"At Morning Blest and Golden-Browed": Unitarians, Transcendentalists and Reformers, 1835–1865' in Wright, *A Stream of Light*, 38; Wright, 'Ministers, Churches and the Boston Elite', 137–8.

4

Orestes Brownson and the Relationship between Reform and Democracy

Naomi Wulf

Introduction

The development of a national reform movement in antebellum America, born with the Second Awakening, was contemporary with the emergence of political democracy and the broadening of suffrage to all white males. Historians such as William McLoughlin have argued for continuity between social reform movements and the birth of democracy, with Finney's perfectionism viewed as 'the millenarian alternative to Jacksonian politics.'[1] Others such as Nathan Hatch see in the religious revivals of the first half of the nineteenth century signs of the growing individualism characteristic of modern liberal democracy.[2] These historiographical trends which focus on the inherent links between reform and Jacksonian democracy are all meant to counter the famous 'social control thesis' developed by Clifford S. Griffin, which sees the spreading of a 'benevolent empire' as a conservative means for declining denominations to recapture their waning influence.[3]

Focus upon the thought of the reformer and political thinker Orestes Brownson makes the relationship between reform and the idea of democracy in the 1820s to 1840s seem more complex. Orestes Brownson, born in 1803, started writing at the beginning of Jackson's presidency. His reflections on democracy offer a provocative response to Tocqueville's oft praised 'equality of conditions'. This Protestant minister and pamphleteer, always looking for the best means to achieve liberty and equality on earth according to the principles of the Founding Fathers, joined a succession of different denominations in his quest:

> The various systems I embraced, or defended, whether social or political, ethical or aesthetical, philosophical or theological, were ... means by which man's earthly condition was to be meliorated ... My end was man's earthly happiness and my creed was progress.[4]

Born to a Congregationalist family in rural Vermont at the beginning of the century, Brownson was briefly attracted to Presbyterianism as a teenager before embracing Universalism, a more liberal form of Christianity, in 1826. He briefly preached this faith in New York State but abandoned this 'moral and intellectual philosophy'[5] after listening to Frances Wright's lectures in the *Burnt-over district*. He then entered his most rational phase, participating in the founding of the New York Workingmen's Movement alongside the British reformers, Frances Wright and Robert Dale Owen, at the end of the 1820s. He nevertheless returned to religion under the influence of Unitarianism and was invited by William Ellery Channing to preach to the Boston working classes in the mid-1830s. There he joined the budding Transcendentalist Club and founded his Society for Christian Union and Progress. The severe economic crisis of 1837 led to a more active involvement in politics: although he defended President Van Buren's Democratic Party, he expressed his growing disagreement with democracy as it was being practised. This criticism of the defects of political democracy culminated in his most famous article, 'The Laboring Classes' (July and October 1840), published in the *Boston Quarterly Review* which he edited from 1838 to 1842.[6] The 1840 elections and the victory of the Whigs over the Democrats provoked yet another turning point; disappointed by the popular vote in favour of the Whigs, he moved away from politics and turned to Catholicism, which he adopted as his true faith in 1844.

During these formative years, Orestes Brownson was always looking for the best means of reform at a time when political democracy seemed to be insufficient to check fast-growing inequalities.[7] He endlessly sought a balance between religion and politics, and a means of guiding reform to meet the requirements of a more just democracy. His frequent denunciations, his numerous changes of direction and his unrelenting dialogue with his contemporaries exemplify in a concrete way the hesitations of his time concerning the relationship that reform should entertain with the individual, with society and with government. Thus Brownson's complicated career invites us to rethink the role of reform in a democracy by prompting a series of questions: through his practice as well as his theoretical writings, he makes us reflect on the necessary complementarity between individual and social reform, and on the limited scope of reform: should it focus on distinct issues or offer more global solutions? And finally he leads us to a reassessment of the relationship between society and government in order to achieve a better democracy.

Reform the Individual or Society?

The reform movement which stemmed from the Second Great Awakening and accelerated after 1812 under the influence of the so-called 'market revolution'[8] was aimed principally at searching for ways of reaching out to individuals outside of any type of governmental structure. From the early missions and education societies to Garrison's Antislavery Society, emphasis was mainly on morally reforming the individual.[9]

Orestes Brownson belongs to this trend. He was a typical product of the religious changes of the beginning of the century and was steeped in religion from his early childhood.[10] Despite this emphasis on the moral regeneration of the individual, the self-taught Brownson, under the influence of writings such as William Godwin's *Political Justice* and the works of Robert Owen, attempted to balance the individual focus of religion with social reform.

This can be seen in his early concern with education. As a young preacher he first spoke out against intemperance,[11] but quickly shifted his interest towards the more social issue of education. As a Presbyterian in the State of New York, he taught young children and later decided to set up a lyceum in his poor Unitarian parish in Canton, Massachusetts.

Together with Frances Wright and Robert Dale Owen he fought for education and the right to instruction for the working classes. This stood together with the demands of the early workingmen's movement for shorter working days and the abolition of imprisonment for debt.[12] While Wright and Owen fostered a 'state guardianship system' at a time when various educational reform experiments were being made in the Northeast,[13] Brownson chose to devote his own newspaper, *The Genesee Republican or Herald of Reform*, to 'the promotion of education' for everyone:

> Without education equal to the other classes, the working men could not maintain the rank to which they are entitled ... The object of the *Herald of Reform* is ... to enquire if the State possess not the means, and whether it be not bound, to give a republican education – an equal education – to all its children, alike to those of the rich and of the poor?[14]

It was to preach, but also to teach the working classes that William Ellery Channing and Brownson's Transcendentalist friend George Ripley invited him to Boston to set up his Society for Christian Union and Progress, which lasted from 1836 to 1842.

From the workingmen's movement to the Transcendentalists, from his religious inspiration to his social concern, Brownson was constantly striving to improve individual moral concerns, while asserting the right to free enquiry together with a strong sense of the social result to be achieved:

> My creed is a simple one. Its first article is, free, unlimited inquiry ... The second article is social progress ... My third article is, that man should labor for his soul in preference to his body ... It would encourage inquiry; It would perfect society, not as ultimate ends, but as means to the growth and maturity of man's higher nature – his soul.[15]

Throughout Brownson's writings and his life one can sense a tension between individual and social reform similar to that experienced by many of his contemporaries. He was attracted to a number of different movements. He was interested in the Transcendentalist emphasis on the individual and morality, as tried out by Bronson Alcott and Elizabeth Peabody in the community of Fruitlands, an education based on self-discovery as opposed to the more mechanistic teachings of the local common schools. He endeavoured to achieve an equilibrium between manual labour and literary studies in setting up manual labour schools in Boston for the working classes, thus trying to counter the division of labor at an early stage. He openly appreciated Horace Mann's stress on the importance of a coherent state educational reform, while expressing his distrust of too centralized a system.[16]

Beyond education, Brownson's aim was to reinject a moral dimension into collective reform and reciprocally to teach the importance of collective effort to preachers who focused solely on individual morality. He wished to dissociate the idea of social progress from the charge of atheism, which he feared had been attached to it by the Enlightenment:

> Before Thomas Paine, no infidel writer in our language, to my knowledge was a democrat ... Since his times, the infidel has been fond of calling himself a democrat, and he has pretty generally claimed to be the friend of the masses and the advocate of progress.[17]

The point was to remind his fellow ministers of the essential egalitarianism contained in the teachings of Jesus Christ – 'He preached fraternal love, peace on earth, and good will to men'[18] – in order to reconcile them with the indissociable character of individual and social reform, of reforming the individual while helping improve the emerging democracy: 'Perfect every individual, and undoubtedly, you would perfect society; but it is necessary that the perfection of both be carried along together.'[19]

Indeed, his goal was to convince the American clergy that 'the real dominant sentiment of our epoch is that of social progress', under the influence of such different thinkers as the Saint Simonians, Robert Owen and Jeremy Bentham.[20]

This in short meant teaching them democracy, reminding them that 'the age is distinguished by its tendency to democracy, and its craving for social reform, [that] the democratic spirit is triumphing.'[21] While he attempted 're-moralizing democracy' – the moral aspect of democracy is characteristic of most writings of the period, from George Bancroft and John O'Sullivan to John Stuart Mill[22] – he strongly expressed his belief in 'the reconciliation between Christians and reformers': 'Religion is taking a social direction, and reform is becoming spiritual.'[23] However, by encouraging his contemporaries to support reform, Brownson was not joining forces with the Evangelicals, for he perceived their benevolent practice to be contrary to democratic principles.

Distinct Issues or Global Solution?

The Evangelical sects which had multiplied since the turn of the century exhibited what Brownson and his *Free Enquirer* friends saw as a form of tyranny. In their weekly journal, as well as in a number of conferences in New York and throughout the country, Frances Wright, Robert Dale Owen and their friends were out to fight 'the Evils of Society' which they attributed to oppressive governments and an oppressive religion. In her famous series of conferences on the 'Causes of Existing Evils', Frances Wright redefined 'evil' not as inherent in man, but the product of institutions which breed superstition and inequalities.[24] Together with Orestes Brownson who had just left the Universalists, they cried out their opposition to the growing influence of Evangelical sects, which they saw as exerting too much 'control', and called out for 'mental independence'[25] and the right to free enquiry: 'Until the people shall be awake to enquiry, reform is impossible.'[26] By resisting this 'mighty tide that sets in from the great Ocean of Religion',[27] they equated true reform and democracy with a freedom of thought which verged towards a *laissez-faire* doctrine: 'We are better off because we are *less governed*. And so will it be found, that all reform consists in the enlarging human liberty and circumscribing governmental authority.'[28]

The distrust of control as they see it, and their insistence on liberty, whether religious or political, stemmed from a strong belief in *laissez-faire*, typical of workingmen as well as the Democratic Party – as opposed to the Whigs and their centralized 'American system'. This conception of reform was reminiscent of the republicanism of the Founding Fathers, which threw off the oppressive government of a despotic monarchy in order to build a virtuous and free republic.

In a more humourous mode, Brownson echoed this attack on the Evangelicals and their reformers and poked fun at those reformers who 'are becoming, it strikes us, a real annoyance':

The land is overspread with them, and matters have come to such a pass, that a peaceable man can hardly venture to eat or drink, to go to bed or to get up, to correct his children or kiss his wife, without obtaining the permission of some moral or other reform society. The individual is bound hand and foot ... He has nothing he can call his own, not even his will.[29]

The freedom of the individual that was so dear to Brownson and to the Jacksonian Democrats was put into peril by what he considered to be mock-reformers, such as the followers of the dietician Sylvester Graham:[30] 'The real idea at the bottom of these institutions, is the control of individual freedom by moral laws ...' and this is what he rejected.[31] In calling for the respect of individual freedom and moderation while wanting to bring about change, Brownson was not rejecting reform altogether. Rather he made a clear distinction between two types of action, individual and global.[32]

What seemed dangerous to him was the excess which characterized the reform effort and which led to dispersion and to a growing separation of the various causes. Beyond the 'nuisance' he complained of, this multiplicity seemed countereffective in fighting the 'evils' that reform set out to eliminate:

All these classes of evils are mutually connected, and no one of them can be cured separately. The cause of them all lies deep in human nature, as now developed, and they must be regarded as inseparable from the present stage of human progress.[33]

Social progress therefore strictly depended on a global view of society. Brownson, in denouncing the reformers as 'short-sighted',[34] was at the crossroads of two conceptions of society: he was confronted by a growing liberal viewpoint which understood society to be an aggregate of individuals, while he believed in a more traditional vision of society as an organic community which transcends the sum of the individuals who compose it. It is on this ground that Brownson finally rejected two of the main movements of his time: educational reform and anti-slavery, as being too limited in their scope.

Is education the main solution to social evils? This is the gist of a long-drawn-out debate which appeared in the workingmen's party at its beginning. 'Knowledge is power', the rallying cry of Wright and Owen throughout the 1820s, is continuously challenged by the reformer Thomas Skidmore, for whom reform of the property system has priority in the fight against inequalities.[35] This debate was taken up by Brownson some twelve years later in his provocative 'Laboring Classes' article, which advocated abolition of the hereditary system of property.[36] Even after moving away from such a radical standpoint, he maintained this viewpoint in his denunciation of education as the priority for achieving success: 'Knowledge is no doubt power ... But knowledge cannot prevent a man from being hungry, from having the heart-ache, nor his coat from becoming rusty or threadbare.'[37] In brief, 'self-culture is a good thing, but it cannot abolish inequality, nor restore men to their rights.'[38] This statement was addressed to 'Dr Channing' and through him to all the Unitarians and Transcendentalists to whom Channing taught the importance of 'self-culture, or the care which every man owes to himself, to the unfolding and perfecting of his nature.'[39] It was also addressed to the British essayist Thomas Carlyle, whose essay 'Chartism', reviewed by Brownson, advocated education as one of the solutions to the ills of the working class in Victorian England, and to all Reformers throughout Europe and the United States.

Brownson's critical approach to abolitionism is along the same lines. Concerning the very sensitive question of slavery in the 1830s and 1840s, he wished not to be misunderstood: 'We are no advocates of slavery, we are as heartily opposed to it any modern abolitionist can be.'[40] Yet the struggle against slavery as it was encouraged by contemporary reformers such as W. E. Channing, called for reflection on the place of this struggle within a broader reform of society. Just as education no longer seemed to have priority, Brownson, whilst denouncing slavery, rejected abolitionism partly because Channing – and even William Lloyd Garrison in a very different way – believed in the personal conversion of slave-owners to abolitionism. In his essay on 'Slavery', Channing had addressed the individual slave-holder's sole responsibility. Brownson responded in a review:

> The evils of slavery do not result from the personal characters of slave masters. They are inseparable from the system ...; indeed, [S]lavery is not an individual but a social institution, and society, not the individual conscience alone, is responsible for it ... This matter of freeing the slaves is a matter for the community, rather than the individual slave-holder.[41]

The question of the interference of the North in the affairs of the South, and of state rights, was developed by Brownson as a central issue of his day and as one of the major obstacles to abolitionism.[42] But did this imply that slavery should be reduced to the personal relationship between slave and master? On the contrary, according to Brownson, it involved the whole community, North and South, the free and the unfree, the masters and the labourers. Slavery was seen as a 'system' which was part and parcel of the American economy and which, like all the other 'evils', had to be treated from a global point of view.

Brownson joined such southern theorists as J. C. Calhoun or G. Fitzugh in analyzing slave labour in direct relationship with free labour, believing that they could not be treated apart from one another. Indeed, as a defender of the working man, Brownson wished to denounce both slavery and what was then called 'wage slavery': 'It were useless to emancipate the slave today, because we would be merely changing the form not the substance of his slavery'.[43] Brownson thus put slavery into perspective and called for a greater involvement of these reformers in more pressing and more general issues – namely poverty and the bad working conditions of 'wage slaves' – which could help improve the young democracy as a whole: 'As yet there is no security given, or capable of being given, that the slave will be a free man even if declared free by the laws. Let this security be obtained before you attempt to emancipate him.'[44]

Reform Must Be Political

Brownson's arguments led to an attack on the apolitical aspect of reform. William Lloyd Garrison's deliberate rejection of any type of political involvement was no secret, and he shared this apolitical stance with many reformers of his time.[45] Brownson exaggerated this feature in a caricature of anti-slavery activists:

> They are not, at least the honest part of them, politicians; but very simple-minded men and women who crave excitement, and seek it in abolition societies and petitions, instead of seeking it in ball-rooms, theatres, or places of fashionable amusement or dissipation. Politics, properly speaking, they abominate, because politics would require them to think, and they wish only to feel.[46]

Brownson himself had been a defender of the 'no-government' position of his party and friends, which was seen as inherently democratic:

> I value a free government, a popular governement, ay, if you will, a democratic government, for I have not a feeling about me that is not democratic. But a free government is powerless without a free people. No matter how much freedom you incorporate into your paper constitutions, you can never have any more practiced than is written in the hearts and on the characters of the people. I therefore expect little from government, I ask little but to be let alone.[47]

Yet he soon turned away from this popular defence of *laissez-faire*, urging on his contemporaries more political involvement as the only true road to more justice: '[Reformers] would have all men wise, good, and happy; but in order to make them so, they tell us that we want not external changes but internal.'[48] Beyond concern for the individual or society, what was at stake was real challenge to the actual political structures of government.

Orestes Brownson tried to reconcile reformers and politics, with a very clear partisan strategy in mind. Reform in the 1820s–1840s was closely tied to the opposition party, the Whigs, who valued a centralized system in all fields, economic, social and political, and openly advocated the necessity for a strong government which intervened in the lives of individuals.[49] In order to counter this partisan monopoly over the idea of reform, Brownson insisted on rallying reformers to the cause of the Democratic Party: 'We wish to see the union consummated between the reformers and the democratic party, so called';

> Are you contending for universal education? ... Are you the advocate of the rights of woman? ... Are you a non-resistant, a peace-man? ... Are you an advocate for the working-man ...? Are you an abolitionist and would you free the slave? ... The democratic party embraces the idea of universal freedom to universal man, and it will realize this idea, just as fast as we can urge onward the general progress of Humanity, and no faster.[50]

At a moment when the political party in its modern form was emerging on the political scene, stimulated by such professional politicians as Martin Van Buren, there was still strong resistance to the very existence of parties, which were seen as contrary to the true republican spirit devoted to the public good and not to private interests. W. E. Channing's plea against party politics as a threat to 'moral independence' is a case in point.[51]

Brownson originally shared this anti-party feeling, typical of his period, but came to believe that 'parties are inevitable', and political action necessary to further the cause of reform.[52] He was not content with social action alone, but had come to understand, ahead of his time, the inherent link between society and government, which had been viewed as separate entities by the heirs of the Enlightenment: 'They who contemplate reforming society without the aid of government, or introducing a state of society in which government will be superfluous, are ... far remote from true practical reformers.[53] Government and society could not be thought of separately from one another. Turning away from his contemporaries' belief in the blessings of *laissez-faire*, Brownson saw government as 'the great and indispensable agent of reform.'[54] Improving society was one of his main concerns, but in order to do so, rather than dissociating government from society, he insisted on their necessary interdependence. Society's role was thus to 'give the law to government', making government the 'agent of society'. There should be no fear of an overly powerful government, for 'government is [society's] servant and subject to its command.'[55]

This conception of the relationship between government and society went beyond Thomas Paine's 'government is but a necessary evil'; Brownson had come to see it as a 'positive good'. True reformers, rather than shying away from what they saw as the intrusiveness of government should understand the protective authority that it could convey. Far from threatening the lives of individuals, this would guarantee individual as well as collective rights:[56] 'Government ... must be an instrument in the hands of society for protecting one individual against another, and in the hands of individuals for protecting themselves against the encroachments of society.'[57]

This resort to a strong government at a time when government was strongly associated with the setting up and maintaining of privilege, pitting the Whigs against the Democrats, directly put Brownson in the conservative camp. Conservative or radical? 'Marxist before Marx' or American Tocqueville?[58] Brownson always seemed to be on the cutting edge between diametrically opposed viewpoints in trying to define what he deemed truly efficient reform.

Always true to his beliefs, Brownson offers a global panorama of the different conceptions of reform of his day. He brings out these multiple coexisting visions at a time when neither reform nor democracy were clearly defined, either separately or in their relationship to one another. By pushing to its utmost logic his conception of the links between politics and religion, between the individual, society and government, he reaches an original understanding of the individual and collective importance of government action and achieves a prophetic vision of the limits of reform within a democracy.

Notes

1. John L. Thomas, 'Romantic Reform in America, 1815–1865,' *American Quarterly* 17 (1965): 656–81, quoted in William McLoughlin, *Revivals, Awakenings and Reform: An Essay on Religion and Social Change in America, 1607–1977* (Chicago: University of Chicago Press, 1978), 129.
2. Nathan O. Hatch, *The Democratization of American Christianity* (New Haven, CT and London: Yale University Press, 1989). For the importance of the Awakening in understanding the Second American Party System, see Daniel Walker Howe, 'Religion and Politics in the Antebellum North', in Mark A. Noll, ed., *Religion and American Politics from the Colonial Period to the 1980s* (New York: Oxford University Press, 1990), 121–45.
3. Clifford S. Griffin, 'Religious Benevolence as Social Control, 1815–1860',

Mississippi Valley Historical Review 44 (December 1957): 423–44. See also John R. Bodo, *The Protestant Clergy and Public Issues, 1812–1848* (Princeton, NJ: Princeton University Press, 1954).

4. Orestes Brownson, *The Convert, or Leaves from my Experience* (New York: Edward Dunigan and Brother, 1857) 102. For more biographical details, see Arthur M. Schlesinger Jr, *A Pilgrim's Progress: Orestes A. Brownson* (1939; reprint, Boston: Little, Brown, 1966).
5. Brownson, *The Convert*, 58.
6. Orestes Brownson, 'The Laboring Classes,' *Boston Quarterly Review* (July 1840): 358–95, is considered Brownson's most famous and provocative article both in the 1840s and today. It is followed by a justification published in the *Boston Quarterly Review* (October 1840): 420–507 [hereafter referred to as 'The Laboring Classes II']. This review is the main journal edited by Brownson from 1838 to 1842. It offered articles on a wide range of subjects, from literature and philosophy to politics and religion. It merged with John O'Sullivan's famous *Democratic Review* in 1843.
7. The 1820s generation saw America's sharpest rise in inequalities. Charles Sellers, *The Market Revolution: Jacksonian America, 1815–1846* (New York: Oxford University Press, 1991), 238. See also Robert Wiebe, *The Opening of American Society* (New York: Knopf, 1984) and *Self-Rule: A Cultural History of American Democracy* (Chicago: The University of Chicago Press, 1995).
8. For a recent discussion of this historiographical concept, see Melvyn Stokes and Stephen Conway, eds, *The Market Revolution: Social, Political and Religious Expression, 1800–1880* (Charlottesville and London: University Press of Virginia, 1996).
9. Ronald G. Walters, *American Reformers, 1815–1860* (1978; reprint, New York: Hill and Wang, 1997), 3.
10. Brownson, *The Convert*, 4; William Gilmore, 'Orestes Brownson and New England Religious Culture, 1803–1827' (Ph.D. diss., University of Virginia, 1971), Chapter 2.
11. Brownson, 'Address on Intemperance' (Walpole, New Hampshire, 26 February 1833).
12. See for example Sean Wilentz, *Chants Democratic: New York City and the Rise of the American Working Class, 1788–1850* (New York: Oxford University Press, 1984).
13. *Free Enquirer*, New York, 1828–1830.
14. *Working Man's Advocate*, New York, 6 March 1830.
15. Brownson, *A Discourse on the Wants of the Times, delivered in Lyceum Hall, Hanover Street, Boston, Sunday May 29, 1830* (Boston, 1836), 21–2.
16. Brownson, 'Brook Farm', *The Democratic Review* (November 1842): 481–96; Brownson, 'Manual Labor Schools,' *The Boston Reformer*, 4 August 1836; Brownson, 'Education of the People', *Boston Quarterly Review* (October 1839): 393–434.
17. Brownson, *Discourse on the Wants of the Times*, 12.
18. Brownson, 'The Laboring Classes', 384.
19. Brownson, 'Education of the People', *Christian Examiner* (May 1836): 160.

20. *Ibid.*, 168.
21. Brownson, *Discourse on the Wants of the Times*, 11.
22. '[John Stuart Mill's conception of democracy] is that it has a moral vision of the possibility of the improvement of mankind', explains C. B. Macpherson, *The Life and Times of Liberal Democracy* (Oxford and New York: Oxford University Press, 1977), 47.
23. Brownson, 'Democracy and Reform', *Boston Quarterly Review* (October 1839): 483.
24. Frances Wright, 'On the Causes of Existing Evils', *Free Enquirer*, 25 March 1829.
25. Brownson, 'Union', *Free Enquirer*, 26 August 1829.
26. Wright, 'On the Causes of Existing Evils.'
27. Robert Dale Owen, *Free Enquirer*, 10 December 1828.
28. *Ibid.*
29. Brownson, 'Ultraism', *Boston Quarterly Review* (July 1838): 108.
30. Brownson, 'Conversations with a Radical. By a Conservative', *Boston Quarterly Review* (April 1841): 153–4, 157; Sellers, *The Market Revolution*, 246.
31. Brownson, 'The Laboring Classes', 381.
32. Brownson, 'Ultraism', 108.
33. *Ibid.*, 110.
34. *Ibid.*, 112.
35. Owen-Skidmore debate, *Free Enquirer*, October 1829-October 1830.
36. Brownson, 'The Laboring Classes', 393–4. See note 6.
37. *Ibid.*, 483. This echoes Thomas Skidmore in *The Rights of Man to Property!* (New York: Alexander Ming Jr, 1829), 369: 'Reformers, if ye prefer that I should call you so, feed first the hungry ...'.
38. Brownson, 'The Laboring Classes', 375.
39. William Ellery Channing, 'Self-Culture', 1838, *Works* (1882; reprint, New York: Burt Franklin, 1972) 12–36.
40. Brownson, 'The Laboring Classes', 368.
41. Brownson, 'The Laboring Classes', 375; Brownson, 'Slavery-Abolitionism', *Boston Quarterly Review* (April 1838): 240–1. See Channing, 'Slavery', *Works*, 725.
42. Brownson, 'Abolition Proceedings,' *Boston Quarterly Review* (October 1838): 485ff.
43. Brownson, 'Democracy and Reform', 514; Brownson, 'The Laboring Classes,' 371. These arguments which tend to reduce the specificity of black slavery in the South have been seen as reflecting the racism of the working class, as in the recent debate led by David Roediger, *The Wages of Whiteness: Race and the Making of the American Working Class* (London and New York: Verso, 1991) and Alexander Saxton, *The Rise and Fall of the White Republic: Class Politics and Mass Culture in Nineteenth Century America* (London and New York: Verso, 1990).
44. Brownson, 'Slavery-Abolitionism', 260.
45. See William Lloyd's famous editorial in *The Liberator*, 1 January 1831.
46. Brownson, 'Abolition proceedings', 492.
47. Brownson, *Address Delivered at Dedham on the Fifty-Eighth Anniversary of American Independence, July 4, 1834* (Dedham: H. Mann, 1834), 17–18.

48. Brownson, 'The Laboring Classes', 373.
49. Daniel Walker Howe, *The Political Culture of American Whigs* (Chicago: University of Chicago Press, 1979); Richard Cawardine, 'Evangelicals, Whigs and the Election of William Henry Harrison', *Journal of American History* 17 (1983): 47–75.
50. Brownson, 'Democracy and Reform', 483, 513–14.
51. Channing, 'Self-Culture', 27. See also Emerson, 'Self Reliance', *Essays, First Series*, 1841 in Joel Porte, ed., *Essays and Lectures* (New York: Library of America, 1983), 261, 281; Martin Van Buren, *Inquiry into the Origin and Course of Political Parties in the United States* (1867).
52. Brownson, 'Democracy and Reform', 517.
53. Brownson, 'Social Evils, and their Remedy', *Boston Quarterly Review* (July 1841): 273.
54. *Ibid.*, 276.
55. Brownson, 'Our Future Policy', *Boston Quarterly Review* (January 1841): 82.
56. Thomas Paine, 'Common Sense', in Michael Foot and Isaac Kramnick, eds, *The Thomas Paine Reader* (New York: Penguin, 1987) 66; Brownson, 'The Laboring Classes II', 486.
57. Brownson, 'Social Evils, and their Remedy', 278.
58. Arthur M. Schlesinger, Jr., 'Orestes Brownson, an American Marxist Before Marx', *Sewanee Review* 47 (July–September 1939): 317–23.

5

Sectarian Perfectionism and Universal Reform: The Radical Social and Political Thought of William Lloyd Garrison

Louis J. Kern

Almost all men condemn the tartness of my expressions; but I am of opinion that God will have the deceits of men thus powerfully exposed; for I plainly perceive, that those things which are softly dealt with in our corrupt age, give people but light concern, and are presently forgotten. If I have exceeded the bounds of moderation, the monstrous turpitude of the times has transported me.

Martin Luther (attrib.)
William Lloyd Garrison,
Letter to Editor [John Campbell] of the *Christian Witness*,
4 December 1846

Remember them that are in bonds, as bound with them; and them which suffer adversity, as being yourselves also in the body.

Hebrews, 13:3

In the early spring of 1866, less than four months after the publication of the final number of *The Liberator*, a group of longtime friends and abolitionist associates met in Boston and proposed that 'there should be a testimonial raised sufficient to put him [Garrison] at ease for the rest of his life.'[1] The result was the National Testimonial to William Lloyd Garrison (1805–1879), which raised over $35,000 by subscription, and paid off the remaining $3,000 mortgage on Garrison's home. He acknowledged the receipt of the funds from the Testimonial Committee on 12 March 1868, accepting them 'in recognition of my labors in the Anti-Slavery cause through a long and perilous struggle.'[2] 'Happily,' he observed,

> I have not had to wait for posterity, for my vindication – a generous and complete vindication. But by the mighty power of a wonder-working Providence, I have been permitted to see the gory system of slavery annihilated, and its four millions of captives set free.

By the abolition of slavery, notwithstanding the pangs and dangers of our present transitional state, we may ultimately hope for all crowning mercies upon our beloved country.[3]

Yet, despite the apparent sense of closure and reconciliation that pervaded his retirement years, Garrison's active abolition career, coterminous with his editorship of *The Liberator* (1 January 1831–29 December 1865), had been marked by bitterness, recrimination and polemical dissension. For three decades his turbulent tactics and ideological intransigence in the anti-slavery cause made him the most notorious and controversial reformer in America. As the nation desperately floundered in its quest for an acceptable compromise solution to the complex political, economic and social dilemmas posed by chattel slavery, Garrison rejected all pragmatic solutions, starkly positing slavery as a moral derangement. He brutally indicted slavery as a national crime; purgation and purification, not mollification and conciliation were needed to expunge its stain from a guilty people. There could be no compromise with sin, and Garrison's tactical expedient of 'moral suasion' necessitated an aggressive assault on the 'conspiracy of silence' that had indulgently indemnified the slave-holding class and their apologists. What immediate, unconditional abolition demanded was confrontation and exposure, not equivocation and concealment.

Garrison announced his radical abolitionist policy of 'come-outerism' and plain speaking in the first issue of *The Liberator*, published 1 January 1831:

> I *will be* as harsh as truth, and as uncompromising as justice. On this subject, I do not wish to think, speak, or write, with moderation ... I am in earnest – I will not equivocate – I will not excuse – I will not retreat a single inch – AND I WILL BE HEARD.

Opponents, even moderate abolitionists, found his language offensive, his tactics extremist and self-defeating, and his personality obnoxious. 'Garrisonianism', which came to be the descriptive epithet for radical abolitionists, was characterized by its adversaries as a wild, disorganized body of 'fanatics, incendiaries, madmen, [and] disturbers of the peace' (William Lloyd Garrison [hereafter cited as WLG] to friends of the Anti-Slavery Movement, Boston, 18 April 1836). Garrison saw himself reviled as 'a terrible, hard-hearted, blood-thirsty monster' (WLG to Helen E. Benson, Boston, 12 March 1834) and a 'cut-throat'.[4]

In the public mind, the man and the movement were conflated; 'Garrisonianism', as one critic put it, 'grows more and more ultra and fanatical' (Joshua Leavitt to James G. Birney, Washington, DC, 14 February 1842).[5] Garrison, many believed, had inappropriately assumed for himself and his movement the claim to divine election as the exclusive champions of the enslaved. An infuriated Gamaliel Bailey (editor of *The Philanthropist*, organ of the Ohio Anti-Slavery Society) expressed the consternation of more moderate abolitionists, writing in a private letter that

> I try to restrain myself, but the disgusting, gross egotism of Garrison, and the loathsome adulation of his idolators are continually urging me to say something in the *Philanthropist* ... He compares himself to an Apostle – he has called out such men as A[rthur] Tappan, J[ames] G. Birney, Gerrit Smith, etc., etc. He is the Atlas of abolition. Had not God made *his* forehead strong against the foreheads of the people, the bark of abolition would have been wrecked on the shoals and quick sands of human expediency. So he says. I believe in my soul, we have overvalued Garrison. And as to himself, pride has driven him mad (Gamaliel Bailey to James G. Birney, Cincinnati, 14 October 1837).[6]

More damningly, an article entitled 'Fanaticism-Disunion' that appeared in the *Philadelphia Commercial Intelligencer* linked Garrison's personal monomania with a broader prospective threat to the stability of the national polity. Alluding to Garrison's recent trip to England to undermine the credibility of Elliott Cresson, agent for the American Colonization Society, the anonymous author of the piece observed that 'he abused his country in language worse than *Benedict Arnold*'. Furthermore, 'this arch disunionist and sanguinary fanatic' was 'lighting the torch of anarchy to flame through the land'. The goal of Garrison and his followers was to corrupt the religious establishment so as to 'incorporate their designs with the religious system of the country'. Once they had subverted the churches, Garrisonians would proceed to overthrow the government, since it was clear that their

> designs are neither more nor less than treason. They contemplate, and *unless speedily checked, will consummate, the downfall of the Government*. This project is not only at variance with the constitution, but with the principles on which it is framed. If they succeed, it must be by revolution.

Garrison was cast as the Robespierre of this Jacobin revolt. He was depicted in *The Liberator* 4.23, 7 June 1834, as 'posting about on his unholy errand of disunion and bloodshed', supporting himself through the country, by the bounty of poor colored servant maids and waiters, to the tune of several thousand dollars yearly.

Garrison's response to his critics was not to deny the substance of what they said, but rather to insist on their inaccurate understanding of the social, political, historical and moral circumstances of the anti-slavery cause, and their indirect (if unwitting) justification of slavery. Writing in 1836, for example, he drew a sharp contrast between public reception of abolitionist arguments then and a scant six years earlier. Looking back to his first public lecture against slavery in Philadelphia in 1830, he observed that

> since that time, a change has come over our land. Other sentiments have become popular, new doctrines have been asserted, new estimates made of men and things, full of novel atrocity and absurd impiety. *Then*, slavery if it found some apologists, could find none to defend it as a righteous system; *now* it is widely vindicated in the Senate chamber, from the pulpit, by ecclesiastical bodies, by theological institutions ... as a system consistent with Christianity, and sanctioned by the Almighty. *Then* it was not disreputable, at least not dangerous, to express abhorrence of the practice of making merchandise of our fellow creatures; *now* he who remonstrates against that practice, is in peril of losing his property, safety, liberty, and life (WLG to William H. Scott, Boston, 20 April 1836).[7]

In the context of the politicization of morality and faith, and their subordination to slavery, Garrison argued that the moral economy of the nation had been inverted; human bondage was not a question of political economy, but fundamentally one of conscience and ethical duty. In the sharply polarized world of moral discourse, the reproachful epithets of his opponents were evidence in Garrison's mind of the validation of his moral vision and a sign of personal justification as well. 'If they should call us honest men,' he wrote,

> discreet citizens, sound republicans, and genuine Christians, it would almost certainly follow that we were as knavish, fanatical, oppressive and corrupt as themselves. In their vocabulary for 'treason' see 'loyalty', for 'insanity' see 'reason,' for 'blood-thirstiness' see 'non-resistance,' for 'malignity' see 'forgiveness.' ... Let us not be alarmed about our reputation: let us rather rejoice that its inherent value is made manifest by the combined slander and scorn of all the wicked in our land. To reign with Christ, we must be crucified to the world; to save our lives, we must lose them; to preserve and enlarge our reputation, we must sacrifice it for righteousness' sake (WLG to William H. Scott, Boston, 20 April 1836).[8]

What his apologia made clear was that while his vision was reductionist and his ideological foundations absolutist, Garrison had profoundly spiritualized American politics; he had introduced religious and moral criteria rather than economic progress and political expediency as the bases for the assessment of the character of the nation and the legitimacy of the socio-political order. He proposed the pre-eminence of the private conscience and personal moral responsibility over ecclesiastical conformity and majoritarian consensus. Over the course of his career, he drew substantially on three major theological traditions which, when united and placed in the service of immediate abolitionism, provided a profound moral challenge to the materialistic values of Victorian America and the self-gratulatory and delusory egalitarianism of Jacksonian democracy – the pietistic, covenantal beliefs of New England Calvinism, the Evangelical enthusiasms of the Second Great Awakening and the antinomianism of the Perfectionist movement. The implacability of his religious vision ultimately led Garrison to reject all secular authority and to deny the legitimacy of the state, which he saw as grounded in the coercion of individual conscience and embodying the legality of human enslavement. His critique of government was in this sense based upon a thoroughgoing philosophical anarchism. At the same time, however, the affective quality of his Evangelical ardour led him to a visionary faith in the prospective regeneration of the human race that found expression in his dedication to universal reform.

Contemporaries in the antebellum years viewed Garrison as either a bigoted and self-righteous fanatic, or, in more generous terms, as an undisciplined, unfocused and ungovernable advocate of social reformation. Only in the years after the Civil War did he become 'the acknowledged spokesman for radical anti-slavery opinion.'[9] Historical assessment has paralleled contemporary opinion: revisionist historians of the 1930s and 1940s blamed Garrison and the radical abolitionists for irrevocably polarizing public opinion, undercutting the possibility of political compromise on slavery and establishing the conditions for an inveterate sectional hostility that made the Civil War inevitable; however, neo-revisionist historians of the 1960s argued that Garrison's tactics of 'moral suasion' provided the basis for a politics of agitation that kept the issue of racial equality before the public after emancipation and provided the tactical foundation for the civil rights movement.[10] The goal of this paper will be, not to weigh the relative merits of the moral and the political in Garrison's thought, or to evaluate the success or failure of his abolitionist efforts in the context of the conflicting secular and spiritual claims that pressed upon him, but rather to interrogate the critical nexus of religion and reform in their application to his quest for the regeneration of mankind. Such an inquest of the fulcrum of moral reform necessitates a more substantive and detailed consideration of what his contemporaries identified as 'Garrisonianism'.

Perhaps the most distinguishing hallmark of Garrisonianism was its use of harsh language. Witness Garrison's editorial creed for *The Liberator*, which he recommended to more lukewarm abolitionists:

> Starve not your epithets against slavery, through fear or parsimony: let them be heavy, robust and powerful. It is a waste of politeness to be courteous to the devil; and to think of beating down his strongholds with straws is sheer insanity. The language of reform is always severe – unavoidably severe; and simply because crime has grown monstrous and endurance has passed its bounds (WLG to *The Liberator*, Liverpool, 23 May 1833).[11]

But what made Garrisonianism so dangerously explosive was his insistence on piercing through the monstrous mask to the real monster beneath, penetrating the veil of collective sin to expose the face of the individual sinner.

Garrison had already adopted this tactic as early as 1829, when he co-edited the Baltimore anti-slavery paper, the *Genius Of Universal Emancipation*. As he declared in connection with a report on the domestic slave trade, 'every one whom I detect in this nefarious business – merchant or master – shall be advertised to the world' (WLG to the Editor of the *Newburyport Herald*, 1 June 1830).[12] In this respect, Garrison prefigured a later generation of radicals; he found the moral (and the political) to be personal, and the personal to be moral (and political). Thus, his rough tongue and rude words were brought to bear not only against hardened sinners (in the tradition of the Evangelical exhorter), but against those who failed to achieve unity of purpose or who lacked essential moral (and political) correctness, as the quirkily inconsistent Gerrit Smith learned in 1835. In a direct communication, published in *The Liberator*, Garrison was characteristically blunt:

> I must be personal, because it is impossible to arraign transgression without implicating the transgressor ... I am accused of harboring ill will towards certain individuals, because I have called them by name, and identified them before the public ... There are occasions when the success of the impeachment depends upon personal identity; there are cases in which general accusations fail to reach individual guilt; and these happen often. Besides, it is far more manly to say, face to face, without circumlocution or equivocation, 'Thou art the man!' than to deal in subtle insinuations and dark imputations (WLG to Gerrit Smith, 31 January 1835).[13]

Both in his direct, uncompromising language and his zeal to expose individual sinners, Garrison adapted the revivalist tactics of Charles

Grandison Finney's 'new measures' to secular reform, thereby evangelizing abolitionism and transforming what had been a discreet, genteel movement into a more democratized and aggressively confrontational moral crusade. He thereby set an example for 'ultraist' reform that was implemented in two of the other great moral crusades of the antebellum era, the temperance and anti-prostitution movements, by George Barrell Cheever and John R. McDowall respectively. Indeed, Garrison followed the careers of these two radical moral reformers who employed his tactics of exposure, and identified with them as fellow victims of ecclesiastical persecution and slavish legalism.[14] Through the medium of his Evangelical anti-slavery crusade, Garrison aimed at nothing less than the moral transformation of America from legalistic to biblical morality; individual regeneration based on the Evangelical model – conviction of sin, conversion and personal salvation – would provide the basis for the redemption of the nation.

As Garrison saw it, the primary problem for abolitionists was touching the hearts of the unconverted, and the key to those hearts was Evangelical education. 'Our cause,' he wrote to a close black abolitionist friend,

> has been retarded, not so much by prejudice and wickedness, as by ignorance and misconception. Just as fast as we get light among the people, and make ourselves heard, and our principles and purposes known, we make converts ... with all their failings, the great mass of the people of this country are *really* the enemies of slavery – really the friends of emancipation (WLG to John B. Vashon, Boston, 22 March 1834).[15]

But anti-slavery truth faced an adamant opponent in the arguments of pro-slavery apologists, whose justifications rested upon '... the logic of Bedlam, the morality of the pirate ship, the diabolism of the pit. They insult the common sense and shock the moral nature of mankind.'[16] Though the struggle was unequal, Garrison became impatient for the triumph of the truth. While his more optimistic Evangelical side evinced a fundamental faith in basic human goodness, his pietistic, puritanical side pushed him towards uncompromising abolitionism and encouraged him to imagine himself a vessel of divine judgment and retribution. There was, he maintained, quite simply no right to property in the bodies and souls of human beings, no possible justification for slavery. Abolitionism was cast as the judgmental power to try a whole nation's moral worth. 'The abolition which I advocate,' Garrison cried,

> is as absolute as the law of God, and as unyielding as his throne. It admits of no compromise. Every slave is a stolen man; every slave

holder is a man-stealer. By no precedent, no example, no law, no compact, no purchase, no bequest, no inheritance, no combination of circumstances, is slave holding right or justifiable.[17]

And Garrison had always championed the moral, the natural law over mere secular legalism. He put the question rhetorically in *The Liberator* in 7 November 1835: 'The first question is, is slavery right? Is it consistent with moral law?' His answer was a resounding condemnation of a corrupt and mammonistic generation. 'The cause which we advocate,' he declared,

> is not ours but GOD's ... Nevertheless it *is* ours to carry forward, instrumentally – but not ours to choose or reject, as we may think expedient. Those who call upon us to suspend our operations, or to keep silence, or to wait till a more convenient season ... make application to the wrong source. They ought to beseech the Creator of heaven and earth to release us from our obligations to himself and to mankind; to reverse all the laws of his moral government ... (WLG to Samuel J. May, Brooklyn [CT], 17 January 1836).[18]

Popular opinion and convenience, however, had set themselves solidly against the moral law and the will of God, and the central institutions of American society – the churches, the government, and the popular press – had reinforced the ethical lassitude of the public mind, while administering palliatives and soporifics to the collective conscience. Opinion makers in the church and politics moulded the views of the mass of the people and effectively obscured and dissimulated the reality of enslavement. The moral and juridical praetors of American society had become the procurators of institutionalized racial bondage. As Garrison put it,

> the pulpit is false to its trust, and a moral paralysis has seized the vitals of the church. The sanctity of religion is thrown, like a mantle, over the horrid system. Under its auspices, robbery and oppression have become popular and flourishing. The press, too, by its profound silence, or selfish neutrality, or equivocal course, or active partnership, is enlisted in the cause of tyranny – the mighty press, which has power, if exerted aright to break every fetter, and emancipate the land. If this state of affairs be not speedily reversed, 'we be all dead men.'[19]

Politics, too, had failed the nation in its moral crisis; the national parties had become little more than conduits for personal ambition and self-perpetuating mechanisms that preserved the continuity of a hypocritical system at the expense of its victims. Garrison's indictment of American politics was appropriately thoroughgoing:

> I perceive little intelligence, and scarcely any conscience, or honesty, or fear of God, at the polls. The politics of this nation, at the present time, are corrupt, proscriptive, and even ferocious; and the leading politicians of all parties fail in their allegiance to heaven and to their country (WLG to the Colored Inhabitants of Boston, Boston, 18 December 1834).[20]

It is clear that by the middle 1830s Garrison had concluded that the American institutional infrastructure had failed and that further attempts at compromise and accommodation were not only futile, but evidence of moral perversity. His most radical and sweeping ideas of national reformation and regeneration rested on a Calvinist substratum – the people had violated their covenant with God; only by subjecting themselves to divine law could they re-establish their erstwhile relationship with the deity; only by repentance and a thorough scourging of the sin of slavery could Americans once again lay claim to a special foederal relationship as the elect. As individuals, Americans had fallen from the covenant of grace; as communities and sections (North and South) they had betrayed the social contract (expressed by the tenets of natural or moral law as set forth in the preamble to the Declaration of Independence); as a nation they had subverted the national covenant, had violated its fundamental conditions, and had thereby forfeited the providential promises contingent upon obedience. The cause of the modern Fall, the root of the profound individual and collective alienation from God and the forfeiture of grace was the national sin – chattel slavery. For Garrison, slavery came to assume the lineaments of the Calvinist's original sin; it was virtually coterminous with the earliest colonial settlements in North America, making it the nation's congenital sin.

Garrison made this point forcefully in an early attack on the American Colonization Society, which he considered at best deeply tainted by racial prejudice and at worst a puppet whose strings were pulled by slave-holding interests. 'I maintain,' he remonstrated in *The Liberator*, 21 December 1833,

> that the guilt of slavery is national, and the obligation to remove it is national. I affirm that Pennsylvania is as really a slave-holding state as Georgia – that the free states are as criminal as the slave-holding states – and that the latter are merely the agents of the former. Hence the people of the United States (not of one portion or territory merely) are wholly responsible, and altogether inexcusable, for the present existence of slavery in that country.

The pervasively insinuating and progressively corrupting quality of the nation's original sin was apparent in his description of the extent of the slave system's grasp. 'The one great, distinctive, all conquering sin in America,' Garrison wrote on the eve of the Civil War,

> is its system of chattel slavery – co-existent with the settlement of the country – for a considerable time universally diffused – at first tolerated as a necessary evil – subsequently deplored as a calamity – now defended in every slave State as a most beneficial institution, upheld by natural and revealed religion – in its feebleness, able to dictate terms in the formation of the Constitution – its strength, controlling parties and sects, courts and legislative assemblies, the army and navy, Congress, the National Executive, the Supreme Court – and having at its disposal all the officials, honors, and revenues of the government, wherewith to defy all opposition, and to extend its dominion indefinitely.[21]

In the text of a letter to Joseph H. Kimble (editor of the Concord, New Hampshire *Herald of Freedom*), Garrison addressed the nation's youth as its last best hope of redemption from the besetting national sin. 'Remember,' he wrote,

> the situation of your country! Recreant to her own heaven-attested principles! Perjured before a horror-stricken world! ... Now fearfully exposed to the exterminating judgments of heaven! Remember that LIBERTY is crucified in your country, and all her true worshippers are branded as madmen, fanatics, and incendiaries! That the constitution is trampled underfoot, 'a blurred and tattered parchment,' by a slave holding faction and their northern adherents. That the 'self-evident truths' embodied in the Declaration of Independence are now ridiculed by the rulers in church and state, as 'rhetorical flourishes' and 'splendid absurdities.'
>
> Remember, then, the high, solemn and affecting responsibilities which now rest upon you – responsibilities which you cannot evade but at the peril of your souls and the certain destruction of your country (WLG to JHK, Brooklyn, CT, 16 August 1837).[22]

It was evident, then, that the national sin must be rooted out from the body politic and expunged from the national and individual conscience. But how could that be accomplished? Garrison's answer was institutionally subversive and individually Evangelical. Like Jonathan Edwards, he called for a renewal of the religious affections that would usher in radical changes in civil and social behaviour, 'an entire revolution in public sentiment,' 'an alteration in the feelings and practices of the people towards the blacks'.[23]

Seeking national redemption and personal sanctification, Garrisonianism assumed a thoroughly anti-authoritarian and anti-institutional stance. Both the state, which presumed to control the body through physical force, and the church, which arrogated to itself supreme power over souls, were illegitimate embodiments of a meretricious orthodoxy. In the spiritual realm, Garrisonian 'come-outerism' was manifested as anti-sectarianism, which effectually meant opposition not to radically dissentient recusancy, but rather to mainstream Protestant denominationalism. Garrison took a stance of moral absolutism towards all established national churches, condemning them as un-Christian, craven violators of the higher law. 'No religious creed,' he asserted, stood firmly against slavery and racial prejudice,

> no form of worship, no evangelical discipline, no heretical liberality, either mitigates or restrains it. Christian and Infidel, Calvinist and Universalist, Trinitarian and Unitarian, Episcopal and Methodist, Baptist and Swedenborgian, Old School and New School Presbyterian Orthodox and Hicksite Quaker, all are infected by it, and equally ready to make an innocent natural distinction the badge of eternal infamy, and a warrant for the most cruel proscription. As a nation sows, so shall it reap. The retributive justice of God was never more strikingly manifest than in this all pervading negrophobia, the dreadful consequence of chattel slavery.[24]

The churches not only assuaged the national conscience on the question of racial servitude, but indemnified the crimes of slave holders and embraced them as fellow communicants. Furthermore, it was not simply an instrumental policy pursuant to ecclesiastical politics and Evangelical interdenominational competition; slavery and racism had infected the very marrow of the churches, giving rise to a symbiotic monster – the slave-church. As Garrison put it,

> the vitality, the strength, the invulnerability of slavery are found in the prevailing religious sentiments and teachings of the people ... At the North, every sect, desirous of national extension, can secure it only by acknowledging slave holders as brethren in Christ. All the great, controlling ecclesiastical bodies and religious denominations in the land – constituting the American Church, comprehensively speaking – are one in sentiment on the subject. All the leading Bishops, Doctors of Divinity, Theologians, Professors, ministers, and religious journalists, find complete justification for slave holding at the South.[25]

Just as the Puritans and enlightened Deists had identified popery and a superstitious priesthood as the twin enemies of a revealed and a rational faith, so too did Garrisonianism lay the responsibility for a corrupt and brutal slave-church squarely on the backs of the institutionalized clerical class. But whereas the sacerdotal villains of an earlier generation had been uniformly Roman Catholic, radical abolitionists inverted the hierarchy of villainy, assigning pride of place to the mainstream, orthodox Protestant clergy, and from within their ranks to the most enthusiastic and Evangelical, since they were considerably more likely to spread the contagion of perversely moralized slavery to those whom they might convert. Late in 1846, the American Anti-Slavery Society made this point most forcefully in adopting a resolution aimed at the American Board of Commissioners of Foreign Mission. The resolution asseverated,

> that this Society rejoices in the present declining state of American religion, inasmuch as it voluntarily comes forth to baptize and to sanctify slavery, which Mahommedanism abolishes, and Catholicism condemns; and that it will endeavor to warn the world, particularly the so-called heathen portion of it, against its influence (WLG to the Editor of the *Christian Witness*, 4 December 1846).[26]

Though frequently viewed as one of his 'extraneous reforms' (Garrison himself sought to distinguish it clearly from his abolitionist crusade) in his guise of 'Universal reformer', Garrison's anti-Sabbatarianism and related theological iconoclasm might better be understood not as a dissipation of his reforming energies, but rather as a plain and visible sign of his creedal dissent from the dogmatic conventions of the slave-church. He seems to have first rendered himself obnoxious to the orthodox establishment in 1836. In early August, he offended the popular religious press by assailing the sanctity of the Sabbath in the pages of *The Liberator*. This resulted, as he told a Quaker abolitionist, in its 'subjecting me to much censure, particularly among the *pious* opposers of the anti-slavery cause' (WLG to Effingham L. Capron, Brooklyn [CT], 24 August 1836).[27]

His orthodox opponents quickly concluded that Garrison, as editor of *The Liberator*, sought 'to overthrow the Christian Sabbath, and the Christian ministry, and the Christian ordinances, and the visible church, and all human and family governments' (WLG to James T. Woodbury, 28 August 1837).[28] Garrison summed up the scope of his 'infidelity' in a negative list of his religious opinions, which had raised such controversy in abolitionist circles by 1840:

> I do *not* believe in the inherent holiness of the first day of the week;

in a regular priesthood; in a mere flesh-and-blood corporation as constituting the true church of Christ; in temple worship as a part of the new dispensation; in being baptized with water, and observing the 'ordinance' of the supper – & & & (WLG to Elizabeth Pease, Boston, 11 June 1841).[29]

In essence, these beliefs constituted a new Puritanism, for while they do not uniformly correspond to a strict doctrinal Calvinism, they do embody its spiritual essence in their attempt to purify a carnal and errant church.[30] But what did a radical faith leave to sustain individuals who, for conscience's sake, had come out from the corrupt body of the slave-church? For Garrison, the answer lay in the social and soteriological doctrines of Charles Grandison Finney. Finney stressed the efficacy of conversion, which resulted in the rebirth of the sinner to 'entire sanctification' or holiness, and which found expression in engaged social action. It was the theology of Finney's 'holiness' religion, more accurately denominated Perfectionism, that provided the spiritual justification for Garrisonian abolitionism.

Garrison professed a non-sectarian, personalist variety of Perfectionism repeatedly, both publicly and privately, and seems to have considered it the outward and visible sign of grace, the seal of membership of the 'true', invisible church, that belied the petty hypocrisies of the sectarian churches. He described his basic creed, for which he had been viciously attacked by more conservative abolitionists, in *The Liberator* (26 October 1838):

> I believe in present and eternal deliverance from sin – that he who is born of God does not commit sin ... I maintain, that the followers of Christ are those who have come out from 'the kingdoms of this world', which are hostile to his kingdom.

That his was an aggressively anti-establishment, 'come-outerist' brand of Perfectionism was clear from a letter Garrison wrote to his longtime friend and loyal financial benefactor, Francis Jackson. 'I am not a Trinitarian,' he wrote,

> Unitarian, Baptist, Methodist, Swedenborgian, Friend, Perfectionist, or member of any other sect, but simply, in profession, ... I believe in passing from death to life – in being born of God – in becoming a new creature in Christ Jesus – in being crucified to the world – in present, perfect, and perpetual deliverance from sin – in unswerving allegiance to the great Lawgiver of heaven and earth, whose glorious name is Love ... (WLG to Francis Jackson, Brooklyn, [CT], 18 June 1838).[31]

In the struggle to attain a personal, absolute grace, a 'perpetual deliverance from sin', most Americans were found wanting; their failure was an inability to unconditionally embrace the law of Love. The spiritual travail of the individual soul in quest of assurance of salvation, what Garrison called 'Christian rest', became in his mind a synecdoche for a profound national incapacity and imperfection, a moral deficiency rooted in the universal sin of slavery. It was on the question of the capacity for perfection that Garrison's theological beliefs and reform programmes came together. His figurative rendering of the tormented and conflicted individual soul excluded from grace in his poem 'Christian Rest' reflects, in its use of the rhetorical device of epanados, the stark polarization of the national conscience over slavery:

> Half saint, half sinner, day by day;
> Half saved, half lost; half bound, half free;
> Half in the fold, and half astray;
> Faithless this hour, the next most true;
> Just half alive, half crucified;
> Half washed, and half polluted too;
> To Christ and Belial both allied!
>
> In thee what contradictions meet!
> Seeing the way, yet groping blind!
> Most conscientious, yet a cheat!
> Allowing what thou dost abhor,
> And hating what thou dost allow;
> Dreaming of freedom by the law,
> Yet held in bondage until now! [32]

Garrison's vision is one of a nation of enslavers themselves enslaved by the sinful system of institutionalized human bondage. Conscious of the evil of slavery, Americans had been, Garrison held, seduced by the legalism of orthodox religion, and thereby excluded from the essential Evangelical sequence of grace, conviction of sin, repentance and spiritual rebirth. The national soul hung in the balance, for, as was also the case for the individual soul, 'If thou should'st fail to find true rest/On earth, thou'lt find it not in heaven.' The urgency, the immediacy of Garrison's abolitionism rested squarely on his perception that there could be no salvation to an unprepared heart; a people, a nation that harboured the horrible sin of slavery in its bosom could never be spiritually free and would never merit grace. His ultimate goal, then, was not only to eradicate the system of chattel slavery and its accompanying racism, but thereby to liberate the national soul and to initiate the rebirth of America. When viewed from this perspective, Garrisonianism assumes the aspect of Evangelical Perfectionism, and becomes a means, a conduit, for a transformatory grace. To find 'true rest' (effective grace) would render the nation

> Perfect in love and holiness;
> From sin eternally made free;
> Not under law, but under grace;
> Once cleansed from guilt, forever pure;
> Once pardoned, ever reconciled;
> Once healed, to find perfect cure,
> And Jesus blameless, undefiled;
> Once saved, no more to go astray;
> Once crucified, then always dead;
> Once in the true and living way,
> True ever to our living Head;
> Dwelling in God, and God in us;
> From every spot and wrinkle clean;
> Safely delivered from the curse;
> Incapable of doubt or fear.[33]

The absolutism of Garrison's Perfectionist vision drove his abolitionist reform toward ultraism and allowed him to brook no compromise with the sin of slavery. It is likely, too, that the psychology of Perfectionist dualism, and the frustration of a decade-long struggle against the national evil of human servitude, led Garrison to conclude that slavery constituted more than an inveterate criminal manifestation in the national character, and that it was no less than a conscious conspiracy against liberty and virtue. The idea of a vast slave conspiracy permeating all American institutions, spiritual as well as secular, provided the conceptual link that brought his religious beliefs and his impetus to social reform into conjunction, providing the logical nexus between absolutist Perfectionism and radical abolitionism.

The slave conspiracy manifested an insatiable appetite for territorial engrossment and power; it covered, Garrison pointed out, 'more than half of the national territory, and aimed at universal empire'; in its expansionist drive, the slave imperium would incorporate Mexico, Cuba, Haiti and the Sandwich Islands (Hawaii).[34] As a national institution, it was of 'colossal size' and power: 'Its existence not only implies,' Garrison warned,

> but demonstrates, universal corruption. It has become organic – a part of the habits and customs of the times. It is incorporated into the State; it is nourished by the Church. Its support is the test of loyalty, patriotism, piety. It holds the reins of government with

absolute mastery – rewarding the venial, stimulating the ambitious, terrifying the weak, inflaming the brutal, satisfying the pharasaical, ostracizing the incorruptible. It has its temple, its ritual, its priesthood, its divine paternity, in the prevailing religion, no matter what may be the title or pretension thereof.[35]

The nation had quite literally incorporated the contagion of slavery; its body politic had been invaded and its soul infected. The disease of sin, the curse of slavery, had eaten away the body of the nation like the bacilli of leprosy, while its soul had been corrupted and enfeebled by the metastasizing cancerous growth of the slave system. The nation had become little better, in Garrison's eyes, than a rotting shell, dead to its own sin. Its former self, its vanished glory, were no longer recognizable. The slave conspiracy, then, was a perverse impediment to reconstituent therapeusis, to personal and national salvation.

With paranoiac and pessimistic intensity, Garrison outlined the depraved state of the union in the last decade before secession:

The present Union, therefore, is one in form, not in reality. It is, and it always has been, the absolute supremacy of the Slave Power over the whole country – nothing more ... while the present Union exists, I pronounce it hopeless to expect any repose, or that any barrier can be effectively raised against the extension of slavery ... with forces never divided, and purposes never conflictive – with a spurious, negro-hating religion universally diffused, and everywhere ready to shield it from harm – with a selfish, sordid, divided North, long since bereft of its manhood, to cajole, bribe, and intimidate ... with the territorial strength and boundless resources of the whole country at its command – it cannot be otherwise than that the Slave Power will consummate its diabolical purposes to the uttermost.[36]

If salvation and salubrity required the separation of the morally healthy from institutionalized religion, they equally mandated the termination of any cooperation with, or collusion in, the affairs of the diseased body of the political order. Garrison's moral ultraism, grounded in Perfectionist theology and manifested in dissociative 'come-outerism', provided the foundation for his radical anarchistic and pacifistic conception of moral duty in the realm of practical politics. His politics were spiritualized politics; his stance in relation to the legalities of government was thoroughly antinomian and led logically to his championing of the peace and nonresistance movements, which necessitated the adoption of a position of complete passivity towards and withdrawal from all political participation. In the 'Declaration of Sentiments' adopted by the Peace Convention in Boston (18 September 1838),

Garrison effectively expressed his spiritualization of the political realm, declaring that 'we cannot acknowledge allegiance to any human government; neither can we oppose any such government by resort to physical force ... [we are bound only by the laws of God's kingdom], which has no state lines, no national partitions, no geographical boundaries; in which there is no distinction of rank, or division of caste, or inequality of sex' (*The Liberator*, 28 September 1838). From its first issue, *The Liberator* had borne the motto 'Our country is the world – our countrymen are all mankind' on its masthead.

Since 'THE POWERS THAT BE, in any government, are [not] actuated by the spirit, or guided by the example of Christ ... they cannot be agreeable to the will of God: and therefore, their overthrow by a spiritual regeneration of their subjects is inevitable.' And, Garrison concluded in *The Liberator*, 28 September 1833, the political duty of the redeemed citizen was non-participation, or nonresistance, as he called it. Because all elected officials require accession to the use of force to sustain the government and its laws, the regenerated must

> voluntarily exclude themselves from every legislative and judicial body, and repudiate all human politics, worldly honors, and stations of authority. If we cannot occupy a seat in the legislature, or on the bench, neither can we elect *others* to act as our substitutes in any such capacity. It follows that we cannot sue any man at law, to compel him by force to restore anything ...

But while complete withdrawal from politics at all levels and voluntary disfranchisement might arguably prove an effective passive means of recalling the polity to its true mission, such tactics would be worse than useless in their effect on the system of slavery, which lay beyond the reach of regional or even national politics. Garrison therefore proposed a more active version of non-association in order to affect institutionalized servitude – the economic boycott. Assuming that profitability was the only rationale for slavery, he argued that

> the consumers of slave goods contribute to a fund for supporting slavery with all its abominations; that they are the Alpha and Omega of the business; that the slave-trader, the slave-owner, and the slave-driver are virtually the agents of the consumer ... that we are imperiously called upon to refuse those articles of luxury [produced by slave labour] ... and that were it not for this [our patronage], they would be compelled by sheer necessity to liberate their slaves – for as soon as slave labor becomes unprofitable, the horrid system cannot be upheld.[37]

Garrison's rationale for resistance as a political strategy, however, was the same for both non-participation (the passive strategy) and economic boycott (the active strategy). His aim was to de-legitimize the institutional supports of human slavery, to subvert them by withholding both consent and cooperation. Such a strategy, he believed, would lead to the eventual collapse of the corrupt infrastructure of the Union. By the late 1830s he saw positive signs of the effects of radical nonresistance on the consciences of the better class of political participants. As a result of nonresistance, he maintained,

> our 'pro-government' brethren have obtained new views of duty at the polls ... they are forced to perceive how hideously defective is the government which they cherish, and to confess that it bears little or no resemblance to the gospel of Christ ... in order to justify their conduct ... they have set themselves to work in good earnest (a small portion only), to repeal wicked and oppressive laws, to soften the severity of the penal code, to elect better men to office, to obliterate the lines of party, and to make conscience and the fear of God attendants at the polls. In all this I rejoice. I hail such an altered state of political feeling as the harbinger of a mighty reformation (WLG to the Editor of *The Emancipator*, 31 May 1839).[38]

Less than a year after Garrison penned these words, the abolitionist movement split, the schism arising to a significant degree out of disputes over the advisability of anti-slavery political action and the appropriate abolitionist role in the presidential election of 1840. The secessionist group formed the Liberty Party in Albany, New York in April of 1840, and in May in New York City nominated one of their number, James G. Birney, as the anti-slavery presidential candidate. Their final split with the Garrisonian American Anti-Slavery Society came at its annual meeting in New York City on 12 May 1840. The seceders formed a splinter organization, anti-Garrisonian in its policies, and politically and religiously conservative in its principles, on 15 May. This group, usually referred to as the 'new movement', called itself the American and Foreign Anti-Slavery Society, and elected Arthur Tappan president. It took with it the official organ of the American Anti-slavery Society, *The Emancipator*, and this journal henceforth contended with *The Liberator* (and the new official journal of the AASS, *The National Anti-Slavery Standard*) for intellectual leadership of the movement and for the allegiance of individual abolitionists.

Garrison took the actions of the 'new movement' abolitionists as proof that they belonged among the unregenerate, that they voluntarily comprised an element of the corrupt political cabal, and that they were in collusion with the slave-church and the slave-power conspiracy.

This episode revealed Garrison at his most paranoiac and conspiratorial, and it impelled him to lead the saved remnant of the 'old movement' in an ever more radical political direction – that of nullification and repudiation of the political and moral legitimacy of the Union. By 1846, Garrison had come to believe that the Union, 'that hideously defective government', had been conceived in sin, embodied in the congenital deformity of 'the "organic" sinfulness of the Constitution' (*The Liberator*, 24 April 1846).

In a three-part article entitled 'The Constitution-Political Action', that appeared seriatim in *The Liberator* (17 and 24 April and 1 May 1840), Garrison posed a more radical strategy for 'no-government' men. 'What,' he asked,

> is the American Union? It is but another name for the American Constitution. Destroy that Constitution, and the Union ceases to exist ... the American Anti-Slavery Society maintains that it is the duty of all who reverence God and abhor oppression, immediately to withdraw from it – to pronounce it unholy and accursed – to conspire for a new and righteous government ...

Lest any think his language figurative only, he made an unequivocal call for disunion:

> The uncompromising friends of emancipation are now earnestly demanding the dissolution of the American Union, as a moral and religious duty, because that union was framed in iniquity, and is cemented with the blood of the slaves, because it is an impious attempt to unite Christ with Belial, holiness with piracy, liberty with slavery.

Garrison consistently supported and sustained the disunionist movement in his home state of Massachusetts, and provided it with broader publicity in the pages of *The Liberator*. He reprinted, for instance, a resolution of the Worcester County Anti-Slavery Society enforcing dissolution of the Union as a 'moral and political duty', and announcing its signatories 'the disunion abolitionists' (*The Liberator*, 24 April 1840). In the issue for 6 May 1842, Garrison published a long editorial entitled 'Repeal of the Union', in which he called the Constitution 'a covenant with death, and an agreement with hell'.[39]

In the wake of the Mexican War, Garrison supported popular petition drives urging the Massachusetts General Court to initiate peaceful secession of the state from the Union (WLG to Richard D. Webb, Boston, 1 March 1847, and WLG to Henry C. Wright, Boston, 1 March 1847).[40] In a symbolic act of protest, on 4 July 1854, he burned a copy of the Constitution, crying, 'so perish all compromises with Tyranny! And let all the people say, Amen!'[41] Finally, in the period of intensifying crisis that followed the Kansas–Nebraska Act and 'Bloody Kansas', he published a call for 'a Convention of ALL THE FREE STATES ... "to consider the practicability, probability and expediency of a SEPARATION BETWEEN THE FREE AND SLAVE STATES"' (*The Liberator*, 24 July 1857). A secession convention in the North on that grand a scale never materialized, due in part to the financial panic, but the call demonstrated Garrison's commitment to withdrawal from the Union.

In contrast to Garrison's Perfectionism, anarchism and disunionism, which his more conventional contemporaries considered 'bigotry' and 'fanaticism', his penchant for universal reform and moral ultraism elicited the epithets 'folly' and 'rashness', (WLG to the Editor of the *Newburyport Herald*, 1 June 1830),[42] and were believed to constitute the fundamental tactical and philosophical contradictions of the moral absolutism of Garrisonianism. Certainly, it played an important role in the splits that occurred in several important reform organizations in which Garrison played a prominent role – the subsumption of the American Peace Society by Garrison's Non-Resistance Society (1838) over the issue of opposition to defensive war (absolute pacifism); the fragmentation of the temperance movement in 1836, resulting from the triumph of ultraism (total abstention and the call for prohibition legislation); and the schisms in the Massachusetts Anti-Slavery Society (1839) and the American Anti-Slavery Society (1840) over Garrison's opposition to political action and his insistence on full participation of female members.

While opposition to slavery remained Garrison's primary objective in the period from 1830–1865, he pursued a dizzying array of reform activities during these years, and considered himself to be a 'Friend of universal reform' (WLG to Samuel J. May, Boston, 17 July 1845).[43] The breadth of his interests had less to do with his schismatical tendencies than with his Perfectionist absolutism and his uncompromising personality. To his credit, he did recognize that his abolition and other reform interests might be at cross purposes, and consequently he tried to make a distinction between his private personality and his public persona as a leading abolitionist. As he wrote to his wife during a trip to Great Britain,

> I did not appear before them [a Chartist group] in my official capacity, or as an abolitionist, technically speaking, but on my own responsibility, uttering such *heresies* in regard to Church and State as occurred to me, and fully identifying myself with all the unpopular reformatory movements in this country. This will probably alienate some 'good society folks' from me, but no matter. I know that the cause of my

enslaved countrymen cannot possibly be injured by my advocacy of the rights of all men, or by my opposition to all tyranny (WLG to Helen E. Garrison, London, 3 September 1846).[44]

However naive his belief that he could effectively separate the private sphere from the public personality, and the cause of universal liberty from the specific instance of manumission, Garrison's range of reform advocacy was extraordinarily broad. He began his career in the late 1820s as a temperance man, and moved on to anti-Sabbatarianism, Perfectionism, pacifism and anarchism. He championed women's rights (including suffrage), supported the ten-hour day, deprecated racism and segregation and advocated the repeal of racial intermarriage laws, denounced the fraud and brutality that characterized the dispossession of the Native American peoples, vigorously contended for free speech and vehemently opposed all forms of censorship, and crusaded against prostitution. He also had time for a variety of popular and more evanescent meliorative ventures – homeopathy, hydropathy, clairvoyance, spiritualism, phonography, and phonotypy. He briefly flirted with, but in the end had little sympathy for, utopian communitarianism, though he remained on friendly terms with abolitionists at the Northampton Association in Massachusetts.[45]

Contemporaries who worried that Garrison dissipated his energies and weakened abolitionism thereby, and historians who have argued that he failed to achieve emancipation peacefully because he 'rejected democratic politics and the idea of compromise', fundamentally missed the point of his crusade. Or, more to the point, they ignored the delicate balance that prevailed between individual conscience and a social and political movement of reform like abolitionism. Garrison claimed that his 'extraneous' reforms were matters of personal moral commitment; an institutionalized reform movement like the American Anti-Slavery Society, he maintained, 'may not coerce or violate the conscience of any man (WLG to the Abolitionists of Massachusetts, 17 July 1839).[46] He insisted on making an 'Important Distinction':

> As individuals, abolitionists may utter sentiments, which, in their associated capacity, they may not express. He who becomes an abolitionist is under no obligation to change his views respecting the duty of going to the polls, or belonging to a sect; they are those of an individual, and not binding at all upon any other member of the anti-slavery society. But if the society itself presume to endorse those views as sound and obligatory on all members, then it violates the spirit of its own constitution ... This distinction between the liberty of an individual and of an association composed of many elements, is important, and essential as much to the harmony of the whole

body as it is to personal free agency (WLG to the Abolitionists of Massachusetts, 17 July 1839).[47]

The 'extraneous' reforms he championed were all outgrowths of the internal dynamics or politics of the abolitionist movement, or extensions of the crusade against human enslavement, as Garrison understood it. Rooted in his Evangelical and Perfectionist convictions and his belief in the efficacy of moral reform, his ultimate goal was 'universal liberation', and he sought, through 'glorious rant and revolutionary fanaticism', to 'bring on a general engagement with the enemies of liberty' (WLG to George W. Benson, Boston, 8 July 1842).[48] But Garrisonian moral reform, characterized by moral absolutism and antinomian anti-institutionalism, could not be contained by the framework of any organized reform movement. It transcended opposition to physical and political bondage; it transcended the crusade against moral bondage to drink and prostitution; it transcended them all. What Garrison ultimately aimed at was the universal regeneration of mankind and the inception of a millennial state; only thus could his vision of universal liberation be fully realized. For,

> the mere abolition of slavery is not the reconciliation of the world to God, or of man to his brother man; though there can never be any such reconciliation without it. I want to see a World's Convention that shall have for its object the recognition and approval of Jesus, the Messiah, as the only King and Ruler on earth – the establishment of his kingdom to the subversion of others – the prostration of all national barriers, castes, and boundaries – the mingling of the whole human race ... the forgiveness of enemies ... the overthrow of all military and naval power ... the adoption of a common language, to the suppression of Babel dialects which now divide and curse mankind ... O for the establishment of a pure religion on earth! (WLG to Maria W. Chapman, 3 June 1840).[49]

For Garrison, then, abolitionism was a necessary pre-condition to the Universal liberation and unification of all mankind under a single moral government rather than an aggregation of competing political principalities. He was a religious revolutionary and a political radical who sought through the spiritualization of human institutional life absolute liberation of the body, mind and spirit from bondage to the powers that be. Although his main concern had to be with the great national sin of racial slavery – the slave-church and the slave-power conspiracy – his moral absolutism led him to see slavery writ large in all the relations of society. To secure the fundamental natural rights guaranteed in the Declaration of Independence and to validate the republican tradition, social and political relations required regeneration. Temperance reform sought to free the body from enslavement to alcohol; the anti-prostitution campaign would redeem the female body from sexual servitude. Anti-Sabbatarianism, anti-sectarianism and Perfectionism sought to free the individual soul from the domination of priestcraft and the denominational churches. Pacifism, nonresistance, nullification, philosophical anarchism and disunionism provided the foundation for the validation of the individual conscience and its liberation from subservience to state power and its enthralment to the use of institutionalized collective force – the police power or military action. Native American peoples were, to Garrison, not so much wards of the state as dispossessed tribal groups that had been defrauded by a hypocritical government that had broken their spirits and imprisoned them on segregated and much diminished territories. Free blacks were the people most analogous to the Native Americans; to call them 'free' was a linguistic travesty; they were simply the shadow of the enslaved blacks, whose chains were forged of links of educational and job exclusion, limitations on suffrage and citizenship rights, segregation and restrictions on social relations and property rights. Their bodies were as effectively controlled as those of slaves.

Garrison's opposition to colonization, residential, educational and occupational discrimination and his championing of 'amalgamation' (racial intermarriage) aimed at liberating the bodies and minds of free blacks by establishing their claim to equality of rights with native-born American citizens. He analogized the condition of white women to that of free Blacks, and strove for their liberation from patriarchal dominance, which exerted similar control over the bodies and minds of women. Opposition to censorship and outspoken support for free speech (both in his own 'immodest language' and his protests against legal and political restraints) effectively made Garrison a champion of intellectual freedom and the legitimation of the freedom of the individual mind.

Garrison was a moral radical who could not tolerate tyranny or hypocrisy, no matter how strongly politicians or churchmen struggled to legitimate them. He refused to accept the idea that persons could be reduced to the status of things by legislative fiat or social custom, and he devoted his life to the liberation of the body, mind and spirit of human beings, regardless of gender, class, colour, or condition, from all forms of oppression and bondage, whatever institutional guise they might assume. Garrison posed the problem of power as a moral question; he was outraged by, and rejected the legitimacy of, laws and authority that violated human dignity and that interposed themselves between the individual and freedom. He assumed the moral right of nullification – to declare such laws unjust and such authority illegitimate, and therefore not worthy of obedience. His rejection of the legitimacy of political authority made it impossible for him to be a 'political action' ('new movement') abolitionist, just as his rejection of the sectarian churches made it impossible for him to be a conventional Christian. It is therefore unreasonable to say that he should have pursued political compromise if he hoped to achieve the emancipation of the slaves. That he supported universal liberation, embodied in a wide range of reforms, did not make him inconsistent or dissipate his energies, but rather testified to his single-minded dedication to his ulterior reform agenda – the liberation of the human race and the regeneration of humankind.[50]

In this respect, Garrison provided a model for later radical opposition to authority based on an antinomian conceptualization of a higher law or a natural law that manifested itself as passive resistance to the state and spirited public opposition to the law of society. Without Garrison, the modern civil rights movement, the anti-Vietnam war movement, the women's movement, the New Left protests, and Black Power would have been very different.[51] Ironically, Garnson's moral absolutism and his anti-authoritarianism, his absolutist nonresistance (the refusal to appeal to violence or governmental intervention to achieve manumission lest the abstract principle of force be legitimized and the authority of power over morality established) – all of which his contemporaries found so fanatical and frequently considered counterproductive to the anti-slavery movement – have proven to be his most enduring legacy to a secular age. His radical advocacy of the cause of human freedom continues to serve as an archetype for, and to provoke and animate, our continuing struggles for justice and equality, as well as to inspire our dreams of an ideal society.

Notes

1. Walter M. Merrill, ed., *The Letters of William Lloyd Garrison*, vol. 5, *Let the Oppressed Go Free, 1861–1867* (Cambridge, MA: Belknap Press, 1979), 366.
2. Walter M. Merrill and Louis Ruchames, eds, *The Letters of William Lloyd Garrison*, vol. 6, *To Rouse the Slumbering Land, 1868–1879* (Cambridge, MA: Belknap Press, 1981), 41.
3. *Ibid.*, 42–3.
4. Louis Ruchames, ed., *The Letters of William Lloyd Garrison*, vol. 2, *A House Dividing Against Itself, 1836–1840* (Cambridge, MA: Belknap Press, 1971), 86; Walter M. Merrill, ed., *The Letters of William Lloyd Garrison*, vol. 1, *I Will Be Heard!, 1822–1835* (Cambridge, MA: Belknap Press, 1971), 291; William Lloyd Garrison, *Thoughts on American Colonization: Or an Impartial Exhibition of the Doctrines, Principles, and Purposes of the American Colonization Society. Together with the Regulations, Addresses, and Remonstrances of the Free People of Color* (Boston: Garrison and Knapp, 1832), 8.

5. Dwight L. Dumond, ed., *Letters of James Gillespie Birney, 1831–1857*, 2 vols (New York: Appleton-Century, 1938), 2:709.
6. *Ibid.*, 428.
7. Ruchames, *Letters of WLG*, 2:86.
8. *Ibid.*, 86–87.
9. Merrill, *Letters of WLG*, 5:l.
10. The two best examples of the revisionist school of abolitionist historiography are Gilbert H. Barnes, *The Anti-Slavery Impulse, 1830–1844* (New York: D. Appleton-Century, 1933), and Avery Craven's *The Coming of the Civil War* (New York: Charles Scribner's, 1942) Barnes concluded that Garrison's radicalism severely impeded the growth of abolitionism and restricted its success, while Craven found Garrisonianism extreme and impractical, skilled in attracting attention and rousing antagonism, but unable to solve the problem of slavery. Stanley Elkins argued, in a revision of revisionism, *Slavery: A Problem in American Institutional and Intellectual Life* (Chicago: University of Chicago Press, 1959), that a healthy democratic society needs moral fervour and fanaticism, and that moderation was, given the brute facts of slavery, not a viable alternative to radical abolitionism. James M. McPherson's *The Struggle for Equality: Abolitionists and the Negro in the Civil War* (Princeton, NJ: Princeton University Press, 1964), is perhaps the best example of the new revisionism. McPherson concedes that abolitionist tactics failed to achieve national conversion to immediate manumission, but argues that their failure was a moral failure of the American people, who have yet to live up to the ideals of the radical abolitionists. Lewis Perry's *Radical Abolitionism: Anarchy and the Government of God in Antislavery Thought* (Ithaca, NY: Cornell University Press, 1973), argues that radical abolitionism failed to relate its anarchism to its broader goals – whether Perfectionist, political, or social – These goals were not extraneous to abolition, however, and were not the product of personal or collective dementia.
11. Merrill, *Letters of WLG*, 1:229–30.
12. *Ibid.*, 102. The case that prompted this outburst was that of a Newburyport merchant, Francis Todd, who was transporting eighty-eight slaves in his vessel, the *Francis*, from Baltimore to Louisiana. Garrison was found guilty of libel and sentenced to pay a $50 fine and costs. Lacking sufficient funds, he was sentenced to imprisonment for a period of six months. He had served only seven weeks when a philanthropist, Arthur Tappan, sent the money to pay his fine and Garrison was freed. For a more detailed discussion of this episode, see Garrison's letters from 12 May 1830 to 6 November 1830 in Merrill, *Letters of WLG*, 1:91–114, and Garrison's tract, *A Brief Sketch of the Trial of William Lloyd Garrison for an Alleged Libel on Francis Todd of Massachusetts* (n.p., n.d., [1830?]).
13. Merill, *Letters of WLG*, 1:437–8. The biblical reference is to II Samuel, 12:7. The rationale of public exposure, an implicit identification of the reformer with divine retribution, may be found in verse 12, where Jehovah tells David, 'for thou didst it secretly: but I will do this thing before all Israel, and before the law'.
14. Cheever (1807–1890), a Congregationalist minister from Salem, Massa-

chusetts, published 'Inquire at Deacon Giles' Distillery' in 1835 (reprinted in *The Liberator*, 21 February 1835). Deacon John Stone saw himself in this satiric piece and sued Cheever for libel. The foreman of Stone's distillery assaulted Cheever in a public street. Cheever was convicted of libel, imprisoned for one month and given a $1,000 fine. Cheever's experience paralleled Garrison's early career, so there was a close bond of identification between them. See *The Liberator*, 14 and 21 February, 4 and 11 July, and 12 and 26 December 1835, and 13 February and 12 March 1836. McDowall (1801–1836) was a Presbyterian minister from Canada and an anti-vice crusader of such moral vigour that he was expelled by his presbytery for 'unministerial conduct' in 1836. On McDowall, see WLG to Isaac Knapp, New York, 11 May 1836, and WLG to Henry E. Benson, Boston, 17 December 1836, in Ruchames, *Letters to WLG*, 2:98 and 192, respectively. The obituary of McDowall in *The Liberator* (12 December 1836) was probably written by Garrison. For personal reflections on Cheever, see WLG to Henry E. Benson, Brooklyn, [CT], 15 December 1835, and WLG to Helen E. Garrison, 28 December 1835, in Merrill, *Letters to WLG*, 1:576 and 589 respectively.
15. Merrill, *Letters of WLG*, 1:299.
16. William Lloyd Garrison, *No Compromise With Slavery: An Address Delivered in the Broadway Temple, New York, February 14, 1854* (New York: American Anti-Slavery Society, 1854), 10.
17. *Ibid.*, 14.
18. Ruchames, *Letters of WLG*, 2:17.
19. Garrison, *Thoughts on American Colonization*, 53–4.
20. Merrill, *Letters of WLG*, 1:426.
21. William Lloyd Garrison, *The 'Infidelity' of Abolitionism* (New York: American Anti-Slavery Society, 1860), 5.
22. Ruchames, *Letters of WLG*, 2:286–7.
23. Garrison, *Thoughts on American Colonization*, 80 and 8 respectively.
24. Garrison, *'Infidelity' of Abolitionism*, 5–6.
25. *Ibid.*, 6.
26. Walter M. Merrill, ed., *The Letters of William Lloyd Garrison*, vol. 3, *No Union With Slaveholders, 1841–1849* (Cambridge, MA: Belknap Press, 1973), 457–8.
27. Ruchames, *Letters of WLG*, 2:172.
28. *Ibid.*, 297.
29. Merrill, *Letters of WLG*, 3:22. Garrison had already offended the popular religious press by assailing the sanctity of the Sabbath in the pages of *The Liberator* in 1836, and he further alienated the orthodox with his call for a 'Church, Sabbath, and Ministry Convention,' *The Liberator*, 16 October 1840. The convention met (17–19 November 1840) at the Chardon Street Chapel, Boston, under the chairmanship of Edmund Quincy. See WLG to John A. Collins, Boston, 1 December 1840, in Ruchames, *Letters of WLG*, 2:724.
30. As orthodox authorities in support of his Sabbatarian stance, Garrison cited Martin Luther (1483–1546), Philip Melancthon (1497–1560), William Tyndale (1492–1536), John (Jean) Calvin (1509–1564), William Paley

(1743–1805), John Foster (1770–1843), Daniel Whitby (1638–1726), Roger Williams (1604–1684), Thomas Belsham (1755–1829), Joseph Priestly (1733–1804), Robert Barclay (1648–1690), George Fox (1624–1691) and William Penn (1644–1718). Garrison's list is somewhat disingenuous since most of these men were religious rebels in their own day, however mainline and orthodox they may have seemed in the first half of the nineteenth century. Indeed, the institutional denominations that sprang from these figures' teachings, with the exception of the Quakers, had uniformly accepted the orthodoxy of Sunday as their official Sabbath. Of these men, Whitby and Foster were the most orthodox. Barclay, Fox and Penn were founders of Quakerism, and Belsham was an early Unitarian. Luther and Melancthon had spearheaded the Protestant Reformation. Priestly had been considered an atheist by many, and later became a millenarian. Paley championed 'natural theology' and was a Deist philosopher. Tyndale was an advocate of the 'new learning', and was executed for his religious views. See WLG to the editor of *Zion's Herald*, 27 August 1842, in Merrill, *Letters of WLG*, 3:98–9.

31. Ruchames, *Letters of WLG*, 2:369. Garrison recognized the effect of John Humphrey Noyes' theological development of Perfectionist doctrines and shared his treatises and copies of his periodical *The Perfectionist* (1834 [New Haven, CT], 1837–1846 [Putney, VT]) with friends and associates. See WLG to Maria W. Chapman, Northampton, [MA], 7 July 1843, in Merrill, *Letters of WLG* 3:24 and 172, respectively. Garrison distanced himself from Noyes' communitarian venture at Putney because of the introduction of 'spiritual marriage' there (*The Liberator*, 27 November 1841). There is no mention of Noyes in Garrison's letters after his formation of the Oneida Community in 1848, but Garrison would have made every effort to dissociate himself from the plural marriage practised there as well as from the radically unorthodox sexological doctrines Noyes espoused under the name 'male continence'. Garrison was much closer theologically to James Boyle, the Evangelical Perfectionist and active abolitionist. Boyle wrote an impassioned defence of Garrison's religious heterodoxy, 'Letter to Wm. Lloyd Garrison, Touching the "Clerical Appeal," Sectarianism, and True Holiness' (*The Liberator*, 23 March 1838), which bore the salutation 'Dearly Beloved Garrison'. Boyle had expressed strong nonresistance and anti-governmental views as early as 1837; the New England Non-Resistance Society (NENRS) was not founded until 1838. Boyle, therefore, as well as the NENRS may well have had significant influence on Garrison's conversion to nonresistance and later to disunionism. Though there is no extant correspondence between Boyle and Garrison, Boyle was a trusted abolitionist associate, and he and his wife Laura seem to have been personal friends of the Garrisons. Boyle figured as a subject intermittently in Garrison's personal letters between 1838 and 1845. Interestingly, Boyle, like Noyes, was associated with the utopian communitarian movement – in Boyle's case, the Northampton Association of Massachusetts. Garrison's close personal friend and editorial collaborator, Oliver Johnson, wrote of Boyle in *The Liberator* in 1840 that 'probably there was no man living whose religious views were more

in harmony with Mr Garrison's.' See Ruchames, *Letters of WLG*, 2:445 n.10.
32. William Lloyd Garrison, *Sonnets and Other Poems* (Boston: Oliver Johnson, 1843), 60. This poem, under its original title, 'True Rest', appeared in *The Liberator* (25 August 1837), and was appended to Boyle's letter (see *supra*, n.31) when Garrison had it reprinted as a pamphlet in 1838. See Ruchames, *Letters of WLG*, 2:446 n.8. The diction of this poem provides an interesting anticipation of Lincoln's 'house divided' speech at the Republican State Convention in Springfield, Illinois (16 June 1858), in which he speaks of a nation 'half slave and half free'.
33. William Lloyd Garrison, *Sonnets and Other Poems*, 61.
34. Garrison, *'Infidelity' of Abolitionism*, 5, and Garrison, *No Compromise with Slavery*, 31.
35. Garrison, *'Infidelity' of Abolitionism*, 3.
36. Garrison, *No Compromise with Slavery*, 30–1.
37. Garrison, *Thoughts on American Colonization*, 76–7. See also Garrison's response to a letter to the editor, 'Products of Slavery', *The Liberator*, 23 April 1831.
38. Ruchames, *Letters of WLG*, 2:483.
39. The reference is to Isaiah 28:15, which announces a retributive divine judgment on the sinful people of Ephraim. Verse 18 promises that 'your covenant with death shall be annulled, and your agreement with hell shall not stand; when the overflowing scourge shall pass through, then shall ye be trodden down by it!' Commencing with the 13 May 1842 issue, Garrison printed a new motto at the head of his editorial column – 'A REPEAL OF THE UNION BETWEEN NORTHERN LIBERTY AND SOUTHERN SLAVERY IS ESSENTIAL TO THE ABOLITION OF THE ONE AND THE PRESERVATION OF THE OTHER.' The 'covenant with hell' statement followed. Garrison had already declared the Constitution 'null and void from the beginning' as early as 1833 in a letter attacking Elliott Cresson, agent of the American Colonization Society, that appeared in the *London Patriot* (6 August 1833). Merrill, *Letters of WLG*, 1:149.
40. Merrill, *Letters of WLG*, 3:470 and 473.
41. Louis Ruchames, ed., *The Letters of William Lloyd Garrison*, vol. 4, *Disunionism to the Brink of War, 1850–1860* (Cambridge, MA: Belknap Press, 1975), 290.
42. Merrill, *Letters of WLG*, 1:l00.
43. Merrill, *Letters of WLG*, 3:303.
44. Merrill, *Letters of WLG*, 3:393.
45. George W. Benson, Garrison's brother-in-law, was a founding member of the community (established in 1842), and James Boyle lived there until 1845. While he recognized its members as fellow workers 'actively engaged in works of benevolence and philanthropy', he objected that 'all this can be brought about by no mere external organization or local colonization ... but [only] by a discernment and hearty embrace of the truth ...' WLG to Louis Humphrey, Boston, 15 December 1843, in Merrill, *Letters to WLG*, 3:235). See also 'Co-operative Associations', *The Liberator* (25 December 1840). The article is signed 'Humanitas'.

46. Ruchames, *Letters of WLG*, 2:501. For the above quoted phrase, see John L. Thomas, *The Liberator: William Lloyd Garrison* (Boston: Little, Brown, 1963), 459.
47. Ruchames, *Letters of WLG*, 2:502.
48. Merrill, *Letters of WLG*, 3:95. It should be noted that *The Liberator* was not the official organ of the American Anti-Slavery Society or of the Massachusetts Anti-Slavery Society, and therefore quite legitimately represented Garrison's own personal reform agenda. While it served as a primary source of Garrison's positions in print, opponents of abolition used its expression of radical ideas on a wide variety of subjects to discredit the anti-slavery movement. In his public speeches, there is some evidence that Garrison strove to separate his advocacy of abolitionism from his enthusiasm for other causes. Any public statement by Garrison, however, was subject to the same distortion and use as his printed words in *The Liberator*, being cited as an ideal type of abolitionist thinking and rhetoric. Garrison's prominence in the movement and the extreme annoyance he presented to pro-slavery apologists made it effectively impossible for him to separate the personal from the public.
49. Ruchames, *Letters of WLG*, 2:632–3.
50. The association of these mistakenly called 'peripheral reforms' with slavery is clear throughout Garrison's writings. A few examples will suffice. See his exposure of the folly of colonization and gradual emancipation programmes by analogizing slavery to inebriety, thus validating immediate abolitionism by comparing it to total abstinence, in Garrison, *Thoughts on American Colonization*, 55. In the 1870s, the European crusade against legalized prostitution spoke of the sex trade as 'a system of slavery for women' and described its adherents as the 'new abolitionists'. *William Lloyd Garrison on State Regulation of Vice* (n.p., n.d. [1879?]), 1). In the 1870s and 1880s, American and English temperance advocates likened alcohol abuse to slavery. See the anonymous pamphlets, *Thoughts on Temperance by American Women* (London: William Tweedie Co., [1875]), and *An Address: Our Next Emancipation: Or, the Coming War with Rum* (Cambridge: William H. Wheeler, 1883).
51. Ernest G. Bormann's position on the relationship between radical abolitionism and the modern civil rights movement was clear in the title of his book – *Forerunners of Black Power: The Rhetoric of Abolition* (Englewood Cliffs, NJ: Prentice-Hall, 1971). His most powerful arguments are in his concluding chapter, entitled 'The Abolitionist Rhetorical Tradition in Contemporary America'. More recently, historians have begun again to reassess the historical significance of radical abolitionism. Daniel J. McInnerney in *The Fortunate Heirs of Freedom: Abolitionism and Republican Thought* (Lincoln, NE: University of Nebraska Press, 1994), argues that the anti-slavery crusaders were the heirs of the revolutionary tradition and that they saw their movement as the manifestation of an ongoing struggle to fully realize and preserve republican values. He concludes that they were prætorians of liberty and the traditions of revolutionary freedom, and yet have a close affinity to modern reform movements as well.

6

'Rational Recreation': Reforming Leisure in Antebellum America

Robert Lewis

Introduction

'In this young and growing country,' Frederick W. Sawyer wrote in 1847, 'it is of vast importance that we early adopt correct views with regard to the bearing of amusements upon our social institutions, and upon the future prosperity and happiness of our country generally. Now is the time ... for us to take the right stand with regard to them.'[1] Two generations before the Progressives warned of the moral danger in unregulated play on city streets and in darkened dance-halls, leisure was a polemical issue. Moralists debated the question of the 'use and abuse' of amusements. Language was significant. All believed in the ideal of 'rational' recreation, as the re-creation of energy and the replenishment of body and soul for further work. But Evangelicals who feared worldliness and a loss of godliness in the increasing devotion to selfish luxury and hedonistic play distinguished between recreation as renewal, and amusement as diversion or dissipation – a waste of time and talents. According to a contemporary dictionary, 'whatever *amuses* serves to kill time, to lull the faculties, to banish reflection.'[2]

Critics, chiefly Unitarian clergy and liberal intellectuals, insisted that Puritan asceticism had impoverished America. Their claims were boldly stated. 'What the church is to our religious natures, and the school is to our intellectual, the theatre may be to our social and moral natures,' declared Sawyer.[3] A crusade to promote beauty and refinement in everyday life would also improve the morals of the people. Public entertainments, appropriately supervised by apostles of taste, would calm the weary and unify the warring classes. Divisions between Evangelicals and liberals were most evident on the practical question of permissible pleasures. Did the theatre or dancing or the circus have a legitimate role in advancing individual moral uplift and regenerating the social order? Were these innocent diversions or vain amusements? And were leisure pursuits which simply gave relief from stressful tasks, and that were in no sense educational, worthwhile? At stake, the more vociferous advocates proclaimed, was the very soul and stability of the young republic.

Commercial Amusements and the Evangelical Response

The Puritans had been wary of selfish pleasures, but permitted 'sober mirth'. As well as more elevated spiritual exercises and educational pastimes, they condoned moderate, productive relaxation in sociable groups in house or tavern. Always, they cautioned against the ever-present dangers of self-indulgent frivolity and idleness. 'I conclude that I cannot serve 2 masters,' John Winthrop wrote in his spiritual diary; 'if I love the world, the love of the father can have no abiding in me.'[4] 'Harmless recreation,' a group of ministers in the greater Boston area advised in 1726, should be 'governed by reason and virtue,' be 'convenient, sparing, prudent,' 'give place to business,' and 'subserve religion.'[5] The Chesapeake gentry were less inhibited: of all the colonies, Virginia had given the theatre most patronage in the eighteenth century.[6]

Nevertheless, there was consensus throughout the colonies north and south that dramatic exhibitions, cock-fighting and games of chance undermined republican virtue during the Revolution. In October 1778, Congress condemned such diversions as 'productive of idleness, dissipation and a general depravity of principles and manners', and agreed to dismiss any office-holder who attended such amusements.[7] After the Revolution, those, like Samuel Adams, who were steeped in the Whig ideology of *Cato's Letters*, worried about the current fashionable taste for gambling and dancing. 'We are exchanging prudence, virtue and economy,' 'Observer' charged in the *Massachusetts Centinel* in 1785, 'for those glaring spectres, luxury, prodigality and profligacy. We are prostituting all our glory as a people, for new modes of pleasure, ruinous in their expenses, injurious to virtue, and totally detrimental to the well-being of society.'[8]

But far more alarming than the private vices of the few was the appeal of commercial amusements to the many. In the urban northeast, the establishment of theatres and dancing academies in the 1790s was greeted with jeremiads to a loss of ancient virtue. Euphemisms became less common. Dancing-masters who had advertized their skilled guidance in 'polite exercise', now openly touted for pupils. In the theatre, much of the old subterfuge about 'histrionic lectures', 'dramatic readings' and 'moral dialogues' disappeared. Showmen became much more brazen and mocked respectabilty. Traditionalists in Newburyport were scandalized when in 1798 Pinchbeck's menagerie advertized that the exhibition of its Pig of Knowledge 'tends to instruct the youth, raise ambition in the tender mind and heart.'[9]

And the public appetite for amusement was contagious. Suddenly, a vibrant and expanding subculture of commercial entertainment threatened to overwhelm traditional opposition to the drama. In the nineteenth century, the theatres, and especially the so-called 'museums' and their eclectic programmes of trivia and meretricious pretension, enjoyed great and growing popularity with all classes in the cities. In New York, the provision of commercial amusement increased even more rapidly than the marked rise in population. In 1850, there were six theatres and probably another sixty general 'palaces' of pleasure accessible to all, rich and poor. Prices of theatre admission dropped by two-thirds from the 1820s to the 1840s. P. T. Barnum realized the limitations of the traditional dime museum and saw the potential of a new mass market. Transformed into a place of respectable family entertainment, Barnum's American Museum became one of the sights for visitors to New York; his theatre disguised as a 'Lecture Room' offered temperance melodramas as well as the staple human 'curiosities' for the middle classes.[10]

Most critical of this entrepreneurial challenge to asceticism was the Evangelical clergy. The leaders of the Awakenings of the eighteenth and nineteenth centuries insisted upon a strict division between the regenerate and unconverted sinners. 'The love of the world', declared Charles Grandison Finney, the leading revivalist of the 1820s and 1830s, 'and the love of God, are directly opposite states of mind, so that to exercise them both at the same time is impossible.'[11] Converts who dedicated and rededicated themselves to God sought perfection by following an uncompromising regime of purification. Membership in congregations of 'strict,' 'precise' or 'exact' Christians carried heavy obligations of holy watchfulness over personal failings and the failings of brothers and sisters in Christ. Congregations were ever-vigilant for transgressions. Vain dissipations of God's time were a frequent cause for censure and discipline. Only by rigorous self-denial and self-discipline, and by following God's law, could the gathered saints avoid the temptations to sin which abounded in the self within and in society without.[12]

Man 'unrenewed' by God's saving grace was depraved. 'The hearts of men, by nature,' wrote the Yale theologian Timothy Dwight, 'need no preparation to commit sin; they are already prepared, they thirst greedily for it, and are not satisfied with less than the utmost exertion of every faculty they possess in their iniquitous career.'[13] Temptations for the unwary were everywhere, and of the most intoxicating kind. 'Worldly pleasure besots the soul,' Edward N. Kirk proclaimed in his sermon in 1854. 'It begets a reckless fearlessness in regard to coming destiny; stifles all spiritual desires and aspirations; hardens the heart in impenitence; keeps it away from Christ; and thus seals it to damnation.'

'Immoral pleasure is self-abandonment. It is the anarchy of the soul; in which the sentinels are recalled, the prudent counsellors are silenced, the legitimate rulers are ejected from power, and the grosser elements of our disordered nature carry the day.'[14]

The theatre had always been viewed as the amusement most inimical to godliness. Evangelicals protested that by its very nature it served depraved tastes. It could never be an innocent diversion. Grog-shops and whorehouses surrounded it: 'these breathing-holes of perdition open their devouring mouths around the theatre as naturally as ashes gather around the crater of a volcano.'[15] Judge worldly amusements by the character of their patrons, the Methodist and Baptist clergy advised. Since the idle, the intemperate, the gambler and the prostitute flocked to the theatre and the dance-hall, these were sources of pollution, and forbidden to professing Christians. Arthur Tappan, the merchant and leading Evangelical reformer, forbade the clerks in his store to attend the theatre; on pain of dismissal. The party of God measured its success by the relative strength of its pleasure-seeking rivals. Evangelicals rejoiced in 1832 when they purchased the lease of New York's Chatham Street Theatre, and transformed it into the Broadway Tabernacle for Finney's revivals. The old pit and saloons were replaced by a lecture-room and a Sunday school. The house of Belial had become the house of God.[16]

The slightest carelessness of the pleasure-seeker might be fatal for hopes of salvation. Thoughtless levity fed natural vanity, and selfish pride produced forgetfulness of God. The *Mother's Magazine*, the organ of the Evangelical maternal associations, published a cautionary tale of how an indulgent mother eager for her children to learn dancing as one of the social graces, sacrificed the innocent: 'rocked in the cradle of worldly conformity, spiritual sleep overpowered their faculties, and then spiritual death benumbed their energies.' Fashionable amusements, the Reverend Gardiner Spring advised, 'may not always prove the school of vice and profligacy, but they are always the school of thoughtlessness and vanity,' where souls were lost to God.[17]

The Evangelical policy of avoiding worldly pleasures was part of a broader reform strategy of moralized non-consumption. Avoiding contamination with everything tainted seemed effective. Without the restraints which only heartfelt religion imposed, men would remain under the sway of their natural passions and seek ephemeral happiness in sensual indulgence. Like the patriots during the colonial crisis of the 1760s and 1770s, Christians committed to improving the morals and manners of the nation believed in exercising consumer choice. By not purchasing the tea of tyrants or slave-grown sugar or cotton or the distillers' products, the godly avoided polluting sin. Disfranchised women might empower themselves and their families, and by influencing others to be selective in market choices, show political will.[18]

In a similar way, non-conformity to the world – not attending the theatre or dancing – promoted Christian republicanism. As one of the leading revivalists warned, at a time when commercial expansion was becoming evident, the stability of the republic was being threatened by a love of pleasure which followed from materialism. Consider the lessons of the past, Lyman Beecher declared: 'No instance has yet occurred, in which national voluptuousness has not trod hard upon the footsteps of national opulence, destroying moral principle and patiotism, debasing the mind and enervating the body, and preparing man to become, like the descendants of the Romans, effeminate slaves.'[19] When the established church in Massachusetts and Connecticut was lost by the 1830s, and the Sabbatarian campaign for a Sunday free from amusements and commerce failed, Evangelicals turned from legislative fiat to persuasion, self-denial and collective will.

Civilizing the City: The Liberal Programme

By mid-century, there was a coherent alternative reform strategy. Those who called themselves liberal Christians challenged Evangelical proscription. No one made a more comprehensive case for a relaxed policy on amusements than Unitarian Minister Frederick W. Sawyer. The traditional New England dislike of pleasure, Sawyer proclaimed in 1847, was primarily responsible for the class divisions which rent American society. Led by the clergy, the Puritans had repressed the normal play of children so that they had grown up 'cold, calculating, and hardened in all the selfish ways of the world'. But the natural instincts of men must have some outlet. 'If every thing festive and social is banished from the fireside, they will seek the enjoyment of each other's society somewhere else,' and usually in the excessive pleasures of the tavern and public resorts of low repute.[20]

Sawyer's *A Plea for Amusements* outlined new priorities for Americans 'to keep our social institutions as liberal as our political'. National holidays, public gardens, gymnasiums, art galleries, music, dancing and the theatre were all potentially useful agencies in refining manners and forging bonds of unity between the classes and the generations. Sawyer consciously thought of his programme of cultural philanthropy as a new reform movement. 'While societies have been formed for almost every purpose under the sun, from that of distributing moral pocket-handkerchiefs, to that of discovering new worlds, no society has ever yet been organized, been designed, in the slightest degree, to foster, encourage, systematize, regulate, or control amusements.'[21]

Sawyer exaggerated the novelty of his programme. In 1792, when the Massachusetts state legislature repealed the 1750 law prohibiting theatrical shows, several Bostonians made specific proposals for a community theatre maintained by public funds. John Gardiner sought commercial advantage for the city over its more liberal rivals, New York and Philadelphia, in the hope that public theatricals would entice pleasure-seeking visitors from the South and the West Indies. William Haliburton's plan for a place of general entertainment with seating for a third of the city's population and three performances weekly was more ambitious. The content of the shows, 'well regulated' by the legislature, would wean the poor, some of whom would be given free admission, from 'slavery of the passions' in vicious amusements, to the path to virtue.[22]

In New York, the merchant and prominent civic leader John Pintard attacked 'an excess of gloomy zeal' and 'the severity of austere rigid piety'. The most effective means of moral instruction and a 'rational amusement' for the urban poor was a system of 'dramatic exhibitions, corrected & restrained'. In a letter to his daughter in 1816, he expanded on his fashionable elite views: 'Mankind cannot always be praying, nor working. Gross dissipation allways [sic] prevails where refinement is not cultivated ... [W]e must aim at giving a proper direction to young minds, find out new resources for occupation & *killing* time, among which Theatres, Operas, Academies of Art, Museums, & c. are to be classed as the means to attract & prevent the growth of vice & immorality.'[23]

By the 1850s, there were comprehensive proposals for public amusements promoting moral welfare and class harmony. Most sympathetic were Unitarian periodicals like the *Christian Examiner* and the *Monthly Religious Magazine*, and urban Unitarian clergymen. In Worcester, Massachusetts, the Reverend Edward Everett Hale declared that the philanthropist who could demonstrate practical ways of innocent relaxation 'will be the greatest benefactor of new England. He is the man whom she most needs'. In so doing, he would address immediately and directly the outstanding issues which affected the poor in cities and succeed where more conventional reformers had failed.[24] In New York, Henry Whitney Bellows praised the theatre and public parks as the main agencies of cultural uplift. He informed his wealthy congregation that 'amusement is a serious, practical interest and concern of society, and not a mere indulgence and weakness to be excused and apologized for. Society is the better, the safer, the more moral and religious, for amusement.'[25]

Through what Bellows called 'the softening influences of elegance and beauty', the apostles of good taste hoped to civilize the new plutocracy and the debased poor, and to reconcile antagonistic classes in the city.[26] This strategy of refinement was a middle ground between the free play of market forces, where the commercial entrepreneur offered immoral or trivial amusements, and the proscription of the Evangelicals, who offered none. Sawyer upheld as the ideal, 'that meridian line, where man is neither scorched by the sunshine of pleasures, nor chilled by their eclipse.'[27]

Bellows, Hale and Sawyer were part of the broad movement of cultural uplift in the mid-nineteenth century. They were proponents of what historians have variously called, gentility, civility, middle-class culture, Victorianism or the humanitarian sensibility.[28] John Kasson has shown how the writers of etiquette manuals believed that European standards of polite behaviour, modified to fit republican society, would civilize, humanize and improve American morals through reforming its manners.[29] Richard Bushman explains refinement: how moralists taught that adorning the middle-class home in the best taste would enhance the nurturing role of the woman as domestic guardian.[30] Leigh Eric Schmidt has shown how Americans invented or introduced festivals and holidays in the nineteenth century, making Easter, Thanksgiving and Christmas occasions for family celebration and fashionable visiting.[31]

In 1857, the *North American Review*, the leading intellectual journal, complained that in America, more than in European countries, 'the nomadic habits of our people' and 'the passion for gain' 'scatter the holy fire of love'. National holidays and universal occasions for celebration offered hope of 'refinement and disinterestedness', transcending divisions of class and locality. 'We could thus infuse a better spirit into our work-day experience, refresh and warm the nation's heart, and gradually concentrate what of higher taste and more genial sympathy underlies the restless and cold tide that hurries us onward, unmindful of the beauty and indifferent to the sanctities with which God and nature have invested our existence.'[32]

Familiarity with European customs often prompted enthusiasm for greater provision of community recreation. The Unitarian Minister Orville Dewey found in England, and especially in France and Italy, a social harmony engendered by public spectacles which was an inspiration. In America, intense competition in business, and especially the 'sanctimonious spirit in religion' which insisted upon Sabbatarianism and suppression of joy, brought misery and intemperance unknown in countries where the liberal 'Continental Sunday' allowed a naturally sober festivity. 'This expansion of social feeling we are particularly liable to want ... Seasons of public amusement, in which all classes engaged, would tend to break up social clanships and to soothe angry collisons.' 'May there be in us and among us,' Dewey concluded, 'restraint without sourness, freedom without licentiousness, refinement without effeminacy, virtue without stoicism, and religion without superstition.' European social liberality would enlarge American political freedom.[33]

Henry Whitney Bellows became convinced in the 1840s that American cities were in moral crisis. The contempt of the Puritans for all pleasures had directed energies into commerce. Unfortunately, materialism offered no solutions to poverty and disorder, and traditional asceticism removed the one potential source of social unity, the natural capacity for relaxation. 'It makes our places of amusement low,' he wrote in 1845, 'divides the thoughtful and the careless, the grave and the gay, the old and the young, in their pleasures.'[34] Eight years later, he argued that luxury, if diffused, made refinement available to all. Apart from domestic comfort and beautiful surroundings, no means of refinement were more effective in inculcating morality than the dramatized lessons of the theatre.[35] Or, Bellows added in 1861, New York's Central Park. Manicured Nature and the music of the bandstand soothed nerves fraught by business; the Promenade was a central meeting-ground or 'assemblage' where the poor could emulate the manners of the genteel. Only an urban park modelled on European precedents could 'teach and induce habits of orderly, tranquil, contemplative, or social amusement' so effectively.[36]

For a small denomination, the Unitarians were unusually prominent in the crusade for refined amusements. They were far more confident than the Evangelicals that control over worldly pleasures was possible. They were deliberately controversial, shocking public opinion. Bellows gave a sermon in praise of actors as a legitimate profession; Sawyer described the theatre as 'another mode of teaching'.[37] They attacked the 'hard moral tendency of Calvinism'. Human nature, according to Bellows, was 'God's work, and not Satan's botch'.[38] Revivals were unnecessary: nurture of man's inner conscience, the moral sense, could give rational control over the 'animal' appetites. Repression of wholesome natural emotions had disastrous consequences.[39]

The main intellectual influence on the Unitarians was William Ellery Channing. In the 1830s, he became convinced that the growing class conflict in Boston and the disorder which resulted from it had no simple solution. The poor needed spiritual rejuvenation and moral reformation more than financial relief. Calvinism abandoned them to the evil forces of commercial amusement. 'A religion,' he wrote in 1837, 'giving dark views of God, and infusing superstitious fear of innocent enjoyment, instead of aiding sober habits, will, by making men abject and sad, impair their force, and prepare them for intemperance as a refuge from depression or despair.'[40] Channing's panacea was middle-class self-culture broadcast by Christian gentlemen. The 'pleasures of a refined taste' he recommended were fine literature, lyceum lectures and graceful music. Dancing was suitable, but not public drama, because of its associations with fashionable dissipation.[41] Channing's disciples were inspired chiefly by his forthright attack on Evangelical theology, but also took his message of social reform in more practical and populist directions.

Unitarians were also part of the urban establishment. The members of Bellows's church in New York included the wealthy businessman Peter Cooper and the literary doyens, William Cullen Bryant and George William Curtis. Unitarians were very conscious of middle-class anxieties – of 'over-work' as one of the great American failings, and of the plight of ambitious young men in cities. Hence, they thought the quiet public relaxation of the 'Continental Sunday' far more effective in promoting social cohesion and individual self-culture than either killjoy Sabbatarianism or the private initiatives of the profit-making entrepreneurs. They were faithful to their class, and marked out a role for the genteel guardians of taste. Elite leadership was essential. Without direction, the public park would be a place for mere 'loitering'. Music – classical music, not discordant brass bands or puerile minstrelsy – would attract the genteel, and teach the poor civility.[42]

Samuel Rodman's Rational Recreation

In everyday life, approval of amusements was usually highly selective – and personal. Samuel Rodman, a New Bedford Quaker merchant, committed to temperance and anti-slavery, provides an example of changing perspectives and the waning of Calvinist prohibitions. The nice distinctions Rodman drew between the acceptable and the banned were highly individual. Not surprisingly, he supported the lyceum. He also approved of the menagerie, and enjoyed exhibitions of a giant and a dwarf, presumably both judged educational. The mainstream theatre, however, he considered immoral, and he did not attend that 'exhibition' in 1840. He prefered the oldfashioned conversational party without music or dancing, and worried that his children frequented a public resort of 'fashionable gaiety'. Change – for the worse – came to New Bedford. On 21 January 1839, he forbade his daughter to attend an evening 'fancy ball' at her uncle's house, 'the first of the kind ever attempted in this place, an innovation on the previous modes of social intercourse which I think promises no advantage.'[43]

Samuel Rodman struggled to make sense of the fashionable amusements in the light of his Quaker religion. The self-appointed guardians of morality who campaigned for a more liberal attitude to amusements reflected more than changing attitudes. By the 1850s, the traditional demarcations between redeeming leisure and mere diversion had been eroded. Edward Everett Hale felt the need for any kind of play as a release from individual or group tensions was so pressing that linguistic precision and outdated moral categories were immaterial. 'Recreation or amusement' he wrote in 1854, 'are but other names for rest.'[44]

Notes

1. Frederick W. Sawyer, *A Plea for Amusements* (New York: D. Appleton, 1847), 275.
2. George Crabb, *English Synonymes* ... (New York: Harper and Brother, 1831), 301.
3. Frederick W. Sawyer, *Hits at American Whims and Hints for Home Use* (Boston: Walker, Wise, 1860), 57.
4. Richard Winthrop, ed., *Life and Letters of John Winthrop*, 2nd edn, 2 vols (Boston, 1869), 1:191, quoted in Charles Lloyd Cohen, *God's Caress: The Psychology of Puritan Religious Experience* (New York: Oxford University Press, 1986), 248.
5. Cotton Mather, et al., *A Serious Address to Those Who Unnecessarily Frequent the Tavern* ... (Boston, 1726), 10, quoted in Bruce C. Daniels, *Puritans at Play: Leisure and Recreation in Colonial New England* (London: Macmillan, 1995), 19.
6. Nancy L. Struna, 'Sport and the Awareness of Leisure,' in Cary Carson, Ronald Hoffman and Peter J. Albert, eds, *Of Consuming Interests: The Style of Life in the Eighteenth Century* (Charlottesville: University Press of Virginia, 1994), 406–43.
7. Nathaniel S. Paine, 'Early American Broadsides, 1680–1800,' *Proceedings of the American Antiquarian Society*, n. s. 2 (1896–1897), 471, quoted in Catharine L. Albanese, *Sons of the Fathers: The Civil Religion of the American Revolution* (Philadelphia: Temple University Press, 1976), 196; J. Thomas Jable, 'The Pennsylvania Sunday Blue Laws of 1779: A View of Pennsylvania Society and Politics During the American Revolution,' *Pennsylvania History* 40 (October 1973): 413–26; Lynn Matluck Brooks, 'Against Vain Sports and Pastimes: The Theatre Dance in Philadelphia, 1724–90,' *Dance Chronicle* 12 (1989): 165–95.
8. Charles Warren, 'Samuel Adams and the Sans Souci Club in 1785', *Proceedings of the Massachusetts Historical Society* 60 (May 1927): 322.
9. James M. Barriskill, 'The Newburyport Theatre in the Eighteenth Century', *Essex Institute Historical Collections* 91 (October 1955): 340.
10. Peter C. Buckley, 'To The Opera House: Culture and Society in New York, 1820–1860' (Ph.D. diss., State University of New York, Stony Brook, 1984), 145–6; Bruce A. McConachie, *Melodramatic Formations: American Theatre and Society, 1820–1870* (Ames: Iowa State University Press, 1992).
11. Charles Grandison Finney, 'Love of the World', in *Sermons on Important Subjects* (New York: John S. Taylor, 1836), 255.

12. See Philip Greven, *The Protestant Temperament: Patterns of Child-Rearing, Religious Experience, and the Self in Early America* (New York: Alfred A. Knopf, 1977), 141–3.
13. Timothy Dwight, *An Essay on the Stage* ... (London: Sharp, Jones, 1824), 34.
14. Edward N. Kirk, *The Love of Pleasure. A Discourse Occasioned by the Opening of a New Theatre in Boston. Delivered in Mt. Vernon Church, Sunday, September 10, 1854* (Boston: John P. Jewett, 1854), 11, 12.
15. Edmund S. Morgan, 'Puritan Hostility to the Theatre', *Proceedings of the American Philosophical Society* 90 (27 October 1966): 340–347; William Pratt Breed, *The Theatre* (Philadelphia, 1868), 13.
16. Joseph A. Scoville, *The Old Merchants of New York*, 5 vols (New York, 1885), 1:230, quoted in Allan S. Horlick, *Country Boys and Merchant Princes: The Social Control of Young Men in New York* (Lewisburg, PA: Bucknell University Press, 1975), 172; Joseph P. Thompson, *The Last Sabbath in the Broadway Tabernacle. A Historical Discourse* ... (New York: Calkins and Stiles, 1857), 10–11.
17. 'On Dancing,' *Mother's Magazine* 14 (1846): 146–7; D. R. Thomason, *Fashionable Amusements* ... (New York: J. Leavitt, 1831), iv; E. R. Keyes, *The Incompatibilty of Amusements with the Christian Life. An Essay* ... (Poughkeepsie, NY: J. H. Hickok, 1867), 5.
18. See Clare Midgley, 'Slave Sugar Boycotts, Female Activism and the Domestic Base of British Anti-Slavery Culture,' *Slavery and Abolition* 17 (December 1996): 137–62.
19. Lyman Beecher, 'The Gospel the Only Security for Eminent and Abiding National Prosperity,' *National Preacher* 3 (March 1829): 147, quoted in John F. Kasson, *Civilizing the Machine: Technology and Republican Values in America, 1776–1900* (Baltimore: Penguin, 1976), 36.
20. Sawyer, *Plea*, 91, 177, 280.
21. Sawyer, *Plea*, 172–3.
22. John Gardiner, *The Speech of John Gardiner ... on ... the Expediency of Repealing the Law Against Theatrical Exhibitions* ... (Boston: Apollo Press, 1792); [William Haliburton], *Effects of the Stage on the Manners of a People; and the Propriety of Encouraging and Establishing a Virtuous Theatre* ... (Boston: Young and Elteridge, 1792). See also, Philo Dramatis, *The Rights of the Drama: Or, an Inquiry into the Origin, Principles, and Consequences of Theatrical Amusements* (Boston, author, 1792).
23. *Letters from John Pintard to His Daughter Noel Pintard Davidson 1816–1833*, 4 vols (New York: New York Historical Society, 1940), 1:25–26, 293.
24. Edward Everett Hale, *Public Amusements for Poor and Rich: A Discourse* (Boston: Phillips, Sampson, 1854), 8.
25. Henry Whitney Bellows, *The Relation of Public Amusements to Public Morality: Especially of the Theatre to the Highest Interests of Humanity* (New York: C. S. Francis, 1857), 8.
26. Henry Whitney Bellows, 'Cities and Parks; with Special Reference to the New York Central Park,' *Atlantic Monthly* 7 (April 1861): 422.
27. Sawyer, *Plea*, 125–6.
28. See Stow Persons, *The Decline of American Gentility* (New York: Columbia

University Press, 1973); Daniel Walker Howe, 'Victorian Culture in America,' in Daniel Walker Howe, ed., *Victorian America* (Philadelphia: University of Pennsylvania Press, 1976), 3–26; Thomas Haskell, 'Capitalism and the Origins of the Humanitarian Sensibility', *American Historical Review* 90 (1985): 339–61.
29. John F. Kasson, *Rudeness and Civility: Manners in Nineteenth-Century America* (New York: Hill and Wang, 1990).
30. Richard L. Bushman, *The Refinement of America: Persons, Houses, Cities* (New York: Alfred A. Knopf, 1992).
31. Leigh Eric Schmidt, *Consumer Rites: The Buying and Selling of American Holidays* (Princeton, NJ: Princeton University Press, 1994).
32. 'Holidays', *North American Review* 84 (April 1857): 362.
33. Orville Dewey, *The Old World and the New; or a Journal of Reflections and Observations Made on a Tour in Europe*, 2 vols (New York: Harper and Brother, 1836), 2:218, 222, 236.
34. Henry Whitney Bellows, 'The Influence of the Spirit of Trade', *American Review: A Whig Journal* 1 (January 1845): 97.
35. Henry Whitney Bellows, *The Moral Significance of the Crystal Palace: A Sermon* ... (New York: G. P. Putnam, 1853), 14.
36. Bellows, 'Cities and Parks', 429.
37. Sawyer, *Plea*, 235.
38. Henry Whitney Bellows, *Restatements of Christian Doctrine in Twenty-five Sermons* (Boston: American Unitarian Association, 1867), 217.
39. Daniel Walker Howe, *The Unitarian Conscience: Harvard Moral Philosophy* (Cambridge, MA: Harvard University Press, 1970); Daniel Walker Howe, 'The Market Revolution and the Shaping of Identity in Whig–Jacksonian America,' in Melvyn Stokes and Stephen Conway, eds, *The Market Revolution in America: Social, Political and Religious Expressions, 1800–1880* (Charlottesville: University Press of Virginia, 1996), 259–81.
40. William Ellery Channing, 'Address on Temperance' [1837], in William Ellery Channing, *Works*, 6 vols (Boston: J. Munroe, 1843), 2:386.
41. Channing, *Works*, 4:274.
42. Bellows, 'Cities and Parks,' 425; [John Sullivan Dwight], 'Popular Amusements,' *Dwight's Journal of Music* 7 (14 July 1855): 117–8.
43. Zephaniah Pease, ed., *The Diary of Samuel Rodman: A New England Chronicle of Thirty-Seven Years, 1821–1859* (New Bedford, MA: Reynolds Printing, 1927), 40, 188, 210, 227, 256, 265–6.
44. Hale, *Public Amusements*, 6.

7

Sabbatarianism: The Intersection of Church and State in the Orchestration of Everyday Life in Nineteenth-Century America

Alexis McCrossen

Introduction

Many studies of reform in nineteenth-century America mention Sabbatarianism: some include it in a list of issues ranging from vegetarianism to abolition; others lump it with temperance and women's rights; and still others consider it a part of the effort to impose Evangelical Christianity on the American state.[1] Like as did most other American reform movements, Sabbatarianism originated in England and first made an impact in America when campaigners began to push for reform after the United States Congress passed a law requiring the transportation and delivery of mail on Sunday in 1810. Mail stages had been moving between towns on Sunday and post offices had been opening (usually after church services) to dispense mail, but the federal government did not have a written policy concerning the matter. When a Presbyterian postmaster in Pennsylvania was expelled from his church in 1809 for opening the local post office on Sunday, he appealed both to his employer, the Pennsylvania postmaster general, and to Pennsylvania's Presbyterian Synod: the postmaster general told him to continue delivering the mail and the Synod upheld his expulsion. Out of this incident, the American Sabbatarian movement was born, although an official Sabbatarian organization was not formed until the late 1820s.[2] At first directed against the interference of the state in what seemed to be local affairs, by the 1840s the Sabbatarian movement was, more often than not, allied with the state (both local, state, and federal) in orchestrating the rhythms of everyday American life.

How did this happen? How did a reform movement that failed in its first efforts, which lasted from 1810 to 1831, gain momentum and state support? How did it manage to inscribe its meanings for Sunday onto America life and into statute law? This essay will briefly describe Sabbatarianism as both a secular and a religious reform movement.

Sabbatarians sought, through methods both coercive and persuasive, to ensure community-wide observance of the Sunday- Sabbath in keeping with their conception of Christian, healthy and patriotic citizenship. Coercion, which Sabbatarians used as early as 1810, included boycotting Sabbath-breaking enterprises, turning to the courts to punish what they defined as 'Sabbath-breaking', and, most importantly, using statute law to define proper ways to observe the Sabbath. Most historians consider Sabbatarianism a religious reform movement that relied heavily on coercion in the form of 'blue laws'. This assessment has a great deal of validity: after all, laws were passed against nearly every practice, from barbering to baseball, that might defile the Sabbath. How then, do we explain the 'dead letter' condition of most of these laws? Do we then argue that Sabbatarianism was not successful, or are there other measures of success?

It is in the realm of persuasion that Sabbatarianism demands attention: Sabbatarians constructed, circulated and deployed theological, therapeutic, scientific and nationalistic meanings for Sunday that effectively ensured that the day would, in most Americans' practices, remain distinct and separate from the other six days of the week. In the end, this is what Sabbatarians aimed for when they expressed outrage at the federal government's insistence on treating Sunday just like any other day of the week. And in the end this is why the Sabbatarian movement largely succeeded.

At first Sabbatarians aimed to prohibit Sunday travel, Sunday mails and other forms of Sabbath-breaking characteristic of an urbanizing, industrializing and expanding nation. It then turned its efforts towards abolishing immigrant styles of Sunday observance, focusing on saloons, theatres, excursions and general rowdiness. After the Civil War, Sabbatarians were faced with new challenges to Sunday in the form of the Sunday-opening movement, rapid technological development, and increased numbers of immigrants. The last decades of the nineteenth century saw Sabbatarians embrace both coercion and persuasion as they fought an epidemic of Sabbath desecration that swept the nation. But toward and after the turn of the century, they began to re-evaluate their goals; they saw that it was possible that Sunday would lose all distinction, and so they ameliorated themselves to the imposition of culture upon Sunday. Little did they realize that their theological and ideological battles over the meaning of Sunday ensured success – that is, if success can be measured in the saving of Sunday from the logic of modernization, which might have obliterated the day, rather than in the prevention of 'Sabbath-breaking'. In this sense, the accomplishments of the Sabbatarian movement challenge historians to reconsider the division between religious and secular reform: Sabbatarianism could be considered as both a religious and a secular reform movement. It not only sought to preserve one of the fundamental components of a Christian life – Sabbath-observance – but also to heighten appreciation of a day of rest, an essential aspect of a secular life regimented by the clock and calendar.

Antebellum Sabbatarianism

Although early American settlers had brought with them codes of Sunday observance that had passed into colonial and later into state and territorial law, Sabbatarianism – the political and religious movement to preserve the Sunday-Sabbath – did not flourish until 1810 when the US Congress sanctioned transportation of mails on Sunday, sparking a controversy that consumed the nation on and off through the 1820s, and leading in 1828 to the formation of the nation's first Sabbatarian organization, the General Union for Promoting the Observance of the Christian Sabbath (GUPCS). With Presbyterian leadership, and wide-ranging Protestant efforts, the first phase of the effort to prevent Sunday mails heralded the first mass petition campaign in American history. A few 'good morals' organizations that had formed earlier included the Sabbath among their interests. In 1812, for instance, Lyman Beecher's New Haven congregation formed a society 'For Suppression of Vice and the Promotion of Good Morals'. Two years later the first society dedicated to improving Sabbath observance was formed in Middlesex County, Massachusetts, and held two meetings, one in Burlington and another in Concord.[3] Some historians, most notably Paul Johnson in *Shopkeeper's Millennium*, have characterized the second phase of the movement, led by the GUPCS, as coercive in its simultaneous reliance on petitions, propaganda and boycotts. These assessments were matched by the outrage of many Americans at the time, who saw it as a violation of religious freedom when fellow-citizens boycotted businesses or services offered by those of a different religious persuasion. Furthermore, Josiah Bissell and the Tappan brothers, GUPCS leaders, went beyond the boycott when they established the Pioneer Line in 1828; this transportation company in upstate New York, which aimed to provide an alternative to Sabbath-breaking canal lines, went bankrupt within a year but although a commercial failure, succeeded in calling attention to the Sabbath. As one of its founders said, it was 'a sermon three hundred miles long'.[4]

Even though the GUPCS failed in its efforts to stop Sunday mails and disbanded in 1832, it set in motion the formation of countless other Sabbatarian organizations, as well as anti-Sabbatarian groups. Furthermore, it began the persuasive work of establishing the Sunday-Sabbath as a distinct day in the week, as part of the American heritage and as an issue of note for those concerned with public health, morality and citizenship. Historians have ascribed the GUPCS's failure to anxiety about the rise of party politics, the 'market revolution,' the spread of Evangelicalism, the strength of the 'godless Constitution,' and the nature of freedom.[5] Richard John, however, has pointed out that the Sunday-mail controversy arose out of the federal government's intervention in the everyday life of ordinary Americans. The relationship between Sabbatarianism and the imposition of commercial and industrial time on both cities and countryside, suggests that the controversy bore even more deeply into American life than many historians have realized.[6]

Sabbatarian influence grew out of the insistence that the Sabbath was meaningful, and out of the movement's largely successful effort to shape the discourse around the Sabbath. Sabbatarians based their convictions on the fourth commandment, arguing that the obligation to observe Sunday was not only perpetual, but also universal (binding on all, not just Jews). It provided the basis, as well as the language, for legislating Sunday as a day of rest during the colonial period and thereafter: well into the twentieth century, many state codes referred to Sunday as the Lord's Day or the Sabbath. South Carolina's 1902 Code, for instance, stipulated that no person 'shall do or exercise any worldly labor, business or work of their ordinary callings upon the Lord's Day (commonly called the Sabbath)'.[7] The first American Sabbatarians, petitioners protesting against Sunday mails, set the precedent by basing their complaints on these grounds.[8] The fourth commandment was responsible for the weekly rhythms of work and rest in nineteenth-century America: 'Without the Sabbath we should have no week at all'. One minister explained, 'Each week is a definite period, having accurate limits, and separated from the period next to it by a sacred day, into which your weekly affairs may not be carried.'[9] In addition to setting aside a day for rest, the fourth commandment also established how much weekly work was necessary. When faced with demands for shorter working weeks and work days, many employers referred to the text of the commandment, 'Six days shalt thou labour', and refused any reform. Six days of work, one day of rest: this was the shape of the week in America, one reinforced by religious, cultural and legal traditions.

Fearful that Americans were failing 'to remember the Sabbath', Sabbatarians formed and disbanded a number of organizations aimed at protecting the Sabbath in the 1840s and 1850s, including the American and Foreign Sabbath Union in 1843, under the leadership of temperance reformer Justin Edwards, the Philadelphia Sabbath Association (1840) and the Baltimore Sabbath Union (1843). The 1840s also witnessed a series of Sabbatarian conventions: the 'Bethel and Sabbath

Convention' in Cincinnati (1840), a Rochester, NY Convention (1842), the National Lord's Day Convention (1844) and the Baltimore and Pennsylvania Convention (1844), as well as fifteen 'General Sabbath Conventions', seven state Sabbath conventions, and twenty-four county conventions in the state of Pennsylvania. Events at the 1844 two-day Lord's Day Convention included an address by John Quincy Adams in which he proclaimed in front of more than 1,700 delegates, that 'So far as propagating opinions in favor of the sacred observance of the Sabbath, I feel it to be my duty to give all the faculties of my soul to that subject.'[10] These conventions were intent on shaping meanings for the Sabbath in an increasingly contentious and fractured religious climate.

In addition to heading one of the most prominent Sabbatarian organizations, Justin Edwards laid out the Sabbatarian case in a widely reprinted and translated Sabbath manual. According to Edwards, God made the Sabbath while Adam and Eve were in paradise; the law of the Sabbath was based on God's law and natural law; its obligation was universal and perpetual; the very word Sabbath meant 'rest'; when Christ rose he shifted the Sabbath from the seventh day to the first day of the week; the weekly Lord's Day was reserved for the celebration of redemption; and 'the Sabbath was designed to commemorate and enforce THE RIGHTS of God.'[11] These assumptions often went disregarded. Some Americans, for instance, ignored biblical mandates, feeling that the building of canals, the repairing of machinery and the ploughing of fields was essential to their own, and the nation's, survival. But the majority assented to beliefs about the sanctity of the Sunday-Sabbath. Through the 1840s, Sabbatarians succeeded in extending their view of the day, in slowing down the rate of its desecration and in spreading the New England Sabbath to the West.[12] Furthermore, they began to formulate several sets of meanings – primarily focused on Sunday as a day of rest – that would become quite powerful. So, after the disappointments in the battle to stop Sunday mails, Sabbatarians found much to rejoice in and on the whole encountered little resistance.

Although largely ineffectual and mostly peripheral, there was a backlash against the heightened Sabbatarian activity of the early and mid-1840s, expressed at a series of meetings, including the Charndon Street Convention (1840), the Anti-Sabbath Convention (1848), the Hartford Bible Convention (1852) and an anti-Sabbatarian meeting in Salem, Ohio (1852).[13] The assortment of radicals and freethinkers who gathered in a hall on Boston's Charndon Street were unable to agree on whether or not the Sabbath was divinely ordained and perpetually binding, suggesting that the Sabbatarian conviction concerning the fourth commandment had wide currency. But less than a decade later, radical abolitionists, including William Lloyd Garrison, Lucretia Mott and Theodore Parker, protested against the 'orthodox Sabbath' at yet another convention held in Boston. This time they unanimously branded the Sabbath a man-made institution.[14] Furthermore, they asserted their conviction that the obligation to observe the Sabbath was not universal: 'the Sabbath, according to the Jewish scriptures, was given to *"the children of Israel"*, – AND TO NO OTHER PEOPLE.'[15] Anti-Sabbatarians insisted that Protestant clergy used the doctrine of the Sabbath as well as the Sabbath itself to perpetuate and spread orthodox beliefs. Several shared memories of the Sunday-Sabbath being 'pressed upon' their 'childhoods'. One speaker, for example, complained that he 'was trained to believe that the Sabbath was a holy day'. He recounted how he was so terrified of breaking the Sabbath that even as he threw off superstition and vowed to bathe on Sunday, his limbs remained paralyzed and he could not 'venture out into the deep'. Though he eventually regained control of his body, he remained outraged at the stultifying theology he had incorporated as a child.[16] Anti-Sabbatarians denounced orthodox strictures concerning the Sabbath as harmful to the spiritual life of children and adults alike, frequently drawing on their personal experiences for verification.

The 'irrationality' of the 'orthodox' Sunday particularly offended anti-Sabbatarians. They criticized the institutionalization of holy days, and especially the efforts to differentiate time, which was a fundamental aspect of Sabbatarianism. William Lloyd Garrison denounced tying 'men up to the idea that one day is more holy than another' and repeated his 1840 plea for the destruction of the Sunday-Sabbath altogether.[17] Labelling Sunday as holy and trying to keep it as such were indicative of an excessive focus 'on outward form', when truly 'there is no Sabbath. It is all humbug and delusion. All days are alike.'[18] It was resistance against Sabbatarian meanings for Sunday rather than blue laws that animated the convention.

When situated within the context of abolitionism, both anti-Sabbatarian and Sabbatarian aims become clear. The historian Lewis Perry observes that abolitionists were intent on saving themselves from 'the slavery of this world'. In that respect, anti-Sabbatarianism became a mode of contesting the church's authority over lifestyles, time and relationships with God.[19] In turn, then, Sabbatarianism, at least in the eyes of contemporary opponents, was about everyday life, not simply about religious observances, customs and rituals. The Anti-Sabbath Convention's dedication to advancing 'strict moral and religious accountability, in all concerns of life, ON ALL DAYS OF THE WEEK ALIKE' was more a bold critique of Protestant churches than an attempt to remake Sunday into 'man's day'.[20] Anti-Sabbatarians stressed that they did not intend to abolish a weekly rest-day; they simply wanted 'the law of rest from labor [to] stand on its true foundation. Let us establish rest-days for the sake of man, and not for the sake of theology and dogmatic religion.'[21] But all agreed on the need to institutionalize and protect rest.

Response to the Anti-Sabbath Convention verged between anger and ridicule. *The Boston Post* ran a notice for an 'ANTI-MONDAY CONVENTION', inviting all laundresses, tub-makers and soap boilers to attend a meeting towards the 'abolition of Monday from the calendar and creation.'[22] Most Americans accepted an order that differentiated between days, and it was within this shared set of assumptions that Sabbatarians were able to persuade a range of Americans of the value of a sanctified Sunday.

Through the late nineteenth century Sabbatarians took the lead in promulgating meanings for Sunday. Furthermore, they continued to form organizations that focused on reforming Sunday observance through persuasive and coercive methods. One of the most active groups, the New York Sabbath Committee (NYSC), was formed in the late 1850s in protest at an array of Sabbath violations, ranging from 'news-crying' to open saloons to the running of railroads.[23] At the same time, Protestant denominations in the North and South took up the issue of Sunday observance, at first hesitatingly, and then by the 1870s, vigorously.[24] Religious authorities who were sympathetic to Sabbatarian doctrine preached strict Sunday observance, published treatises concerning theological points of dispute and protested whenever an innovation such as street cars or reading rooms imposed itself on Sunday. These were organized attempts to inscribe Sabbatarian meanings onto Sunday. Sabbatarian doctrine continued to affirm the perpetuity and universality of the fourth commandment: to see Christ as fulfilling, not abrogating, the law; and to find new energy in biblical texts concerning Sabbath-observance, such as Isaiah 58:13, which promises delight in the Lord if the Sabbath-keeper will turn from doing his 'pleasure' on the 'holy day'.[25]

During the last quarter of the nineteenth century, when confusion and doubt concerning the applicability of the fourth commandment rose to its highest pitch, Sabbatarians turned to history and natural law for support. For instance, they argued that evidence that civilizations as diverse as the Assyrian, Egyptian and Anglo-Saxon had observed a day of rest and worship proved that at creation a Sabbath was instituted for all the tribes, not just the Jews.[26] Allusions to archaeological, historical and literary evidence proved to Sabbatarians that the Sabbath was not a religious institution *per se*, but a human, and therefore historic, institution. They also relied on natural law to demonstrate that mankind needed one day of rest in seven. They formulated a natural law of weekly rest which co-existed with 'a divine law, vested, like all other of God's laws, with divine authority and obligation.'

True, they used natural law to justify blue laws: if the Sabbath was 'a natural institution' then the state had the right to legislate Sunday observance.[27] But natural law assumptions left room for a wide range of interpretation and controversy over the relationship between rest and Sunday. Sabbatarians frequently reiterated the conjunction of the Sabbath with man's need to rest, emphasizing both the idea of 'one day of rest in seven' and placing a stress on rest that would reshape much of twentieth-century American life. Until after the Civil War, Sabbatarians sought and gained a great deal of influence over the meaning of Sunday; no doubt this was due not only to their efforts, but to widespread sympathy for their beliefs growing out of a shared Protestant inheritance.

Winter of 1879–1880

The winter of 1879–1880 heralded a new period of intense conflict for authority over Sunday's meanings. In October 1879, Sabbatarians from Massachusetts, New York, Philadelphia, New Haven and Providence gathered for two meetings at which papers concerning a 'rationale' for the Sabbath, 'the Sabbath in history,' and the 'Sabbath in state and in society' complemented a range of topical addresses concerning Sunday observance.[28] Although the conference had convened 'with some degree of depression and misgiving', it rejuvenated the Sabbatarian counter-offensive against liberalized meanings for Sunday.[29] Liberal theologians had succeeded on many fronts in turning Sunday into 'man's day' throughout the 1870s: public libraries, afternoon concerts in parks and lecture series characterized Sundays in many urban areas. Such reforms had not been easily won, Sunday-opening controversies having occupied a great deal of political, religious and social energy between 1860 and the mid-1890s. In addition, those outside the American Protestant tradition altogether – Catholics, Jews and certain European Protestants – who had never regarded Sunday as anything more than a holiday or an inconvenience, were gaining in power and numbers in many urban areas.[30] Mainstream Protestant disagreement over the day further eroded Sabbatarian hegemony. Still, Sabbatarians retained a significant amount of political power, leading to renewed enforcement of Sunday laws.[31] Numerous articles, sermons, and tracts along with Sabbatarian meetings marked several decades of full-fledged conflict over Sunday.

In the face of the combined challenges to the sanctity of the Sunday-Sabbath, Sabbatarians formed associations, held innumerable meetings, petitioned national legislative bodies for strict Sunday laws and published countless tracts. It has been observed that during the last two decades of the nineteenth century, Sabbatarianism, along with temperance, was 'the subject of more attention by Protestants than any other social concern.'[32] Between 1874 and 1913, numerous local, state and national Sabbatarian organizations were formed, including the Sabbath Union of New Jersey (1874), the Philadelphia Sabbath Alliance (1877), the International Sabbath Association (1878), the American Sabbath Union (1888), the New York State Sabbath Association (1890), the Massachusetts Sabbath Union (1891), the New England Protective Sabbath League (1895) and the Women's National Sabbath Alliance (1895), which had correspondents in every state.[33] Every president of the United States from Grant to Coolidge endorsed the Sabbatarian cause, while senators and congressmen proposed Sabbatarian measures including closing World's Fairs on Sundays and prohibiting government work on Sundays. In 1888 Senator H. W. Blair of New Hampshire introduced a bill 'to secure to the people the enjoyment of the first day of the week, a day of rest, and to promote its observance as a day of worship.' On just one day during the following year, Blair presented Sabbatarian petitions representing the opinion of thirteen and a half million citizens.[34] Despite efforts such as these, Sabbatarian efforts to write and enforce more Sunday laws failed; their opposition to liberalized meanings for Sunday, however, points to a larger failure, one that they could not fully reverse once they assented to plural meanings for Sunday.

Sabbatarians and the 'Liberal Sabbath'

Sabbatarians found liberalized meanings for Sunday so dangerous that they turned to the police and courts for enforcement and protection of their ideal Sabbath. They sought increasingly restrictive laws that would make the day resemble their vision of a sanctified Sabbath. Religious liberals such as Robert Collyer, Henry Ward Beecher and Washington Gladden did not call for the complete repeal of all blue laws; they wanted laws that would protect the liberty to rest, instead of enforcing church attendance or other narrow visions of what constituted a day of rest.[35] To be sure, they hoped that the day would be spent in uplifting activity or in the comfort of the home, and most abhorred the saloon and other places that complete liberty might have kept open on Sunday. Nevertheless, religious liberals saw Sunday laws as necessary to protect individual liberty, whereas Sabbatarians considered Sunday laws necessary for the protection of their version of religious liberty.

Many critics felt that Sunday laws created a false relationship between the individual and God. Religious liberals hoped to foster individual commitment to the Sunday-Sabbath because they believed that legally enforced religious behaviour suffocated the Christian spirit. A professor of theology speaking at a Sunday Rest-Day Congress in California on the eve of American entry into World War I explained:

> We shall never win the Sunday that we need, by means of negations and prohibitions – 'touch not, taste not, handle not' – walk not, call not, play not, auto not, read not this nor that, go not here nor there. To rely on such negations will only defeat itself. Prohibitions have their place but reliance upon them means failure to be true to the Gospel of power and of love and of a sound mind.[36]

Christians had to rely on powers of persuasion to improve Sabbath observance; ministers who failed to make church and the Sabbath appealing were part of the Sunday problem. Believing that forced church attendance was worse than none at all, religious liberals expressed optimism that their version of religion, encompassing both a sacralized world and the church, would keep Christians in the faith.

Sabbatarians, on the other hand, were not so sure. The world was full of temptations, and without reverence for binding laws, men and women would surely take up evil ways. Their discomfort flared as blue laws began to be challenged as unnecessary and restrictive. If few would heed the teachings of the 'Lord of the Sabbath', then the arm of the state was required to enforce morality. Still Sabbatarians were convinced that without demonstrating the 'Divine Authority' behind the special status of Sunday, Christians and non-Christians would continue to flout civil laws.[37] Gradually their theology that a binding covenant compelled strict Sunday observance lost validity, especially when religious liberals began to provide Protestants with other ways of thinking about Sunday observance that allowed faith in the sanctity of Sunday to continue without demanding that believers abandon the world every seventh day.

Liberalized meanings for Sunday harboured a vision of uplift at the heart of Progressivism and the social gospel that challenged Sabbatarianism's division between sacred and profane. The opportunity to expose working people to 'Culture' and 'Nature', whose beauties could open the spirit to the saving grace of Christianity, was irresistible to some Protestants. If the Sabbath was made for man, as Christ declared, then it was made for his higher nature. This vision of uplift led to a complicated cultural logic, with some kinds of music being allowed to be performed on Sunday and other kinds banned; a logic that sanctioned the screening of certain movies and censored others, and so on. Nevertheless, unhinging Sunday from the strictures of the fourth commandment, and seeing in the texts of the New Testament testimony to the Christian Sabbath's purpose as useful and beneficial to mankind, allowed for a wide range of practices to enter into Sunday's timetable without a majority of the population becoming unchurched: the proportion of churchgoers rose during the years between 1850 and 1930.[38] Nevertheless, Sabbatarians perceived in these developments significant incursions into the special meaning and purpose of Sunday.

To maintain and rebuild support for the Sunday-Sabbath, Sabbatarians redirected the understanding of its foundations away from biblical demands and towards notions of health – of the body, of the community and ultimately of the state. During the last decades of the nineteenth century, Sabbatarians joined religious liberals in suggesting that Sabbath-keeping was vital for day-to-day existence. Both groups redefined Sunday as a sanitary waystation – a tonic for men's bodies and minds, a preventative measure against social degeneration and an essential requirement for nation-building. The contest over Sunday turned to the meanings of rest and uplift, both concepts at the heart of the American Sunday.

The Scientific Sabbath

Eventually the large and internally inconsistent group committed to promoting Sunday as a day of rest turned away from the fourth commandment and pleas for national health; and towards physiological and scientific justifications for periodic rest. Throughout the eighteenth and nineteenth centuries, ministers and others had referred to natural law as proof that the necessity of Sunday rest was universal: it was admitted that the Sabbath had a spiritual meaning, use and obligation, 'but these all grow up from the root of the original physical law that man requires one day's rest in seven'.[39] Sunday was ordained to give men and women a day to rest (as God had rested after his six days' labour during creation) as well as to worship. Many assented to the physical necessity of one day of rest and quickly attached that necessity to the obligation to observe the Sabbath. Nevertheless few could agree on what constituted physical rest, and natural law did little to alleviate this confusion. Sabbatarians maintained that worship was the only way that men and women could obtain meaningful and lasting rest.[40] Others found rest in amusements, recreations and even idleness.

A chart depicting the 'Natural Law of the Weekly Rest-Day' provided many Sabbatarians with a visual representation of the hypothesis that Sunday was necessary for man's physical well-being.[41] Efficiency experts concurred with Sabbatarians; for example, Richard T. Dana in an influential study, *The Human Machine in Industry* (1927), advised avoiding *Sunday* work to assure 'complete recovery from fatigue.'[42] In sum, fatigue studies suggested that a periodic rest-day was fundamental as 'preventative medicine', but failed to establish that Sunday was a better day for rest than any other day of the week. Sabbatarians stressed the importance of *Sunday* rest by focusing on the positive relationship between Sunday observance and mental health, domestic happiness, industrial prosperity and political stability.

In the 1880s ministers began to replace references to natural law with citations of scientific evidence concerning the necessity of Sunday rest. Arguments concerning the physiological basis of the Sabbath had sporadically appeared in England in the 1830s, when some physicians performed 'experiments' to prove the necessity of a periodic rest-day. With few exceptions, such arguments were rarely produced in the United States until the twentieth century. One exception was Robert Patterson's 1870 tract *The Sabbath: Scientific, Republican, and Christian*, in which he argued 'that the Sabbath is a fact of chemistry'. Patterson conceived of God as a scientist who 'measured out' the weekly Sabbath as the exact proportion of holy rest men required, not simply for the fitness of their bodies, but for the salvation of their souls.[43] In the 1880s and 1890s other Sabbatarians articulated still more pseudo-scientific formulations about the necessity for Sunday rest. For instance, the indefatigable Sabbatarian Wilbur F. Crafts claimed 'that Sabbath rest brings some benefits even to the vegetable and mineral kingdoms'. He favourably cited a Bishop Mallaliew who found good evidence that wood, iron, and steel last longer when used only six days out of seven. Comparison with machinery that periodically had to be shut down for repairs established man's need for rest: 'Are not needed repairs to wasted bodies, minds and morals an equal emergency?' Following these findings, doctors located periodic rest as central to preventative medicine and public health.[44] The 'scientific Sabbath' was a popular panel at congresses concerning Sunday; it was here that Sabbatarians could share scientific arguments for the rest-day, thereby promulgating still more powerful meanings for Sunday.[45]

The Civil Sabbath

In the 1880s Sabbatarians responded to claims that Sunday laws were no different from biblical laws; in doing so they articulated their vision of the relationships between the state, Sunday, and rest. They argued that the 'Christian and the American Sabbath' were like two arms on the same man – 'they resemble and cooperate, and yet are by no means the same'. Sabbatarians pointed out that even though crimes and sins often resemble one another – take murder and adultery – this similarity did not undermine civil law. Blue laws prevented Sunday work and Sunday dissipation, which Sabbatarians believed to be 'crimes against man'. Civil law only enforced 'man's duties to man', not to God. These distinctions developed out of the fourth commandment's unique position as 'the transition commandment that connects what are chiefly duties to God with what are chiefly duties to man'. When Christ declared 'the Sabbath was made for man, not man for the Sabbath' (Mark 2:27) he split Sabbath-keeping into a religious and a civil obligation. Therefore, it was 'only man's part in the Day that American Sabbath laws' defended.[46]

It was out of these ideas that the term 'civil Sabbath' was coined. The discourse on the civil Sabbath was meant to connect liberty (the liberty to rest) with the prohibition of Sunday amusements and recreations. A popular Sabbatarian slogan was that 'the law of rest for all is necessary to the liberty of rest for each'.[47] When working people frequented places of amusement or took excursions they jeopardized their right to a day of rest. As one minister asked, 'If a man may rightfully be called upon to drum or to declaim on Sunday, why may he not as rightfully be called upon to stand behind a counter, to lay rails or to make barrels?'[48] The Sabbatarian definition of rest excluded all but church attendance in the neighbourhood and communion with the family in the home (the twin pillars of the Protestant Sunday-Sabbath): the liberty to rest reflected biblical more than American constitutional law. The emphasis on the liberty to rest was partially an attempt to keep the American Sunday close to the Sabbath of the fourth commandment. But the emphasis on rest tapped into one of the most contentious issues of modernizing America – the balance between rest and work.

To supplement the affinity with biblical law, Sabbatarians also constructed the liberty to rest as vital to the health of the individual and the nation. Rest was vital in the process of character *and* nation formation – in fact, more important than business hours: 'Any people who spend their Sabbaths partly in toil and the remainder in dissipation or childish play can never develop enough manhood to safely govern themselves.' Prominent Sabbatarian Wilbur F. Crafts argued that the state ought to prohibit Sunday amusements as a defence measure: Sunday amusements 'destroy the Rest Day itself and so the body politic also.'[49]

The discourse of the civil Sabbath, particularly its focus on liberty and the state's health, appealed to those in the organized labour movement. Crafts encouraged the Knights of Labor, at one time the nation's largest labour union, to 'make a new Declaration of Independence' by insisting on Sunday rest. In the attempt to connect Sabbatic obligation to the promises of the American state, he asserted that 'Labor's right to the weekly rest is part of the right to life, liberty and the pursuit of happiness'. Developing the patriotic theme further, Crafts described how the Sabbath was the workingman's college, without which 'toilers could not qualify themselves for self-government, but would remain like the adult infants of Continental Europe, content to take Sunday amusements in place of liberty.'[50]

Eventually most Sabbatarians stopped calling Sunday 'the civil Sabbath' and introduced the term 'rest-day', thereby fully eliminating the religious texture of the term 'Sabbath'. Still, they did not abandon their religious convictions about the nature and importance of Sunday. At the turn of the century an International Sunday Rest Congress adopted a 'Basis' containing two planks, 'one recognizing the religious, and the other the civil side of the Sabbath institution.' Although the battle for the preservation of Sunday was 'conducted mainly on civil lines', the Congress's organizers declared that most of its advocates were Christian men who knew that 'the real foundation of Sunday rest' was in 'Divine appointment'.[51] The Congress's sessions were organized into categories that arose out of the distinctions implicit within the civil Sabbath. More than half addressed the physical, mental, moral, industrial, domestic, social, civic and national relations of Sunday rest. But when the Congress shifted to celebrating the religious foundations of the Sunday-Sabbath, it abandoned these appeals to the health of the individual and nation, raising instead the duty to worship. Herein we see the failure of Sabbatarianism to be persistent and consistent in adapting the meaning of Sunday to the nation's shifting needs.

1893 World's Fair

It was not only in texts and speeches that Sabbatarians worked to shape Sunday and to orchestrate everyday life, but also through direct political action. Numerous examples fill the decades between 1870 and 1930. The most dramatic and illustrative effort began in 1890 with the campaign to force the Columbian Exposition to close on Sundays. Throughout the week before the first Sunday of the fair, Sabbatarians rallied. The First United Presbyterian Church in Boston telegraphed President Cleveland: 'Guard the gates next Sabbath *with troops* if necessary'.[52] When this Boston church sent its missive, its members joined millions of other Americans in efforts to keep the Chicago World's Fair closed on Sunday. The massive protest against opening the fair on Sunday was the culmination of decades of tensions over what was known as 'the Sunday-opening movement', which began in Boston in the 1860s when some residents demanded that the public library's reading rooms open on Sunday afternoons. Throughout the 1870s it simmered in cities across the nation as demands for the opening of public libraries and museums increased. Erupting with some force in the mid-1880s, the movement called forth an array of concerned citizens in New York City, who saw in the Sunday opening of the Metropolitan Museum of Art either grave danger or great good. The telegraph rallying US troops to keep the World's Fair closed on Sunday is but one of many artifacts from the battle over the imposition of culture upon the holy time of Sunday. But it was a losing cause; by 1915 the Sunday opening of libraries, museums and fairs was standard practice.

It was on the shores of culture that Sabbatarianism lost its war to save the Sabbath. However, on these same grounds the movement bolstered Sunday's unique place in American life, thereby fulfilling one of its larger goals. Throughout the nineteenth century, ideals concerning the uplifting potential of culture circulated, but it was not until the Sunday-opening movement that these ideals clashed with an older conception of culture as beneficial to the elite but corrupting to the masses. Religious and social conservatives embraced culture as an arena of education only for the wealthy. Younger members of the 'metropolitan gentry' whose own religious affiliations were either Episcopalian, or in Boston, Unitarian, proposed a newer programme which defined culture as a tool for uplifting the masses. In cities across America this group began to withdraw from politics, focusing its authority on the formation of cultural institutions. Inheriting from the Whigs an ambivalence about democracy, one faction of the metropolitan gentry had envisioned culture as a privilege of an educated elite. But under the influence of religious liberals and genteel reformers, some within this group embraced culture as a tool for refining and uplifting the electorate in whose hands rested the fate of democratic politics. This more liberal but well-connected generation – the metropolitan gentry – contended that opening institutions of culture could expand 'the means of grace' available each Sunday.[53]

The battle over the 1893 World's Fair revived earlier arguments, fears and hopes surrounding Sunday. Metropolitan gentry and religious liberals suggested that opening the fair on Sunday would have the same positive effects as opening public libraries and museums. At a hearing about opening the World's Fair, for instance, a senator from Nebraska stated that 'he saw no objection to the art galleries being open so that people might quietly go there and be instructed, as well as interested, by gazing at the works of the great masters'.[54] Yet to others, an open fair was 'a reproach to everything in the name of Christianity'. The 1893 Columbian Exposition was conceived of as glorifying the nation's economic, political and cultural achievement. Those for and against Sunday opening each claimed that they sought to glorify the Sabbath as well as the nation. Sabbatarians considered a closed fair a symbol of the integrity of the Christian republic and an open fair as a threat to the nation's moral and physical health. A coalition of religious liberals, workingmen and metropolitan gentry, on the other hand, believed that a closed fair symbolized the nation's hypocrisy, selfishness and disregard for republican and Christian values. They believed that an open fair would sanctify the day. It would, in the words of that great proponent of uplift, Matthew Arnold, 'diffuse sweetness and light, make the reason and the will of God prevail'.[55] Those in favour of Sunday opening agreed that the Sabbath had to be 'put to the best uses of man', and that the best uses included anything that would 'rouse the soul to an appreciation of what is good and beautiful and true'.[56] The debate was fraught with moral and religious opinions that made compromise, let alone civil and reasonable discussion, impossible; for more than three years vicious, frequently hysterical, accusations punctured the discourse.

Sunday-opening opponents formed organizations, signed thousands of petitions sent to congressmen and senators, sent fifty members of the American Sabbath Union to Chicago to meet with the fair's board, sponsored rallies and assemblies, planned boycotts of the fair and telegraphed President Cleveland with advice about the controversy. Presbyterians and Methodists led the movement. A national meeting of Methodist Churches in Omaha held a large rally against Sunday opening and, after the fair had opened in 1893, many of the Methodist clergy threatened to boycott it. Some Baptists, Congregationalists, Episcopalians and Presbyterians were also opposed to Sunday opening, despite dissent within these denominations.

Extradenominational groups were the primary locus of the anti-Sunday-opening movement: the 1892 Christian Endeavor Convention made Sunday closing their centrepiece; the American Sabbath Union agitated on a local and national level; a National Committee on Sunday Closing of the World's Fair was formed out of a coalition of the American Sabbath Union, the Women's Christian Temperance Association, Christian Endeavor societies and five state Sabbath associations. They had learned that in order to close the fair, they had to deploy political acumen, not theological erudition. When the question of Sunday opening first arose, influential Sabbatarians went immediately to the fair's directors and commissioners. After their personal appeals failed, they organized a grassroots effort that resulted in (literally) miles of petitions being sent to congressmen and senators demanding that the World's Fair be closed on Sundays. At one point during a debate, one senator asked the clerk to read from the Bible the words, 'Remember the Sabbath day to keep it holy'. Apparently this caused a good deal of titillation in the chambers; nevertheless, the petitions had some influence, in that the Senate and House of Representatives voted to amend their appropriation of five million dollars for the World's Fair with the clause that the gates close on Sundays.[57] The fair's directors had no choice but to accept this condition since they were in somewhat in desperate financial straits.

Those against Sunday opening expressed their fears about 'the entering wedge' of the Continental Sunday, about ceaseless rounds of labour, and above all about the nation's Christian identity. The latter topic received heated emphasis; Sabbatarians constructed Sunday as 'the cornerstone in the foundation and the citadel in the defenses of our free institutions'. They tried to depict the contest as one for the nation's well-being. Sunday closing was most certainly a symbol, for no one complained about the exposition grounds (which were under construction) being open to the paying public on Sundays since the summer of 1892. Sabbatarians conflated national with Evangelical needs relentlessly, predicting that the damage done to Sunday by an open fair would be equal to epidemic and war.[58] Despite a congressional declaration to close the fair, religious and cultural leaders continued to speak in favour of Sunday-opening; newspapers still speculated that Congress would rescind the clause, and the fair's directors went to the courts, where they were able to secure Sunday opening.[59] At first hundreds of thousands came to the fair, but rather quickly attendance diminished.

The press did its best to valorize the opening of the fair. Reporters noted the absence of rowdyism, drunkenness and disorderly conduct, citing this as evidence that the Continental Sunday had made no headway.[60] They emphasized the crowds' lack of interest in the Midway Plaissance; it was only 'thronged' because 'so much had been written about it'. Meanwhile, families from diverse backgrounds packed the Art Building and other exhibitions: 'As to the eyes of Columbus dawned an unknown continent, so to them was this an undiscovered country full of miracles preaching the gospel of sweetness and light'.[61] In sum, as the papers would have it, 'the Plaissance only piqued curiosity; the main exhibition satisfied the soul'.[62] Reporters noted that the crowd had little money to spend, was so thrifty that the concessionaires were sorely disappointed, but was as well-dressed as the middle-class crowds on weekdays.[63] In addition to the immense good the fair wrought for its visitors, most saloons and 'cheap amusements' were reportedly deserted, utterly disconcerting Chicago's 'rumsellers'.[64]

Papers also depicted the fair as an adjunct to the nation's churches and Christianity itself: 'It was plainly the people's holy day.'[65] Sousa's Marine Band played sacred and popular music through the day and into the evening, providing an emblematic narrative. One version or another of this narrative turns up in nearly all the reports about the first open Sunday at the fair, even in fair director Henry Higginbotham's dry and precise report to the directors. There must be a kernel of truth in the tale, but even if entirely fabricated, its relevance is that the described moment encapsulates a version of the ideal Sunday, as a holy day and a holiday, that many hoped would triumph. A reporter for the *New York Times* wrote:

> One of the most impressionable incidents happened at night. Sousa's Band was surrounded by a crowd of 20,000 or 30,000 people while the illumination was in progress. The programme included sacred and popular music. Some of the airs were in waltz time. The young people enjoyed these immensely, and tapped their feet on the walks impatiently, as if wishing that they might dance.

All reported that none danced, a respect for the Sabbath being deeply and universally felt.

> Suddenly the strains of the hymn 'Nearer My God, to Thee' floated out over the immense concourse of people. Instantly every head was uncovered, and in silence, in the peaceful moonlit night, surrounded by the marvelous beauty of the exposition buildings in their robes of electrics, the assemblage listened to the song hallowed by the tenderest memories. When the music died away there was deep silence for several minutes. Then the audience applauded with their hands, because everybody there wanted to emphasize the fact that the opening of the fair on Sunday had not made the hearts of those present callous, nor driven away all religious feeling.

Clearly those present belonged to, and respected, a common Protestant culture that held Sunday sacred. The *Chicago Tribune* was more explicit in its construction of this seminal moment: 'It was at the Fair grounds that these people, with look and act, paid homage to the Creator ... The evening prayer, involuntary, unexpected, had been said.'[66]

After the first open Sunday, Evangelical protests seemed to disintegrate; neither threatened boycotts nor doomsday prophesies materialized. One newspaper editor summed up: 'The United States are still in existence, no thunderbolt has rived the Union and no deluge of water or shower with burning sulpher [*sic*] has erased the American people from the face of the earth; yet the gates of the World's Fair were open on Sunday.'[67] Nevertheless, six weeks later attendance was so disappointingly low that the directors voted to close the Fair on future Sundays; the headlines on 24 July read 'White City's Gates Closed: Even Scrubwomen Were Barred'. The defenders of Sunday-opening had disappeared and, in their place was 'a drink-flushed individual mounted on a box across the street from the Fifty-Seventh Street entrance in the forenoon, calling vociferously for 100 volunteers to aid him in tearing down a section of the fence in order to allow poor laboring men to see the Fair free.' A policeman 'stopped the harangue'.[68] So, we are left asking, who won the battle over Sunday-opening?

Conclusion

Sabbatarians often returned to the fourth commandment when other legitimations for a certain kind of Sunday rest collapsed. Modernizing America had become inundated with productive and entertainment industries that could not be stilled every seventh day. Attempts to return to the fourth commandment, although frequent, failed because lists of 'necessities and mercies' grew longer and longer and because of the inability, and unwillingness in many cases, to enforce jumbled and contradictory laws.

Justifications put forward for Sunday observance by religious liberals had loosened the day from its religious roots, and therefore can be understood as enabling the persistence of many Sunday laws, as one by one these laws were challenged on the grounds of violating the separation of church and state. In the view of many, Sunday legislation, because of its roots in physical and moral grounds, 'simply creates a holiday'. Therefore any court in the land could uphold the constitutionality of Sunday laws.[69] By the 1960s the Supreme Court found that although the blue laws had their origins in religious longings and desires, they had been 'secularized', and therefore did not violate the constitutional guarantee of a separation of church and state.[70] Since liberal theology multiplied the reasons why Sunday should be observed to include temporal realities, such as the benefits of a common day of rest, it provided a non-religious basis for continuing to set Sunday aside from the rest of the week. In their effort to realize their vision of a day set apart from the world, Sabbatarians lost the battles but won the war: the state does not treat Sunday like the other days of the week. More importantly, neither do the American people.

Notes

1. Scholarly studies of Sabbatarianism published in the 1990s include: Isaac Kramnick and R. Laurence Moore, *The Godless Constitution: The Case Against Religious Correctness* (New York, 1996), 131–43; Paul Conkin, *The Uneasy Center: Reformed Christianity in Antebellum America* (Chapel Hill, NC, 1995), 116–17 and 142–6; Richard John, *Spreading the News: The American Postal System from Franklin to Morse* (Cambridge, MA, 1995), 169–205; Michael J. McTighe, *A Measure of Success: Protestants and Public*

Culture in Antebellum Cleveland (Albany, NY, 1994), 62–5 and 139–40; Robert Abzug, *Cosmos Crumbling: American Reform and the Religious Imagination* (Oxford, 1994), 105–24; Richard John, 'Taking Sabbatarianism Seriously: The Postal System, the Sabbath, and the Transformation of American Political Culture,' *Journal of the Early Republic* 10 (1990): 517–67.

Scholarship published in the 1980s includes: James Rohrer, 'Sunday Mails and the Church–State Theme in Jacksonian America,' *Journal of the Early Republic* 7 (1987): 54–74; Morton Borden, *Jews, Turks, and Infidels* (Chapel Hill, NC, 1984), 103–29; Robert T. Handy, *A Christian America: Protestant Hopes and Historical Realities* (Oxford, 1984), 42–6, 73–7, 125–7, 172–4, 183–4; Lewis Perry, *Childhood, Marriage, and Reform: Henry Clarke Wright, 1797–1870* (Chicago, 1980), 147–50.

Scholarship published through the end of the 1970s includes: Dennis Lynn Pettibone, 'Caesar's Sabbath: The Sunday-Law Controversy in the United States, 1879–1892' (Ph.D. diss., University of California at Riverside, 1979); Paul Johnson, *A Shopkeeper's Millennium: Society and Revivals in Rochester, New York, 1815–1837* (New York, 1978), 74–5, 83–94, and 129; Paul Carter, *The Spiritual Crisis of the Gilded Age* (Dekalb, IL, 1971); Bertram Wyatt-Brown, 'Prelude to Abolitionism: Sabbatarian Politics and the Rise of the Second Party System,' *Journal of American History* 58 (1971): 316–40; Roy Zebulon Chamlee, 'The Sabbath Crusade, 1810–1920' (Ph.D. diss., George Washington University, 1968); Oliver W. Holmes, 'Sunday Travel and Sunday Mails: A Question Which Troubled Our Forefathers,' *New York History* 20 (1939): 413–24; A. C. Cole, *The Irrepressible Conflict, 1850–1865* (New York, 1938), 253–5; Frederick Bronner, 'The Observance of the Sabbath in the United States, 1800–1860' (Ph.D. diss., Harvard University, 1937); and Harold S. Jacoby, 'Remember the Sabbath Day?' (Ph.D. diss., University of Pennsylvania, 1945).

2. John Wigley, *The Rise and Fall of the Victorian Sunday* (Manchester: Manchester University Press, 1980), Chapters 1 and 2.
3. Will C. Wood, 'Historical Sketch', in Will C. Wood, ed., *Sabbath Essays* (Boston: Congregational Publishing Society, 1880), 433. For more details on these earlier 'Sabbatarian' organizations see Chamlee, 'The Sabbath Crusade,' 101–24.
4. Lewis Tappan, *Letter to Eleazor Lord in Defense of Measures for Promoting the Observance of the Christian Sabbath* (1831), 22.
5. Wyatt-Brown focuses on Sabbatarianism as part of the shift to party politics (1971); McTighe considers 'the Sabbath cause' part of the battle between religion and mammon (1994); Rohrer focuses on it as part of the rising tide of Evangelicalism (1987); Kramnick and Moore see the controversy a part of the effort to remake the 'godless Constitution' (1995); and Johnson considers Sabbatarianism as an assault on freedom (1978).
6. John, 'Taking Sabbatarianism Seriously' and *Spreading the News*.
7. *Twenty-Second Annual Report of the Commissioner of Labor. 1907: Labor Laws of the United States* (Washington, DC: GPO, 1908), 1232.
8. Lyman Beecher, 'Pre-Eminent Importance of the Christian Sabbath', *The National Preacher* 3 (1829): 155–60; Beecher, 'Mr Johnson's Report on

Sabbath Mails', *The Spirit of the Pilgrims* 2 (1829): 145–50; and *An Account of Memorials Presented to Congress During Its Last Session* (Boston, 1829), 9–12. Thanks to Richard John for sharing these documents with me.
9. Henry A. Nelson, *Benefits of the Sabbath* (Philadelphia: Presbyterian Publication Committee, 1867), 10. For more details about the Protestant reformation of the religious calendar see Peter Burke, *Popular Culture in Early Modern Europe* (New York: Harper and Row, 1978), 207–43. For details about the importation of the Puritan Sabbath into all the American colonies see Winton Solberg, *Redeem the Time* (Cambridge, MA: Harvard University Press, 1977).
10. See Wood, 'Historical Sketch,' 435–6.
11. Emphasis included in text. Edwards, *Sabbath Manual*, 23. Publishers in Philadelphia Boston, and New York circulated Justin Edwards' *Sabbath Manual* in many different forms between 1844 and 1870. It was also translated into French, German and Dutch: *Le Manuel du Sabbat* (Philadelphia: Presbyterian Board of Publications, n.d.); *Le Manuel du Sabbat* (New York: Jean A. Ackley, 1860); *Gendenke de Sabbathtages* (New York: Amerikanischen Tractat-Gesellschaft, 1860); and *Het Sabbath's Handboekje met Inbegrip van de Sabbath eene Familie-instelling* (New York, 1853). Edwards 'was prominent' in one of the first Sabbath Conventions, the Middlesex County Convention. Wood, 'Historical Sketch,' 433.
12. Chamlee, 'Sabbath Crusade,' 134–5 and Bronner, 'Observance of the Sabbath', 287–328.
13. Bronner, 'Observance of the Sabbath', 228–36. See also Edmund Quincy, 'History of the Church, Ministry and Sabbath Convention,' *The Liberator* (19 March 1841). Cited in Dean Grodzins, 'Theodore Parker and Transcendentalism' (Ph.D. diss., Harvard University, 1993), 410. Thanks to Dean Grodzins for sharing his research concerning this early anti-Sabbatarian gathering. Theodore Parker maintained that the Sabbath was an institution full of promise for mankind. In another sermon that probably resembled the speech he gave at Charndon Street, Parker sought to stress the improvements that Christians could make in their observance of the day, such as taking a walk or indulging in cheerful conversation. See Parker's sermon 'Some Thoughts on the Most Christian Use of the Sunday Delivered January 30, 1848' and 'Remarks of the Rev. Theodore Parker at the late Anti-Sabbath Convention in Boston,' *The Liberator* (12 May 1848).

For a critical description of the Charndon Street convention see Amos Augustus Phelps, *The Sabbath* (New York: American Society for the Promotion of Christian Values, 1842) and Amos Augustus Phelps, *A Sketch of the Proceedings of the Convention for the Discussion of the Sabbath, the Ministry, and the Church* (New York: American Society for the Promotion of Christian Morals, 1842).
14. Lewis Perry's interpretation of the convention focuses on the intersection of abolitionism, radicalism and anti-Sabbatarianism. See Lewis Perry, *Childhood, Marriage, and Reform: Henry Clarke Wright, 1797–1870* (Chicago: University of Chicago Press, 1980), 147–52.
15. Emphasis in the original. Henry M. Parkhurst (reporter), *Proceedings of*

the *Anti-Sabbath Convention Held in the Melodeon* (Boston: Andrews and Prentice Printers, 1848), 5–6.
16. Henry C. Wright, Parkhurst, *Proceedings*, 32, 78–81.
17. Parkhurst, *Proceedings*, 28–9.
18. Henry C. Wright and Stephen S. Foster quoted in Parkhurst, *Proceedings*, 81, 87, 93.
19. Perry, *Childhood*, 147. See also Lewis Perry, *Radical Abolitionism: Anarchy and the Government of God in Antislavery Thought* (Ithaca, NY: Cornell University Press, 1973) and William Hutchison, *The Transcendentalist Ministers* (Hamden, CT: Archon Press, 1972, 1959). For an earlier example of how religious radicals used the Sunday question to contest ecclesiastical claims, see 1848 Anti-Sabbath Convention participant William Logan Fisher's *The History of the Institution of the Sabbath Day* (Philadelphia: John Penington, 1845).
20. Emphasis in original. Parkhurst, *Proceedings*, 8.
21. John W. Browne, Parkhurst, *Proceedings*, 34.
22. Appendix, Parkhurst, *Proceedings*, 142.
23. See the many documents published and distributed by the New York Sabbath Committee (hereafter cited as NYSC), such as *The Sabbath: As It Was and As It Is* (New York: NYSC, 1857); NYSC, *Railroads and the Sabbath* (New York: Edward O. Jenkins, 1858); Russell S. Cook, *The Sabbath in Europe: The Holy Day of Freedom – The Holiday of Despotism* (New York: NYSC, [1859]); NYSC, *Plea for the Sabbath in War* (New York: NYSC, [1861]); NYSC, *Sunday Theatres, 'Sacred Concerts', and Beer Gardens* (New York: NYSC, 1866); William Wallace Atterbury, *Sunday Laws and Sunday Liberty* (New York: NYSC, n.d.); NYSC, *Sunday Observance in the United States As a Civil Institution* (New York: NYSC, 1897); NYSC, Legislative *Hearings at Albany* (New York: NYSC, 1909); *Bulletin of the NYSC for the Years 1914–1922* (New York: NYSC, 1923); Duncan J. McMillan, *Influence of the Weekly Rest-Day on Human Welfare: A Scientific Research* (New York: NYSC, 1927).
24. Wood, 'Historical Sketch', 436–7; Wilbur F. Crafts, *The Sabbath for Man* (New York: Funk and Wagnalls, 1885), 587–93; and Chamlee, 'Sabbath Crusade,' 250–67.
25. For a compendium of nineteenth-century Sabbatarian interpretations of Isaiah 58:13–14 see Crafts, *Sabbath for Man*, 536–7. For Sabbatarian interpretations of other biblical texts see Crafts, *Sabbath for Man*, 531–43. See also Talbot W. Chambers, 'The Scriptural Authority of the Sabbath,' *The Independent* 47 (1895): 2; Charles Elliott, *The Sabbath* (Philadelphia: Presbyterian Board of Publications, 1867), 62–5; Henry Lummis, 'Obligation of One Rest-day in Seven', in *Sabbath Essays*, 143–55; Edmund K. Alden, 'The Sabbath and the Lord's Day,' in *Sabbath Essays*, 156–81.
26. Frederick Peake, 'The Religious Basis of Lord's-Day Observance Historically Justified', in *Sunday Rest*, 171. Peake was the Secretary of the Lord's-Day Observance Society (London).
27. William Wallace Atterbury, 'The Natural Law of Weekly Rest', in *Sabbath Essays*, 37 and Elliott, *The Sabbath*, 99–100.
28. These addresses are reprinted in Wood, *Sabbath Essays*. For an anti-

Sabbatarian report of the convention see Charles K. Whipple, 'Help for the Sunday-Sabbath', *Index*, 10 (1879): 537.
29. Alexander McKenzie, 'Opening Address,' 7.
30. On the Catholic position concerning Sunday, see: James Cardinal Gibbons, 'The Place of Sunday Observance in Christianity,' in *The Sunday Problem* (New York: Baker and Taylor, 1893), 248. This essay is reprinted as 'The Dangers of Sunday Desecration', *The Independent* 47 (1895): 1. See also Alexander Doyle, 'The Catholic Church and the Sunday Saloon', *The Independent* 47 (1895): 10; M. J. Lavelle, 'The Attitude of the Catholic Church Towards the Lord's Day', in *Sunday. The World's Rest Day*, 126–33; Archbishop Ireland, 'Sunday For All', in *The Sunday Problem*, 311–18; and 'Letter from the Third Plenary Council at Baltimore', in *The Sunday Problem*, 248–54.

On the relationship between Jews and Sunday see: B. Felsenthal, 'The Sabbath in Judaism,' in *The Sunday Problem*, 266–7; Henry Gersoni, 'How the Orthodox Jew Observes the Sabbath', *The Independent* 47 (1895): 7; Bernard Drachman, 'The Jewish Problem of the Sabbath in a Christian Land,' in *Sunday. The World's Rest Day*, 516–28; 'The Sunday-Sabbath Movement in Reform Judaism', *American Jewish Archives* 34 (1982): 75–88; 'Sunday and the Jews in the Nineteenth Century', *Judaism* 20 (1971): 490–3; and Benjamin Kline Hunnicutt, 'The Jewish Sabbath Movement in the Early Twentieth Century', *American Jewish History* 69 (1979): 196–225.
31. An early defence of Sunday laws can be found in D. W. Bond, *The Power of the Legislature to Enact Sunday Laws* (Northampton, MA: Metcalf and Company, 1870). See also Will C. Wood, *Five Problems of State and Religion* (Boston: H. Hoyt, 1877); *The Right of the People to Their Sunday Rest* (New York: NYSC, 1880); Rev. Dr Shipman, 'Sermon', *New York Times* (hereafter cited as *NYT*), 25 December 1882; Edward E. Hale, *The Sunday Laws* (Boston: Geo. H. Ellis, 1880); Henry E. Young, 'Sunday Laws', in *Report of the Third Annual Meeting of the American Bar Association* (Philadelphia: E. C. Markley and Sons, 1880): 109–47; Leonard Woolsey Bacon, *The Sabbath Question* (New York: G. P. Putnam's Sons, 1882); George Strobridge, 'Degradation and Desecration of the Christian Sabbath', *NYT*, 26 June 1880; George Gardiner, 'Shall We Have a Sabbath and How?', *Baptist Review* 2 (1880): 584–93; and G. Stanley Hall, 'Philosophy in the United States,' *Mind* 4 (1879): 89–105.
32. Pettibone, 'Caesar's Sabbath,' 2–6.
33. Jacoby, 'Remember the Sabbath Day?' 10–11.
34. Bill S. 2983, *The Congressional Record*, vol. 19 (1888): 1455. The 13.5 million citizens were represented by the American Sabbath Union, the Brotherhood of Locomotive Engineers, the Knights of Labor, the Presbyterian General Assembly (North), the Convention of Christian Workers, the Women's Christian Temperance Union and the Roman Catholic Church of America. Between 1886 and 1896 senators and congressmen presented thousands of petitions and memorials in favour of Sunday legislation which provide an excellent record of the broad coalition in support of a 'closed Sunday'. See volumes 17–24 and volume 28 of *The Congressional Record*. These volumes represent the business of the 49th–54th Congresses.

35. See 'Massachusetts Sunday Laws,' *The Index* 16 (26 February 1885): 415–16 and Frederick May Holland, 'Our Sunday Laws,' *The Index* 16 (2 September, 1885): 147–8.
36. John Wright Buckham, 'The Sacred Day in Social Relations,' in *Sunday. The World's Rest-Day*, 123.
37. Crafts, *Sabbath for Man*, 357.
38. Judith R. Blau, Kenneth C. Land, and Kent Redding, 'The Expansion of Religious Affiliation', *Social Science Research* 21 (1992): 329–52.
39. Vincent, *Pleasure-Sunday*, 4. For a compilation of arguments against relying on natural law as support for Sunday as a day of rest see, Thomas B. Brown, *Thoughts Suggested by the Perusal of Gilfillan, and Other Authors on the Sabbath* (New York: American Sabbath Tract Society, 1869), 41–3.
40. For an example of the insistence that only Sunday could provide meaningful rest, see J. O. Peck, 'The Sabbath. A Necessity to All Forms of Social Regeneration,' in *Sabbath Essays*, 47–63.
41. Dr Haegler's chart is reprinted in the following texts: W. W. Atterbury, 'The Natural Law of Weekly Rest', in *Sabbath Essays*, 34; Wilbur F. Crafts, 'What Are Innocent Sunday Recreations?', in *Sunday Rest in the Twentieth Century*, 120; McMillan, 'The Necessity of the Day of Rest', 203; Theodore Gilman, 'The Day Which Divine Love Established and Human Love Must Preserve', in *Sunday. The World's Rest Day*, 289; and Duncan J. McMillan, *Influence of Weekly Rest-Day on Human Welfare* (New York: NYSC, 1927), 36.
42. Richard T. Dana, *The Human Machine in Industry* (New York: Codex Books, 1927), 196. Dana suggested that the 'sense of staleness that comes from working continuously through Sunday after Sunday is even more harmful than the fatigue produced'.
43. Robert Patterson, *The Sabbath: Scientific, Republican, and Christian* (Cincinnati, OH: Western Tract Society, [1870]). See also John Robert Floody, *Scientific Basis of Sabbath and Sunday* (Boston: Turner, 1906, 1901).
44. Crafts, *Sabbath for Man*, 490, 513–14 and Samuel B. Lyon, 'The Physiological Basis of Sunday Rest', in *The Sunday Problem* (New York: Baker and Taylor, 1894), 21–39.
45. Wood, *Sabbath Essays*, 25–94 and Lyon, 'Physiological Basis', 21–5. The papers delivered at the 1915 Congress were: G. Frederick Wright, 'Periodicity. A Law of Nature'; William J. Gies and Collaborators, 'Studies of the Physiological Influence of a Weekly Day of Rest'; E. G. Martin, 'The Day of Rest in Nature and Human Nature'; Duncan J. McMillan, 'The Necessity of a Day of Rest'; and Mrs Robert Bruce Hull, 'Woman's Responsibility Toward the Sabbath'. These are found in Duncan J. McMillan, ed., *Sunday. The World's Rest Day* (New York: Doubleday, Page, and Co., 1916), 154–215.
46. Wilbur F. Crafts, 'The Civil Sabbath The Friend, Not the Foe, of Liberty', in Wilbur F. Crafts, ed., *Addresses on the Civil Sabbath* (Washington, DC: The Reform Bureau, 1890), 19–21.
47. For use of the phrase 'the law of rest for all is necessary to the liberty of rest for each' see Leonard Woolsey Bacon, 'The Law of Rest', in Wood, *Sabbath Essays*, 306–17; Marvin Vincent, *The Pleasure-Sunday a Labor-*

Sunday (New York: Rufus Adams, [1886]), 10; *Work and Rest* (New York: Concord Co-operative Printing, n.d.); W. S. Rainsford, *The Rest Day* [1902], 8–9; Gardiner Spring, *The Sabbath: A Blessing to Mankind* (New York: American Tract Society, n.d.), 15; 'Sunday and Trades-Unions', *Outlook* 55 (1899): 337–8; George H. Fellows, *Sunday and the Workingman* (New York: NYSC, n.d.), 6–7; Crafts, *The Sabbath for Man*, 190–266, 602.

48. Vincent, *Pleasure-Sunday*, 8–9.
49. Crafts, 'Fair Play and Sunday Plays', in *Addresses on the Civil Sabbath*, 47–9.
50. Crafts, 'Labor's Right to the Weekly Rest Day,' in *Addresses on the Civil Sabbath*, 31–4. He delivered this address in Scranton, Pennsylvania on 20 October 1889.
51. Alexander Jackson, Introduction, in Alexander Jackson, ed., *Sunday Rest in the Twentieth Century* (Cleveland: International Federation of Sunday Rest Associations of America, 1905), 22–3.
52. Emphasis added. The telegraph was reprinted in an article titled 'Not This Sunday, Some Other,' *NYT*, 20 May 1893. A few days earlier the Evangelical Alliance telegraphed the Attorney General, 'The presence of United States troops at Fort Sheriden holds the Chicago Anarchists in check. Cannot the administration notify the Directory [of the World's Fair] that those troops will be promptly used, if necessary, to maintain inviolate the Nation's authority and keep the Fair closed on the Lord's Day?' 'Against Sunday Opening', *NYT*, 16 May 1893.
53. The term 'metropolitan gentry' comes from Thomas Bender, *New York Intellect* (New York: Alfred A. Knopf, 1987), 172–202. See also Helen Horowitz, *Culture and the City* (Lexington: The University Press of Kentucky, 1976), 47.
54. *NYT*, 12 July 1892. See also, 'Sunday at Chicago Next Year', *Nation* 55 (8 December 1892): 425 and James De Normandie, *Sunday at the Columbian Fair* (Boston, 1892), 11.
55. Alonzo Trevier Jones, *The Captivity of the Republic* (Battle Creek: International Religious Liberty Association, 1893), 8. Matthew Arnold, *Culture and Anarchy* (Cambridge: Cambridge University Press, 1869, 1988), 71.
56. See *NYT*, 14 May, 13 September, 25 October, 26 October, 4 December 1892, 27 February, 22 May and 4 June 1893; *Chicago Tribune*, 29 May 1893; *Washington Post*, 30 May 1893; *New Orleans Times Picayune*, 29 May 1893; *Detroit News*, 29 May 1893; *St. Louis Dispatch*, 29 May 1893; *The Atlanta Constitution*, 29 May 1893; Henry N. Higginbotham, *Report of the President to the Board of Directors of the World's Columbian Exposition: Chicago 1892–1893* (Chicago: Rand, McNally and Co., 1898); 'Sunday at Chicago Next Year', *The Nation* 55 (1892): 425; Henry C. Kinney, *Why the Columbian Exposition Should Be Opened on Sunday* (Chicago: Rand, McNally and Co, 1892), 10–12; Henry C. Potter, 'Some Exposition Uses of Sunday', *Century* 23 (1892): 138–41; Henry C. Potter, 'Sunday and the World's Fair', *Forum* 14 (1892); 'Jesus, The Church, and the World's Fair', *The Arena* 6 (1892): 250–60; Bishop J. L. Spalding, 'Why the World's Fair Should be Opened on Sunday', *The Arena* 7 (1892): 45–7; and Rev. O. P. Gifford, 'Why the World's Fair Should Be Opened on Sunday', *The Arena* 7 (1893): 193–6.

57. The roster of those against Sunday opening can be compiled by looking through the *NYT* between 1891 and 1893. *NYT*, 2 September 1891, 15 and 16 October 1891, 23 May, 30 May, and 19 June 1893. See *NYT* report titled 'Several Miles of Petitions', 3 May 1892. For reports about extradenominational resistance to Sunday opening see *NYT*, 7 March, 8 July, 10 July, 21 October 1892, 14 May, 16 May, 17 May, 20 May, 22 May, 23 May, 30 May, 6 June and 16 July 1893. For reports of the congressional debate concerning the Sunday-opening amendment to the fair's appropriation bill, see *NYT*, 27 May, 10 July, 12 July, 14 July, 15 July, and 7 August 1892.
58. The Reverend R. V. Hunter to the Christian Endeavor convention, quoted in *NYT*, 8 July 1892.
59. Edwin Walker, *The Litigation of the Exposition* [pamphlet] (Chicago: Bench and Bar of Chicago, 1894).
60. See the 29 May 1893 issues of *NYT*, *Chicago Tribune*, *Washington Post*, *New Orleans Times-Picayune*, *Detroit News*, *St. Louis Dispatch*, and *Atlanta Constitution* for reports about Sunday at the fair.
61. *Chicago Tribune*, 29 May 1893.
62. *NYT*, 29 May 1893.
63. *Chicago Tribune*, 29 May 1893.
64. Most of the papers had separate articles reporting that saloons, hotels and attractions did their poorest Sunday-business in history.
65. *Chicago Tribune*, 29 May 1893.
66. Some papers carried what appears to be reports lifted from the *Chicago Tribune*, like *St. Louis Dispatch*.
67. *St. Louis Dispatch* (editorial) 29 May 1893.
68. *NYT*, 24 July 1893.
69. J. Ramage, 'Sunday Legislation', *Sewanee Review* 4 (1895): 122.
70. See the 1961 Supreme Court decision upholding blue laws, *McGowan v. Maryland*, 366 US (1961).

8

The Woman's Christian Temperance Union Reform Movement in the South in the Late Nineteenth Century

Valeria Gennaro Lerda

Introduction

This paper briefly examines the Woman's Christian Temperance Movement (WCTU), a body that combined both religious and secular aspects and was innovative in becoming the first mass woman's movement. Its focus is on the South, where the WCTU became not only a vehicle of social reform but also an instrument that helped women (mainly white and Protestant) to develop new roles in a changing society. The postbellum defeated South was poverty-stricken but nostalgic for an earlier era of opulence and patriarchal order, and torn between its need for modernization and its attachment to the old values that had shaped antebellum social and economic structures in the plantation system. In such an impasse any kind of project to redress social ills was desirable and needed.

From the beginning churches led the way in the philanthropic crusade along with some secular organizations, the woman's club movement being an important one. They originated a widespread commitment to social justice in a broad programme of charity and social action. The WCTU was ecumenical in scope – the word 'Christian' being indicative of its openness toward a wide view of moral and social reform; it was 'outside denominational fences', and broad in its geographical representation. Organized around the main and immediately controversial issue of temperance, and advocating in some instances total abstinence from alcoholic beverages, it soon became involved in the most important areas of social action, from prison reform to public health, from education to women's rights, attracting such an impressive membership that Ruth Bordin defines the WCTU as 'the leading women's organization in the United States' from 1873 to 1900.[1]

Beginnings of Temperance Movements

The rules of the Methodist Church written by John and Charles Wesley, which forbade the manufacture, sale and use of alcoholic beverages, were instrumental in bringing many to see intemperance as an evil and to legislate against it. As early as 1766 the Presbyterian Church was invited to oppose intemperance by Benjamin Rush of Philadelphia, who wrote a treatise on 'The Effects of Ardent Spirits Upon Human Body and Mind'. In Georgia the Baptist Churches of Eatonton and Columbus organized the first Temperance Society (1827), and in the so-called 'Petition Year', 1838, citizens in many states, including Georgia, began to petition their legislatures to repeal liquor licence laws.[2] Despite the failure of this initiative due to the opposition of the press and of many politicians, the campaign was useful in stimulating awareness of the damage connected with the use and abuse of liquors. During the first half of the nineteenth century the basic aim of reformers was 'to persuade' and convince people to reduce or to give up the drinking of alcohol. The association called the Sons of Temperance, and the affiliated Daughters of Temperance who joined the activities of the 'Sons' but did not share in its governance, started a new campaign aimed at securing state prohibition laws.

The Civil War was a watershed in the temperance movement because liquor was sometimes issued to soldiers; at the same time, the importation of liquor was cut off, so that many started to distill their grain and fruit into whisky. In 1862 Governor Joseph E. Brown sent a message to the General Assembly of Georgia recommending that a law be enacted restricting distillation in order to save grain for the army. After the end of the war, however, the distillers grew strong again. Drinking and drunkenness increased, and the number of saloons grew. According to Ruth Bordin, in 1873 the state of Ohio supported a saloon for every two hundred citizens, and by 1900 one out of every 116 Americans was employed in one way or another in the liquor industries. Over a half million people were engaged directly in the liquor trade.[3] As a consequence, the Order of Good Templars was formed to press for 'absolute prohibition of the liquor traffic and for the election of good, honest men to administer the laws'.

In the South the United Friends of Temperance established its own rules, among which were a guarantee of states' rights and of separate orders for whites and blacks, and the prohibition of political and sectarian discussions in the Order.[4] It is interesting to note that Henry Grady, the spokesman of the New South Creed, and the Governor of Georgia, William Northen, himself a promoter of New South economic awakening and industrialization, belonged to the United Friends of

Temperance, thereby showing that they considered the measures to control the liquor traffic to be progressive.

In the aftermath of the Civil War social conditions changed the burden of housekeeping for the majority of southern elite white women. No longer engaged in the demanding care of black families, their clothing and health, and at the same time more free to use the abundant labour force of former women slaves who performed housework for very low wages, southern ladies managed to profit from the increase in leisure time and moved from the microcosm of the plantation household to the wider sphere of community life. At the same time the social conditions of both poor whites and blacks in their communities stimulated their growing tendency to social activism and charitable work. The new reality encouraged churches to provide an opportunity for women to invest their time and resources. Moreover, the church, by permitting women to organize, gave them a greater appreciation of their ability and self-worth. Thus began a process of self-consciousness that was destined to be the strength of the woman's movement and, at the same time, of a large part of the movement for social justice which characterized Progressivism in the South.

The Role of Churches in the Women's Reform Movements

As John Patrick McDowell suggests, the history of southern Christians includes a deep concern for social reform, epitomized by the Home Mission movement among women in the Methodist Episcopal Church, South. Southern women distinguished this from Foreign Mission work because it addressed problems and needs within their own nation, and in some respects within their own region, the South. The period of mission work lasted from 1886, when women began their first denomination-wide home mission work, to 1940, when the mission came under the authority of the newly formed Methodist Church, resulting from the merging of the First Methodist Episcopal Church and the Methodist Protestant Church.[5]

Foreign Mission work is too large a subject to be discussed here at length, but it must be remembered that since 1848, when the Ladies' China Missionary Society of Baltimore was launched – considered by Noreen Dunn Tatum as the first society to bear a distinctively southern label – women's groups interested in foreign missions were springing up throughout the South. Their scope was generally educational and addressed to the improvement of public health and housing, along with conversion to Christianity.[6]

The depth of the relationship between everyday life and religion that characterized the southern reform movement of the nineteenth century may find an explanation in the widespread Evangelical spirit. Evangelical meetings were moments of collective and individual regeneration: after the intense experience of public conversion, life appeared to be a mission to pursue with optimism as a call of God. Samuel Hill, the leading historian of religion in the South, speaks of the diversity of southern Protestantism, which often caused an awakening of individual desire for perfection, expressed through philanthropy. Ted Ownby in his study of religious and lay ceremonies in the South, shows how the mass meetings became, in his words, 'festivals that celebrated the church-centered, home-centered values of evangelical culture'.[7]

Women, while working to alleviate the sufferings and injustices of the postbellum society, became convinced that they, as well as men, were given a divine command to extend the kingdom of God on earth. They started their struggle for self-improvement by asking for an expanded role and recognition within the Methodist denomination, where they lacked the right to serve the church in all the capabilities open to male lay members. As Methodist women began to organize, they pioneered their own emancipation and, long before the term 'status of women' was used, they began to press for their own rights of representation in the government of the Missions' programmes.[8] Aside from the gender struggle within their church, women soon became committed to eradicating conditions that they considered detrimental to family stability and to eliminating the social wrongs caused by poverty, illiteracy, poor health conditions and drunkenness.

During the more than half century of organized home mission work, women's efforts were indeed diversified and far-reaching and played a large role in the widespread Evangelical awakening. At the beginning the Home Mission movement focused on the West, where it was difficult to establish new churches. For that reason the first task assigned to women by the Methodist General Conference in 1886 was to collect funds for building parsonages, with Mrs Lucinda Helm, a renowned activist, being elected general secretary of the Woman's Department of Church Extension. Only in 1890 did the General Conference agree to the request of Miss Helm to let the Woman's Department of Church Extension become a separate organization known as The Woman's Parsonage and Home Mission Society. From 1896 to 1910 Miss Belle Harris Bennett was the president of the new representative governing Board.[9] In 1910 The Woman's Missionary Council resulted from the merging of the Woman's Board of Foreign Missions and the Woman's Home Missionary Society, and two departments were organized for home and foreign missions.

The WCTU: 'The Golden Key ... The Generous Liberator ... The Developer of Southern Women'

In order to understand this definition of the WCTU given by one of the leaders of the southern crusade for temperance, Belle Kearney from Mississippi, we must not forget the rules of southern patriarchal society to which all elite women had to conform. Among them was the rule of silence banning women from speaking in public places, even in church.[10]

When the temperance wind swept the South as 'a prairie fire',[11] women learned how to overcome these Victorian codes of behaviour and to move from the 'shelter' of homes to defend their homes imperilled, as they believed, by drunkenness. It was not an easy task, and the leaders of the movement repeatedly recalled their embarassment and fear at their first experiences of public speaking against the liquor traffic.

Belle Kearney, who became a national and international speaker and a leader of the Mississippi WCTU, remembered feeling stunned when, in 1884, she attended a lecture by Julia Ward Howe and saw a woman, upon a platform, delivering a speech! She also recalled her own paralyzing fear when she had to respond in public to the call of Frances Willard to organize the Loyal Temperance Legion, a juvenile society for temperance in Mississippi, and to accept appointment as state superindendent of the Young Woman's Christian Temperance Union.[12]

A great aid in overcoming the prohibition against speaking in public came from the Methodist Church, which supported the WCTU work from the beginning. It not only approved the strategies and goals of temperance women but quite often hosted the WCTU Conventions, offering a 'proper' platform for women to address a public audience. For instance, the 7th Annual Convention of the Georgia WCTU was held at St John's Methodist Church in Augusta (April 1889). There a series of important resolutions were approved: to petition the State Legislature to enact a law prohibiting the sale of liquor within a radius of three miles of all state institutions of learning; to gather funds for the establishment of an Industrial School for Girls in Milledgeville and to establish a State Reformatory for penitent fallen women.[13]

Another important convention was held in Atlanta on the suggestion of Methodist Rev. Samuel V. Small. Governor Northen was a strong opponent of the liquor traffic, and he was glad to offer the opportunity to the WCTU women to gather in the State Capitol; to that meeting Union leaders came from all over the United States, showing that the prohibition crusade could cross sectional boundaries and denominational lines.[14] Among the issues discussed was the need for scientific temperance instruction laws. On that occasion hundreds of Georgians had the opportunity to recognize that a woman could speak in public and 'not only retain her womanly dignity, but become in the hands of God a mighty agency for good'.[15] A number of other reforms were supported by the WCTU and successfully enacted: the age of consent was raised from ten to fourteen years in all English-speaking countries; the number of schools teaching the evils of alcohol on public health increased; National Temperance Hospitals were built, where the use of alcohol as a medicine was prohibited; temperance education in Sunday Schools became accepted. Their success allowed women to have a WCTU exhibit at the Atlanta Cotton Exposition of 1895.

Frances Willard's 'Do Everything Programme'

The wide range of issues offered by WCTU women reformers may be better understood by briefly describing Frances Willard's intense programme of activities and goals. Willard was the first national organizer of a broad agenda of charity and of social activism. Through her lecture tours, she also showed how a woman inflamed with the spirit of reform could overcome all sorts of difficulties, including fatiguing travels, uncomfortable lodgings and lack of funds. Her stamina and courage made it possible for her to cross the United States, covering every state, travelling on cold trains, even freight trains when necessary, without granting herself a break except for Christmas. In the spring of 1881, Willard realized one of her most ambitious goals, that of bringing the gospel of temperance to the South. She went to every southern state and to over fifty cities, receiving tributes to her charisma and feminine, persuasive style.

As the historian Ruth Bordin has emphasized, Willard's success in the South was due to the fact that she was able to offer an image of womanhood and femininity, despite addressing such controversial topics as prohibition, political corruption and prison reform. Moreover, Willard's trip to the South received the blessings of President James Garfield who had invested her with the responsibility of uniting 'the two sections with sweet ties of sympathy and mutual help in philanthropic work'.[16] Willard perfectly understood the kind of mission that was bestowed on her and used the strategy and the words of reconciliation and harmony repeatedly and convincingly. The warm hospitality she received, and the flattering reports in local newspapers, made her a heroine for southern ladies who continued to feel the strain of speaking in public and who learned from her the skills of eloquence and elegance. Willard's speeches were in fact considered 'literary gems', her language was declared 'chaste', and her dresses 'tasteful'. Her commitment became an encouragement and opened new fields of social activism, which she synthesized in the slogan 'do everything', meaning to prove that women could widen their fields of social activism and become a part of a national movement.

Southern women had first learned how to organize in the Foreign and Home Mission movement; when leaders like Frances Willard and other prominent lecturers went to the South, they were encouraged to become militant reformers.[17] Ruth Bordin argues that part of Willard's success in the South was the considerable autonomy the national WCTU allowed to local unions. Bordin considers the 'do everything' programme as the key to the success in the South. It 'was operationally possible because of the large measure of organizational local autonomy that the constitution of the WCTU provided from the beginning'.[18] Local autonomy in fact allowed members not to implement a part of the programme if it violated southern values and political or social standards. Even dress reform, an important area of interest in the WCTU's agenda, was not intended to force local unions to conform to the fashion and rules suggested as proper for WCTU members. Neither was Willard's growing ecumenical outreach to the Catholic community meant to be accepted unanimously.

Temperance remained the unifying issue around which a wide range of social reforms was eventually organized, such as nurseries, industrial schools, police matrons for women prisoners, health reforms, juvenile reformatories, convict camps and prison reforms, and woman's suffrage. By 1896, twenty-five departments out of the total of thirty-nine into which the national WCTU was organized, were dealing with non-temperance issues, along with the abolition of the production and sale of alcoholic beverages.[19] Indeed, the WCTU motto is indicative of the aims and expectations of women reformers: 'Woman will bless and brighten every place she enters, and will enter every place'.[20]

'The Angel of the Stockades': Julia Tutwiler

One of the most active among southern WCTU members was Julia Tutwiler of Alabama, where she put into practice the 'do everything' programme and, indeed, entered 'every place' to improve the welfare of Alabama's inhabitants.

Tutwiler was born in 1841 in a cotton-producing area. The atmosphere of her large family was cultured and hospitable and, most important, conducive to learning. Her father, Henry Tutwiler, was a planter, a schoolteacher and a promoter of public education and of co-education in the South. He was an openminded gentleman who believed that girls too should be educated. Therefore, Julia was allowed to attend the academy in co-educational schools, and, for a couple of winters, was sent to Philadelphia – a rare opportunity, because southern children were never encouraged to go north to receive their education.

The Tutwilers lived through the Civil War and, when the war was over, Julia wished to continue the education started in Philadelphia. After attending Vassar College she returned to Alabama to become a full-time teacher. In 1873 she decided to go to Europe, where she spent three years studying the new educational methodologies and theories of Pestalozzi and Froebel. It was only upon her return to her home state that she started her practical reform activity, working throughout her life for the development of teacher training, for vocational schools and for the admission of women to the state university. The long and successful campaign she conducted to support co-education and women's right to higher education was recognized in 1907 when the University of Alabama awarded her an honorary doctorate in law. As president of the Livingston Normal College she not only supervised educational programmes and found opportunities for needed girls but, as an active administrator, worked tirelessly to improve the campus with new and modern buildings, and sought in every way to enhance the facilities for students, often advancing her own money.[21]

Her contribution was not limited to educational reform. Julia Tutwiler was also one of the southern women reformers, along with Rebecca Latimer Felton of Georgia, who committed time and energy to penal reform. It took a lot of courage for a southern lady to confront the difficulties of visiting prisons and convict camps, but she went, riding night trains to reach the camps near Birmingham in the early mornings to inspect the physical conditions of convicts. In 1879 she started a campaign to activate educational and corrective programmes in prisons, profiting from an earlier experience in Germany at the Institute of Deaconesses at Kaiserswerth, where she had learned how to organize charitable and corrective programmes. In both camps and prisons Julia conducted religious services and brought books and Bibles to both black and white prisoners. As a consequence of such charitable and educational efforts she was soon named 'The Angel of the Stockades', and the local WCTU invited her to serve as chairman of prison work in Alabama. With the support of the WCTU she then started her crusade for the abolition of the convict-lease system, an institution that was profitable for both the state and for private entrepreneurs, but was racially brutal and degrading for blacks who were the main workforce in the coalmining and iron industry.[22]

After many years of commitment, Julia Tutwiler found some satisfaction in a series of Acts, 1883, 1885, 1886, of the Alabama Legislature by which the governor was given authority to define the rules for the treatment of prisoners. Among others, she had asked for the separation of criminals according to age, sex and the seriousness of their offence. She also led the way in the establishment of juvenile reformatories, and, realizing that legislators were indifferent to the problem, she succeeded, as a first step, in establishing prison schools by an act eventually passed in 1887, which made Alabama the first southern state to create prison schools in convict camps.

Encouraged by this success, Tutwiler continued to advocate prison schools for women and girls, and reformatory schools for boys. Through cooperation with Miss R. D. Johnston of Birmingham, a WCTU member and her co-worker in WCTU prison-visiting, the Boys Industrial School was built at East Lake. Two other such institutions were established, the Reform and Industrial School for Negro Boys, and a school for the training of white girls at Mount Meigs. In addition to such intense reform activity in the crucial fields of education and prison reform she was active in campaigning for prohibition and also in the International Peace Movement.

Tutwiler defined as her 'dearest pleasure' the charitable work and the private liberality and generosity that she pursued all her life, a time that spans the era of King Cotton, Reconstruction and the New South. She was one of the leading figures in the Progressive movement of the South, an untiring WCTU member, and a protagonist in the 'do everything' programme of Frances Willard. An educator and 'an ardent spirit', as her biographers Ann Gary Pannell and Dorothea E. Wyatt have considered, Julia Tutwiler can rightly be taken as a symbol of the 'New Women of the New South', as southern ladies came to be called by historians of the woman's movement and of the Progressive movement in the South.[23]

'... Lucifer Is Let Loose When King Alcohol Reigns and Rules'[24]

Women reformers in the South became aware that, in order to accomplish their goals as social workers without risking ostracism by their communities, they should avoid infringing the principles on which southern society was still organized, despite the changes brought about by the Civil War and Reconstruction.

First of all, in their vision of a better society, the leaders of the WCTU and of other reform movements committed themselves to social justice crusades, not in order to reject women's domestic status or the proscriptions against women's exposure in the public sphere, but to enhance the rights of women to have their domestic world protected and improved. The defence of home included the moral duty to maintain the sexual purity of girls, to care for health and education and to fight against vice and violence. Women's task, in this perspective, became a maternal one, and their stepping out of the home's protective walls became an extension of motherhood. Moreover, their opposition to political corruption became, not a way to intrude directly into the world of men, but rather a means to ask men to legislate in support of children and women's welfare.

Children indeed were central to the organization of the reform agenda of WCTU and the other women's organizations. As Linda Gordon has written in a recent study of maternalism and welfare in the early twentieth century: 'Women were influential in formulating and popularizing the view that promoting the welfare of the nation should begin with children.' Gordon also underlines the fact that 'putting children first arose with putting forward motherhood as women's claim to respect and power'.[25] In Gordon's analysis, 'maternalist reformers developed a more coherent approach to social betterment that became known as "social work."' She also maintains that in the 1890s, social work 'grew from traditional charity, largely religious and denominational.' All this social reform impetus had a female character in the Progressive Era.[26]

As an example of the maternalist approach to reform we can analyze Rebecca Latimer Felton's life and activity, as one among many other WCTU reformers. After acting as campaign organizer and secretary to her husband, William Felton, a farmer and politician, she almost inadvertently found herself involved in a wide range of social crusades: 'I found myself suddenly in the thick of a campaign. I did not stop to think what a radical change this was for a young woman reared on an old-fashioned Southern plantation ...'[27] She soon decided to join the WCTU, hoping through that organization, first of all to capture new forces in her battle for the abolition of the convict-lease system. Raised in a Methodist family, Rebecca Latimer Felton was also biased against the 'Demon Liquor' and became convinced that only legislative action could cure what she considered to be a calamity as tragic as war.[28] She was aware that the WCTU's first phase, under the leadership of Annie Wittenmyer (1874–1879), had directed efforts toward 'moral suasion', a strategy that proved too weak to solve the plague of alcoholism. Felton therefore followed the more radical programmes of Frances Willard, who succeeded Wyttenmyer and presided over the WCTU from 1879 to 1898.

Willard maintained that women should be granted suffrage as a 'weapon to protect the home', and although the Georgia WCTU took a stand against woman's suffrage in 1893, Rebecca Felton became a supporter of woman's right to vote. In Felton's mind the vote was needed in order to obtain laws aimed at protecting children and women. 'I believe a woman has a multitude of rights,' she wrote '... I want her to have and enjoy the right to choose her own rulers, such rights as a sober home and a decent upright husband.' Children had their rights too: 'Among the foremost and prominent rights inherent to the little child, is to be born into a sober home without diseased blood in his little veins.'[29]

Both in the battle against the liquor traffic and in the campaign to abolish the convict-lease system, Rebecca Felton was convinced that she was fighting to defend human rights in the name of motherhood. She took every opportunity in public speeches and in meetings of the WCTU to remind her audiences about the cost of alcoholic beverages to American society: 'The Drink Evil,' she convincingly informed, 'demands nine hundred millions of dollars of tribute per annum.' In the same speech she directly accused men of allowing such a waste: 'Men,' she asked, 'and this you call progress? ... I will stand up against this injustice and inhumanity while God gives me breath!'[30]

Along with the social and physical damages of alcohol, reform of the penal system was Felton's priority. Again, children were her main concern, because the penal system did not provide separate areas for juvenile criminals. Especially in the convict camps, where the convicts were kept during construction work, women and men were 'hoarded together'. Children were born in captivity and Rebecca Felton again and again, in hundreds of letters and newspaper articles, denounced the shame and the corruption of politicians who profited from such leases and were blind to the tragedy of the victims. When eventually the Georgia Legislature outlawed the convict-lease system in 1908, Rebecca Felton proudly recalled the part that she played in the battle: 'I should be given consideration,' she claimed, 'for the incessant fusilade I kept upon this subject ... I was never too busy or too tired to ventilate the atrocity when I could find a place to publish my criticism.'[31]

The WCTU became, indeed, the place where women reformers could use their power to rebuild in a new moral vision their communities and their society. The WCTU was 'The Sword of the Spirit',[32] but it was a double-edged weapon, because both the crusade against liquor traffic and the campaign for woman's suffrage were Progressive measures and at the same time measures to control the black population.

Southern Traditions and Social Reforms: A Paradox of Southern History

The WCTU campaigns against the use of, and traffic in, alcoholic products from 1873 to 1900 achieved some important goals for three main reasons: first, the link established between Christian morality and abstinence sanctioned women's work outside the domestic walls as an 'organized mother's love', and as an extension of their maternal duty to keep their enlarged families, communities and cities physically and morally healthy; second, the defence of the family from the devastating consequences of men's drunkenness enhanced the feminine, maternal role of southern women; third, their crusade against mental diseases and the other damaging effects of alcohol on children became part of the more general movement for the betterment of public health, a major concern of the Progressive reformers.

Among some of its achievements were the 'local option' laws, by virtue of which every county could prohibit the sale of 'intoxicating beverages' within its borders – measures that raised strong opposition because they reduced the states' income from liquor licences and also reduced the profits of both producers and sellers; the 'Four Miles Law', a measure adopted in some states to prohibit the sale of liquors at four miles from schools; and the Scientific Instruction Bill (Georgia, 1901) relating to scientific instruction in Sunday Schools.

Of course, all the measures were small steps, quite often left to the goodwill of individual legislators. None was adequate completely to solve the problems arising from the production, the sale and the use of alcohol. Too often the measures were taken in isolated small places, country stores, villages, little towns, and not where big business was involved. In some cases, federal laws were indirectly a support to temperance, for example the Pure Food and Drug Act (1906),[33] but everyone in the nation was aware that only a federal amendment could make prohibition a national measure. Until 1900 the WCTU was the leading temperance organization; then another organization, the Anti-Saloon League, led the movement to the Eighteenth Amendment. Churches were, as in the past decades, strong allies of the new organizations and offered financial support, organizational work, propaganda and support in publications like the *South Atlantic Quarterly* and the *Sewanee Review*. Rightly, the Anti-Saloon League was defined as 'a political ecclesiastical machine'.[34]

World War I became a decisive turning point in the long crusade for temperance and prohibition. In 1913 the Anti-Saloon League, along with members of the WCTU, marched in Washington to bring to the Congress a draft of a National Bill, but it took four more years for the government to enact, in 1917, a Selective Service Act that defined the 'dry' zones around military camps (May 1917). Subsequently, the Lever Food and Fuel Control Act (August 1917) aimed to protect grain supplies by preventing their distillation into liquors. Finally, the War Prohibition Act (21 November 1918) included wine and beer among the prohibited beverages, and even before passage of the Eighteenth Amendment and the Volstead Act (January 1920) the American people experienced a degree of prohibition.

The historian Thomas Terrill concluded that 'prohibition conquered the South ... because it offered a simple, moral solution to disturbing social ills ... It afforded an opportunity to attack moral and political corruption and it reaffirmed the evangelical ideals of Southern Protestantism.' It was also, Terrill argued, 'a coercive reform with strong racial and class overtones.'[35] The paradox of southern history is evidenced in the woman's WCTU movement and in the fight to 'moralize' society. While in the first phase of the Methodist Church reform movement some efforts had been directed toward reducing racial tensions, and the church eventually became involved in campaigns to end lynchings, the most famous leaders and lecturers of the WCTU, such as Rebecca Felton and Belle Kearney, did not hesitate to proclaim the necessity of protecting southern white women from blacks and from the drunkenness of blacks, the poorest segment of southern society.

Recently Glenda Elizabeth Gilmore has found evidence of early experiments in bi-racial cooperation in the WCTU in North Carolina, but, 'when the white supremacy campaign at first discouraged black voting and then disfranchised African Americans, white women's concern with black temperance ended, and they readily recast their former WCTU allies as part of the "Negro problem."'[36] Consequently, the crusade to moralize southern society was also a crusade to prevent blacks from drinking alcohol and thus becoming even more dangerous to the purity and safety of southern womanhood. In the name of women's protection, women like Rebecca Felton and the Mississippian Belle Kearney became suffragists, on the basis that the vote was the only means to enact laws against forces that could endanger the family and the community.

Belle Kearney, undoubtedly one the most influential WCTU national and international southern lecturers and leaders, frankly admitted that southern women wanted the 'home protecting vote' to cancel the black vote. From one of her platforms at the NAWSA meeting in New Orleans (March 1903), she openly called for the enfranchisement of women who could meet educational and property qualifications as a means by which white supremacy could be forever ensured. Kearney saw the right to vote for white women as an instrument to settle the race question in politics, and she did not hesitate to proclaim that 'Anglo-Saxon is the standard of the ages to come. It is, beyond all else, the granite basis of the South. Upon that its civilization will mount; upon that it will stand unshaken ...'[37]

The principle of states' rights was another cornerstone of southern political culture designed to maintain white supremacy. The fear of any federal interference in state laws intended to control the black population accelerated the passage of prohibition laws in many states:

Georgia, in 1907; Tennessee in 1909; Virginia in 1914; Alabama, Arkansas and South Carolina in 1915, without waiting for a federal amendment. Many southern reformers did not accept the idea of federal amendments, especially on the issue of women's suffrage. For them the progressive demand for women's suffrage was based on the need to counterbalance African American votes at the polls.[38] Ruth Bordin maintains that the WCTU women were slower than suffragists to ask for the vote, but that nineteenth-century WCTU activism opened the way to success for the suffrage movement in the twentieth century. WCTU reformers joined the suffragists in the South only after segregation laws were passed by state legislatures; and white women could hope that the same strategies that were used to keep black men from voting would be applied as well to black women in case of a federal amendment for universal suffrage.

In the rhetoric of women's social mission at the end of the nineteenth century, women's leaders spoke of stepping into the public arena in order to clean the 'house of politics'.[39] Their moralizing view of their maternal duty included pressing for better schools for whites and blacks better housing for blacks, and protection of public health for all. Elizabeth Fox-Genovese has recently written that 'as segregation shaped the experience of white and black women, so it shaped attitudes toward woman suffrage', and she also contends that 'the causes with which women associated themselves and the issue of suffrage were ever more likely to intertwine as growing numbers of women insisted that they must themselves be able to defend their interests and the interests of women less fortunate or independent than they.' *Noblesse oblige* 'and echoes of older paternalism underscore an emphasis upon the responsibilities for the elite rather than upon the rights of the poor.'[40]

Conclusion

The WCTU was indeed the 'Golden key and the developer of Southern women' as defined by Belle Kearny when she became 'a New Woman' able to accomplish her desire for an independent life. Following the charismatic example of Frances Willard, she was able to overcome all the boundaries of southern culture and liberate herself, reaching – not without effort and personal strain – public recognition even beyond her expectations. Indeed, she travelled throughout the world to spread the gospel of temperance and, after the Federal Amendment for Woman's Suffrage, ran immediately for public office. Despite being defeated by James K. Vardaman in the competition for the US senate, she ran a few months later for senator in the state of Mississippi. She was successful and became the first woman senator in the Mississippi

Legislature. When she died in 1939 at the age of seventy-five, she received public tributes as 'Senator Belle Kearney, Lecturer, Writer and Stateswoman'.

Many other prominent southern ladies who became public figures or who entered the political arena started their adventure as WCTU leaders: Nellie Nugent Somerville (Mississippi), Rebecca Latimer Felton (Georgia), Laura Clay (Kentucky), to name just a few. From the single issue of temperance and prohibition, they were able to expand their activities in almost all of the main fields of Progressive reforms for social justice.

But in the world of Jim Crow they could not overcome the paradoxes of southern Progressivism, and they accepted segregation. We may agree, however, with Elizabeth Fox-Genovese when she argues that 'Southern post-bellum racism embodied the fears and tensions in a world in which whites and blacks competed directly for scarce resources', while, at the same time, 'as white southerners set about pulling together the remnants of their lives and their region, many clung more fiercely to the values and habits they could salvage.'[41] The devastation of the war made it difficult, if not impossible, in the years of the WCTU's crusade, to face a revolution in the relations between whites and blacks. Therefore women, who fought their own uphill battle for self-emancipation, accepted the rules of their bi-racial society.

Notes

1. Ruth Bordin, *Woman and Temperance. The Quest for Power and Liberty, 1873–1900* (Philadelphia: Temple University Press, 1981), xviii. Membership, in Bordin's figures, reached 150,000 in 1892.
2. Dr Adiel Sherwood was the Eatonton leader and Dr J. H. Campbell was the Baptist organizer in Columbus, Georgia. See J. J. Ansley, *History of the Georgia WCTU, 1885–1907* (Columbus, GA, 1914).
3. Bordin, *Woman and Temperance*, 6. According to the *United States Bureau of the Census, Historical Statistics of the United States, Colonial Times to 1957* (Washington, DC: Government Printing Office, 1960), 179, Americans spent $1.8 billion on alcoholic beverages in 1909, in contrast to $2 billion on all products and non-alcoholic beverages combined. See Bordin, *Woman and Temperance*, 6.
4. Ansley, *History of the Georgia WCTU*, 32.
5. John Patrick McDowell, *The Social Gospel in the South. The Woman's Home-Mission Movement in the Methodist Episcopal Church, South, 1886–1939* (Baton Rouge and London: Louisiana State University Press, 1982), 116 ff.
6. Noreen Dunn Tatum, *A Crown of Service. A Story of Woman's Work in the Methodist Episcopal Church, South, from 1878 to 1940* (Nashville, TN, 1960), 21 ff.

7. Ted Ownby, *Subduing Satan. Religion, Recreation, and Manhood in the Rural South, 1865–1920* (Chapel Hill and London: The University of North Carolina Press, 1990).
8. Dunn Tatum remembers the role of Belle Harris Bennett as a 'farsighted leader' in the movement for laity rights and indicates 1906 as a turning point in the movement due to Bennett's proposal to form a General Council, composed equally of men and women, to administer all missionary affairs of the church (page 38). The General Conference voted 77 for and 144 against laity rights for women. Bennett kept the struggle going in the following years, until 1918 when, by a vote of 265 to 57, the General Conference granted laity rights to women. Mrs Luke Johnson, Chair of the Council Laity Committee in 1918, commented upon the long awaited victory with words of gratitude toward Mrs Bennett, and explained that women, taking place by the side of the laymen of the church, came 'not to do their work or to receive their crown, but to stand shoulder by shoulder with them, in ministering to the suffering, sorrowing and dying of all earth' (page 40).
9. Dunn Tatum, *A Crown of Service*, 27–8.
10. In 1893 the Southern Presbyterian Church issued a decree that 'the session must absolutely enforce the injunction of scriptures forbidding women to speak in churches, or in any way failing to observe the relative subordination to men that is thought in I, Corinthians 11:13 and other places'. For an in-depth analysis of the position of women in southern churches see Jean Friedman, *The Enclosed Garden: Women and Community in Evangelical South, 1830–1900* (Chapel Hill: The University of North Carolina Press, 1985); and, by the same author, 'Southern Women and Reform', in Valeria Gennaro Lerda, ed., *Città e campagna nell'Età dorata: gli Stati Uniti tra utopia e riforma* (Roma: Bulzoni, 1986), 93–103. For an excellent and insightful analysis of Victorian culture see Louise L. Stevenson, *The Victorian Homefront. American Thought and Culture, 1860–1880* (New York: Twayne Publishers, 1991).
11. The metaphor was used by Frances Willard, the leading authority of the American WCTU and national president from 1878 until her death in 1898. Quoted in Bordin, *Woman and Temperance*, 15.
12. Belle Kearney, *A Slaveholder's Daughter* (London and New York: Abbey Press, 1900), 107–8. Kearney felt inadequate to the exposure of appearing before a group of women: 'My voice was choked, my eyes were clouded with the mist of unshed tears' (page 142). Frances Willard, in order to help her to overcome the difficulties of speaking in public, urged her to study oratory under Mrs Frank Parker of Cooke County Normal School (Illinois). Mrs Parker was a gifted student of the Boston School of Oratory. In 1893 Belle Kearney also enrolled in Dwight L. Moody's Chicago School for a six-month course in 'practical Gospel Work', where she also took lessons in 'voice culture' from Mrs Parker, and in physical training from Baron Nils Posse, head of the Boston institution for 'body development'. Reassured by the training, Belle Kearney became a traveller and an indefatigable lecturer. In 1906, for example, she lectured crossing the United States five times in one year! She also became a lecturer of the

Chautauqua Circuit, where she could address crowds of people from three to five thousand, and where she defended southern ideals. See Nancy Carol Tipton, 'It Is My Duty: The Public Career of Belle Kearney' (BA thesis, University of Mississippi, 1975), 60–3. On the Chautauqua movement see Joseph E. Gould, *The Chautauqua Movement: An Episode in the Continuing American Revolution* (New York: State University of New York, 1961).

13. Ansley, *History of the Georgia WCTU*, 119.
14. *Ibid.*, 131. Six hundred delegates went to Atlanta.
15. *Ibid.*
16. Quoted in Bordin, *Woman and Temperance*, 77.
17. In 1879 Eliza Stewart, chairman of Southern Work, visited Kentucky, Tennessee, and Georgia in 1883; J. Ellen Foster spoke in eleven southern states; Sallie Chapin, president of the Ladies' Christian Association and a teacher in Sunday Schools, lectured frequently on behalf of the WCTU.
18. Bordin, *Woman and Temperance*, 98.
19. *Ibid.*
20. Frances Willard, 'The Work of the WCTU', in Annie Nathan Meyer, *Women's Work in America* (New York, 1891), 410.
21. See, for example, Julia Tutwiler Papers, University of Alabama Library, Mss. Collection. Julia Tutwiler to Judge Norman Jarman, Trustee of Alabama Normal College, Livingston, 11 July 1908 (handwritten letter), and 'A Business Statement. Report to the Board of Trustees of Alabama Normal College' (typescript, 5 pages).
22. For an insightful analysis of the convict-lease system in southern coal mines, see Alex Lichtenstein, 'Through the Rugged Gates of the Penitentiary: Convict Labor and Southern Coal, 1870–1900,' in Melvyn Stokes and Rick Halpern, eds, *Race and Class in the American South Since 1890* (Oxford: Berg Publishers, 1994), 3–42.
23. See Marjorie Spruill Wheeler, *The New Women of the New South: The Leaders of the Woman Suffrage Movement in the Southern States* (New York: Oxford University Press, 1993). Surprisingly for such a prominent leader in the Progressive movement, the only biography of Julia Tutwiler dates back to 1961. The authors, Ann Gary Pannell and Dorothea E. Wyatt, to whom I am indebted for the information and data on Julia Tutwiler's life and activity, offer a thorough description of Julia's contribution to Alabama social improvement. *Julia Tutwiler and Social Progress in Alabama* (Alabama: University of Alabama Press, 1961).
24. Rebecca Latimer Felton Papers, University of Georgia Library, Special Collections (hereafter quoted as Felton Papers), manuscript, n.d., written for the campaign of Mayor Bacon.
25. Linda Gordon, 'Putting Children First: Women, Maternalism and Welfare in the Early Twentieth Century,' in Linda H. Kerber, Alice Kessler Harris, Kathryn Kish Sklar, eds, *U.S.History as Women's History: New Feminist Essays* (Chapel Hill and London: University of North Carolina Press, 1995), 65–86 (quote on page 63).
26. Gordon, 'Putting Children First,' 69.
27. Quoted in Josephine Bone Floyd, 'Rebecca Felton, Political Independent',

Georgia Historical Quarterly 21 (March 1946): 14–34. Rebecca's husband was a leader of the Independent Democratic party. The WCTU was never an exclusively white organization, even in the Gulf States, although it was a segregated one. According to Bordin, 'even if southern blacks and whites were not members of the same local Unions, organization of black women proceeded fairly equally alongside that of white women in the South'. See Bordin, *Woman and Temperance*, 82–3.

28. Felton Papers, speech delivered before the Woman's Christian Temperance Union, n.d.
29. *Ibid.*
30. Felton Papers, speech delivered in a WCTU Convention, n.d.
31. Felton Papers, 'Georgia Convict-Lease System', manuscript, n.d. See also the chapter 'History of the Reformatory Movement in Georgia', in Rebecca Felton, *My Memoirs of Georgia Politics, Written by Mrs William H. Felton* (Atlanta, 1911), 581–623.
32. Anastasia Sims, 'The Sword of the Spirit: The WCTU in North Carolina', *North Carolina Historical Review*', 64 (October 1987): 394–415.
33. The Pure Food and Drug Administration Act established that, on every medicine shipped through Interstate Commerce, the percentage of alcohol or other drugs be declared, and on every bottle of whisky a label should declare 'straight whiskey,' 'rectified whiskey', or 'blended whiskey'.
34. Quoted in John Lee Eighmy, 'Religious Liberalism in the South during the Progressive Era,' *Church History* 38 (September 1969): 359–72. Philanthropy helped the Anti-Saloon League, and also J. D. Rockefeller contributed to the League from 1900 to 1919. See James H. Timberlake, *Prohibition and the Progressive Movement, 1900–1920* (Cambridge, MA, 1963), 148.
35. William J. Cooper and Thomas Terrill, *The American South: A History* (New York: McGraw Hill, 1991), vol. 2, 597.
36. Glenda Elizabeth Gilmore, '"A Melting Time": Black Women, White Women, and the WCTU in North Carolina, 1880–1900,' in Virginia Bernhard, Betty Brandon, *et al.*, *Hidden Histories of Women in the South* (Columbia and London: University of Missouri Press, 1994), 153–72.
37. Quoted in Tipton, 'It Is My Duty,' 47–8.
38. Kenneth R. Johnson, 'Kate Gordon and the Woman Suffrage Movement in the South,' *Journal of Southern History* 38 (August 1972): 365–92.
39. Felton Papers, manuscript, n.d., scrapbook, no. 117.
40. Elizabeth Fox-Genovese, 'Afterword,' in *Hidden Histories*, 224–38 (quotes on 229–31).
41. Fox-Genovese, 'Afterword,' 236–7.

A Note on Sources

Rebecca Latimer Felton Papers. University of Georgia Library, Special Collections, Athens, Georgia. The rich collection includes private and public letters handwritten by Mrs Felton (1835–1930), clippings and the minutes of her speeches as a WCTU leading member, related to the fields in which she campaigned to abolish the convict-lease system, to establish juvenile reformatories, to defend women's and children's rights against the evils of the widespread heavy use of alcoholic beverages, to include in the school curricula the Scientific Instruction on the damages of alcohol on health, to convince the legislators of the need of Local Option measures, in order to prevent the selling of alcohol, and even to ask for woman suffrage, despite the fact that the Georgia WCTU never had a Suffrage Department and did not endorse the woman suffrage crusade of the national WCTU. Collections Nos. 81 and 82 are particularly rich for the issues of temperance and convict-lease. A large part of her correspondence is addressed to politicians, a way out for Rebecca Felton from the so-called 'proper sphere' into the public arena, where she suffered ostracism and criticism and where she challenged southern traditions. Rebecca Felton also wrote two interesting memoirs where she expressed her feelings both of nostalgia for the Old South and of hope for the New South, despite the widespread corruption: 'My Memoirs of Georgia Politics, Written by Mrs William H. Felton' (Atlanta, Georgia, 1911), and 'Country Life in Georgia in the Days of my Youth' (Atlanta, Georgia, 1919).

Julia Tutwiler Papers. University of Alabama Library, Mss. Collection, Alabama. Julia Tutwiler (1841–1916), did not leave a large collection of letters, therefore her papers contain clippings, many of her poems and some of her articles.

Belle Kearney Papers. Mississippi Department of Archives and History, Jackson, Mississippi. Miss Belle Kearney (1863–1939), besides letters and clippings, wrote a memoir in which she recounts her life as a 'southern Belle' who refuses the role of an ornament on a pedestal and, longing for higher education and culture, builds up a career at first as a teacher (against her father's opinion that a southern young woman should not work outside the protected walls of home), and later on as a WCTU lecturer and leader, and as the first woman senator in Mississippi: Belle Kearney, *A Slaveholder's Daughter* (New York: Abbey Press, 1900).

The national organ of the WCTU was the *Union Signal*. Founded in 1883, it became the most popular temperance journal, published by the Woman's Temperance Publishing Association (a stock company for women only, founded by Matilda Carse, president of the Chicago Central Union). In 1903 the national WCTU purchased the *Union Signal* and its juvenile periodicals. Frances Willard assumed regular editorship in 1892, deciding broad editorial policy and writing contributions. The journal became the mouthpiece of temperance campaigns, home-protection ballot and woman suffrage. The *Union Signal* campaigned for a wide range of social reforms and broad social issues. Articles on everyday life, household, dress fashion, public health, education, prohibition and kindergartens make of the journal the mirror of Frances Willard's 'do everything' programme and of the whole WCTU broad programme of reform.

9

War in the Social Order: The Great War and the Liberalization of American Quakerism

Howell John Harris

Introduction

When, or if, historians think of the American branches of the Religious Society of Friends, we probably think of them as quintessential representatives of the social activist tradition within American Protestantism. Our views may be affected by experience of the liberal, welcoming meetings which are a feature of so many college towns. But they are also, perhaps, influenced by the thought that one can draw a direct, unbroken line from the pioneering anti-slavery advocates of the late eighteenth century, through the supporters of a wide variety of reform causes in the nineteenth century (particularly equal rights for women and other oppressed groups – including 'Indians', prisoners and the mentally afflicted), to some of the founding members of the Committee for a Sane Nuclear Policy (SANE) in the 1950s, and even as far as the Freedom Riders of the early 1960s. Here, it seems, is an (Anglo)-American religious tradition with much to attract modern secular liberal historians – one that has remained faithful to the core values of pacifism, egalitarianism and respect for individual human dignity and moral autonomy, which are rooted in its radical dissenting origins.[1]

But wait a moment. The denomination which gave the United States Woodrow Wilson's attorney general, A. Mitchell Palmer, architect of the Great Red Scare, and two Republican presidents, Herbert Hoover and more surprisingly Richard Nixon, cannot have had an unproblematic relationship with American liberalism during this century. Clearly there are tendencies within American Quakerism which do not fit easily within the picture of theological radicalism and social reformism presented above. For there were many Friends who came of age in the late nineteenth century, after the dramas of the Civil War era had ended, and who dropped their moral reformist politics along with the other peculiarities of language and dress which had once marked them out. Palmer was a product of this comfortable conformist milieu. And there was a whole different world of Quakerism beyond the

Appalachians, where rural migrants became absorbed into the dominant local Protestant patterns of belief, worship and church organization. Hoover's and Nixon's roots were in this evangelicized soil, not that of the Atlantic seaboard cities and their hinterlands, where Friends remained closer, spiritually and geographically, to their beginnings.[2]

My purpose in this paper is to address the above apparent paradox, by exploring and explaining when, how and why *parts* of American Quakerism re-established its historic identification with political dissent and reform, and coloured the enduring public image of the whole denomination. This question is not one which came to me very naturally. I am not a religious historian. The research project which drew me to the study of American Friends was a history of anti-unionism in the American metal trades – in particular, a case-study of the battles waged on behalf of employers' sovereign authority by two generations of industrialists in America's third-largest manufacturing city, Philadelphia, from the 1890s through the New Deal.[3]

In the course of this work, I encountered some interesting, anomalous men – Republican entrepreneurs who organized relief programmes for the families of striking and destitute coalminers in the lean years of the 1920s and through Mr Hoover's depression, serving as labour arbitrators and acting as advisors in the creation of the federal Social Security system during the turbulent years of the 1930s, and making private pilgrimages to Germany in a desperate attempt to influence the Hitler regime to allow Jews to emigrate. In the 1920s, they had been leading figures in one of the most successful (but non-violent) anti-union organizations in American industry, the Metal Manufacturers Association of Philadelphia (MMA), which was my principal interest. But they were also among the founders, key activists, and chief financial supporters of the American Friends Service Committee (AFSC) during and after the Great War.[4]

It was this experience, and this organization, which did more than anything else to reconnect American Quakerism with its own radical past, and to forge new links with the overlapping worlds of Social Gospel Protestantism and secular liberal reform. Explaining why some of the leading Philadelphia businessmen I encountered had such unusual and ambivalent political commitments and wide-ranging social concerns required that I examine the beliefs they had in common, which distinguished them from their capitalist friends and neighbours. They were at the heart of the AFSC; it was the key player in the lasting redefinition of what it meant to be a Friend. Religious renewal and reformist convictions came together in the crucible of war, in a 'church' without ministers or creeds, where 'lay' activism had to be the dominant force.

This paper will begin by sketching in a description of American Quakerism at the turn of the century. It will then concentrate on the interplay between religious commitment, pacifist ideals, social criticism and social action among the prosperous and formerly quite conservative Friends who forged the AFSC, situating them in a transatlantic religious milieu, and explaining the catalytic role of the war experience in their longer-term intellectual evolution. Finally and more briefly, it will explore the lasting consequences of the redefinition of Quakers' critical role in American society whose origins it will have explored.

The Background

Late-nineteenth-century American Quakerism was a denomination in crisis. Of its circa 100,000 adherents, about two-thirds were to be found west of the Appalachians, while a quarter still lived in the Atlantic seaboard cities and their hinterlands, from Baltimore to southern Maine. Quakers were divided into two main groups as an enduring result of a doctrinal schism in 1827. Hicksites – the schismatics – made up about 17 percent of the total and were the largest group in the mid-Atlantic states. The Orthodox were themselves further subdivided among conservatives, Wilburites, Gurneyites and the far more numerous Evangelicals who had sprung from the latter camp but had diverged so far that they 'risked becoming, as one British Friend put it, "a second-rate holiness sect."'[5]

Sectarianism flourished among American Quakers, but the denomination itself stagnated. Midwestern Friends' numbers were comparatively buoyant as a result of the Evangelical impulse; but the Hicksites and the eastern Orthodox were slowly fading away. These well-educated, bourgeois Friends, particularly the original core communities of American Quakerism, the Philadelphia region's circa 4,000 Orthodox and 11,000 Hicksites, still represented the greatest concentrations of wealth, intellect and organized influence within their small, scattered, fissile denomination. They financed and controlled most of its magazines, its prestigious schools and colleges and its reformist agencies, notably the Friends' Freedmen's Association, the Indian Rights Association and the Peace Society. But they did not strive to make converts, were not especially welcoming to the few outsiders who wished to join, and, crucially, disowned anybody who married outside their particular branch of Quakerism. They also suffered demographically as a paradoxical result of their commitment to women's education and active benevolence. These offered satisfying careers and ways of life outside of marriage, a choice which was itself rendered difficult by the rules of endogamy; so about 40 percent of their female members remained single. It did not take a rocket scientist to work out that theirs was a denomination with more past than future.[6]

The Challenge of Modernity

The crisis of eastern seaboard bourgeois Quakerism was more than demographic; it was also spiritual. In a denomination utterly dependent on lay activism and personal commitment, about half of its members were Quakers through family tradition rather than real conviction; these nominal 'birthright Friends' scarcely participated in its religious or benevolent activities. Its younger members were also exposed to the intellectual challenges to Christian belief which afflicted Protestants on both sides of the Atlantic: critical Bible scholarship and modern scientific, in particular Darwinian, interpretations of the natural world and humankind's place within it. The midwestern Evangelical majority was less threatened and took easy refuge in Fundamentalism when it took notice of the problem at all. But well-educated younger Quakers in the seaboard cities and in Britain, to which they remained closely attached, felt the need for, in the words of the key English modernist manifesto, 'a reasonable faith', some way of reconciling their traditional beliefs with contemporary thought and of making their religion once again meaningful in their lives.[7]

Most of the forces for regeneration showed themselves in Britain first. This was partly because of the greater intellectual openness of younger British Friends, who were firmly embedded within provincial Nonconformity, closely tied to Wilhelmine Germany and not afflicted by their American counterparts' chilling memories of earlier but enduring schisms resulting from doctrinal disagreements. British Friends wholeheartedly embraced theological modernism; they actively recruited a small, new working-class membership through the Adult School Movement, which engaged the energies of a generation of Friends, and, together with their other benevolent activities, introduced them to the realities of life across the class divide; they adopted a Christian Socialist or at least a Social Gospel perspective; and they became increasingly involved in the overlapping worlds of Fabian Socialism and the 'New Liberalism' in late Victorian and Edwardian England. A renewed commitment to social service and activism gave Friends a sense of religious purpose, as participants in the common liberal Protestant design to perfect the Brotherhood of Man and to begin building the Kingdom of God on earth by the unselfish efforts of men and women of reason and goodwill. At the same time as it took them out of their sectarian isolation, they were also able to interpret this work as re-establishing their connection with original and historic Quakerism.[8]

British and mid-Atlantic Friends were closely linked by bonds of family, visiting, common denominational magazines and even by business, so it was natural that the modernizers' solutions to common problems of faith would swiftly be disseminated among the Americans.[9] The principal agent of change among, first, the Philadelphia Orthodox, and later American Quakerism more generally, was Rufus M. Jones (1863–1948). Jones served from 1893 as instructor in, and later professor of, philosophy at Haverford College, where most of the male Orthodox proceeded on graduating from the Friends' day or boarding schools in the Philadelphia region; he was also editor of *The American Friend*, the leading denominational monthly. He collaborated closely with the British modernizers in a common project aimed at renewing Quakers' theology, spirituality and sense of a distinctive religious identity and purpose.[10]

Jones's task was in some ways easier than his British Friends, at least as far as reaching the Philadelphia Orthodox was concerned: the latter were a small, concentrated community of overlapping family groups, relatively homogeneous in social background and outlook, and when their young men went to Haverford, they all had to take at least one course with him.[11] In other ways, it was much harder: American Quakerism's divisions prevented the modernist impulse from spreading far beyond the mid-Atlantic city-regions; even in Philadelphia itself, ethnic, religious and class barriers made it much more difficult for bourgeois WASPs to reach out to, or even sympathize with, their working-class immigrant neighbours, than in more culturally homogeneous milieus like the Cadbury family's Birmingham or the Rowntrees' York.[12]

In addition, American Friends did not at this time experience as great a revitalizing challenge to their most distinctive core conviction. For them, pacifism remained fairly unproblematic, unexamined, a commitment without cost; in Britain, a great imperial power engaged in the brutalities of the Boer War of 1899–1902, then embroiled in the international rivalries and arms races leading up to World War I, members of a denomination devoted to the removal of force from human affairs were compelled to begin some hard thinking. Their opposition to the Boer War revealed to Friends that, though in most respects they existed comfortably within the world of provincial Liberal Nonconformity, their unwillingness to go along with imperialism and militarism set them apart from their community. Becoming 'outsiders' was a price many were willing to pay for their religious convictions; and, having become outsiders on one great issue, some of them felt free, even compelled, to embark on wide-ranging social criticism. Faith in the inevitability of human progress was soon questioned: the material prosperity of Atlantic capitalism provided reasons and resources for international conflict as well as the potential for social advancement. Capitalism itself came to be viewed through a Hobsonian, even Leninist frame of reference: it rested on inequality and exploitation at home and resulted in conflicts between individuals, classes and nations. The connected challenges of the Boer War, the pre-war social unrest and the uneasy Edwardian peace therefore encouraged a thoroughgoing modernization of British Quakerism which extended well beyond its original areas – theology, spirituality and the details of denominational practice – to include an extensive engagement with radical, or at least reformist, politics.[13]

No such changes occurred in the United States. The most that happened was a faint impulse toward Progressivism – stronger, it seems, among Quaker women making their way in the worlds of the settlement house and social work, and in some ways substituting the religion of reform for their ancestral faith, than it was for their male contemporaries.[14]

Encounters with Progressivism

Philadelphia Friends before the Great War were generally politically conservative – if they involved themselves in public affairs at all. Their most sustained commitment was to successive, largely futile attempts to clean up the city's notoriously corrupt Republican political machine.[15] Most proved resistant to Rufus Jones's social gospel, at the same time as many accepted him as a modernizer of their religious beliefs. As late as 1912, he was still bemoaning American Quakerism's failure of political imagination:

> [S]ocial service is an inherent part of our heritage from the past, but ... we as a religious people are not awake to the call of this age for spiritual light and leading in the solution of the great social and economic problems that confront us ... For the most part Friends have not yet caught the vision nor have they prepared themselves for what is to be one of the most impressive undertakings of the Twentieth Century, the conquest of unnecessary disease, the banishment of unnecessary poverty, the transformation of environments which breed and foster disease and sin, the spiritualizing of both capital and labor and the recovery of faith in the actual coming of the Kingdom of God in the world.[16]

But the social gospel message was actually striking chords with some in his audience. One of the most influential among them was Morris Evans Leeds (1869–1952), a leading member of the local Quaker and business elites. Leeds was a scientist, a successful entrepreneur and a deeply-committed birthright Friend; educated in Friends' schools and at Haverford, he chose his wife, golfing and vacation companions, closest business associates and partners in a wide range of charitable endeavours – all from within the narrow confines of the Orthodox community. By the late 1900s, Leeds was backing Jones's call, and in some ways developing it, because as a businessman and an employer of labour he was daily confronted by a whole series of moral and practical questions about how a convinced liberal Quaker ought to make his religion operative in his everyday life.[17]

To begin with, Leeds's argument sounded like that of a technocratic Progressive. The application of inanimate sources of power and of scientific knowledge to industrial production was creating a revolution in economic and social organization and ushering in an age of abundance, of limitless possibilities for improvement.[18] But this materialistic analysis led smoothly to a moral conclusion: since poverty was no longer inevitable, 'economic justice and the best interests of the race as a whole, demand that every individual who is willing at the proper age to do his fair share of the world's work, should always be in a position to earn at least the necessities of life, in exchange for a reasonable amount of work performed under healthful conditions.' This condition of affairs was now possible; it was desirable – but it was not normal. Bad housing, poor education, child labour, low and irregular wages, excessive hours, industrial accidents, seasonal and cyclical unemployment – all of these blighted workers' lives. Leeds did not blame the poor for their poverty and had moved beyond the old certainty that it resulted from their 'idleness and vice'; rather, the moral failings of the poor, as well as their material insecurity, were the result of 'lack of opportunity'. Leeds had become a thoroughgoing environmentalist, not at all given to the individualistic-moralistic or hereditarian explanations of poverty and inequality so common among his entrepreneurial contemporaries.[19]

Leeds's conclusions about the nature of the good society were profoundly egalitarian – 'the existence of pressing need for a more equitable distribution of the world's wealth needs no argument'. They were deeply rooted in personal religious convictions, whose detailed content one can trace in the summary of the teachings of Jesus which he wrote for his own guidance during a return trip across the Atlantic in 1912–1913:

> Wealth is a very great hindrance to righteousness and should be disposed of and used for the public good. Efforts to accumulate it are at least dangerous and perhaps wrong ... The poor, the hungry and the mourners are promised compensation in the future and are pronounced blessed, and a reversal of condition is also foretold for the rich, happy and well fed.[20]

Leeds, and the contemporaries who shared his beliefs, were driven in part by the guilt of people who had come to think of themselves as the too-comfortable members of an imperfect society, whose private privilege depended on the very structures of inequality they saw as the greatest obstacles to its perfection. Doing *something* became a moral obligation. The question was, what? And how? Liberal Quakers' theology might be radical, but their politics were at best reformist, and they were strongly inclined toward moderate, gradual, rational change.

Leeds himself was neither a socialist nor a believer in the simple redistribution of surplus wealth. He was, first and foremost, an employer and saw the solution in the making available, somehow, of more good jobs within the existing capitalist system. But how? What could individuals do toward this end? As consumers they could of course shun 'establishments which do not treat their employees fairly and thus bring pressure to raise the standard'. But Leeds offered a rather dismissive judgment on this key strategy of the National Consumers' League, considering that Quaker women were among its leaders and loyal followers. Their method, inspired by Abolitionists' boycotts of slave-made goods, was good for the soul and useful as a publicity technique, but no more than superficially effective. Concerned Quakers had to become more than discriminating shoppers. They had to be active citizens, abandoning their conservatism and quietism to reach out beyond their meeting communities and enter fully into the Progressive coalitions then forming:

> Reforms of the fundamental character which we are considering can best be advanced by organized effort ... [I]t is by aiding such organizations, where their methods are right and deserve support, that we have the best opportunity to advance the cause of social and economic justice.[21]

They should favour bodies promoting protective legislation for women and children, which could be considered to be an unproblematic extension of established Quaker concerns for oppressed or disadvantaged minority groups; they should even support labour unions, despite reservations about their conflictual tendencies.

Finally, Quaker employers like himself had a special opportunity and responsibility to initiate improvement within the spheres they could influence directly: the companies they owned and ran. They 'may do considerable to further the cause of economic injustice [*sic*] in spite of the limitations placed on them' by competitive pressures. Welfare capitalism therefore became a personal obligation, given that businessmen – particularly in America, with its weak state regulation and feeble unions – had more control over working conditions than anyone else.[22]

Quaker masters were traditionally required to take responsibility for the material and moral welfare of their servants: just as Leeds's Progressivism blended the technocratic and the moralistic, so too his search for an ethically defensible relation between employers and employees would build on this domestic model and adapt it to the demands of a bureaucratic and democratic age. And, just as modernist Quakerism was a transatlantic project in which, essentially, the British took the initiative and (some) Americans followed, here too Leeds and his fellows would have their cousins' experience to build on.

English Quaker confectionery manufacturers – the Rowntrees of York and Cadburys of Bournville – turned the 1900s into a Chocolate Age in the development of British personnel management by their early and comprehensive innovations in employment relations and employee welfare. These and other non-Quaker American and European pioneers (notably Ernst Abbé of the Carl Zeiss optical works at Jena, which Leeds had visited as a graduate student) were Leeds's mentors. He advised other Quakers to 'help the cause of economic justice ... by keeping in touch with the[se] very interesting commercial experiments ..., so as to help in the dissemination of knowledge about them ... Such experiments ... are in the nature of preventive [sic] medicine for the ills of the social body and where they succeed their methods should become known and be copied as widely as possible.'[23]

And copy them he did, when in 1915 he introduced what were, in American terms, pioneering welfare measures and personnel management programmes once his firm grew too large for him to manage employee relations personally. Leeds combined an 'efficiency' and a 'social justice' agenda within his reforms and also began to cede his personal ownership and control by sharing them with his associates and employees. His aim was to find a way to motivate, reward and include his co-workers as co-owners of a growing company which was evolving away from being a small, simple proprietary enterprise. Management and controlling ownership would broaden out and remain united in the same persons; absentee capital would be deprived of any right to anything more than a fair return. In particular, unsympathetic outside investors would be deprived of any power to subvert the 'co-operative commonwealth' Leeds was intent on creating within a dynamic company driven by scientific research and ethical imperatives.[24]

In all his work and thought Leeds was the very model of the active citizen, the enlightened businessman, the middle-class Christian as Progressive. He was cautious and moderate, aware of the complexity of the problems he was confronting and of the constraints under which he and his liberal associates operated. '[J]ustice is by no means a simple matter and ... the desire to do right is not in itself enough, but ... we must make a serious effort to find out what is right'. His aim was to encourage 'orderly evolution rather than revolution'. No total solution of the social problem was imminent, but 'a reactionary position and failure to support' agencies working toward it could 'but encourage the more radical and revolutionary proposals of socialists and other doctrinaire schools'.[25]

Driven by serious internalized convictions, by his commitment to moderate social change and by his belief in the possibilities of progress, directed by men and women of education, reason, and goodwill, towards the achievement of some portion of the Kingdom of God on earth, Leeds developed his ideas further in the pre-war years. He was responsive to the *Zeitgeist* and became a minor prophet, a 'minister of reform', ready to stand at Armageddon and battle for the Lord, convinced that, as a movement, Friends should shift their attention from individual sin to social redemption. They should join the forces of social reform wholeheartedly,

> an army which has perhaps been poorly organized and disciplined, but which has nevertheless been engaged in successful warfare and which needs more than anything else a carefully worked out plan of campaign and the loyalty and devotion of a large body of men and women who do not only have consciences sensitive to all kinds of injustice, but that enduring conviction which comes from thorough and wide experience ... [Friends must] fit ourselves to play our part in helping society so to mould its conscious will that it will proceed with orderly activity to progressive steps of social betterment.[26]

But before Friends had time to come round to a group commitment to this new definition of their social activist responsibility, something happened to wrench the ground of reason, gradualism and measured optimism from under their feet. That something was total war involving the two countries, Britain and Germany. War as brute reality, not metaphor, created massive problems for the Quaker community and was of the greatest cultural importance to educated Friends. Ironically, what finally galvanized them to accept, belatedly but with enduring effect, the message Rufus Jones had preached and Leeds and others had clearly endorsed, was not the years of Progressive persuasion, but rather the shock of war. For most of those Protestants – particularly ministers and theologians – who emerged from the war experience as convinced pacifists, their route to this destination led from an initial Social Gospel concern. For Quakers, uniquely, their particular road went mostly in the other direction.[27]

War and Reconstruction

Philip Benjamin stressed that 'If the pacifist testimony was the most singular of Friends' religious tenets, it was the least tested in the late nineteenth century'. They had protested against the oppression of Native Americans, the war against Spain and against proposals for universal military training in Pennsylvania high schools. But in pre-war America, with its tiny, volunteer armed forces and free security, they had not had to lay their consciences on the line. Their pacifism, in Charles Chatfield's judgment, 'was often nominal and passive, and with few exceptions, they merged into the broad peace movement of the Progressive Era'.[28]

As Martin Ceadel describes their Edwardian British 'pacificist' contemporaries, they were 'in favour of peace and arbitration and opposed to militarism and settling disputes by war'. This undemanding creed was rooted in a thoroughly optimistic analysis of the international relations of modern liberal capitalism. As societies became more complex, nations more economically interdependent, populaces more rational (and, if you were an Evangelical Protestant, more godly), and leaders more far-sighted, so the possibilities of war receded and the attainability of peace through diplomacy increased. This genial worldview was shattered by the events of 1914–1918. Friends were unable to remain for long apart from and above this battle. Eventually they were compelled to declare themselves for or against the powerful currents of national sentiment sweeping America toward active involvement in the war on the Allies' side.[29]

The Philadelphia Orthodox were the most solid in maintaining their traditional 'witness to peace' right through this ordeal. The effect was to separate them further than usual from their fellow-citizens and even from their upper-middle-class milieu. They found themselves projected beyond the bounds of the national consensus, keeping strange and unrespectable company, thinking new and challenging thoughts. In the opinion of their Military Intelligence watchdogs, it was 'curious that the Quakers, who of all people, have scrupulously tried to preserve themselves from contamination with [sic] the world, should find themselves comfortable in the company of enemies, traitorous citizens, political profiteers of the Socialist type, and with some whose associates grade into the criminal classes.' But, pejorative epithets aside, it was more or less true. The organizations they founded or supported, including the Fellowship of Reconciliation, the Collegiate Anti-Militarism League, the Liberty Defense Union and National Civil Liberties Bureau (forerunners of the American Civil Liberties Union), and the Women's International League for Peace and Freedom, were all suspect in the eyes of the government. Their names found their way into Military Intelligence files because of the causes they backed and the periodicals to which they attempted to subscribe, some of which were declared unmailable. Their neighbours reported on subversive teaching in Friends' schools. Pillars of the community and leaders in mugwumpish civic reform like publisher John Winston and banker J. Henry Scattergood found their companies raided, bank accounts raked over and meetings in the privacy of their own homes betrayed to the authorities.[30]

The Philadelphia Orthodox's response to the war mirrored that of their British Friends, who had already been forced to confront the implications of their pacifism more seriously than their American counterparts even before the war, and then had to deal with growing pressures on young men to enlist in the armed forces, and eventually with the compulsory draft. Part of their answer was to provide a form of alternative service, an idea promoted by the country banker William C. Braithwaite who '[r]ealiz[ed] the difficulties of many young men whose principles forbade them to fight and who yet wanted to help their country, and could not bear to remain in safety whilst others were hazarding their lives'. Out of this perception came the Friends' Ambulance Unit, for which American Friends raised at least $5,000 a month, and for which Rufus Jones selected volunteers; the Friends' War Victims Relief Committee; and the Friends' Service Committee, set up to provide 'help and counsel to those who were suffering for their faith as conscientious objectors'.[31]

All too soon, Philadelphia Friends had to deal with the same forces – a belligerent public opinion, an all-devouring wartime state. They also had to cope with the way in which the conflicting demands of conscience exacerbated traditional divisions within their community. The Hicksites, being less separate in doctrine and lifestyle than the Orthodox from the Philadelphia Protestant mainstream, did not officially renounce pacifism, but they often did not cling to it either. Swarthmore was the only Quaker college to establish an Army Training Corps; Hicksites denounced Orthodox pacifists and their own to Military Intelligence; the Hicksite Attorney-General A. Mitchell Palmer displayed scant regard for the civil liberties of opponents of war. Most divisively, a large group of prominent Hicksites attacked the Orthodox position in a widely-reprinted public statement which was an odd combination of philosophical argument and scathing rhetoric. They ended up by calling on Jesus, 'a religious teacher in *normal* times' [emphasis in original] in their support, throwing in His more warlike sayings, and lining up squarely behind the 'Cause of Civilization' and 'the President of the United States', which were, for all practical purposes, indistinguishable. Not surprisingly, this onslaught on the continuing relevance of traditional Quaker beliefs was welcomed by

Woodrow Wilson himself. It was also encouraged (and perhaps got up in the first place) by Military Intelligence, who were delighted to have a way of undermining the moral effect of the (largely Orthodox) Quaker witness to peace in a country demanding total submission to the dictates of war.[32]

Their manifesto illustrated the breadth of the divide separating many of the Hicksites from most of the Orthodox on this issue. But it does not seem to have had much effect. It was in essence a response to the *success* of absolutist Quaker pacifism in winning broad support within its own community, and even a grudging tolerance outside of it. The way the leaders of Orthodoxy managed this was by taking another leaf out of their British cousins' book. They offered unconditional support and encouragement to those of their young men who would not enlist or fight; and they provided alternative service opportunities to make this course more acceptable to the draft resisters themselves, to the public and to the government. As Charles Chatfield suggests, this kind of activity mitigated pacifists' isolation from the shared idealism of the democratic war effort and limited the risk that such enthusiasm would prove contagious and undermine their commitment.[33]

Rufus Jones became chair of the American Friends Service Committee (AFSC), set up at the end of April 1917 to give effect to this plan. As he later explained, 'Friends could not accept exemption from military service and at the same time do nothing to express their positive faith and devotion in the great human crisis'. The Philadelphia Yearly Meeting had laid out the theological argument for this service commitment in their public statement a month earlier, that opposition to war did not entail

> a weak neutrality toward evil. For us, as for [Christ], it means a life of action devoted to the heroic purpose of overcoming evil with good. The unspeakable sufferings of humanity are now calling us and all men to larger sacrifices and more earnest endeavors to put this faith into practice. To such endeavors we dedicate ourselves.[34]

The AFSC offered, in its historian Lester Jones's words, 'a unified leadership to which that somewhat dazed and inarticulate mass [the Quaker community] gladly turned for direction'. Divided though they were on the question of absolute pacifism, they were nevertheless able to unite in support of the AFSC's programme of unproblematic good works. The Orthodox, the Hicksites, and to a much lesser extent the more numerous Evangelical Friends of the Mid- and Far West, poured in more than a quarter of a million dollars in 1917 and twice that amount in 1918. The main original objective was to aid the British Friends' work, but when America entered the war and started its own draft, the direct provision of alternative service became even more vital. Rufus Jones and Haverford President Isaac Sharpless wrote repeatedly to Woodrow Wilson seeking guarantees that the work the AFSC proposed (reconstruction of devastated areas in eastern France) would be acceptable to the authorities. The War Department's eventual readiness to cooperate, which resulted in only a very few absolutely uncompromising Quaker draft-resisters going to prison, was probably helped by the fact that the official in charge of these matters was an old Haverfordian.[35]

In order to finance this massive effort, and to organize it, the 'spiritual' leaders of the AFSC, including Sharpless, Jones, Jones's brother-in-law, neighbour and fellow-Haverford theologian Henry J. Cadbury, and Cadbury's father-in-law Thomas Brown, the former headmaster of the leading Orthodox boarding school, naturally turned to the high-minded Orthodox businessmen who were their friends and relatives, former students, golf and canoeing partners and usual companions in philanthropy.

As a result, the latter became deeply involved with the AFSC's work. Morris Evans Leeds joined J. Henry Scattergood, his company's financial backer, on an exploratory visit to France and England in June 1917. They returned with a firm plan of action, whose implementation in the field was overseen by paper box-making machinery manufacturer Charles Evans, while Leeds handled the Philadelphia end of the AFSC's operations. Nor did the altruistic capitalists' commitment decline with the end of the war: plumbing fittings manufacturer Bob Yarnall left his own business in 1919–1920 to help J. Henry's brother Alfred with the *Kinderspeisung*, the AFSC's great child-feeding effort in a starving Germany. He was joined in that enterprise by his old crew companion from Penn, and successor as leader of the Philadelphia engineering community during the years 1910–1920, Arthur C. Jackson of Miller Lock, who had already served as the AFSC's purchasing agent. In 1924, when the Friends' Germany-Austria programme was coming to an end, box-manufacturer Henry Tatnall Brown, married to a Scattergood, went to organize its wrapping-up.[36]

Leeds, Evans, Yarnall and others absented themselves from businesses which were booming because of the war economy, thereby imposing a burden on their partners and associates who were left managing the shop. This was a real sacrifice by proprietors of firms with at most a handful of policy-making executives. Companies like these could not avoid benefiting from the war, even though they were not directly involved in munitions making. Giving freely of their time to the AFSC, and doubtless of their money too, was one way for their owners to deal with their resulting sense of guilt.[37]

But it was not enough. The AFSC represented, as Philip Benjamin wrote, 'the culmination of the trend toward activism already at work in Philadelphia meetings' before the war, and 'generated an excitement in the Quaker community which had not been felt since the programmes for Indians and the freemen' after the Civil War. However, the aroused consciences of the Philadelphia Orthodox were not satisfied with merely palliative action to help the victims of war. Instead, they turned a sharp critical attention on what was wrong in their society that it should have produced such a calamity in the first place.[38]

Here, too, they were inspired by the British example. In 1911, London Yearly Meeting had adopted a new 'query' to guide its members' conduct: 'Do you seek to understand the causes of social evils and do you take your right share in the endeavour to remove them?' In Britain, theological modernism and social activism were closely linked before the end of the nineteenth century. Growing dissatisfaction with a merely do-gooding engagement with 'social problems', and close contact with a burgeoning working-class membership encouraged Friends' gradual radicalization. This cause was fostered by the Socialist Quaker Society (whose socialism was mostly of the moral, not Marxist, variety). Its analysis of capitalism was rhetorically blunt. Capitalist societies were soiled and riven by inequality, oppression and injustice; they rested on force; their internal failings produced international conflict; they violated Friends' conceptions of the inherent worth and equality of all humans. Capitalism was a form of 'economic slavery' against which Quakers should struggle as they had against chattel slavery.[39]

The Socialist Quakers were only a ginger group before the war, but the conflict seemed to confirm their analysis. Witnessing to peace in time of total war alienated many English Friends from middle-class respectability and its old certainties, and from the Liberal Party itself. Collaboration in draft-resistance brought them into unprecedentedly close contact with members of the Labour Party and the labour movement, revolutionizing both their political behaviour and their attitude toward industrial relations. They became convinced that their commitments to peace, equality and community must permeate all aspects of their life. So in 1915, London Yearly Meeting established a new committee on War and the Social Order to think through its response to the crisis.[40]

Two years later, Philadelphia Yearly Meeting followed suit. A group including Leeds, Yarnall, his friend and partner Bernard Waring, Alfred Scattergood, Henry Brown and other executives, petitioned the meeting, stressing the growing 'realization ... that we should more completely live up to the ideals suggested in our Queries' and that Quakers 'should seek more fully to recognize what is implied by our stand against all war.'

The war in Europe has laid bare the fact that Twentieth Century Civilization falls far below the standard of Christ in industrial and national as well as in international life. We have discovered the seeds of war in our social order. If Love can and should be trusted to the uttermost and made the ruling principle of action in international affairs it follows it can be and should be made supreme in social and industrial life. It seems therefore, that part of the great task before us is to discover what practical steps the Society of Friends should take in applying Christ's teaching of love and brotherhood in business, in the home, in politics and in all other relations of life.

They were 'baffled and perplexed', but also surprisingly hopeful:

We believe that a great opportunity lies before us at this time. The world is in deep need of light and leadership ... If with the sin and agony of the world pressing on our hearts, with the vision of so many men and women in Europe laying down their lives for the right as they see it, we also are willing to give our time, our possessions, our lives to establish the Kingdom of God on earth, who can say what great work God may accomplish ...[41]

Yearly Meeting responded by setting up a 'Committee on Social and Industrial Problems' (soon shortened to 'Social Order Committee'), whose active membership and that of the AFSC overlapped, and which was full of the usual suspects from the Military Intelligence 'enemies lists'. Bernard Waring was its chair, Morris Leeds its secretary. They were charged 'to weightily consider the part which the religious Society of Friends should take in the present day application of efforts to promote the Kingdom of God on earth, particularly as it relates to social, political and industrial conditions'. Their agenda was quite explicit: the critical analysis of the competitive and wage systems, that is, of basic capitalist institutions which were at variance with Friends' beliefs.[42] But what did this mean in practice?

Two members, moved by the millennarian spirit common on the secular as well as the religious left, argued that fundamental social change was possible because of the war, and that it was 'surely more necessary to avert war between classes than between nations'. Others were not so radical: agricultural machinery manufacturer Samuel Leeds Allen suggested that they should explore possibilities for change *within* the existing social order. It was 'impossible to eliminate all troubles, but let us commence by hoping they may be alleviated'. The patriarchal Allen recommended a mix of state and private action: legislation for minimum wages and maximum hours; provision of public work when the market economy could not sustain full employment; and welfare work conducted in a Christian spirit by employers. Haverford's President Sharpless responded to the group's evident uncertainty by advising Leeds to pursue open-ended investigation of 'the various efforts that have been made in the past to correct [capitalism's] evils, or replace it entirely with a better order of society,' aided by 'lectures on the subject by people who know more about the subject than you do, if that supposition is possible'.[43]

The Committee accepted Sharpless's suggestion. It divided its work among several different interest groups which discussed matters most directly concerning them. The groups in turn organized programmes of lectures by a roll-call of social reformers, enlightened businessmen, trade union leaders, educators, and others from the Progressive centre and non-revolutionary left, which became a regular feature of the social and intellectual life of Philadelphia Quakerism thereafter. But it would be wrong to dismiss the Social Order Committee as having resulted in little more than the creation of a series of talking-shops. This was a voluntary and quite effective programme of political re-education, which produced (for example) a renewed, active and thereafter unbroken commitment to the cause of racial equality, and a somewhat less full-blooded commitment to 'industrial democracy' which was of immediate practical significance.

One of the Social Order Committee's largest and most active groups of supporters, whose wealth and generosity underpinned the rest of its work, was its Business Problems (originally Managing Employers) Group, set up in October 1917.[44] The creation of the Business Problems Group was a natural response to the class backgrounds of the Philadelphia Orthodox, and to the social criticism in which some of them were so deeply engaged. In 1920, 87 percent of those in paid work, and whose occupations were known, were professionals (39 percent), in salaried employment (24 percent), proprietors and senior executives of businesses (15 percent), or professors and teachers (9 percent). Of those not in paid work, about half were non-wage earning homemakers, and most of the remainder were rentiers. The community was overwhelmingly composed of members of the comfortable middle class, doing rather well out of the very social order of which some of them were so critical. The uneasiness this caused many of them rarely resulted in political radicalization, but there was a more moderate response possible, which their leaders pointed out. As the Committee summed it up,

> When [the Society of Friends] has perceived wrongs in institutions in which it has been involved it has tried first of all to clear itself of complicity in those wrongs. It has believed that permanent good to society can best be brought about by the influence of conviction and

example which spreads from the individual to the group and from the group to the community. This was Jesus' teaching and method of work.[45]

The Son of God's method of social change – with which who could disagree? – was 'an appeal to the conscience and the arousing of a sense of duty in the favored class, not a call to rebellion or to an assertion of their rights on the part of the poor'. And, Henry J. Cadbury pointed out, 'As the membership of the Friends lies almost wholly in the favored class it is all the more important that we observe this technique of Jesus.' The employing capitalists among them bore a specially heavy responsibility to 'stir our own consciences and appeal to our own sense of duty'. Out of this stern self-examination and inner direction concrete results could follow, because they owned and controlled the firms they ran. Leeds, Samuel Allen, Bob Yarnall and Bernard Waring, the Scattergood brothers, Charles Evans, Arthur Jackson and other AFSC activists were the Business Problems Group's leaders or among its founder members.[46]

What did they do? Over the next several years, and indeed throughout the 1920s, as the prospects for large-scale social reconstruction receded, some of them (notably Leeds) turned their companies into nationally-renowned examples of welfare capitalism combined with a growing measure of employer-inspired industrial democracy. They lobbied within the business organizations they joined, like the MMA and its national counterparts, to win them round, too, to some less troublesome Progressive causes, notably the crusade against insecurity and unemployment. In general, they helped keep alive the flickering flame of liberal optimism through a bleak time. Morris Leeds and his fellows enjoyed great prestige in the New Era, and even erstwhile labour-liberals and future New Dealers attached their realistically-limited hopes for social progress to them and their projects. In John Fitch's words, Progressive employers 'constitute[d] merely an oasis in a great desert. But it is an oasis that is very cheering and full of promise. I have faith to believe that it will grow.'[47]

Conclusion

In fact, it did not: the Depression destroyed welfare capitalism and business Progressivism, whether their inspiration had been religious or secular, and ushered in a new and uncomfortable era of class politics and government intervention. Leeds and his friends' day was past, but they played their part in easing the tensions of change, acting as conciliators in labour disputes who enjoyed both sides' trust, helping to smooth the transition from welfare capitalism to welfare state. As war clouds gathered over Europe, they also attempted to capitalize on the goodwill they hoped the *Kinderspeisung* had won them by trying to intercede with the Nazis and buy the privilege of emigration for more Jews. Within the United States, they worked to ease the immigration and assimilation of these refugees, and joined themselves to a variety of liberal groups for whom the challenge of totalitarianism had increased their sensitivity to civil liberties and race relations issues, where the AFSC and associated 'Quakerly' organizations like the Fellowship of Reconciliation had taken a leading role since the war.

In all these ways, they helped complete the process, begun in the 1890s, whereby American Quakerism transformed itself from a marginal, declining collection of mutually hostile sects, into a religious movement with broad social purposes, a continuing this-worldly meaning for its members and prestige and influence far outweighing its small (but no longer shrinking) size. Curiously, given the divisive immediate effects of the Great War, one of the lasting benefits of the shared pride in, and identification with, the AFSC's continuing work, was the healing of the Hicksite/Orthodox schism. As a result, the combined influence of the seaboard Quaker communities was enhanced, and they, not the more numerous but less distinctive conservative Evangelicals of the Mid- and Far West, came to stand and speak for the whole diverse Religious Society of Friends in the minds of outsiders. It was their kind of Quakerism which exerted powerful attractions on a stream of new adherents. These 'Quakers by convincement' were gathered from co-workers in the variety of civil liberties, social justice, and pacifist causes to which seaboard, metropolitan, and college town Quakers have continued to devote their efforts ever since the Great War brought them out of their sectarian shells, and thereby, perhaps, saved them from ordinariness and oblivion.

This paper has gone some of the way towards explaining this outcome. Clearly, the Great War was the catalyst for change rather than its underlying cause. The basic forces for change were generated by the transatlantic modernizers' response to the spiritual crisis of the Gilded Age, and their identification of social activism as a way of making their religion once again meaningful. Much of the argument and programmatic content of the Quaker social gospel was scarcely distinguishable, and largely derived, from their liberal Protestant and secular Progressive contemporaries. And yet Quakers' distinctive religious convictions did make a difference: in particular, the commitments to equality, community and peace made them peculiarly sensitive to issues of domestic social injustice, and exposed them to public hostility during times of international conflict. The first such major war in the American Century was from 1917 to 1919; ironically, one might argue that the resultant lasting revitalization of (parts of) American Quakerism, with its incalculable benefits for the subsequent course of American liberalism, has been a significant positive by-product of the fact that injustice and conflict have never since been absent, for those with eyes to see.

Notes

1. Hugh Barbour and J. William Frost, *The Quakers* (Westport, CT: Greenwood, 1988), esp. Chapters 17–20; Carol and John Stoneburner, eds, *The Influence of Quaker Women on American History: Biographical Studies* (Lewiston, ME: Edwin Mellen, 1986); James M. McPherson, *The Abolitionist Legacy: From Reconstruction to the NAACP* (Princeton, NJ: Princeton University Press, 1975); Milton S. Katz, *Ban the Bomb: a History of SANE, the Committee for a Sane Nuclear Policy, 1957–1985* (Westport, CT: Greenwood, 1986); Douglas McAdam, *Freedom Summer* (New York: Oxford University Press, 1988), 174.
2. Stanley Coben, *A. Mitchell Palmer: Politician* (New York: Columbia University Press, 1963); George H. Nash, *The Life of Herbert Hoover: The Engineer 1877–1914* (New York: Norton, 1983); Roger Morris, *Richard Milhous Nixon: The Rise of an American Politician* (New York: Holt, 1990).
3. Howell J. Harris, *The Rise and Fall of the Open Shop: Masters, Unions, and Men in the Philadelphia Metal Trades, 1890–1940* (New York: Cambridge University Press, forthcoming – 1999).
4. The most prominent of these were Morris Evans Leeds, Bernard G. Waring and D. Robert Yarnall, for whom see William P. Vogel, *Precision, People and Progress: A Business Philosophy at Work* (Philadelphia: Leeds and Northrup Co., 1949) and C. Elliott Barb, *The Yarway Story: An Adventure in Serving* (Philadelphia: Yarnall-Waring Corporation, 1958). For the AFSC, see Rufus M. Jones, *A Service of Love in Wartime: American Friends' Relief Work in Europe, 1917–1919* (New York: Macmillan, 1920); Lester M. Jones, *Quakers in Action: Recent Humanitarian and Reform Activities of American Quakers* (New York: Macmillan, 1929); Mary Hoxie Jones, *Swords Into Ploughshares: An Account of the American Friends Service Committee 1917–1937* (New York: Macmillan, 1937); and Clarence E. Pickett, *For More Than Bread: An Autobiographical Account of Twenty Two Years' Work With the American Friends Service Committee* (Boston, Little, Brown & Co., 1953).
5. Figures calculated from Barbour and Frost, *The Quakers*, 234–5. For the history of Quaker divisions, see esp. Robert W. Doherty, *The Hicksite Separation: A Sociological Analysis of Religious Schism in Early 19th Century America* (New Brunswick, NJ: Rutgers University Press, 1967); H. Larry Ingle, *Quakers in Conflict: The Hicksite Separation* (Knoxville: University of Tennessee Press, 1986); and Thomas D. Hamm, *The Transformation of American Quakerism: Orthodox Friends, 1800–1907* (Bloomington: Indiana University Press, 1988). For the quote, see Hamm, 'The Legacy of Allen Jay', *Quaker Life* 27.1 (January–February 1986): 13–15 at page 15.
6. Philip S. Benjamin, *The Philadelphia Quakers in the Industrial Age* (Phila-

delphia: Temple University Press, 1976), 159. There were about as many Quakers in the Philadelphia region alone as in all of Great Britain.
7. For contemporary developments in Britain, see esp. Elizabeth Isichei, *Victorian Quakers* (Oxford, England: Oxford University Press, 1970); quote from Francis Frith *et al.*, *A Reasonable Faith: Short Religious Essays for the Times* (London: Macmillan, 1884).
8. The most recent and accessible discussion of the modernization of British Quakerism is Hope Hay Hewison, *Hedge of Wild Almonds: South Africa, the 'Pro-Boers' and the Quaker Conscience* (London: James Currey, 1989), esp. 22–3, 43–8. See also J. Wilhelm Rowntree and Henry Bryan Binns, *History of the Adult School Movement* (London: Headley Bros., 1903) and Peter d'A. Jones, *The Christian Socialist Revival 1877–1914: Religion, Class, and Social Conscience in Late-Victorian England* (Princeton, NJ: Princeton University Press, 1968), 367–89. For the best recent account of this postmillenial vision, see Paul T. Phillips, *A Kingdom on Earth: Anglo-American Social Christianity, 1880–1940* (University Park: Penn State University Press, 1996).
9. See e.g. Edwin B. Bronner, *'The Other Branch': London Yearly Meeting and the Hicksites 1827–1912* (London: Friends Historical Society, 1975).
10. For Jones, see his memoir *The Trail of Life in the Middle Years* (New York: Macmillan, 1934) and Elizabeth G. Vining, *Friend of Life: The Biography of Rufus M. Jones* (Philadelphia: Lippincott, 1958).
11. For the sectarian and clannish nature of Philadelphia Quakerism, see esp. Margaret Hope Bacon, *Let This Life Speak: The Legacy of Henry Joel Cadbury* (Philadelphia: University of Pennsylvania Press, 1987), 3; E. Digby Baltzell, *Philadelphia Gentlemen: The Making of a National Upper Class* (Glencoe, IL: Free Press, 1958), esp. Chapters 10–11; Logan Pearsall Smith, *Unforgotten Years* (London: Constable, 1938); Francis J. Stokes, Jr, *Stokes Cope Emlen Evans Genealogy: Genealogical Charts of Four Closely Associated Germantown Families* (Philadelphia: author, 1982), 3–4.
12. Iolo A. Williams, *The Firm of Cadbury 1831–1931* (London: Constable, 1931) and Charles Dellheim, 'The Creation of a Company Culture: Cadburys, 1861–1931', *American Historical Review* 92 (1987): 13–44; Anne Vernon, *A Quaker Business Man: The Life of Joseph Rowntree, 1836–1924* (London: George Allen and Unwin, 1958), Elfrida Vipont, *Arnold Rowntree: A Life* (London: Bannisdale Press, 1955) and Asa Briggs, *Social Thought and Social Action: A Study of the Work of Seebohm Rowntree 1871–1954* (London: Longmans, 1961); Gillian Wagner, *The Chocolate Conscience* (London: Chatto & Windus, 1987) – for the two remarkable families at the heart of Quaker 'progressivism' in Britain.
13. Hewison, *Hedge of Wild Almonds*, esp. Chapter 8, and Jones, *Christian Socialist Revival*, 367–89.
14. For leading women Progressives who were brought up as Quakers, and in some cases returned to the religion of their ancestors after the religions of reform and even socialism had disappointed, see Stoneburner and Stoneburner, eds, *The Influence of Quaker Women on American History*.
15. Philip S. Benjamin, 'Gentleman Reformers in the Quaker City, 1870–1912,' *Political Science Quarterly* 85 (1970): 61–79.

16. Quoted in Vining, *Friend of Life*, 144; cf. Joshua Rowntree, *Social Service: Its Place in the Society of Friends – the Swarthmore Lecture 1913* (London: Headley, 1913).
17. Vogel, *Precision, People, and Progress* and 'Morris Evans Leeds 1869–1952', *The Cooperator* 9.11 (March 1952): 3, 15. For the key Orthodox educational institutions he and his closest associates attended, see Watson W. Dewees, compiler, *A Brief History of Westtown Boarding School* (Philadelphia: Sherman & Co., 1888) and Helen G. Hole, *Westtown Through the Years* (Westtown, PA: Westtown Alumni Association, 1942); Committee of the Haverford College Alumni Association, *A History of Haverford College for the First Sixty Years of Its Existence* (Philadelphia: Porter & Coates, 1892) and Isaac Sharpless, *The Story of a Small College* (Philadelphia: John C. Winston Co., 1918). Leeds's papers are Accession No. 1127 in the Quaker Collections, Haverford College (hereafter cited as QCHC) – see esp. his letters to his wife; his 1951 'Personnel Security Questionnaire', which lists his affiliations and associates; offprint, John Van Schaick, Jr, 'Cruising Cross the Country, V: The Four Way Lodge', *Universalist Leader* (31 January 1925): 6–7 (an Orthodox Quaker retreat Leeds helped found in the New Jersey Pine Barrens); and *'Down the Fairway' and in the Rough with the Ozone Club from 1901 to 1927* (Philadelphia: privately printed, 1927) – his Orthodox Quaker golf club.
18. This was the heretically optimistic message of Simon Patten, professor at the Quaker-endowed Wharton School of Finance and Commerce at the University of Pennsylvania, and an intellectual leader for the city's reformers – see Daniel M. Fox, *The Discovery of Abundance: Simon N. Patten & the Transformation of Social Theory* (Ithaca, NY: Cornell University Press, 1967).
19. 'The Attitude of Friends Toward Industrial Conditions,' typescript circa 1909, Leeds Papers, box 9.
20. *Ibid.*; Holograph MS, pages 3–6, in file 'New Testament Study', Leeds Papers, box 9, F. 4.
21. Leeds, 'Attitude of Friends.'
22. *Ibid.*
23. *Ibid.*; for the influence of Abbé and Rowntree, see letter to Hadassah Leeds, 26 June 1923, in Leeds Papers, box 5, and typescript MS, 'Ernst Abbé and the Karl Zeiss Stiftung', n.d. (1912 latest date within document), page 4, box 9, F. 3.
24. Daniel Nelson, '"A Newly Appreciated Art:" The Development of Personnel Work at Leeds and Northrup, 1915–1923,' *Business History Review* 44 (1970): 520–35 and 'The Company Union Movement, 1900–1937: A Reexamination,' *Business History Review* 56 (1982): 335–57, are generally reliable, but neglect Leeds's religious motivation, as does C. Canby Balderston, *Executive Guidance of Industrial Relations: An Analysis of the Experience of 25 Companies* (Philadelphia: University of Pennsylvania Press, 1935), 141–54; Vogel, *Precision, People, and Progress*, esp. Chapter 3. Leeds's friends Yarnall and Waring also inaugurated a profit sharing plan in 1915 – Barb, *Yarway Story*, 52.
25. Leeds, 'Attitude of Friends'.

26. Leeds, 'The Social Order: Why Should Friends Study It' (to Germantown Group Preceding Social Order Committee), n.d. but pre-1917, unpaginated twenty pages typescript, Leeds Papers, box 9.
27. John K. Nelson, *The Peace Prophets: American Pacifist Thought, 1919–1941* (Chapel Hill: University of North Carolina Press, 1967), 22–3.
28. Benjamin, *Philadelphia Quakers*, 192; Margaret E. Hirst, *The Quakers in Peace and War: An Account of Their Peace Principles and Practice* (London: The Swarthmore Press, 1923), 450; Chatfield, *For Peace and Justice*, 8; cf. Jones, *A Service of Love in War Time*, 3, and C. Roland Marchand, *The American Peace Movement and Social Reform, 1898–1918* (Princeton, NJ: Princeton University Press, 1972), xiv, 18.
29. Martin Ceadel, *Pacifism in Britain 1914–1945: The Defining of a Faith* (Oxford: Clarendon Press, 1980), 3 (quote), 29; Jones, *Quakers in Action*, 16, esp. 163; cf. A. Neave Brayshaw, *The Quakers: Their Story and Message* (Harrogate: Robert Davis, for the 1905 Committee of Yorkshire Quarterly Meeting, 1921), 132; James Dudley, *The Life of Edward Grubb 1854–1939: A Spiritual Pilgrimage* (London: James Clarke & Co., 1946), 103.
30. Maj. John W. Geary to Col. M. Churchill, 'Quaker Pacifist Activities in Philadelphia: Report,' 16 August 1918, file 99-35, box 137, and attachments – 'The Peace Committee of Philadelphia Yearly Meeting of Friends', 'Fellowship of Reconciliation', 'Collegiate Anti-Militarism League', 'Liberty Defense Union', all 1 August 1918, and 'National Civil Liberties Bureau', 12 August 1918, with consolidated mailing lists for pacifist organizations and magazines; Maj. W. C. Smiley to General Churchill, 'Subject: Radical Activities,' 24 April 1919, and Capt. J. S. Cottrell to Brig. -Gen. Churchill, same title, 16 May 1919, files 10110–92–53 and 60, box 2792 (Quaker schools). Scattergood's acquaintances denounced him as 'entirely too radical' and 'almost insane', though intelligence operatives admitted that as long as he confined himself to his normal philanthropies 'he does good work, but when he crosses over to pacifism or socialism or Christian Love, he begins to utter very dangerous sentiments'. His problem was that 'while well balanced in other ways', he was 'a fanatic on the idea that Christian Love can end the war', and that his family had 'always been rabid Pacifists and wealthy enough to indulge in their propensities in this line.' See file 10175–292, box 2891 – quotes from Office of MI Service to Col. Churchill, 'Subject: John C. Winston Co.,' 12 August 1918, Capt. John W. Geary to Lieut. Col. Churchill, 14 June 1918, file 9771–24, box 2184, and Maj. John W. Geary to Brig. Gen. Churchill, 4 November 1918, file 10175–292. All references to MID Corr., RG165, US National Archives.
31. Isichei, *Victorian Quakers*, 151–2; Edward Grubb, *Does War Promote Industry? An Answer to 'Can We Disarm?'* (London: Headley, 1899); John W. Graham, *War from a Quaker Point of View* (London: Headley, 1915); Anna L. B. Thomas and Elizabeth B. Emmott, *William Charles Braithwaite: Memoir and Papers* (London: Longmans, Green, 1931), 75; Jones, *A Service of Love in Wartime*, 4–5
32. Benjamin, *Philadelphia Quakers*, 203–6; Elbert Russell, *The History of Quakerism* (New York: Macmillan, 1942), 510–5; Copy of Horace

Lippincott to 'Esteemed Friend', 7 February 1918 and 'Some Particular Advices for Friends and A Statement of Loyalty for Others: Being the Views of Some Members of the Society of Friends Regarding Its Attitude toward the Present Crisis. Third Month, 1918,' file 99–35, box 137, MID Corr., RG165, US National Archives; Wilson to Lippincott, 24 April 1918, in Arthur S. Link et al., eds, *The Papers of Woodrow Wilson* (Princeton, NJ: Princeton University Press, 1966–1994), 47:415–16; Maj. John W. Geary to Col. M. Churchill, 'Subject: Quaker Pacifist Activities in Philadelphia,' 19 August 1918, Lieut. J. R. Winterbotham to Geary, 30 August 1918, Geary to Churchill, 10 September 1918, and Churchill to George Creel (chair, Committee on Public Information), 17 September 1918 – all in file 99–35, box 137, MID Corr., RG165, US National Archives.

33. Chatfield, *For Peace and Justice*, 38.
34. Jones, *A Service of Love*, 8–9 (quote), 49; *A Statement by Philadelphia Yearly Meeting of Friends Third Month 29th, 1918*, copy in file 99–35, box 137, MID Corr., RG165, US National Archives; cf. Jones, *Quakers in Action*, Chapter 2.
35. Jones, *Quakers in Action*, 21, 157; Russell, *History of Quakerism*, 516–17; Woodrow Wilson to Newton D. Baker [Secretary of War], 16 August 1917; Baker to Wilson, 22 August 1917; Wilson to Jones, 28 August 1917, in Link et al., eds, *Papers of Woodrow Wilson*, 43:492, 44:29, 75; Jones, *Quakers in Action*, 16–17.
36. Bacon, *Let This Life Speak*, Chapter 3; Jones, *Swords Into Ploughshares*, 16–17; Jones, *A Service of Love*, 12–15, 62, 72, 119–20; Jones, *Quakers in Action*, 47–8; Jackson remarks in verbatim transcript, Memorial Meeting for Worship, 7th day, 9th. Month 16, 1967, in D. Robert Yarnall Papers (copy in author's possession, supplied by D. Robert Yarnall, Jr); Brown entry in *Dictionary of Quaker Biography* (typescript, QCHC).
37. Leeds & Northrup shipments increased from $149,000 in 1914 to $1,015,000 in 1919 – 'Estimate of Production Capacity', Executive Committee Minutes, 25 July 1919, L & N Papers, Hagley Library; Yarway's went from $91,000 to $428,000, 1914–1920. 'Shipments 1908–1959,' Yarnall Papers.
38. Benjamin, *Philadelphia Quakers*, 202–3.
39. Lucy Fryer Morland, *The New Social Outlook: The Swarthmore Lecture, 1918* (London: Headley Bros., 1918), 14; Edward Grubb, *Social Aspects of the Quaker Faith* (London: Headley Bros., 1899); Rowntree, *Social Service*; Mary O'Brien Harris (Clerk, Socialist Quaker Society) in Committee on War and the Social Order, *Facing the Facts: Being the Report of the Conference of 'The Society of Friends and the Social Order' Held by Direction of the Yearly Meeting at Devonshire House, Bishopsgate, London, 19–22 October 1916* (London: Headley Bros, 1916), 103.
40. Committee on War and the Social Order, *Social Thought in the Society of Friends* (London: n. p., [circa 1922]), esp. 1–3; cf. Catherine Anne Cline, *Recruits to Labor: The British Labour Party 1914–1919* (Syracuse, NY: Syracuse University Press, 1963); Committee on War and the Social Order, *'Whence Come Wars?' First Report* (London: Headley Bros, 1916) and *Facing the Facts*.

41. 'To the Yearly Meeting,' March 1917 (month names used in footnote references, not in originals), in Social Order Committee (hereafter cited as SOC) Minutes, SOC Records F4.18, QCHC.
42. Vining, *Friend of Life*, 79.
43. Extract from the Minutes of Yearly Meeting, 26–30 March 1917; Charles A. Ellwood and Agnes Tierney to SOC, 24 April 1917; SOC Minutes, 8 May 1917; Sharpless to Leeds, 20 April 1917 – all in SOC Records, F4.18, QCHC.
44. Benjamin, *Philadelphia Quakers*, 208–12; Minutes of the SOC, 13–14 October 1917, in SOC Records, F4.18; SOC Report to the Yearly Meeting, Third-Month 1920, page 2, in SOC Records, F4.13; Minutes of the SOC, 15 June 1922, page 1, in SOC Records, F4.18, QCHC.
45. Occupational Census in SOC Minutes 10 January 1921; SOC, Second Annual Report, 1919, page 5, in SOC Records, F4.18, QCHC.
46. SOC Annual Conference (November 1926), page 5; SOC Minutes, 13–14 October 1917, page 6, 11 March 1918, page 1, 9 April 1918, page 2, all in SOC Records, F4.18, QCHC.
47. Vogel, *Precision, People and Progress*, 40; John Fitch, 'An Oasis That is Full of Promise,' *American Assocation for Labor Legislation Review* 17 (1927): 242–3 at page 242.

10

Progressivism, Poststructuralism, and the Writing of American History

Melvyn Stokes

Introduction

Much of the appeal of 'the Progressive years' to contemporary historians, it has been alleged, arises from the fact that they witnessed the birth 'of an order that seems recognizably ours'. Among the features of modern life that emerged in the period from roughly 1880 to 1920 were 'new corporate forms; the advent of political capitalism and governmental interference in the economy; mass warfare; mass consumption; the rise of universities; the spread of education to masses of people; the growth of bureaucracies, professions and new technical strata.'[1] It is not only, however, in relation to economic, social and political characteristics that the Progressive Era seems 'recognizably ours'. The same could be said of much of American intellectual life. In this essay, I shall propose a number of ways in which thinkers and reformers of the Progressive Era anticipated some of the crucial elements of modern poststructuralist thought.[2] I shall advance a suggestion as to why this happened and try to explain why these 'poststructuralist' aspects of Progressive thought were almost completely ignored by later historians.

Foucault's and Derrida's Poststructuralist Assumptions

'Poststructuralism' is the general name given to a range of concepts and positions that have emerged to challenge the structuralist tradition in European thought associated with Ferdinand Saussure, Claude Lévi-Strauss and the early Roland Barthes. Though it has had many followers in the United States including Paul de Man and J. Hillis Miller, it has been, in the main, a continental European phenomenon. Its champions have included the later Barthes, Jean Baudrillard, Jacques Derrida, Michel Foucault, Julia Kristeva, Gilles Deleuze and Jean-François Lyotard. In the United States itself, however, the principal advocates of poststructuralism are widely seen as Foucault and Derrida, and this essay will concern itself with their work.

Foucault and Derrida have shared a number of poststructuralist assumptions: that there are no authors, only discourse; that meanings are always contingent and provisional, never fixed and final; that all thinking is characterized by fragmentation and incompleteness; that there are no real universal categories or grand, totalizing theories. Apart from these hypotheses, the emphasis of their work differed. Foucault (who died in 1984) was principally interested in the study of power. He perceived it, not as simple downward-leaning authority in a hierarchical system, but as a 'capillary' or 'net-like organization', functioning through acceptance rather than simple repression. Turning his back on what he saw as Hobbes's concern for the central will of the state, Foucault elected to analyze the way in which the *subject* of power was persuaded to acquiesce and assist in its operation. The subject was conditioned – in a sense 'constituted' – by a 'multiplicity' of institutions that went to make up social life. These institutions were governed by 'discourses' which, on the basis of internal rules and classifications, created their own views of what was true or false. Truth, therefore, to Foucault, was a social product rather than a metaphysical phenomenon. It varied according to the 'regime of truth' – the types of discourse that were permitted to flourish by society. Discourse was not, however, stable. It shifted and changed. Such changes were often arbitrary, abrupt and distinguished by consequences that were both paradoxical and unforeseen.[3]

Derrida's main preoccupation has been with meaning in its relation to text. To structuralists, the linguistic sign has no meaning as a result of its own qualities, but only as a consequence of its position as part of the pattern of contrasts and comparisons which make up a particular language. Meaning, however, as Derrida argues, is never functionally *present* in language: it is subject to an endless process of differing and deferral. Language itself works on its own to create meaning. Derrida created the term 'différ*a*nce' to describe the series of relations developing out of this dissemination, this continual play of difference. Since the author has no control over language, or the meaning of what has been written, the text itself is all-important. Derrida advocates 'deconstructing' the basic dualisms in structuralist thought – such as signifier and signified, conscious and unconscious, mind and body – which he perceives as false and sustained simply as a consequence of social practice. To him, deconstruction involves focusing on the inconsistencies, marginalia, footnotes, side issues and key omissions in the text. It can help reveal both the manner in which language systems are constructed, and the way in which they contribute to the preservation of relations of domination through their tendency to privilege one side of a binary opposition over the other.[4]

American Progressives and Elements of Poststructuralist Thinking

Many of these conceptions, of course, are far from new. For example, Foucault's perception of power as a 'capillary' or web-like phenomenon in which a variety of institutional discourses guarantee the acquiescence and acceptance of the subject bears a striking resemblance to the notion of social control which first occurred to American sociologist Edward A. Ross in 1894, and was expanded by him in a series of articles and his famous book *Social Control* of 1901. The sub-title of the book, *A Survey of the Foundations of Order*, explains Ross's purpose in writing it. Disturbed by the growing evidence of social and class conflict in an American society increasingly fragmented by urbanization and industrialization, he set out to identify the various means through which society disciplines its members. Foucault's concept of 'power' and Ross's of 'social control' have many aspects in common. They are both perceived as complex developments to cope with changes that had destroyed older, simpler methods of holding society together. Both agree that control and power were the result of internal as well as external constraints. Both distinguish between coercive power and authority which is regarded as rightful, and therefore accepted as legitimate: Ross regards the cruder forms of control as repression, Foucault as strategies of domination. Ross sees institutions as enjoying their own values; Foucault perceives institutions as blessed with their own discourse.[5] The two may also have shared a subjective interest in some of the issues they explored: Ross's experience as an orphan growing up on the plains of Iowa may have left him anxious for stability, whether in institutions or human relationships; Foucault was accused by Derrida of writing his book *Madness and Civilization* to ward off 'the ... terror of going mad'.[6] There are also, of course, a number of differences between the two. Ross regards control as a conscious process that can be utilized in making society 'better'.[7] Foucault sees power as something that merely exists. It is not presumed to operate, like social control, on the basis of values which are constants because ultimately based on human nature. The similarities, however, suggest that Ross was asking much the same kind of questions - and arriving at much the same kind of answers - as Foucault nearly three-quarters of a century earlier.

Foucault defined his main objective from the 1960s to the 1980s as being the clarification 'of the different modes by which, in our culture, human beings are made subjects'.[8] Such 'subjectification', as Paul Rabinow terms it,[9] is the result of a long process of personality formation in which the individual takes an active part. The formation of subjects was also a major preoccupation of Progressive thought. There were, in fact, two principal ways in which they considered it to occur. The first was through socialization. John Dewey, for example, believed school discipline should evolve naturally out of classroom activities and the manner in which they were conducted, rather than being imposed on pupils via the authority of the teacher. When obliged to work with each other, children gain the self-discipline that comes from subordinating their own impulses to the needs of the group. This change, in the end, Dewey argued, would also help transform society, as external restraints on behaviour were supplemented by an acquired inner predisposition toward cooperation and service.[10] Some Progressives considered the same approach could work in the area of juvenile crime. Judge Ben B. Lindsey, for example, developed the suggestion made by psychologist G. Stanley Hall that, though a strong correlation existed between juvenile gangs and crime, the gangs themselves were not wholly bad. Through his juvenile court in Denver, Lindsey set out to create 'law-and-order' gangs. His strategy depended in part upon securing the loyalty of the gang leader, but also in part on the exploitation and the refocusing of those very qualities (cooperation, loyalty, and friendship) which had made the gang into a social unit in the first place.[11] The second mode of subjectification took place by means of internalization. It occurred when individuals were persuaded, as a result of appeals to their personal pride and sense of honour and self-esteem, to modify pre-existing patterns of behaviour. This approach substituted inner restraints or 'chains unseen' for external constraints: Lindsey showed how it could work with his successful policy of sending convicted young offenders, alone and unsupervised, on the long journey to their reform school.[12]

Foucault also laid considerable emphasis on the links between power and truth. 'Truth', however, he regarded as a construct within the discourse of a particular institution or institutions – a discourse that itself functioned within the limits set by society at large. This was an issue which increasingly preoccupied a number of Progressives from the 1890s onward. The growing commercialization of society had brought with it an increasing propensity for institutions to censor (or have censored) some of the ideas with which their members were associated, in order to maintain good relations with the local community or to attract funding from wealthy sponsors. This tendency first showed itself in universities through a number of 'academic freedom' cases. If economist Richard T. Ely's famous 'heresy' trial at Wisconsin in 1894 raised the different issue of what could be taught in an institution dependent on public funding, the dismissals of Edward W. Bemis from Chicago in 1895, John R. Commons from Syracuse in 1899 and Edward A. Ross from Stanford in 1900 seem to have occurred in part at least for patronage reasons. Bemis had offended the administration of his new university because of his criticisms of the commercial interests on which it depended for funding. Commons was told he was being fired because his presence at Syracuse made it harder for the university's chancellor to raise money from wealthy contributors. Ross was disposed of because he had offended Mrs Julia Stanford, widow of his university's founder and its principal benefactress.[13]

A second wave of sackings, beginning in 1915 with the dismissal of Scott Nearing from the University of Pennsylvania, and continuing with the removal of James M. Cattell and Henry W. D. Dana from Columbia in 1917, inspired several observers to analyze the causes of, and the issues raised by, the relation between power and knowledge in the universities. Randolph Bourne saw this relationship as deeply influenced by the replacement of ministers with businessmen on boards of trustees. Business trustees ran universities in the same way as their industrial and financial corporations. Professors were increasingly treated in the same way as corporate employees. If, through their work or actions, they made it harder for a university corporation to administer its 'invested capital', explore new sources of funding or attract students, they were liable to be dismissed. Bourne also pointed out the increasing tendency for such dismissals to be based (in common with the value of corporate securities) on unsupported press allegations or unsubstantiated rumours.[14]

Much of Bourne's analysis was developed and extended by Thorstein Veblen. In *The Higher Learning in America* (1918), Veblen argued that such learning took 'its character from the manner of life enforced on the specialist group [employed to further it] by the circumstances in which it is placed'. He launched a sharp attack on business influence in universities. Business-dominated trustee boards and alumni associations, he argued, increasingly selected presidents of universities on the basis of their 'business qualifications'. Such men saw universities as 'corporations of learning' and sought to follow the business model in their conduct of affairs. If not captains of industry, they operated as 'captains of erudition'. Under their influence, 'the dry-rot of business principles' came to replace 'the disinterested pursuit of knowledge'. Universities competed with one another for benefactors and students. This produced proliferating courses and 'student activities', building programmes, and 'scholarly pageants' – none of which, Veblen asserted, was relevant to the main purpose of a university, which he saw as the pursuit of learning and scientific discovery. It also brought a pronounced limitation on professorial freedom. 'An institution,' Veblen remarked, anticipating to an extent the modern view of discourse, 'is ... a prevalent habit of thought.' This controlling habit of thought in universities was dictated by several things. Business-oriented 'directorates' were eager not to offend potential donors or possible students. They thus expected researchers in 'the so-called moral and social sciences' to avoid contradicting 'the views and prepossessions prevalent among the respectable, conservative middle-class'. Administrative pressures of this kind, however, were only part of the story. A 'truculent quietism' was also produced by the internal structures of the disciplines concerned. Professional considerations helped impede research which might have led to radical conclusions. For in these subjects, Veblen bitterly noted, 'a clamorous conformity to current prepossessions ... or an edifying and incisive rehearsal of commonplaces' could easily pass 'for scholarly and scientific merit'. A professor who, despite these differing pressures, insisted on showing scepticism towards established ideas in his work would probably have to be dismissed. If a 'voluntary' resignation could not be secured, the university administration set out (as happened in Veblen's own case) 'delicately to defame his domestic life, or his racial, religious or political status'. Wider opinion, enforced by administrative power, consequently set out to control not just professors' teaching and research, but also their private lives as well.[15]

Colleges, churches and charitable foundations were the principal institutions in which freedom of thought seemed increasingly limited. In March 1905, Congregationalist Minister Washington Gladden launched a campaign against the decision of the Congregational Church's Foreign Missions Board to accept a gift of $100,000 from John D. Rockefeller. The controversy brought together two strands in Gladden's thought. The first was based on traditional morality: the belief that corporate wealth in general, and Rockefeller's in particular, had been gained by iniquitous means. It was thus, in the term Gladden had coined a decade earlier, 'tainted money'.[16] To accept financial aid from such a source would be tantamount to condoning the methods used to acquire it. The second and more important strand was concerned with the wider effects of such wealth on society. Philanthropy, Gladden believed, helped manipulate public opinion, presenting a far more favourable view of the man or corporation doing the giving, while at the same time encouraging – through institutional pressures, both direct and indirect – professors and ministers who might otherwise have criticized such wealth to remain silent. As early as 1879, Gladden had objected to what he considered the excessive deference paid by many colleges to wealthy donors or potential donors of questionable reputation. In the article in which he first talked of 'tainted money', he criticized it for polluting the stream of public opinion, enabling 'pirates of industry' to be treated with respect and subservience by the very institutions which should have been condemning them and their methods.[17] Gladden's view of the complicated way in which philanthropy used a mixture of internal and external restraints to influence – though he did not use this word – the 'discourse' of institutions marks him out as a precursor of poststructuralist thought so far as power is concerned.

Progressive and modern poststructuralist perceptions, of course, were far from being always the same. One way of demonstrating this is to analyze their differing views of science. To Progressives, science was the great door to the promise of the future. At colleges in the 1870s, 1880s and 1890s, science was by far the most glamorous subject on the curriculum. Not only was it endowed with the prestige of the great natural scientists – Darwin, Huxley, and Tyndall – but it brought with it an exciting new methodology: the approach characterized in the phrase 'look-and-see'. Moreover, the speed of scientific discovery in the twenty-five years before World War I was quite amazing: X-rays, wireless telegraphy and the cinema, for example, in 1895; electrons and the radioactive properties of radium and uranium in the late 1890s; the quantum theory of energy, Einstein's special theory of relativity, Rutherford's theoretical model of the atom and the birth of genetics in the course of the next few years. The same quarter-century saw the growing tendency for horse-drawn modes of transport to be replaced by motor-driven vehicles, the first electricity transmissions over long distances, the design of the first diesel engine, the advent of new industrial processes such as hydrogenation and the advent of powered flight. By 1914, of the great innovations which have transformed the modern world, only nuclear power, television and computers remained yet unknown.

These influences and new discoveries fostered an uncritical acceptance of science as a means of improving American society and the American way of life. From Gifford Pinchot's call for a 'scientific' forestry through the 'scientific' investigations of poverty by Jane Addams and Robert Hunter to the enthusiasm on the part of Louis D. Brandeis and Herbert Croly for 'scientific management' in industry, science was identified with optimism and progress.[18] To Foucault, by contrast, science was in many ways the enemy: it had helped impose the idea of a hierarchy of knowledges, conferring power on some discourses at the expense of others. He himself was more interested in what he described as 'subjugated knowledges', or knowledges pushed to the margins of history by the baleful consequences of science.[19] *Madness and Civilization* (1961), his first major book, deals with themes such as these. In the Middle Ages, Foucault argued, the insane had been treated with respect and allowed to roam at will. They were presumed to have some special clarity of vision or quality of insight that could account for their condition. From the eighteenth century onward, however, in a triumph of 'misguided philanthropy', the mad had been treated as sick and incarcerated in institutions. Foucault regarded this apparently humane and enlightened application of new scientific knowledge as nothing more than a repressive form of power.[20]

A second major issue dividing early Progressives and modern poststructuralists is the Progressives' belief in the rational, autonomous individual. The individual tends to disappear in poststructuralist thought: he or she is constituted through the discourse of institutions, submits to power and is reduced to little more than cipher by the free play of language. Progressive thought – and particularly the perception of democracy it embraced – was centred on the idea of individual action. Long before Charles Beard's *An Economic Interpretation of the Constitution* was published in 1913, Progressives had concluded, either on the basis of evidence produced by scholars such as Orin Libby, Algie M. Simons and J. Allen Smith or – more probably – as a consequence of their own experience, that the institutions of the American state were designed to prevent democracy rather than to express it. 'Our troubles,' future muckraker Ray Stannard Baker noted in his personal diary in 1902, 'arise not because we are democratic but because we are not democratic.'[21] The early years of the twentieth century witnessed a growing readiness on the part of Progressives to hand policy-making over to the collective action of the individual voter. This was reflected in efforts to give voters more control over elected representatives, either at the stage of nomination and election (the Australian or secret ballot, the party primary, the direct election of US senators) or after the representatives had been installed in office (the referendum, the recall). It was also reflected, in its most radical form, in proposals for direct law-making as a result of the initiative.

In its staunch assertion of the right to majority rule, the initiative came close to being, in the words of municipal reformer Frederic C. Howe, 'a movement for government by public opinion'.[22] Behind this conception lay a rapidly-growing faith in the ability of the individual to pursue the interests shared with his fellows by rational means. The swiftness with which this change happened can be seen, for example, in the evolving thought of Herbert Croly. In *The Promise of American Life*, which appeared in 1909, Croly demonstrated his continuing adherence to the positivism in which he had been reared by proposing that the Hamiltonian but democratic state he advocated could best be realized through the leadership of an intelligent and idealistic elite. Croly's next book, *Progressive Democracy*, published only five years later, showed the distance Croly himself had travelled. It was based, like his earlier work, on the analysis of two competing traditions. But the new book, instead of the famous divide between Hamilton and Jefferson, analyzed the conflict between the idea of popular sovereignty and the restrictions imposed on the democratic will by the constitutional system and the practice of law. If people had faith in their own destiny, Croly argued, they should dispense with these props and act on their own. He predicted the weakening of the party system and appeared much more favourably disposed towards the new democratic mechanisms, though he warned against placing too much reliance on them.[23]

The difficulty with Croly's book was his conviction that the popular will was inherently good. It was also assumed to be rational. Both of these assumptions, but particularly the second, were challenged by Walter Lippmann in his *Preface to Politics* (1913). Still only twenty-three years old, Lippmann had already studied at Harvard, worked as a researcher for muckraker Lincoln Steffens and served as an assistant to the socialist mayor of Schenectady, New York. His main intellectual influences, however, were European. From Henry Bergson and Georges Sorel he learned of intuition's superiority over reason and the power of myths in persuading men to abandon thought and take action. Through Graham Wallas's *Human Nature and Politics* and Sigmund Freud's *Interpretation of Dreams* he was exposed to convincing portrayals of the irrational side of human behaviour. In *Preface to Politics*, Lippmann argued that political institutions were out of joint with human nature. Paradoxically, after Lincoln Steffens, he saw the political machine in favourable terms as a 'natural sovereignty' which had defeated that 'really rigid and mechanical thing', the city charter. When an institution produced by social or economic change, such as the trust, came into conflict with the law, Lippmann suggested that the fault might be that of the law for being 'stupidly obstructive'. Above all, he argued that politics must adapt itself to a recognition of the importance of men's emotions and subconscious drives. A desire was a form of energy, neither good nor bad. It could be directed into socially useful channels by the political equivalent of Freud's theory of 'sublimation'. Lippmann praised William James and Jane Addams for proposing, respectively, 'moral equivalents' to war and vice. In order to discover the most effective means of sublimation, he recommended acting on experimental, pragmatic lines. It would sometimes be inevitable, he conceded, that action would be taken on the basis of 'half-knowledge, illusion and error'. But in the end, experience would 'reveal our mistakes; research and wisdom may convert them to wisdom'.[24]

By the time of his second book, *Drift and Mastery* (1914), Lippmann had reached the conclusion that emotion and action by themselves were insufficient grounds on which to base a political philosophy. These natural tendencies only led to aimless drift. What was needed in order to produce a superior civilization was control, mastery and discipline. Science could establish the true nature of desire, he wrote, and what people want could be examined to find out what they *should* want.[25] Lippmann had no notion that empirical analysis might offer a decidedly cool alternative to the warmth of emotion in politics, and might in consequence be far less effective. But at this stage his theorizing about thought and reason, action and will, was interrupted by that major outbreak of unreason: World War I.

From one point of view, as Daniel T. Rodgers has pointed out, the war was 'a massive act of will: a dramatic instance of the Progressives' faith in public opinion'.[26] But in its brutality, its inhumanity, its irrationality, it drove Lippmann and many others to question the efficacy of pragmatic intelligence as a guide to political conduct. Further, Lippmann went on to question a basic principle of pre-war Progressivism – the idea that knowledge should be tested in action. In *Public Opinion* (1922), he asked how it was possible for men to change the world before they could be sure of understanding it correctly. Lippmann began the second chapter of his book with an account of a French staff conference during the battle of Verdun. What was at issue was not the plan of campaign but the words of the communiqué in which the events of the day would be reported to the press. The critical battle in war, as in politics, Lippmann realized, was now the struggle over language and morale.[27] That battle was waged by creating pictures or images in people's minds: fictions, symbols and simplifications, all claiming to be representations of reality. As a consequence, the true location of sovereignty in modern society had passed from legislatures to the press and the media in general, since it was the institutions of communication that created the basis in modern society for 'manufactured' popular consent and political action. With this book, Lippmann took a major step into poststructuralist territory: the use of words, the interpretation and meaning of signs and symbols, the ways in which institutions and the discourses associated with them formed the character and opinion of the individual subject.

The Influence of Nietzsche on Progressives and Poststructuralists

If it is accepted that American Progressives anticipated elements in the poststructuralist thinking of Derrida and Foucault, there are two possible lines of explanation for such a coincidence. The first is that the French thinkers read and were familiar with American writers of the Progressive Era. While this is not completely fanciful,[28] it is less convincing than the second: that both Progressive writers and French poststructuralists were, in a real sense, members of the same intellectual world. They addressed similar issues and were influenced by the same thinkers who had already grappled with those issues.

If one thinker more than any other influenced the work of Foucault and Derrida, for example, it was Nietzsche. Foucault, writing in the preface to the first edition of *Madness and Civilization*, projected a lifework to be carried out 'under the sun of the great Nietzschean quest'.[29] Andreas Huyssen and Cornel West listed Nietzsche as a major interest of the two men. To Jürgen Habermas, they were included among 'Nietzsche's followers'.[30] Foucault and Derrida both accepted and developed what John McGowan refers to as the 'extreme skepticism' displayed by Nietzsche toward 'traditional philosophical concepts such as substance, truth, and reason'.[31] Nietzsche repudiated the Enlightenment idea that truth could be achieved by means of reason. There was, he believed, no such thing as truth, since it depended on an exact fit between subjective representations (words, images) and an external reality. In both science and philosophy, there were no true 'facts'. There were only endless interpretations, all subjective and all, therefore, to an extent illusory. Foucault no doubt had this in mind when, lecturing on Nietzsche's theory of knowledge, he depicted 'truth' as the result of 'a primary and always reconstituted falsification'. Each human being, Nietzsche believed, was formed by a series of rules, statutes, customs, categories and institutions, in all of which he acquiesced. But the herd-like mores they embodied would have to be overcome before a more noble 'authentic man' might appear. Nietzsche was particularly scathing about Christian morality and other 'slave ethics'. He evoked the idea of an *Übermensch* who would emerge once man had managed to transcend such social constraints through the exercise of his 'will to power'.[32]

Nietzschean thought also had a major impact on many Progressive writers. The German philosopher enjoyed a pronounced vogue in America during the Progressive period. Publicists of his work included, in New York, H. L. Mencken and Randolph Bourne and in Chicago George Burnham Foster, Ben Hecht and Clarence Darrow.[33] But those American Progressives who wrote about Nietzsche tended to emphasize only those parts of his work that fitted their own preconceptions. To Darrow, professional agnostic and legal champion of unpopular causes, Nietzsche was useful because he had argued 'that whatever a majority believed must necessarily be untrue' and, in dismissing the idea of God, had 'swept away the cob-webs of superstition.'[34] Some Americans, including Mencken, wrote favourably of Nietzsche because of what they saw as his Darwinian outlook. Others attacked him for the very same reason: Edward Ross criticized what he called Nietzsche's 'ultra-Darwinist' critique of Christianity for the restraints it imposed on the strong.[35] Walter Rauschenbusch, the principal theologian of the 'Social Gospel', similarly found Nietzsche's philosophy repugnant for applauding 'the strong man's self-assertion' and depicting 'Christian virtues as the qualities of slaves', though he also conceded that Nietzsche had deeply touched 'the ethical thought of the modern world'.[36]

Randolph Bourne, in particular, fell under Nietzsche's spell. Many of the titles of his essays acknowledged the debt: 'The Puritan's Will to Power' reflected Nietzsche's view that the main essence of human life was the pursuit of power; 'Twilight of Idols' was borrowed from Nietzsche's similarly-titled book of essays, published in 1888.[37] Bourne, like other Progressive writers, responded to Nietzsche in ways which were allied to his own perceptions. He mobilized Nietzschean ideas in two major ways behind his drive for artistic and cultural liberation. First, he argued that the 'will to power' in American Puritanism profoundly restricted artistic expression, but could itself be surmounted by the individual's own will to power. Second, like Mencken, he utilized Nietzsche in the assault on the stultifying strength of the 'Eastern, upper-class, Anglo-Saxon cultural monopoly'.[38] Yet there were crucial points where he disagreed with Mencken. Bourne, while conceding that it was Mencken's book on Nietzsche (published in 1908) 'from which a majority of the Americans who know about Nietzsche seem to have gotten their ideas,' reproved Mencken for not spending sufficient time 'in understanding the depth and subtleties of Nietzsche'.[39]

One writer whom Bourne believed to have a true understanding of Nietzsche was ethnologist Elsie Clews Parsons. In a review of her *Social Rule*, published in 1917, he praised Parsons's grasp and application of Nietzschean ideas. In his comments on the work of this 'thoroughgoing Nietzschean', Bourne anticipated in many ways the later preoccupations of poststructuralists such as Michel Foucault. Parsons, he wrote approvingly, 'sees that the business of understanding life is very largely a matter of sensing the manifold ways in which people get their desire for power satisfied'. She 'makes it very clear that the power dogma is only a realistic diagnosis of life'. Parsons, Bourne noted, argued 'that we classify people because it gives us power over them ... Classification is the weapon with which one group dominates another.'[40] She was also aware how subjects were constituted (at all events, in social terms) by means of language and how they themselves acquiesced in that constitution: 'Your victim,' Bourne paraphrased Parsons's argument, 'gets born into a social category ... His label is all prepared for him by society. Moreover, he assents to his own subjugation. A social category makes everybody take for granted this relation of power.'[41] In his *Genealogy of Morals*, Nietzsche had questioned the possibility of 'human sciences'. Parsons, according to Bourne, had extended this idea in two directions. She had attacked the claim to the monopoly of knowledge on the part of scientists 'who express their will-to-power by trying to lock science up'. Using ethnographical evidence, moreover, she had undermined the supposedly 'scientific' basis of certain 'religious, social, or sex taboos' by demonstrating that they were 'one with the irrational attitude of primitive peoples'.[42]

'Poststructuralist' Aspects of Progressive Thought Ignored by Historians

In retrospect, it seems that writers of the Progressive Era frequently addressed themes that have attracted the attention of modern poststructuralists such as Derrida and Foucault. They were interested in issues to do with language and the construction of meaning. Power, its structure and its operations, was a matter of real concern to them. They often became absorbed in the question of who controlled, and therefore defined, knowledge. But the doors opened onto these matters by Ross, Gladden, Dewey, Lindsey, Bourne, Lippmann and others were effectively closed by later historians of Progressivism. In order to understand how this happened, it is necessary to construct a typology, or more accurately a genealogy, of various historical approaches to Progressivism and Progressive thought.

In 1915, Benjamin Parke De Witt defined Progressivism as a movement aiming to abolish political corruption, democratize the machinery of politics and employ government in the improvement of social and economic conditions.[43] While later historians provided more information on who the 'Progressives' themselves actually were,[44] the fundamental dualism of De Witt's approach – reformers versus corrupt businessmen and politicians – would survive for more than thirty years as the principal means of interpreting the politics of the Progressive Era.

Between the 1930s and 1950s, however, a series of massive events – the Great Depression of the 1930s, the rise of Fascism, World War II, the Holocaust, the appearance of nuclear weapons, the start of the Cold War – emphasized the distance between the modern world and the innocence and credulity of a world in which, at least to Theodore Roosevelt and his supporters, Armageddon appeared to threaten in 1912. They also set the scene for the arrival of a more pluralistic interpretation of the American past. In particular, social scientists, many of them former radicals, set out to show how the processes of industrialization, urbanization and immigration in the United States had fragmented political power, undermined old elites and created a society made up of many different groups. This profusion of groups with conflicting interests made it very hard for any one group on its own to acquire dominance. It also discouraged the rise of mass movements committed to radical change. The New Deal, which had helped to revive American capitalism, re-establishing it on 'a reasonable and stable basis', had in any case made such movements unnecessary. It also symbolized the need for a more rational, instrumental politics, in which groups sought to achieve their own interests through compromise and negotiation.[45]

The most important of these writers in influencing the interpretation of Progressivism was the historian Richard Hofstadter. Once briefly a member of the Communist Party, Hofstadter had become by the 1950s a defender of the New Deal order: one of those liberals, he wrote in *The Age of Reform* (1955), who were now 'more conscious of those things they would like to preserve than ... of those things they would like to change'. While Americans attempted to uncover 'some way out of the dreadful impasse of our polarized world', he did not believe they should give up what they had 'gained and learned' or tear down 'the social achievements of the past twenty years'.[46] Hofstadter was opposed to the 'Radical right' of the early 1950s: a loose coalition made up of conservatives wanting to 'roll back' the New Deal legacy, old-style isolationists and supporters of McCarthyism.[47] What was new about his analysis was that he set out to show that the origins of these ideas lay, not in conservative thought – Hofstadter quoted Lionel Trilling's observation in *The Liberal Imagination* (1950) that most American conservatives only engaged in 'irritable mental gestures which seek to resemble ideas'[48] – but in the tradition of liberal reform itself.

It was Hofstadter's argument that the reform tradition, up to but not including the New Deal, had included both reactionary and reformist elements. Tendencies 'in American life [such] as isolationism and the extreme nationalism that usually goes with it, hatred of Europe and Europeans, racial, religious and nativist phobias, resentment of big business, trade–unionism, intellectuals, the Eastern seaboard and its culture ... have been found not only in opposition to reform but also at times oddly combined with it.' According to this line of reasoning, what Hofstadter called the 'cranky pseudo-conservatism' of the time could be linked to the fact that 'a large part of the Populist-Progressive tradition has turned sour'.[49] When it came to Progressivism itself, it seemed to Hofstadter that the movement had been essentially backward-looking in its aims. Its 'general theme', he asserted, 'was the effort to restore a type of economic individualism and political democracy that was widely believed to have existed earlier in America and to have been destroyed by the great corporation and the corrupt political machine.'[50] Those involved in this effort had become involved for what Hofstadter saw as principally selfish motives. The Progressives were, he wrote, 'men of the Mugwump type – the old gentry, the merchants of long standing, the small manufacturers, the established professional men, the civic leaders of an earlier era.' This particular social group had suffered a good deal from the economic changes of the later nineteenth century. Accustomed to deference and power in their local communities, they had watched their influence being dwarfed as a result of the emergence of a new elite: 'the newly rich, the grandiosely or corruptly rich, the masters of great corporations.' They turned to political reform in response to this 'status revolution', hoping by this means to restore their earlier influence and prestige.[51]

As a way of preparing the ground for the distinction he was intent on making between Progressivism and the New Deal, Hofstadter described the emergence, during the Progressive Era, of 'two thoroughly different systems of political ethics'. The first, linked to 'indigenous Yankee-Protestant political traditions', was that of most Progressives. At its base was an idealized perception of 'the superior disinterestedness and honesty of the average citizen'. It emphasized ideas of morality and civic virtue, of continuous participation in public affairs, of placing the general good before sectional interests. The second system of ethics was primarily an outgrowth of immigrants and their European backgrounds. According to this system, people participated in politics in order to meet individal or family needs; personal obligations mattered far more than civic responsibilities; and 'strong personal loyalties' replaced 'allegiance to abstract codes of law or morals'. The institution that came closest to operating on the basis of the second system was the political machine.[52]

From the late nineteenth century to the 1950s, the ruling historical interpretation of the political machine was what David C. Hammack termed the 'patrician elite' theory. This saw the machine in much the same way as upper-class reformers had done: as the dominant force in, and principal corrupter of, urban politics. Supported by the most ignorant and venal elements of the population, it had been opposed by those who were better educated, better off and apparently more virtuous.[53] The first important dissent from this view came in functional sociologist Robert K. Merton's book, *Social Theory and Social Structure*, published in 1949. Merton's view of the political machine was conditioned not by moralism but by the methods of social science. He argued that the machine maintained its grip on power not so much by means of corruption as through the satisfaction of 'latent functions'. It took on the task of 'humanizing and personalizing' aid to the 'deprived classes' while providing alternative routes to social mobility.[54] Merton's rehabilitation of the political machines was continued by Oscar Handlin and Richard Hofstadter. Handlin, in *The Uprooted* (1951), depicted the political machine as an important medium of immigrant acculturation. Urban bosses, themselves usually drawn from an immigrant background, protected immigrants from the law, helped them over issues to do with daily life (such as housing), and sometimes found them jobs.[55] Hofstadter, much influenced by Handlin,[56] saw the immigrant as coming from societies with no tradition of active citizenship; as comparatively slow to exercise his ballot after naturalization had been gained; and as doing so finally solely in response 'to immediate needs arising out of his struggle for life in the American city'. Encouraged by professional politicians to see politics as an area in which 'one could legitimately pursue one's interests', he voted in anticipation of 'concrete and personal gains.'[57]

In Hofstadter's account of urban politics, the 'patrician elite' theory was turned on its head. It was the boss rather than the reformer who was dealt with most sympathetically. The reformer, indeed, was depicted as ineffective and remote. In his dedication to abstract principles and his involvement in campaigns such as those for temperance, Sunday laws or women's rights, he seemed 'a mystery' to the immigrant. The boss was the very opposite of the reformer: he appeared approachable and friendly, sympathetic to immigrants' needs and a pragmatic source of practical help. It was, as Terrence J. MacDonald has pointed out, no coincidence 'that these bosses looked a lot like Franklin D. Roosevelt'.[58] Like the bosses, FDR was 'a seasoned practical politician'. His approach to politics was characterized by an 'opportunistic virtuosity'. He showed himself 'thoroughly at home in the realities of machine politics and a master of the machine techniques of accommodation'. Indeed, the New Deal as a whole, with its opportunism, its experimental quality, its practicality, its furtherance of 'human needs over inherited notions', and its concern for results, seemed far closer in spirit, as Hofstadter depicted it, to the political machine than to its critics and opponents.[59]

If Hofstadter, in describing how political machines served the interests of their constituents, was trying to provide a 'usable past' for interest group liberalism,[60] his criticism of the 'insistent moralism' of Progressive reformers was in many ways an indirect attack on McCarthyism.[61] He clearly distinguished between the political machine/New Deal and Progressive/McCarthyite traditions in American politics. The first represented a politics based on self-interest and accommodation. Both groups and individuals regarded politics as a means of economic gain, and decisions on how available resources should be allocated between competing interests were made by politicians. The second tradition was one of mass movements, often irrational in character because they arose from the belief of many Americans 'that there is some great but essentially very simple struggle going on, at the heart of which there lies some single conspiratorial force'. Instead of trying to educate the public out of this belief, 'political and intellectual leaders' pretended that demands to destroy the evil concerned were 'altogether sensible' and tried 'to find ways to placate them'. The result of this failure of nerve on the part of the country's elite was 'periodical psychic sprees that purport to be moral crusades': the McCarthyite attack on an internal communist threat was all of a piece with the Progressives' attempts to curb big business, remove political corruption, or completely eradicate liquor interests and the saloon.[62]

Hofstadter's interpretation of Progressivism in *The Age of Reform* was dominated by two principal approaches, each concerned with inner responses to external tendencies and events. The first was the attempt to explain why Progressivism's middle-class leadership had been driven to embrace reform during a period of apparent prosperity. He found the answer to this in many middle-class professionals' anxieties concerning their social status. The second was the effort to understand why so many others had supported such a leadership. His answer to this question was a complex one, but much of it emphasized the clash of traditional doctrines of morality and personal responsibility with new, emerging forms of economic and political organization. By posing his analysis in these terms, Hofstadter set aside a good deal of the thinking which Progressives themselves had considered important, and which made them into forerunners of the poststructuralists.

There was almost no attention in Hofstadter's work to issues of power. Although he mentioned 'the entire system of underground government' investigated by 'crusading journalists', his analysis of the political machine was confined to its functional role rather than its central position in the urban power structure.[63] In examining Progressive thought, he devoted most time to analyzing the way Progressives reacted to the challenge mounted by social and economic change to traditional moral values, rather than to the way they were controlled and persuaded to acquiesce in the operations of power. He paid no attention to the ways in which the individual was constituted by varying methods of social control, including socialization. His analysis of the reformist role played by ministers and professors concentrated more on changes in their social status than on limitations on free speech ('discourse') in churches and universities.[64] Moreover, while anticipating the Foucaultian notion of discursive shifts by demonstrating how linguistic usage changed from Progressivism to the New Deal, the value of this insight in terms of Progressivism was weakened by his failure to compare the language of the Progressives with that used by the reformers and non-reformers who had preceded them.[65]

Hofstadter set the agenda for much of what was written on Progressivism in subsequent decades. The earliest critiques of his view of Progressivism stressed the implausibility of anxieties about social status as a motive for commitment to political reform.[66] Other scholars extended Hofstadter's pluralistic interpretation of the New Deal back into the Progressive Era, seeing Progressivism not as a monolithic middle-class movement so much as a series of differing and different coalitions.[67] These coalitions included at varying times lower-class and ethnic groups,[68] organized labour,[69] businessmen and their organizations,[70] and, on some issues, the political machines.[71] Other historians, who would become known as the 'organizational' school, saw reform as an amalgam of middle-class experts, bureaucrats, managers and professionals, seeking to respond to the problems caused by modernization through the use of their varied professional skills.[72]

The political and intellectual conflicts of the 1960s, which undermined the general consensus approach to history, did not bring about a substantial departure from this broad framework. Argument principally revolved around which interest or group had exercised most influence in the adoption of particular policies or specific pieces of legislation. Gabriel Kolko's *The Triumph of Conservatism* (1963), which attempted a major reappraisal of the Progressive Era, simply altered the nature of the coalition and the objectives it sought to achieve through political means. Kolko saw large business corporations as successfully lobbying for legislation to meet their own commercial needs. Kolko's book confined its analysis to the national political scene. Other students of Progressive Era legislation at the state level either supported Kolko's principal thesis or saw law-making as far less susceptible to the influence of business corporations alone than he had done.[73]

The pluralist approach, for most scholars, made irrelevant the issues of knowledge, language and power that had interested some Progressive Era thinkers. Two different interpretative approaches to Progressivism in recent years, however, have begun to address these issues again. Closest to the priorities and concerns of the poststructuralists has been the work of James Weinstein and Martin J. Sklar. They have examined the changes and movements of the Progressive Era from a Marxist perspective, as revised and updated by Gramsci, dedicating themselves to showing how a dominant corporate class consolidated its hegemonic power by co-opting the forces of reform and protest. This approach, however, has meant that power, language and the constitution of the subject are regarded merely as a product of class relations, a considerably narrower view than that to be found in poststructuralist writings, or in the work of a number of Progressives.[74]

The second approach, though linguistic in orientation, owes much more to the efforts of historians such as Quentin Skinner and J. G. A. Pocock to 'contextualize' political ideas than to poststructuralist thinkers.[75] Its principal adherent has been Daniel T. Rodgers. At the heart of Progressivism, Rodgers claimed, could be found not a united, single ideology, but three 'social languages' (the term 'discourse' is avoided) that Progressives of all types could draw upon in order to advance their 'discontents' and 'social views'. These languages – antimonopolism, social bonds and social efficiency – had different roots; they did not arrive on the scene together, nor did they lose currency at the same time; and all were typified by 'mutual contradictions'.[76]

In a sense, Rodgers' study of the way words are used in politics may be perceived as supporting the idea of hegemony. As he concedes, words 'legitimize the actual frame of politics; they create those pictures in our heads which make the structures of authority tolerable and understandable'. By means of these 'word pictures', men and women can be adjusted to 'realms of power beyond their reach'. But Rodgers actually dismisses hegemony, 'a single, class-based worldview', together with the earlier consensus approach, because they failed to take account of 'the deep, continuous elements of conflict in our political life'. Various elements in politics had fought over the use and interpretation of words; Americans' political vocabulary, Rodgers asserted, 'is contested terrain and always has been'.[77]

Language and power, as Rodgers maintains, are closely linked. This was clear to some American Progressives decades before modern poststructuralists began to focus on such matters and the relationship which exists between them. Issues such as the nature of power, the manner in which people are constituted as subjects, the construction of meanings and the control of knowledge were often addressed in Progressive discourse. But later historians of Progressivism, in pursuit of their own agendas, either ignored or distorted what the Progressives had to say on these matters. Much of this legacy of historical writing will consequently have to be set aside if we are to understand more fully what might be called the 'poststructuralist' aspects of Progressive discourse. The Progressive era may have more to offer than is currently believed.

Notes

1. Joseph Featherstone, 'John Dewey and David Riesman: From the Lost Individual to the Lonely Crowd', in Herbert J. Gans *et al.*, eds, *On the Making of Americans: Essays in Honor of David Riesman* (Philadelphia, 1979), 3–5 (quote on 5).
2. There have, of course, been other efforts at establishing an American ancestry for poststructuralism. Richard Poirier maintains that poststructuralist views of language are prefigured in Emerson, James, Whitman, Frost and Stevens. Cornel West sees Emerson and the pragmatists as foreshadowing some poststructuralist notions, in particular anti-realism. Richard Rorty and Giles Gunn also regard the pragmatists as precursors of poststructuralism, a view recently challenged by John Patrick Diggins. See Richard Poirier, *The Renewal of Literature: Emersonian Reflections* (London, 1988); Cornel West, *The American Evasion of Philosophy: A Genealogy of Pragmatism* (London, 1989); Richard Rorty, *Consequences of Pragmatism* (Brighton, 1982); idem, *Contingency, Irony, and Solidarity* (Cambridge, 1989); Giles Gunn, *Thinking Across the American Grain: Ideology, Intellect, and the New Pragmatism* (Chicago, 1992); John Patrick Diggins, *The*

Promise of Pragmatism: Modernism and the Crisis of Knowledge and Authority (Chicago, 1994).
3. Michel Foucault, 'Lecture Two: 14 Jan. 1976,' and 'Truth and Power', both in Michel Foucault, *Power/Knowledge: Selected Interviews and Other Writings 1972–1977*, ed. Colin Gordon (London, 1980), 96–8, 106, 111–13, 119, 131. On Foucault generally, see James Miller, *The Passion of Michel Foucault* (London, 1993) and Didier Eribon, *Michel Foucault*, trans. Betsy Wing (Cambridge, MA, 1991).
4. Christopher Norris, *Derrida* (London, paperback ed., 1987), 15, 80; Jonathan Culler, *On Deconstruction: Theory and Criticism after Structuralism* (London, 1983), 89–110; John R. Searle, 'The World Turned Upside Down', in Gary B. Madison, ed., *Working Through Derrida* (Evanston, IL, 1993), 171. For Derrida's own discussion of the usage of terms such as 'deconstruction' and 'différance', see Raoul Mortley, *French Philosophers in Conversation: Levinas, Schneider, Serres, Irigaray, Le Doeuff, Derrida* (London, 1991), 96–100.
5. See Edward A. Ross, *Social Control: A Survey of the Foundations of Order* (1901; reprint, Cleveland, OH, 1969).
6. *Ibid.*, introduction to *Social Control*, by Julius Weinberg, Gisela J. Hinkle and Roscoe C. Hinkle, xii; Derrida, quoted in Miller, *Passion of Michel Foucault*, 120.
7. See Ross, *Social Control*, 173, 195, 296–7, 328, 339, 340–2, 360–3, 365.
8. Michel Foucault, 'The Subject and Power', in Hubert L. Dreyfus and Paul Rabinow, eds, *Michel Foucault: Beyond Structuralism and Hermeneutics* (Chicago, 1982), 208.
9. Paul Rabinow, ed., *Michel Foucault: The Foucault Reader* (London, 1984), 11.
10. John Dewey, *The School and Society*, in Jo Ann Boydston, ed., *John Dewey, The Middle Works, 1899–1924, Volume 1: 1899–1901* (Carbondale, IL, 1976), 10–13, 19–20, 53, 55. Dewey saw occupations of a mainly manual variety as according the best means of educating children 'in cooperative and mutually helpful living'. They would also prepare children for the industrial jobs awaiting them when they left school (Dewey, *School and Society*, 9, 13, 16–19, 81). But Dewey's insistence on the significance of occupations was much criticized. By producing a more skilled and tractable workforce, it was contended, it would operate mainly to the advantage of employers. It would also, it was maintained, institutionalize social divisions by educating the children of industrial workers on the assumption that that they too would be industrial workers.
11. G. Stanley Hall, *Adolescence: Its Psychology and Its Relations to Physiology, Anthropology, Sociology, Sex, Crime, Religion and Education*, 2 vols (London, 1905), 1:360–2. For Lindsey's approach in operation, see Lindsey to 'Dear Gang', 22 January 1910, Ben B. Lindsey Papers, Library of Congress; cf. Ben B. Lindsey and Rube Borough, *The Dangerous Life* (New York, 1931), 120–31. For accounts of the creation of 'law-and-order gangs', see Lindsey, *Dangerous Life*, 131–8, and Lindsey and Harvey O'Higgins, *The Beast* (New York, 1910), 144–6. For another believer in such gangs, see Jack M. Holl, *Juvenile Reform in the Progressive Era: William R. George and the Junior Republic Movement* (Ithaca, NY, 1971), esp. 64–73.

12. See Lindsey, *Dangerous Life*, 167–202.
13. Burton J. Bledstein, *The Culture of Professionalism: The Middle Class and the Development of Higher Education in America* (New York, 1976), 302–3 n. 23; John R. Commons, *Myself* (New York: Macmillan, 1934), 58; Edward A. Ross, *Seventy Years of It: An Autobiography* (New York, 1936), 62–3, 67–72, 81–5.
14. Randolph Bourne, 'Who Owns the Universities?'; 'Those Columbia Trustees'; 'The Idea of a University', all in Lillian Schlissel, ed., *The World of Randolph Bourne* (New York, 1965), 72–8, 84–8.
15. Thorstein Veblen, *The Higher Learning in America: A Memorandum on the Conduct of Universities by Business Men* (New York, 1918), 3, 34, 81, 85, 87–9, 107–8, 111–12, 118–19, 143–7, 158–9, 163–4, 176–9, 183–4, 236, 273.
16. Washington Gladden, 'Tainted Money', *The Outlook* 52 (30 November 1895): 886–7.
17. Gladden in *Sunday Afternoon* 3 (August 1879): 761–2, Washington Gladden Papers, Ohio Historical Society; Gladden, 'Tainted Money,' 886–7.
18. See Samuel P. Hays, *Conservation and the Gospel of Efficiency: The Progressive Conservation Movement, 1890–1920* (Cambridge, MA, 1959); Jane Addams et al., *Hull-House Maps and Plans* (Chicago, 1895); Robert S. Hunter, *Poverty* (New York, 1904); Samuel Haber, *Efficiency and Uplift: Scientific Management in the Progressive Era, 1890–1920* (Chicago, 1964), esp. 53–4, 58, 80–2, 89–90.
19. Foucault, 'Lecture One: 7 January 1976', in *Power/Knowledge*, 81–5.
20. Michel Foucault, *Madness and Civilization*, trans. Richard Howard (New York, 1965).
21. Ray Stannard Baker, *Notebook C*, 1902, page 90, Baker Papers, Library of Congress.
22. Frederic C. Howe, *The City: The Hope of Democracy* (New York, 1905), 171.
23. Herbert Croly, *The Promise of American Life* (New York, 1909), esp. 38–46, 138–9, 146–7, 153–4, 169, 214, 427–41; Herbert Croly, *Progressive Democracy* (New York, 1914), esp. 42–4, 51–3, 55, 61–2, 129–32, 174–7, 220, 225–30, 245–66, 306–8, 342–4.
24. Walter Lippmann, *Preface to Politics* (New York, 1913), 18, 22–3, 34–6, 38–40, 43, 46–51, 79, 105–7.
25. Walter Lippmann, *Drift and Mastery: An Attempt to Diagnose the Current Unrest* (New York, 1914).
26. Daniel T. Rodgers, *Contested Truths: Keywords in American Politics since Independence* (New York, 1987), 198.
27. Walter Lippmann, *Public Opinion* (London, 1922), 35–8.
28. Foucault could read English with no difficulty by the early 1970s. Didier Eribon asserts that he knew historian Peter Brown's book on St Augustine 'almost by heart'. Didier Eribon, *Michel Foucault*, trans. Betsy Wing (London, 1992), 313–14. Interestingly, while lecturing in Brazil in 1974, Foucault himself credited his conception of language as a 'game' to the work of various 'Anglo-American philosophers'. Miller, *Passion of Michel Foucault*, 416 n. 28. Derrida, of course, was familiar with the writings of

a number of American philosophers. See, for example, his comments on Charles S. Peirce in *Of Grammatology*, trans. Gayatri Spivak (Baltimore, 1976), 48–9.

29. Michel Foucault, *Folie et déraison* (Paris, 1961), iv–v. Foucault would also admit Nietzsche's influence on his thinking in the last interview he gave, two months before his death. Michel Foucault, 'Final Interview,' trans. Thomas Levin and Isabelle Lorenz, *Raritan* 5.1 (Summer 1985): 9.

30. Andreas Huyssen, 'Mapping the Postmodern', *New German Critique* 33 (1984): 39; Cornel West, 'Black Culture and Postmodernism', in Joseph Natoli and Linda Hutcheon, eds, *A Postmodern Reader* (Albany, NY: State University of New York, 1993), 391–2; Jürgen Habermas, *The Philosophical Discourse of Modernity: Twelve Lectures*, trans. Frederick Lawrence (Cambridge, MA, 1987), 97, 104, 241–65, 278, 307.

31. John McGowan, 'Excerpts from *Postmodernism and Its Critics*', in Natoli and Hutcheon, eds, *A Postmodern Reader*, 215.

32. This summary of Nietzschean thought is drawn from several sources: Bernd Magnus and Kathleen Higgins, eds, *The Cambridge Companion to Nietzsche* (Cambridge, 1996), Chapter 1; Keith Ansell-Pearson, *An Introduction to Nietzsche as Political Thinker: The Perfect Nihilist* (Cambridge, 1994); Alexander Nehamas, *Nietzsche: Life as Literature* (Cambridge, MA, 1985); Michael Tanner, *Nietzsche* (Oxford, 1994). For Foucault's comment on truth as recurrent falsification, see Miller, *Passion of Michel Foucault*, 269.

33. Henry F. May, *The End of American Innocence: A Study of the First Years of Our Own Time* (London, 1960), 166, 206–10, 255, 256, 303, 376. On the Nietzschean vogue in America, see Robert C. Bannister, *Social Darwinism: Science and Myth in Anglo-American Social Thought* (Philadelphia, 1979), 201–11 and Bryan Strong, 'Images of Nietzsche in America, 1900–1970,' *South Atlantic Quarterly* 70 (1971): esp. 575–81.

34. Clarence Darrow, 'Nietzsche,' *The Athena* (1916), quoted in Kevin Tierney, *Darrow, A Biography* (New York, 1979), 74.

35. Edward A. Ross, *Foundations of Sociology* (New York, 1905), 330–1. On the far from simple relationship between Nietzsche and Darwinism, see Bannister, *Social Darwinism*, 202–3.

36. Walter Rauschenbusch, *Christianity and the Social Crisis*, ed. Robert D. Cross (1907; reprint, New York, 1964), 315–16.

37. Both essays are reprinted in Olaf Hansen, ed., *Randolph Bourne, The Radical Will, Selected Writings, 1911–1918* (New York, 1977), 301–6, 336–47. Nietzschean passages are scattered across Bourne's writings.

38. May, *American Innocence*, 251.

39. For example, Bourne considered that – in opposing Comstockery – Mencken had failed to understand this was not 'a function of American culture' so much as a result of 'the current moralism of our general middle-class civilization'. The solution, therefore, would have to be 'as Nietzsche made it, on that moralism rather than on its symptoms'. Randolph Bourne, 'H. L. Mencken,' in Hansen, *Randolph Bourne*, 474.

40. Randolph Bourne, 'A Modern Mind,' *The Dial* 62 (22 March 1917): 239; cf. Paul Rabinow, 'Introduction,' *The Foucault Reader*, 8–9.

41. Bourne, 'A Modern Mind,' 239; cf. Rabinow on Foucault's 'subjectification', *The Foucault Reader*, 10–11.
42. Bourne, 'A Modern Mind,' 239–40. Foucault, of course, had attacked supposedly scientific disciplines as part of a technology of normalization.
43. Benjamin Parke De Witt, *The Progressive Movement: A Non-partisan, Comprehensive Discussion of Current Tendencies in American Politics* (New York, 1915), 4–5.
44. See, for example, Harold U. Faulkner, *The Quest for Social Justice, 1898–1914* (New York, 1931).
45. The movement towards pluralism in academic thought in the United States is covered in Michael Paul Rogin, *The Intellectuals and McCarthy: The Radical Specter* (Cambridge, MA, 1967), 9–31 (quote on 9).
46. Eric Foner, 'The Education of Richard Hofstadter', *The Nation* (4 May 1992): 597; Richard Hofstadter, *The Age of Reform: from Bryan to F.D.R.* (1955; reprint, London, 1962), 13–14.
47. See Daniel Bell, ed., *The New American Right* (New York, 1955).
48. Hofstadter, *Age of Reform*, 12.
49. *Ibid.*, 19–20.
50. *Ibid.*, 5.
51. *Ibid.*, 135–40 (quote on 137), 146–8.
52. *Ibid.*, 8–9, 255.
53. David C. Hammack, 'Problems in the historical study of power in the cities and towns of the United States, 1800–1960,' *American Historical Review* 83 (1978): 323–49.
54. Robert K. Merton, *Social Theory and Social Structure: Toward the Codification of Theory and Research* (Glencoe, IL, 1949), 71–4, 76–7.
55. Oscar Handlin, *The Uprooted* (New York, 1951), 210–13, 221.
56. For Hofstadter's acknowledgement of his debt to Handlin, see *Age of Reform*, 181 n. 1.
57. *Ibid.*, 180–3. Though Hofstadter did not acknowledge Merton's work directly in the same way as Handlin's, it seems very likely that he was influenced by it. Merton had argued, for example, that voters considered public issues 'abstract and remote', while private problems were 'concrete and immediate' – substantially the same point Hofstadter would later make in distinguishing between the political priorities of Progressives and immigrants. Merton, *Social Theory and Social Structure*, 73; cf. Hofstadter, *Age of Reform*, 9, 180–4. Hofstadter later included, in a list of the influences which had helped undermine the 'scheme of polarized conflict' advanced by the Progressive historians, 'functional analysis in society, especially as made accessible in the work of Robert Merton'. Richard Hofstadter, *The Progressive Historians: Turner, Beard, Parrington* (New York, paperback ed., 1970), 442–4.
58. Hofstadter, *Age of Reform*, 176, 180–4, 267; Terrence J. McDonald, 'The Burdens of Urban History: The Theory of the State in Recent American Social History,' *Studies in American Political Development* (1988): 15.
59. On Roosevelt as a 'machine' politician, see Hofstadter, *Age of Reform*, 305, 317. On his preparedness to work with political bosses, see *ibid.*, 308. On 'machine' characteristics of the New Deal, see *ibid.*, 305, 314–15, 322 n. 7, 323, 325.

60. Terrence J. MacDonald, 'The problem of the political in recent American urban history: liberal pluralism and the rise of functionalism,' *Social History* 10 (1985): 332.
61. On the moralism of the Progressives, see Hofstadter, *Age of Reform*, 5, 15–16, 181, 257, 274, 314–15, 317, 323 (quote on 322 n. 7). Hofstadter, as a former member of the Communist Party, was too vulnerable himself to attack McCarthyism directly. His criticism in *The Age of Reform* coded with great care. Moreover, he also distanced himself from 'totalitarian liberals' who, while attacking Fascism, had excused the existence of similar evils in the Soviet Union. *Ibid.*, 15–16.
62. See *ibid.*, 16–17.
63. See *ibid.*, 173–4 (quotes on 174), 182–4.
64. While referring to the replacement of clergy by businessmen on the trustee boards of colleges and universities (in the same way as they were taking over from 'men of the Mugwump type' who had once dominated the ruling boards of 'philanthropic and cultural institutions'), Hofstadter presented this as having more to do with the loss of status by the groups concerned than with the growing limitations on institutional discourse. See *ibid.*, 137, 151.
65. *Ibid.*, 318.
66. One tactic of historians was to compare the social origins of the Progressives with that of their conservative opponents. For a review of this literature, together with his own findings on Wisconsin and more general doubts about using social status as a means of explaining political behaviour, see David P. Thelen, 'Social Tensions and the Origins of Progressivism,' *Journal of American History* 56 (1969–1970): 323–41.
67. Peter G. Filene, in a famous article, suggested that support for Progressive measures was too diverse and inconsistent to allow meaningful use of the term 'Progressive movement'. Peter G. Filene, 'An Obituary for "The Progressive Movement",' *American Quarterly* 22 (1970): 20–34.
68. J. Joseph Huthmacher, 'Urban Liberalism and the Age of Reform,' *Mississippi Valley Historical Review* 49 (September 1962): 231–41; J. Joseph Huthmacher, *Senator Robert F. Wagner and Urban Liberalism* (New York, 1968); John D. Buenker, *Urban Liberalism and Progressive Reform* (New York, 1978).
69. Irwin Yellowitz, *Labor and the Progressive Movement in New York State, 1897–1916* (Ithaca, NY, 1965).
70. Robert H. Wiebe, *Businessmen and Reform* (Cambridge, MA, 1962); James Weinstein, 'Organized Business and the City Commission and Manager Movements,' *Journal of Southern History* 28 (May 1962), 166–82; Samuel P. Hays, 'The Politics of Reform in Municipal Government in the Progressive Era,' *Pacific Northwest Quarterly* 55 (October 1964): 157–69.
71. John D. Buenker, 'The Urban Political Machine and the Seventeenth Amendment,' *Journal of American History* 56 (1969–1970): 305–22.
72. See Samuel P. Hays, *The Response to Industrialism, 1885–1914* (Chicago, 1957); Robert H. Wiebe, *The Search for Order, 1877–1920* (New York, 1967).
73. Gabriel Kolko, *The Triumph of Conservatism: A Reinterpretation of American*

History, 1900–1916 (New York, 1963). For studies of state reform see, for example, Stanley P. Caine, *The Myth of a Progressive Reform: Railroad Legislation in Wisconsin, 1903–1910* (Madison, WI, 1970); Joseph F. Tripp, 'An Instance of Labor and Business Cooperation: Workmen's Compensation in Washington State (1911),' *Labor History* 17 (1976): 530–50.

74. Martin J. Sklar, *The Corporate Reconstruction of American Capitalism, 1890–1916: The Market, the Law and Politics* (Cambridge, 1988); James Weinstein, *The Corporate Ideal in the Liberal State, 1900–1918* (New York, 1968).

75. The main assumption behind this approach is that words have different meanings in different contexts. See for example J. G. A. Pocock, *Politics, Language, and Time: Essays on Political Thought and History* (New York, 1971); Quentin Skinner, 'Some Problems in the Analysis of Political Thought and Action,' *Political Theory* 2 (1974): 277–303.

76. Daniel T. Rodgers, 'In Search of Progressivism', in Stanley I. Kutler and Stanley N. Katz, eds, *The Promise of American History* (Baltimore, 1982), 123–7.

77. Rodgers, *Contested Truths*, 5, 8, 11.

11

The Cultural Foundations of Democracy: The Struggle between a Religious and a Secular Intellectual Reform Movement in the American Age of Conformity

Jan C. C. Rupp

Introduction

Among historians and sociologists the conviction is gradually taking root that the traditional way of thinking about America's twentieth-century periodicity – the age of progress and reform (1890–1940),[1] the age of consensus (1940–1964),[2] and what may be called the 'age of dissent' (1964–1980) and the 'no-nonsense era' (1980–1990) – has to be revised. When reassessing the progressive, conformist, dissenting or no-nonsense character of the various periods in American twentieth-century history, it might be helpful to distinguish between specific levels of analysis: the level of the era, the level of the social movement and the level of the individual actor. For example, the 1890–1940 period might still be called the Progressive Era, although its most important social movements, on a closer look, appear to have been far from progressive in all their activities and opinions; and the individual careers of spokesmen and women, on further inspection, might demonstrate a mixture of opinions and attitudes or a change over time from one form of radicalism to another.

Edward Purcell Jr summarized the traditional characterization of the politico-cultural tone of the decades after the beginning of World War II to the early 1960s as 'the belief that the special and enduring strength of the United States grew from a socially unifying national culture which embodied practices, attitudes and values that uniquely nourished both scientific inquiry and democratic government'.[3] Tolerance, pragmatism and openness as norms of social interaction inoculated Americans against ideological fanaticism and created the conditions that enabled diverse groups to live together peacefully and cooperatively; they also demonstrated the virtue and superiority of American culture. This concept of consensus implies a view and a 'construction'[4] of the America of the 1940s and 1950s, not only as an orderly, pacified society, based upon some degree of general consensus over norms and values such as pragmatism, social tolerance and non-dogmatic habits, but also as the – postindustrial,[5] end-of-the-ideology,[6] pluralist – model democratic society called to overcome, and capable of overcoming, any form of totalitarianism and absolutism in the world.[7]

Recently, American historians have been emphasizing the complexities, conflicts and unrest of the 'age of conformity' as bearing the seeds of the dissenting 1960s and 1970s.[8] I agree with the Dutch historian Tity de Vries that the consensus was at least a complex one.[9] She suggests significant differences among the New York intellectuals on issues such as the moral foundation of politics, anti-anti-communism, end-of-ideology and conformism and mass culture. The extent to which opinions in America disagreed on educational philosophy becomes perfectly clear when studying the post-war Report of the United States Education Mission to Germany. According to the assistant secretary of state for public affairs, in the United States there was 'no common body of educational thought, which can be adequately interpreted by any ten individuals, applied to the present situation'.[10]

In the line of work previously done by Philip Gleason and David Hollinger,[11] the thesis of my paper is that the so-called consensus-driven Forties and Fifties demonstrated a considerable range of often conflicting and antagonistic 'approaches to national unity' discourses, in particular when discussing what was seen as necessary post-war reforms of democracy in its (global) war for survival. For a revision of this era, the focus of attention has to be turned away from the deradicalization ('conformization') of pre-war radical (New York) intellectuals [12] to what was going on in the mainstream of American academia. In fact, as Gleason put it, by 1939 a 'mighty democratic revival was under way which continued into the wartime years and shaped the outlook of a whole generation.'[13] Within this broad movement for democracy, various organizations emerged with often conflicting views and producing a flood of publications that were dedicated to defining, defending and promoting democracy. In the intellectual arena the major contestants were, on the one hand, the *Conference on Science, Philosophy and Religion in their Relation to the Democratic Way of Life*, a religious reform movement, stressing the need for a (Christian) spiritual foundation for democracy in its battle with totalitarianism; on the other hand, various secular reform groups, the most important of which was the *Conference on the Scientific Spirit and Democratic Faith*, stressing scientific naturalism and the experimental approach as the basics of democracy.

My first proposition is that in the so-called age of conformity in mid-century America these intellectual reform movements presented *cultural* agendas with respect to the foundations of democracy. So far the views of these reform movements have been seen as conflicting and bitterly opposed, some authors writing of their conflicts as *Culture Wars* or *Kulturkämpfe*.[14] But they agreed upon one thing: the moral foundations of democracy were to be sought in the cultural domain rather than in (socio)economics or politics. Democracy was not seen as intrinsically anchored morally by its constitution, its procedures and 'checks and balances'.[15] Neither was credence attached to the 'invisible hand' of the free-market economy, which from the days of Adam Smith onwards should have brought people and nations together by reinforcing interdependency and its civilizing process; nor to the institution of a system of social security as the moral base of democracy.[16] The debate was held in *cultural* terms, and religion and science played a key role in it.

The mid-twentieth century cultural discourses were – and that is the second point I wish to make – only partly American in their origins. The religious, 'personalist' discourse was French, and French Thomist in particular. Personalism was a Christian Reveil movement with a double programme. It was a *political programme* suggesting a (typically European) combination of Christendom and socialism, against individualism (capitalism, liberalism) and collectivism ('mass-society', Communism, Fascism); and also a *French anti-Enlightenment programme* that radically opposed religion to science and to the Enlightenment. The political programme of personalism was very influential in the post-war intellectual debate in the Netherlands, although it was finally rejected because of its exclusively Christian and therefore intolerant nature.[17] The anti-Enlightenment programme of personalism was influential in the United States [18] and was responded to by John Dewey and others in the tradition of American pragmatism and of the American Enlightenment.

A Religious Discourse

World War II in America stimulated reflection upon the foundations of democracy and upon the task of the universities and of science in society. The protagonists of a religious discourse were united in the *Conference on Science, Philosophy and Religion in Their Relation to the Democratic Way of Life*.[19] Among the initiators were Robert M. MacIver, Pitirim A. Sorokin, Mortimer J. Adler, Jacques Maritain, Albert Einstein and Harald D. Lasswell. They enrolled seventy-nine leading scholars as 'founding members' in June 1940, and organized a series of symposia. There was a consensus among the founders that no common culture existed throughout the world which provided an adequate basis for the maintenance of democracy, peace and security. Ethical and spiritual ideals had to be instilled if the world's culture was to provide a suitable environment for democracy and a free world society. The only scale of values which provided a key for coping with the spread of pockets of totalitarianism within the United States and without was that reflected in Christianity.[20] Democracy could only exist in a Christian state, in spite of history and all contemporary facts to the contrary.[21] The gatherings of the conference were held at the Men's Faculty Club of Columbia University annually through the war years and for over a decade thereafter. The proceedings of each symposium were published.[22] In 1939, under the auspices of the Roman-Catholic University of Notre Dame, Indiana, they founded a journal, *The Review of Politics*. The spiritual father of this intellectual reform movement was the French neo-Thomist Jacques Maritain, who emigrated to the United States in the late 1930s.

Maritain's personalism was influenced through his participation in the *Catholic Worker*, an American movement led by Dorothy Day, a convert introduced to Catholic social thought by the French peasant philosopher Peter Maurin in the 1930s. Day integrated orthodox Catholicism with radical social thought and developed an American version of personalism.[23] A 'personalist revolution in self and society' was necessary, in which the love of Christ forced Christians toward personalist commitment to see Christ in His poor. She 'consistently practiced and promoted the voluntary spiritual disciplines of prayer, worship, retreat, and fasting, insisting on the "primacy of the spiritual" as the necessary foundation of any lasting personal and social transformation.'[24] The movement lost its influence in the 1940s because of its pacifism. During the war, Jacques Maritain was one of the initiators of the establishment in 1942 of the École Libre des Hautes Études at the New School for Social Research in New York. This autonomous, self-governing French university in exile followed the model for German, Italian and Austrian scholars established in 1933 at the same school.[25]

The keynote article, 'Integral Humanism and the Crisis of Modern Times', in the first issue of *The Review of Politics* came from Maritain's hand. Maritain argued that Fascism, Nazism and Communism formed the latest phase of forms of the Enlightenment, rationalism and humanism. In their anthropocentric view of man and culture, religious life (prayer, miracle, suprarational truths, the idea of sin and grace, the Evangelical blessings, the necessity of ascesis and contemplation, and the ways of the Cross) was put in brackets or denied. In the concrete government of human life, reason was not open for, but was isolated from, the supra-rational. Maritain saw Fascism and the other totalitarian movements as substitute religions, as the 'anti-Christ'.[26] He and other Roman Catholic intellectuals emphasized the need for spiritual values in a secular, dechristianizing society and the crucial contribution of Christian religion to democracy.

Significantly, Maritain did not introduce his personalism in America as a way of combining Christendom and socialism, nor as a political programme against (capitalistic, 'American') individualism and (German and Soviet-Russian) collectivism (Nazism and Communism), which in his view were equally to be condemned. This was done in the second issue of the *Review of Politics* by Goetz Briefs, who reviewed Wilfrid Parsons' book *Which Way, Democracy?*[27] Briefs agreed with Parsons that 'neither the Jews nor the Communists nor the Nazis were the villains of the crisis of democracy', but the decline of Christianity. According to the Founding Fathers, religion should be a man's private affair. The separation of church and state, which they proclaimed for the sake of tolerance, was later on transformed into the right of the government to control the public sphere exclusively. Politics and business dominated public life, preventing religion from sharing in it. Immense harm was done when deep issues of family, marriage and education were at stake. 'Whenever these issues turn up, they are decided according to the majority principle, not according to Christian tenets and morals any more.' What Communism and Fascism had in common with the Catholic Church was that they believed in principles. No secular democracy had the power to cope with them. Democratic institutions did not in themselves wield a 'magic power of salvation'; there was no inherent virtue in rule by the people. Democracy, cut adrift from natural law and from religious sanctions, was in danger of becoming a technique of government. The inherent weakness of democracy was its being too closely allied to liberalism. The fateful legacy of democracy linked with individualism was the destruction or weakening of the sub-political and social units and institutions. Their normal hierarchically-graded functions could no longer be fulfilled by them. A narrow path was open, 'leading between individualistic capitalism and collectivism of one kind or another'. Government had to care for the common good. The New Deal represented an attempt in this direction. 'With all its shortcomings, it shows that there is a way to disregard Liberalism and yet avoid Communism or Fascism.' It would be a disaster if it were otherwise. In the whole Western world there was left only one genuine and uninterrupted tradition of common welfare and of the vital requirements of human society: in Catholic social philosophy.

In America, Maritain's personalism was primarily directed against the Enlightenment:

> Neither Locke, nor Jean-Jacques Rousseau, nor the Encyclopedists can pass as thinkers faithful to the integrity of the Christian heritage. There, too, everything indicates that a great renewal of spirit is being prepared, which tends to bring democracy back to its true essence and purify its principles.[28]

The contribution of science and technology to the moral foundation of society was seen as very dubious.[29] We have to remember here that, in contrast to the American and also the Dutch and the Scottish Enlightenments, which were primarily directed against political power,[30] religious i.e. Roman Catholic authority was the main target of the French Enlightenment. Personalism was a kind of revenge of Christian religion, challenging the French Enlightenment's equation of religion with fanaticism, intolerance and reaction.[31]

American Catholic scholars, from Georgetown University in Washington DC in particular, launched an offensive against America's most illustrious secular scholars and intellectuals, such as Justice Oliver Wendell Holmes Jr and John Dewey. Oliver Wendell Holmes Jr (1841–1935), a justice of the US Supreme Court, did more than any other American thinker to develop and popularize the insight that law is a living, changing part of culture, responsive to shifting circumstances with which societies must cope.[32] According to Father Francis E. Lucey SJ, a regent of the Georgetown University School of Law, 'the inevitable result of Holmesian jurisprudence was a rather disagreeable (ugly) conclusion; one which is causing a Second World War.' His ultimate philosophy of law and life was a 'crude form of totalitarianism'.[33] According to Father Stephen MacNamee SJ, a professor of ethics at Georgetown, John Dewey and other American non-Catholic university professors had, for the most part, been 'sappers instead of architects and builders of democracy'. The irony was, in MacNamee's view, that the person who was seen as the intellectual leader and the leading philosopher of democracy had in fact, by denying God and man's God-given rights, been undermining the very principles of American democracy.[34]

Among the protagonists of the religious discourse, Robert M. Hutchins, president of the University of Chicago, another bulwark of Catholicism, was the spokesman for university reform.[35] In his Aristotelian-Thomistic educational theory, metaphysics is the highest wisdom and the unifying principle of all academic subjects and of all academic institutions.[36] 'It is the highest science, the first science, and as first, universal.' Referring to Plato, Aristotle and Aquinas and claiming that 'knowledge is truth, and the truth is everywhere the same', Hutchins like Maritain was not arguing for any specific theological or metaphysical system, but for revitalizing metaphysics, the study of the first principles on which the social sciences and natural sciences were dependent, and restoring it to its central place in higher learning, so that 'we may be able to establish rational order in the modern world as well as in the universities'.[37]

Hutchins propagated a reform of liberal education in terms of the '100 great books tradition,' the shibboleth of cultural conservatives in

America and an alternative to American pragmatism and utilitarianism. The 'Chicago Plan' was the main reference at the Ninth Symposium of the *Conference on Science, Philosophy and Religion*.[38] Its main opponents were what Hutchins called the 'cults' of naturalism, scepticism, relativism, materialism and utilitarianism which would have 'captured' American culture, the state and education.

> The liberal arts are the arts of freedom. To be free a man must understand the tradition in which he lives. A great book is one that yields up through the liberal arts a clear and important understanding of our tradition. An education which consists of liberal arts as understood through great books and of great books as understood through liberal arts would be one and the only one which would enable us to understand the tradition in which we live. It must follow that if we want to educate our students for freedom, we must educate them in the liberal arts and in the great books.[39]

This curriculum would form the first step in a spiritual revolution, 'the moral, intellectual and spiritual reformation' for which the world waited.[40] One could not take part in this revolution, as Hutchins tells us, 'if one believes that men are no different from brutes, that morals are another name for the mores, that freedom is doing what you please, that everything is a matter of opinion, and that the test for truth is immediate practical success.'[41]

For educationalists, the attractiveness of Maritain's personalism was that it gave place to 'interests and recognized the importance of a creative approach to life and that it is a function of education to help people deal with their environment.' Maritain, as one of his opponents said, had 'everything in fostering the growth of personality, including creativeness and originality, provided you came out in the right way as regards dogmas at the end.'[42] With the breakdown of neo-Thomism in the 1950s, and the rise of the new social movements in the 1960s, personalism lost its attractiveness.

A Secular Discourse

Initially, membership of the *Conference on Science, Philosophy and Religion in Their Relation to the Democratic Way of Life* included religious traditionalists as well as Progressive thinkers like John Dewey, Horace Kallen, Eduard C. Lindeman, Jerome Nathanson and Herbert W. Schneider. Dissatisfied with the strong religious orientation of this conference, these protagonists of a secular discourse founded in 1943 the alternative *Conference of the Scientific Spirit and Democratic Faith*, placing a plainly polemic emphasis on the words 'spirit' and 'faith'.[43] John Dewey, eighty-four years old, was the spiritual father of this secular intellectual reform movement. Unfortunately, the proceedings of only two meetings were recorded and printed. Against the 'absolutists', according to whom the survival of democracy depended upon the return to (Christian) belief and to the eternal philosophical and social truths, the 'relativists' posed a democracy that was related to scientific naturalism and the experimental approach.[44] The debate, however, was not held in terms of 'pluralism versus Christendom', in the sense of 'pluralism against religion', as the work of some recent authors suggests.[45] In the tradition of the American Enlightenment, science is not the negation of religion; the American Enlightenment placed religion in the background of the public sphere and theology to the fringe of the universities. Maritain's French anti-Enlightenment diatribes implied absolutist claims for the Christian religion. The relativists were against any form of absolutism and its implied intolerance and anti-Semitism. They were – much to their credit – strongly opposed to the exclusive Christian character of personalism. They challenged not only Nazism, but also the absolutist Roman Catholic doctrine and the Communist movement because of their strong 'religious character'. Science, as David Hollinger put it, offered these American intellectuals a welcome ideological refuge. They related the adjective 'scientific' to 'public rather than private knowledge, with open rather than closed discourses, with universal rather than local standards of warrant, with democratic rather than aristocratic models of authority.'[46]

Robert Merton's work was very influential, most of all his controversial 'A Note on Science and Democracy', first published in 1942 in the *Journal of Legal and Political Studies*.[47] Merton was a sociologist who saw science as an institution under attack, restraint, and repression in Fascist regimes, but not only there. Anti-intellectualism threatened to become epidemic. According to Merton, universalism, Communism, disinterestedness and organized scepticism comprised the ethos of modern science. Universalism meant that truth-claims, whatever their source, were to be subjected to pre-established impersonal criteria, consonant with observation and with previously confirmed knowledge. 'Particularly in times of international conflict, when the dominant definition of the situation is such as to emphasize national loyalties, the man of science is subjected to the conflicting imperatives of scientifc universalism and of ethnocentric particularism.' 'Communism' is to be understood as common ownership of goods; the findings of science are a product of social collaboration and are assigned to the community. They constitute a common heritage. Science is part of a public domain. 'Disinterestedness' refers to the virtual absence of fraud in the annals of science, a quite exceptional phenomenon when compared with the record of other spheres of activity. The cause lies in science itself, in its public and testable character. Finally, in Merton's view, organized scepticism is both a methodological and an institutional mandate. The temporary suspension of judgment and the detached scrutiny of beliefs have brought science into conflict with other institutions. The scholar does not preserve the cleavage between the sacred and the profane. Organized scepticism had brought science in conflict with religious interests, and with economic and political groups. Merton's formulation of the scientific ethos was located in the defence of democracy. The moral qualities science stands for were seen by him as intrinsic to the practice of science.

Influence was also wielded by Mark May, director of the Yale's Institute of Social Relations, and one of the speakers at the first meeting of the *Conference of the Scientific Spirit and Democratic Faith*.[48] His paper on the moral code of scientists was not so much directed at Fascists as at Catholics. Although, as Hollinger has emphasised, some Catholics did hold Progressive views, and some were themselves victims of Protestant prejudice, 'the Protestant, Jewish and agnostic intellectuals who rallied to the banner of science and democracy had strong reasons for believing that Roman Catholic priests and their fellow-travelling intellectuals were a genuine and formidable obstacle in a struggle over the future of American culture.'[49] Substantial sections of the Catholic hierarchy in the United States were openly sympathetic to the Fascist cause. Notions of a 'Christian' culture had still strong anti-Semitic connotations. According to May, the morality of science consists of six imperatives: (1) absolute honesty with oneself and one's fellow scientists; (2) fearless acceptance of verified facts regardless of the personal consequences of such acceptance; (3) the results of science are common property to men everywhere; (4) the contributors to this common store of knowledge are to be recognized as such, and not victimized by the pirating of their ideas; (5) controversies among scientists are to be settled by an appeal to facts rather than by *ad hominem* arguments, personal vituperation or an appeal to authority; and (6) full freedom of inquiry.

After the war, best known were the 'red book' of Harvard University, *General Education in a Free Society*, and James Conant's *On Understanding Science*.[50] In these publications science was seen as the foundation of the spiritual values of a democratic humanism, and it was declared that American democracy needed citizens with 'the habit of forming objective, disinterested judgments based upon exact evidence'. The Christian ethos which had so long dominated the American colleges was in their view an anachronism. People felt lost in modern society not because they did not hold on any longer to the belief of their ancestors, but because they 'failed to assimilate science into their culture'. In Conant's concept of a secular culture it is not the scientist who is put on a pedestal.[51] Conant's heroes were those who were able to think and judge as scientists without the continuous, careful supervision of peers and without the support of a 'self-propagating social phenomenon', that made impartiality for the working scientist an unheroic routine. His great examples were Petraca, Machiavelli, Rabelais and Montaigne, free-thinking critics of religious orthodoxy, together with various 'honest explorers and hard-headed statesmen and military commanders' who, without the advantage of institutional reinforcement, courageously came to reason-based decisions. The point was not, as David Hollinger summarizes Conant's concept, to imitate the life of scientists, but to operate in a scientific way in social environments, which in many respects differed from the scientific world. McCarthyism enhanced these views. In their *The Development of Academic Freedom in the United States* of 1955, Hofstadter and Metzger upheld the practice of science as the tradition to which mankind owed more than to all other historical influences 'tolerance and honesty, publicity and testifiability,' 'universalism' and 'disinterestedness'.[52]

The problem of the pragmatic-relativist theory of democracy and the significance of the scientific enterprise for democracy was that, unnoticed, American democracy and – given the presupposed intimate connection between science and democracy – the American (social) sciences could be proclaimed as the norm for the world. Participants in the second *Conference of the Scientific Spirit and Democratic Faith* such as F. Allport and A. Carlson stated blatantly: 'The scientific way is also the democratic way. Science and democracy cannot flourish without each other' and 'There is absolute harmony between the scientific spirit and our fundamental democratic faith in the principles and processes of democracy.'[53] Whereas John Dewey and Sidney Hook saw democracy as a hypothesis, an experiment, of which the practice had to be tested over and over again by criteria of social equality and justice,[54] empiricism was conceived by them as a 'commitment to a procedure, not a theory of metaphysics'. 'The cluster of values we bring to the situation is the result of prior experience and reflection. They are not arbitrarily postulated.' The temptation to turn democracy into something absolutely valid in and for itself, and requiring no justification, should be avoided. They did not oppose religion as such, but rather absolutist claims from the side of Christians. The earlier problem had been how to breed tolerance in America between people adhering to so many denominations; the problem had now become how to cooperate on an international level with nations having an economic system and political traditions that were fundamentally different from the American ones.[55]

John Dewey spoke strongly against the separation, propagated by Hutchins *et al.*, between liberal education and vocational training.

As far as such a separation exists in fact, it is an inheritance from the earlier class structure of human relations. It is a denial of democracy. At the very time when an important, perhaps the most important, problem in education is to fill education having an occupational direction with a genuinely liberal content, we have, believe it or not, a movement, such as is sponsored, for example by President Hutchins, to cut vocational training off from any contact with what is liberating by relegating it to special schools devoted to inculcation of technical skills. Inspiring vocational education with a liberal spirit and filling it with a liberal content is not a utopian dream. It is demonstrated possibility in schools here and there in which subjects usually labelled 'practically useful' are taught, charged with scientific understanding and with a sense of the universal social-moral applications they potentially possess.[56]

Democracy was, in Dewey's view, not an easy road to take and follow. The biggest task ahead was to humanize science, a task which could not be accomplished without also humanizing the fruit of science which is named technology.

Conclusion

The importance of the two intellectual reform movements in the American Era of Conformity is their contribution to the debate on the foundations of democracy. They put the cultural domain on the agenda, alongside the political and the economic domains. It was Daniel Bell who expressed so well the contradictory consequences of what I would call 'the three domain theory of democracy' on the level of the individual scholar and intellectual, by portraying himself as a conservative in cultural affairs, a liberal in politics and a socialist in economics.[57] Opinions still differ widely over the question of the relative importance for democracy of the cultural domain compared with the political, the economic and the military spheres. The cultural domain certainly is a controversial one, an arena moreover with many contestants: science, religion, the arts and the media. The most substantial contribution to the study of the values underpinning democracy was Merton's formulation of the scientific ethos. Critical as one can be of his formulation, his analysis of values implied in scientific behaviour illuminates science and its relation to democracy.

The debate incited in mid-twentieth century America by the two intellectual reform movements made clear that Americans hate but tend to tolerate radical religious belief (fundamentalism) as much as radical rationalism. The 'real' problem is not the relationship between science and religion, but the division of powers between cultural authority, economic exploitation and political power.

Notes

1. Richard Hofstadter, *The Age of Reform. From Bryan to F.D.R.* (New York: Vintage Books, 1955).
2. Irwin Howe, 'This Age of Conformity', *Partisan Review* 21 (1954): 7–33; Daniel Boorstein, *The Genius of American Politics* (Chicago: Chicago University Press, 1953).
3. Edward A. Purcell, Jr., 'Consensus', in Richard Wightman Fox and James T. Kloppenberg, eds, *A Companion to American Thought* (Oxford: Blackwell, 1996), 140–1.
4. In contrast to postmodernist orthodoxy, I do not consider every view, opinion or theory to be a social construction, but only those with definable social and political implications and consequences.
5. Daniel Bell, *The Coming of Post-Industrial Society* (New York: Basic Books, 1973).
6. Daniel Bell adopted an anti-ideological perspective, but not a conservative one. In response to the Marxist ideologies, he said, many intellectuals began to fear 'the masses' or any form of social action. 'But a repudiation of ideology, to be meaningful, must mean not only criticism of the utopian order but of existing society as well.' Daniel Bell, *The End of Ideology. On the Exhaustion of Political Ideas in the Fifties* [1960] (Cambridge, MA: Harvard University Press, 1988), 16.
7. The view of consensus as creating both social order and a national mission has much in common with Gunnar Myrdal's concept of the American creed and with R. N. Bellah's use of the Durkheimian concept of civil religion. The concept of civil religion refers to the beliefs, symbols, rituals and institutions which legitimate the social system, create social solidarity and mobilize a community to achieve common political objectives. Bryan S. Turner, *Religion and Social Theory* (London: Sage, 1991), 52–6; R. N. Bellah, *Beyond Belief, Essays on Religion in a Post-Traditional World* (New York: Harper and Row, 1970); Gunnar Myrdal, *An American Dilemma. The Negro Problem and Modern Democracy* (New York: Harper, 1944).
8. John P. Diggins, *The Proud Decades: America in War and Peace, 1941–1960* (New York: Diggins, 1988); David Halberstam, *The Fifties* (New York: Harper and Row, 1993); A. Jamison and R. Eyerman, *Seeds of the Sixties* (Berkeley: Berkeley University Press, 1994).
9. Tity de Vries, *Complexe consensus. Amerikaanse en Nederlandse intellectuelen in debat over politiek en cultuur 1945–1960* ['Complex Consensus: American and Dutch Intellectuals Debate on Politics and Culture 1945–1960'], Ph.D. diss., University of Amsterdam (Hilversum: Verloren, 1996).
10. *Report of the United States Education Mission to Germany* (Washington, DC: US Government Printing Office, 1946), iv.

11. Philip Gleason, 'World War II and the Development of American Studies', *American Quarterly* 36 (1984): 343–58; David A. Hollinger, 'Science as a Weapon in *Kulturkämpfe* in the United States,' *Isis* 86 (September 1995): 440–54; also included in his: *Science, Jews, and Secular Culture. Studies in Mid-Twentieth-Century American Intellectual History* (Princeton, NJ: Princeton University Press, 1996): 155–74.
12. Richard Pells, *The Liberal Mind in a Conservative Age. American Intellectuals in the 1940s and 1950s* (New York: Harper and Row, 1985); Terry A. Cooney, *The Rise of the New York Intellectuals: 'Partisan Review' and Its Circle, 1943–1945* (Madison: University of Wisconsin Press, 1986).
13. Gleason, 'World War II', 345–6.
14. Hollinger, 'Science as a Weapon'. Although James Davison Hunter did not pay very much attention to the mid-century discussions, his distinction between the *impulse toward orthodoxy* and the *impulse towards Progressivism* fits remarkably well with mine between a religious and a secular discourse. Orthodoxy, adhered to by religious people from all kinds of denominations, is, in Hunter's view, the commitment to an external, definable and transcendent authority. The progressivist world view, adhered to mostly by secularists, is the tendency to resymbolize historic faiths according to the prevailing assumptions of contemporary life. James Davison Hunter, *Culture Wars: The Struggle to Define America* (New York: Basic Books, 1991), 43–5. Although the mid-twentieth century religious ('personalist') discourse was formulated by Roman Catholics, it attracted an almost ecumenical crowd and precluded religious pluralism that would rise soon after the war. In my view, religious pluralism is the logical outcome of the struggle of religions versus secularism in the modern era. Religions sharing the fate of being in decline and under secular attack all over the world, tend to cooperate and to tolerate each other. In the contemporary Netherlands, the Roman Catholic Church strongly supports the establishment of mosques for Islamic immigrants; it is better to adhere to a religion, even if that religion is Islam, than to be irreligious or nonreligious.
15. See for this constitutionalist view Michael Walzer, 'What Does It Mean to Be an "American"?,' *Social Research* 57 (1990): 591–614.
16. In a famous mid-century Dutch report, both religious-ethical and economic and political motives are put forward for the development of a universal system of social security. It was a matter of social justice, of the increase of productivity and a more even purchasing power (redistribution of social income), and of the removal of causes of internal and international conflicts and wars. *Sociale Zekerheid*. Rapport van de Commissie, ingesteld bij beschikking van den Minister van Sociale Zaken van 26 Maart 1943 (London, 1944): deel 1, 14–18.

In contrast to the very succesful Beveridge Report of 1942 in Great Britain, in which the 'welfare state' was opposed to the Nazi 'warfare state', the report of the American National Resources Planning Board was rather badly received. 'The NRPB proposed major organizations and extensions of US policies that would accompany measures to sustain a full-employment economy. With the Democrats in nominal control and President Roosevelt in office, reformers hoped to use the war to complete the New Deal. But their aims were not to be realized. New Deal public employment agencies were phased out, and the comprehensive plans of the National Resources Planning Board were thwarted.' Margaret Weir, Ann Shola Orloff and Theda Skocpol, eds, *The Politics of Social Policy in the United States* (Princeton, NJ: Princeton University Press, 1988), 82. The only substantial improvement was the 1944 GI bill for veterans and their families. National Resources Planning Board, *Security, Work and Relief* (Washington, DC: US Government Printing Office, 1942).

17. In the Netherlands, W. Banning, professor in the sociology of religion at Leiden University and Christian-socialist, defined the personalist discourse, with the help of which the pre-war Socialist Party (Sociaal Democratische Arbeiders Partij) was transformed into a Social-Democratic Party (Partij van de Arbeid). His own and his followers' attempt to get a so-called 'central department of philosophy, psychology and pedagogics' instituted at the universities, to breed a common spiritual foundation of Western (Christian) civilization in the minds of all students, was rejected because of its exclusive Christian character, excluding Jews, Humanists, Muslims and others. In the view of Banning, the Netherlands could play an important role on the post-war world scene by being a personalist (Christian-socialist) nation, mediating between, and superior to, liberalism and collectivism. See J. C. C. Rupp, *Van oude en nieuwe universiteiten. De verdringing van Duitse door Amerikaanse voorbeelden van wetenschapsbeoefening en hoger onderwijs in Nederland, 1945–1995* ['The Transformation of the University. The Superseding of German by American Influences on Scholarship and Higher Learning in the Netherlands, 1945–1995'] (Den Haag: SDU, 1997), Chapters 5–6.

18. Philip Gleason, *Keeping the Faith: American Catholicism Past and Present* (Notre Dame: University of Notre Dame Press, 1987); Mel Piehl, 'Catholicism', in *A Companion to American Thought*, 105–10.

19. *Proceedings of Conference on Science, Philosophy and Religion in Their Relation to the Democratic Way of Life* (New York: The Conference, 1940–1955).

20. Donald C. Stone, 'The Function of the University in a Free Society', in Lyman Bryson, Louis Finkelstein and R. M. Maciver, eds, *Goals for American Education* (New York: The Conference on Science, Philosophy and Religion, 1950), 235–41, esp. 239–41.

21. *Science, Philosophy and Religion, Second Symposium* (New York: Conference on Science, Philosophy and Religion in Their Relation to the Democratic Way of Life, 1942), 210.

22. Including a final meeting in 1960, sixteen symposia were held. Harold Lasswell and Harlan Cleveland, eds, *The Ethic of Power. The Interplay of Religion, Philosophy and Politics* (New York: The Conference on Science, Philosophy and Religion in Their Relation to the Democratic Way of Life, 1962), 491–2.

23. Mel Piehl, *Breaking Bread: 'The Catholic Worker' and the Origin of Catholic Radicalism in America* (Philadephia: Temple University Press, 1982); Nancy L. Roberts, *Dorothy Day and 'The Catholic Worker'* (Albany: State University of New York Press, 1984); Mary Jo Weaver, *New Catholic Women* (New York: Harper and Row, 1985).

24. Mel Piehl, 'Dorothy Day', in *A Companion to American Thought*, 168–70.
25. Peter M. Rutkoff and William B. Scott, *New School. A History of the New School for Social Research* (New York: The Free Press, 1986), 86–106, 153–71.
26. Jacques Maritain, 'Integral Humanism and the Crisis of Modern Times', *The Review of Politics* 1 (January 1939): 1–17. See also Goetz A. Briefs, 'The Crisis of Our Age', *The Review of Politics* 4 (1942): 315–26.
27. Rev. Wilfrid Parsons, S.J., *Which Way, Democracy?* (New York: MacMillan, 1939); Briefs, 'Crisis of Democracy', *Review of Politics* 1.2 (1939): 350–6.
28. Thomas F. Woodlock, introduction to *Democracy: Should it Survive?* (Milwaukee, WI: Bruce Publishing Co., 1942), 8.
29. Hollinger, 'Science as a Weapon', 442.
30. Sheldon Rothblatt argues that the Scottish philosophical school of Common Sense, imported into the United States at the end of the eighteenth century, provided a reasonably succesful means of integrating a liberal arts curriculum of classical languages, modern languages, modern social science and some methods of experimental science. 'It should be pointed out that neither the Scottish nor American version of the Enlightenment were anti-clerical.' Sheldon Rothblatt, 'The Limbs of Osiris: Liberal Education in the English-Speaking World', in Sheldon Rothblatt and Björn Wittrock, eds, *The European and American University since 1800* (Cambridge: Cambridge University Press, 1993): 19–74, esp. 42–3; Joseph Ellis, ed., 'An American Enlightenment,' *American Quarterly* 28 (1976): 147–271; Henry May, *The Enlightenment in America* (New York: Oxford University Press, 1976); James T. Kloppenberg, 'Enlightenment,' in *A Companion to American Thought*, 207–9; Margaret C. Jacob and Wijnand W. Mijnhardt, eds, *The Dutch Republic in the Eighteenth Century. Decline, Enlightenment and Revolution* (Ithaca, NY: Cornell University Press, 1992).
31. James Hunter wrongly applies the French definition of the Enlightenment to the American situation. This equation contradicts his own observation that 'anticlericalism and general opposition to religious institutions and sensibilities were both extreme and violent in France after the Revolution; Americans who heard about the terrors of French republicanism feared that the French experience might be replicated in America.' Hunter, *Culture Wars*, 41, 351 n.
32. David A. Hollinger and Charles Capper, eds, *The American Intellectual Tradition. Volume II 1865 to the Present* (New York/Oxford: Oxford University Press, 1993), 127.
33. Francis E. Lucey, 'Natural Law and American Legal Realism: Their Respective Contributions to a Theory of Law in a Democratic Society', *Georgetown Law Journal* 30 (April 1942): 498–533. Quoted in: Edward A. Purcell Jr, *The Crisis of Democratic Theory. Scientific Naturalism and the Problem of Value* (Lexington: The University Press of Kentucky, 1973), 168.
34. Stephen MacNamee, S.J., 'Presidential Address,' in *Phases of American Culture* (Worcester, MA, 1942), 11–12. Quoted by Purcell, *The Crisis of Democratic Theory*, 180.

35. Robert M. Hutchins, *The Higher Learning in America* (New Haven, CT: Yale University Press, 1936); Robert M. Hutchins, *Education for Freedom* (Baton Rouge: Louisiana State University Press, 1939).
36. Purcell, *The Crisis of Democratic Theory*, 148–9.
37. Hutchins, *The Higher Learning in America*, 105.
38. During this conference the 'Chicago Plan' was introduced and discussed by ten scholars: Lyman Bryson (Teachers College, Columbia University), T. V. Smith (professor of philosophy, Syracuse University), Alain L. Locke (professor of philosophy, Howard University), Howard Mumford Jones (professor of English, Harvard University), Mordecai M. Kaplan (professor of the philosophy of religion, The Jewish Theological Seminary of America), George N. Shuster (president, Hunter College of the City of New York), John U. Nef (chairman Committee on Social Thought, University of Chicago), Earl J. MacGrath (dean of the College of Liberal Arts, State University of Iowa), Ordway Tead (chairman Board of Education, City of New York), and George B. de Huszar's (history editor, *American People's Encyclopaedia*). Lyman Bryson, Louis Finkelstein and R. M. Maciver, eds, *Goals for American Education* (New York: The Conference on Science, Philosophy and Religion, 1950).
39. Hutchins, *The Higher Learning in America*, 14.
40. Hutchins and the philosopher Mortimer J. Adler started an adult education programme in 1941. In 1948 some forty thousand or more people were taking part in the classes. It was hoped that the number would increase in geometrical progression from year to year until it reached into the millions. John U. Nef, 'The Goal of American Education,' in *Goals for American Education*, 243–60, esp. 253.
41. Hutchins, *Education for Freedom*, 47.
42. *The Authoritarian Attempt to Capture Education.* Papers from the 2nd Conference of the Scientific Spirit and Democratic Faith (New York: King's Crown Press, 1945), 85.
43. Gleason makes mention of a couple of other organizations advocating support of democracy against totalitarian threats. One of these was the Committee of Fifteen, which published a manifesto entitled *The City of Man: A Declaration on World Democracy* (1941). Among its members were Alvin Johnson, Thomas Mann, Lewis Mumford and Reinhold Niebuhr. Gleason, 'World War II', 347–8.
44. For the distinction to be made between the pragmatic naturalism of John Dewey and the naturalism of logical positivists (many of them German emigrés like Rudolf Carnap, Herbert Feigl and Hans Reichenbach), see Henry Samuel Levinson, *The Religious Investigations of William James* (Chapel Hill: University of North Carolina, 1981); Richard Rorty, *Contingency, Irony and Solidarity* (Cambridge: Cambridge University Press, 1989); Henry Samuel Levinson, 'Naturalism', in *A Companion to American Thought*, 480–3.
45. Hunter, *Culture Wars*. See also the discussion in *Culture*, Newsletter of the Sociology of Culture, Section of the American Sociological Association, 10 (1996) and 11 (1997).
46. Hollinger, 'Science as a Weapon', 444.

47. Robert K. Merton, 'A Note on Science and Democracy (Science and Technology in a Democratic Order)', *Journal of Legal and Political Studies* 1 (1942): 115–26. Later publicized as 'The Normative Structure of Science,' in *The Sociology of Science* (Chicago: Chicago University Press, 1973), 267–8. For a critique see S. B. Barnes and R. G. A. Dolby, 'The Scientific Ethos: A Deviant Viewpoint,' *Archives Européennes de sociologie* 11 (1970): 3–25; and also, for a more balanced view, Richard McKeon, 'Democracy, Scientific Method, and Action', *Ethics* 55.4 (July 1945): 235–86. McKeon, a professor at the University of Chicago, contributed this essay to the symposium 'Is Scientific Method Neutral to Democracy?', which was held at the New School for Social Research under the auspices of the Conference on Method in Philosophy and the Sciences in New York on 11 April 1943.
48. Mark A. May, 'The Moral Code of Scientists', in Eduard C. Lindeman, ed., *The Scientific Spirit and Democratic Faith* (New York: King's Crown Press, 1944), 40–6.
49. Hollinger, 'Science as a Weapon', 159.
50. Paul Buck, et al., *General Education in a Free Society* (Cambridge, MA: Harvard University Press, 1945); James Conant, *On Understanding Science: An Historical Approach* (New Haven, CT: Yale University Press, 1947).
51. Hollinger, 'Science as a Weapon', 445–6.
52. Richard Hofstadter and Walter P. Metzger, *The Development of Academic Freedom in the United States* (New York: Columbia University Press, 1955).
53. *The Authoritarian Attempt to Capture Education*, 52–65, 66–73.
54. Yervant H. Krikorian, ed., *Naturalism and the Human Spirit* (New York: Columbia University Press, 1944), 1–16, 33–64.
55. *The Authoritarian Attempt to Capture Education*, 24, 85. Eduard C. Lindeman, professor in social philosophy at Columbia University and chairman of the first conference, during the discussions took great care that the 'Progressive educators' would not neglect the relevance of religion for culture.
56. *The Authoritarian Attempt to Capture Education*, 8.
57. Daniel Bell, *The Cultural Contradictions of Capitalism* (New York: Basic Books, 1976).

12

Evangelicalism, Social Reform and the US Welfare State, 1970–1996

Axel R. Schaefer

Introduction

The resurgence of Evangelical and Fundamentalist Christianity constitutes one of the most significant and striking developments in American religion since the 1930s, and in US politics since the 1960s.[1] This paper argues that a closer analysis of the political and cultural impact of the revival is crucial in understanding the development of the welfare state and the dynamics of social policy in the United States.

The focus of this presentation, however, is not on the New Christian Right and its attempts to dismantle the welfare state.[2] Rather, the emphasis is put on the resurgence of Evangelical social activism and the way in which it helped both preserve a federal role in the realm of social provision and perpetuate the contradictory nature of the US welfare system.

The first part of the paper addresses the problems of defining Evangelicalism and its political impact, explores the social reform impulses of the resurgent Evangelical movement and examines the relationship between charities and the federal government. Part two of the presentation is devoted to a discussion of the contradictions embedded in US social policies and the role religious narratives and sensitivities play in constructing this paradox.

Issues in Defining Evangelicalism

Many observers of the current debate on federal social provision in the United States view the attack on the social welfare state as growing out of the combined efforts of Evangelical Christians, who claim that welfare undermines individual self-discipline and rewards immoral behaviour, and economic conservatives, who view any infringement on the workings of the market as idolatry. In common parlance, the New Right and Evangelical Christianity are often used interchangeably, especially by liberal opponents who conjure up the spectre of an unholy alliance of Christian Fundamentalists, conservative Republicans, wayward southern Democrats, and the extreme Right fringe.[3] In the same vein, these critics tend to view the recent changes in the welfare system as examples of the insidious power of the Right, and a hapless attempt of disoriented Democrats to reclaim lost political territory by second-guessing the Republicans.

While these contentions hold widespread appeal, they are difficult to sustain on two grounds. First, the welfare state has essentially remained intact, due to both congressional resistance and organized pressure by a broad coalition of popular groups that organized in the wake of previous expansions of welfare programmes and included nonprofits, social workers, local government groups, and clients' organizations.[4] As a result, the Reagan administration's main successes were confined to weakening regulatory controls on business and to reducing or eliminating programmes benefiting the poor and minorities.[5]

Second, the link between theological and economic conservatism is tenuous at best. Evangelicalism is, by all accounts, a highly diverse and complex movement. As Robert Wuthnow concludes, at least two-thirds of the critical studies of conservative religion failed to discover a link between theological conservatism and other forms of conservative beliefs.[6] 'It is no exaggeration to say that capitalism has been one of the most divisive issues within American evangelicalism in recent decades', Craig Gay maintains. While Evangelicals at one point may have been unified as defenders of capitalism, 'a vociferous evangelical left ... has become increasingly influential over the last twenty years,' and even the Evangelical mainstream 'has become troubled by the issue of capitalism'.[7]

These divergent interpretations indicate that there is little consensus on defining the word 'Evangelical'. George Gallup's famous finding that 31 percent of Americans and 44 percent of Protestants are 'born-again' Christians remains intriguing, but controversial.[8] Theologically, a dozen distinct and frequently antagonistic traditions are typically grouped under the umbrella term 'American Evangelicalism', ranging from Pentecostals and the Holiness movement to Adventists and Mormons.[9] Socially, there is much debate about the role of class and status in the revival of religious conservatism. Politically, Evangelicalism consists of numerous groups with distinct social and economic views. Both Pat Robertson and Jesse Jackson are Evangelicals. Hence, Donald Dayton recently called Evangelicalism an 'essentially contested concept' and even suggested doing away with the term completely.[10]

Theological Diversity

For those scholars who focus on the power of belief itself and refuse to reduce religion to its social function, theological categories and beliefs remain at the centre of the Evangelical phenomenon.[11] Thomas Askew regards affirmation of the Bible as the sole authority, salvation through faith, conversion as a personal experience necessary for beginning a deliberate Christian life, the self-conscious nurture of spirituality, and both Evangelical mission and social witness as the basics of Evangelical conviction.[12] James Davison Hunter argues that biblical inerrancy, belief in the divinity of Christ, faith in Jesus as the only hope for salvation, and/or a powerful religious experience still important in everyday life are the marks of Evangelical identification.[13]

As self-evident and clear-cut as the theological approach may seem, it spells trouble nonetheless. Donald Bloesch, a conservative Evangelical, for example, rejects biblical absolutism because it places God's word 'in the power of man, since words and propositions can be mastered by reason'. For him, the Fundamentalist assumption of inerrancy runs counter to Evangelical mysticism.[14] Likewise, the conservative political scientist Stuart Rothenberg doubts that belief in inerrancy of the Bible is useful as a defining criterion. He found that 52 percent of born-again Christians and 54 percent of Fundamentalists do not agree with a strict interpretation of the Bible.[15] He also questions that the status of being 'born-again' is a necessary condition for classifying Evangelicals. Instead, he concludes that the descriptors 'born-again', 'Evangelical' and 'Fundamentalist' do not identify the same people.[16]

Conservative Protestantism is thus marked by deep theological divisions. In addition to a plethora of doctrinal differences, the key distinction emphasized in the critical literature is between Evangelicalism and Fundamentalism. While the 'theology of the word', meaning the adherence to literalism, legalism and formal doctrine, tends to identify Fundamentalists, the 'theology of the spirit,' meaning the emphasis on the intuitive, mystical Christian experience, forms the core of Evangelicalism.[17] Michael Lienesch thus sees Evangelicals primarily as traditionalists, while he considers Fundamentalists to be militant conservatives.[18] Likewise, Donald Dayton concludes that Fundamentalism can be considered an exclusivistic substratum within Evangelicalism.[19] Ernest Sandeen's argument, that dispensationalist premillennialism identifies twentieth-century Fundamentalists, lends support to this differentiation. Since premillennialism teaches that Christ's imminent second coming will mark the end of a long period of worldly corruption and decline, and dispensationalism sees the current 'church age' as marked by the corruption of the large churches of Christianity, Fundamentalists urge separation from the mainstream churches and elevate individual piety over social witness.[20]

Historically, Evangelical revivalism antedates separatist Fundamentalism and continues to be nurtured from different theological and political sources. Dayton traces American Evangelicalism to three major historical struggles that still inform Evangelical self-identification in the United States today. First, he credits the Reformation with promoting a biblical Christocentrism, justification by faith, and Augustinian anthropology with themes of election and bondage of the will. Second, the Great Awakenings of the eighteenth and nineteenth centuries brought a new quality to Evangelicalism, with the emphasis placed on personal conversion and being 'born-again', low-church mass evangelism, world mission and commitment to the doctrine of sanctification. In the third phase, Fundamentalism emerged from the Fundamentalist-modernist controversies of the early twentieth century, allying itself with political and social conservatism.[21]

The key is that these three stages form not only a historical sequence, but also an alternate presence, and continue to shape Evangelicalism today. I would agree with Dayton that we should 'preserve the label "Evangelical" for those expressing the ethos of the awakenings and revivals and continue to use the word "fundamentalist" to designate the descendants of the more recent conservative party.'[22]

In the 1940s, the rift between Fundamentalism and Evangelicalism was institutionalized in the formation of competing organizations. On the one hand, Carl McIntire's American Council of Christian Churches (1941) demanded strict separatism and doctrinal purity. On the other hand, the National Association of Evangelicals (1942) focused on evangelism and on creating a broad interdenominational evangelical basis (Harold John Ockenga, Carl F. H. Henry, Billy Graham).[23]

Social Characteristics

As far as common social characteristics of Evangelicals are concerned, the picture is equally blurred. Heeding Henry Steele Commager's old quip that well into the twentieth century religion in the United States prospered while theology went slowly bankrupt, many scholars discount the argument that the religious revival can be understood as a theological phenomenon and seek instead social and economic explanations. They find vindication in the fact that religion in the United States apparently does not change peoples' lives to the degree that one would expect from the level of professed faith. In addition, knowledge about the Bible remains limited among most Americans.[24]

However, interpretations which see Evangelicalism as linked to rural, older, poorer and less educated people have also been partially refuted.[25] Although it appears that lower social classes are more traditional in their belief, firmer in their conviction and more vigorous if they are involved in religious activities, and that Evangelicals are predominantly southern, midwestern and female, the data provides little conclusive evidence for matching Evangelicalism with class or social stratum.

Even the definition of conservative Christians as unreconstructed traditionalists harking back to pre-modern times is highly questionable.[26] The enlightenment paradigm that posits the inexorable appearance of the modern, which would ultimately undermine the hold of religious ideas and institutions, can work in wondrous ways.[27] Thus, James Davison Hunter regards Evangelicalism as part of an accommodation to cognitive and normative assumptions of modernity, replicating a process that liberal Protestantism underwent in the early part of the century. In his view, the personalization of the religious message in Evangelicalism constitutes a shift from 'a concern with the proclamation of an objective and universal truth to a concern with the subjective applicability of truth', and thus an 'alignment to the normative codes ... spawned by the contemporary milieu of pluralism'.[28]

Other modernist elements of Evangelicalism are its organizational emphasis on mobility, the absence of strong traditions and institutional ties and the embrace of Christian faith as an actively chosen status.[29] Similar parallels between the modern temper and the Evangelical mindset can be found in the voluntaristic spirit, the denial of authority and the deliberate air of spontaneity.[30] As Donald Dayton points out, the churches of the National Association of Evangelicals have also acted as social innovators. They are in the vanguard of the ordination of women, have a high percentage of female ministers and have introduced innovative and creative church experiments.[31] In addition, religious conservatives are eager to embrace the rationalized techniques of modern advertising and promotion. Historically, Evangelicals were masters of the modern technique of mass mailing and skilful in the use of the airwaves and television. The careers of Charles Finney, Dwight Moody, Billy Sunday, Carl McIntire, Charles Fuller and Billy Graham attest to this.[32]

Evangelicalism and the Politics of the Welfare State

These ambiguities have led some observers to conclude that Evangelicalism is best described as a temper or an ethos suffusing American culture, as in Bob Dylan singing 'He not busy bein' born is busy dying'.[33] This ranges from Alberoni's distinction between nascent and institutional religion, which extends into social and political life as an alternation between states of exhilaration and states of routine, to William McLoughlin's interpretation of American history as a series of revivals.[34] In the same vein, Michael Lienesch views redemptive campaigns that occur with regularity on the American political scene as stemming from a revivalist undercurrent that desires to confess sins, seek conversion and pursue a spiritual revolution.[35]

This raises the issue of the political meaning of Evangelicalism. A closer analysis of the political impact of Evangelicalism in the context of the development of social policies can add substance to this vague concept of an Evangelical temper. Post-1960s Evangelicalism can be considered a distinct and diverse political undercurrent that is equally suspicious of recent economic conservatism and of post-war liberalism. Though conservative Evangelicalism is most prominent in US politics as a result of a tremendous organizational effort and skilful lobbying, radical and liberal Evangelicals continue to vie with the conservatives for political influence.[36] While the New Right was able to tap into the anti-liberal sentiment and moral concerns of Evangelicals, its embrace of *laissez-faire* is one of its weakest planks, because capitalism itself helped undermine 'traditional values'.[37]

In his book *The True and Only Heaven*, Christopher Lasch sheds light on the political and cultural meaning of the revival of Evangelical religion. He views conservative moral indignation that decries permissiveness, pornography, abortion, welfare dependency and softness on crime as growing out of a lower-middle-class sense of decorum. According to Lasch, sincere concern about moral values in a self-indulgent consumer culture that lost its ethical bearings and brought socio-economic decline to the lower-middle and working classes was the cultural and intellectual basis of the backlash of the 1970s.

Invoking Reinhold Niebuhr's critique of liberalism, Lasch contends that liberals lack a tragic conception of life, a sense of limits, loss and defeat. He charges that they cling to a blind faith in progress and in the beneficent results of technology, economic growth, moral relativism and consumerism. This explains, in his opinion, why the New Right's focus on so-called 'social issues' struck a chord with the lower-middle-class ethic of personal accountability and neighbourly self-help, and its culture organized around family, church and neighbourhood.[38] The New Right was able to deflect traditional lower-middle-class resentment against corporate America and to cover up the fact that capitalism itself undermined the traditional values cherished by the petty-bourgeois classes.[39] However, according to Lasch, this should neither distract us from the movement's deeply-felt alienation from liberalism, nor from its potential to find 'moral inspiration in the popular radicalism of the past'.[40]

Lasch's argument is supported by the findings of political scientists who attribute the backlash of the 1970s and 1980s to a crisis in the Democratic Party and its post-war social agenda, rather than to a serious shift to the right in the electorate. As Michael K. Brown explains, New Deal and Great Society party building effectively precluded the development of a viable welfare state coalition.[41] What emerged instead was a 'segmented welfare state' in which federal income support programmes, non-wage benefits due to unionized welfare capitalism, and a plethora of federal and local in-kind transfer programmes served different social groups based on separate administrative mechanisms.[42]

Although Lyndon B. Johnson had hoped that the Great Society's dissolution of the boundary between contributory and assistance programmes would unite the social programme clientele, his policies actually heightened animosities between the poor and the middle classes. Since none of the programmes were financed through redistributionist tax policies, Kennedy, Johnson and Nixon 'shifted an increasing share of the burden of paying for the reduction in poverty to wage and salary earners, including the working poor'.[43] When inflation and tax increases began to eat up the real income of the lower and middle classes in the 1970s, a fateful schism between the New Deal and the Great Society wings of the Democratic Party developed.[44]

Evangelicals' traditional affinities with the Democratic Party fell victim to this political crisis, but their identification with traditional Democratic policies survived relatively unscathed. George Wallace's insurgent campaign in 1968, for example, attracted a significant Evangelical following with a platform that eschewed economic conservatism. His American Independent Party called for social security increases, better health care and a reaffirmation of the right to collective bargaining, prompting *National Review* to call Wallace's approach 'Country and Western Marxism'.[45] Likewise, Paul Weyrich, one of the architects of the New Right, felt intellectually much closer to William Jennings Bryan than to Friedrich Hayek.[46]

Jimmy Carter's political stance equally illustrated that it was not necessary to be a political conservative to be a full-fledged Evangelical.[47] He started the policy of deregulation, but was not adamantly committed to *laissez-faire* economics. He was a born-again Christian and a southerner, but also a defender of racial equality and a social reformer. Carter embodied the moderate, Niebuhrian, neo-Evangelical spirit of the resurgence of theological conservatism in the 1970s. It was the disenchantment with his presidency, rather than with the role of government in general, that ushered in the right-wing resurgence in the form of a coalition of neo-conservative intellectuals (Buckley, Podhoretz, Kristol, etc.), political conservatives (Paul Weyrich, Richard

Viguerie, Howard Phillips) and the New Christian Right (Falwell, Robertson, Robison).[48]

The political shift from Carter to Reagan, however, was not accompanied by a fundamental reorientation in the political views of many Evangelicals.[49] George Gallup found in the late 1980s that while Evangelicals were generally more conservative on matters of lifestyle than non-Evangelicals, they were slightly more liberal on some economic issues. While 74 percent of non-Evangelicals favoured raising the minimum wage, 83 percent of Evangelicals did. Seventy-two percent of Evangelicals and 71 percent of non-Evangelicals favoured increased spending on programmes for the elderly. Only 8 percent of Evangelicals (9 percent of non-Evangelicals) supported cutting entitlement programmes to reduce the deficit.[50] Large minorities of Evangelicals identified with causes such as environmentalism (39 percent) and civil rights (33 percent), and two-thirds supported the ERA.[51]

The polls revealed that non-Evangelicals and the religiously unaffiliated were the ones who were most clearly opposed to expanded government programmes. The 1988 election, George Gallup maintained, 'suggests that Democratic candidates are not hurt by, and are actually helped by relatively liberal economic programs.'[52] He saw the future of the party in crafting a platform defending traditional democratic economic policies and promoting a moderate image on social issues, especially on crime. In conclusion, political Evangelicalism's embrace of social conservatism does not automatically translate into support for conservative economic policies.

The Revival of Evangelical Social Reform and the Evangelical Left

In the 1970s, Evangelicals not only preserved their commitment to the basic welfare state, they also engaged in renewed charitable social activism. This constitutes one of the least studied aspects of the religious upsurge since the 1970s, mainly because the thesis of the 'great reversal' of Evangelicalism – the alleged switch from the nineteenth-century emphasis on social reform to a twentieth-century focus on personal piety and evangelism – had captured the imagination of most scholars. In addition, the media attention lavished on the apostles of the New Christian Right has made it difficult to divorce post-1960s revivalism from the images of pro-life demonstrations, anti-gay initiatives and Moral Majoritarianism.

Observers back in the 1970s, however, had a very different view of these events. In his classic study *It Seemed Like Nothing Happened*, Peter Carroll referred to the 'crossroads of possibility' of the period, and argued that the revival of conservatism was matched by the rise of what he calls 'community populism'.[53] Both movements were nurtured by widespread frustration with government, Vietnam and Watergate. However, while the conservatives 'forecast a world of endless opportunity and growth, the community populists predicted an era of roots and limits'.[54]

By the late 1970s, Carroll maintained, twenty million Americans participated in neighbourhood improvement organizations.[55] According to the journalist Robin Garr, only a few dozen viable community development organizations were in existence in 1970, whereas '[t]oday there are many thousands, from community development corporations to food banks, homeless shelters to self-help credit unions, job training organizations to banks'.[56] Other studies have shown that two-thirds of all social service nonprofits were formed after 1960.[57]

The community impulse of the early 1970s fitted into the personal contacts/small-group culture of Evangelicalism. Evangelicals had an advantage, because they already had a network of mutual aid societies, hospitals and other social service institutions in place. They were also skilled in modern promotion and organization geared to addressing problems emerging from a spiritual crisis.[58] But although many observers still consider involvement in social action the clearest difference between theological liberals and conservatives, the numbers do not bear this out.[59] As James Hunter reminds us, 'though liberals emphasize social concern rhetorically, it is the conservatives who are, in actual dollars, far more generous', giving approximately 47 percent more than the liberals.[60]

The rise of an Evangelical Left was instrumental in giving direction and vigour to the social activism that accompanied the religious resurgence.[61] A new generation of Evangelical Christians who rejected the social and political conservatism of established Evangelicalism without giving up the orthodox Christian faith emerged in the early 1970s. Attacking the blatant racism, sexism, militarism and indifference to economic injustice on the part of white churches and the political establishment, these insurgent Evangelicals such as Jim Wallis, John Howard Yoder, Clark Pinnock, Dale Brown and Art Gish made social action the distinguishing mark of their religious commitment.[62]

Two factors were crucial in this emergence. First, the changing composition of the Evangelical movement itself. Dominated since World War II by the National Association of Evangelicals, Billy Graham and the Evangelical Theological Society, the movement was predominantly white, middle-class, Calvinist and politically conservative. In the 1970s, however, a growing number of Evangelicals were recruited from minority groups, the poor, gays, intellectuals, Catholics, Wesleyans, and political liberals and radicals.[63] With the support of many older Evangelicals they formed organizations such as Evangelicals Concerned, the National Black Evangelical Association, Evangelical Women's Caucus and Evangelicals for Social Action.

Second, college campuses and religious seminaries became places where left-wing Evangelicals gained influence and visibility by appealing to zealous and highly educated students organized in the Inter-Varsity Christian Fellowship and similar groups.[64] Their efforts culminated in the 1973 Chicago Declaration, which attracted the support of such staunch Evangelical traditionalists as Carl F. H. Henry and Rufus Jones.[65] With Fuller Theological Seminary and other leading Evangelical training grounds as their strongholds, the left-wing Evangelicals challenged traditional teachings ranging from the subordination of women (Paul K. Jewett) to the doctrine of inerrancy (Daniel P. Fuller).[66] Theologically, the Evangelical Left rejected the theology of the word in favour of the theology of the spirit. With Karl Barth, Dietrich Bonhoeffer and Reinhold Niebuhr as their theological heroes, their focus was on the transforming power of the Bible, not on scripture as the retainer for divine truth.[67]

The new Evangelical Left developed in a number of ways. On the one hand, Arthur Gish, Jim Wallis and others emphasized the need to form alternative communities for living, worship and care for the poor. On the other hand, Paul B. Henry, Richard Pierard, Mark Hatfield and John Anderson strove for responsible participation in the political process and for the use of government to advance the cause of social justice. However, the hopeful beginnings of the early 1970s gave way to despair and fragmentation in the latter part of the decade. By the late 1970s, Left-liberal positions had become a rarity. However, the communitarian spirit remained alive and well, as Sojourner Community in Washington DC and other examples show.[68]

With the active support of the Evangelical Left, Evangelical social service activities became more formalized and attained a more prominent position in Evangelical rhetoric. In addition, at least four major parachurch social relief agencies were established.[69] Many existing Evangelical relief organizations, such as Medical Assistance Program, Compassion and World Relief Commission experienced significant growth in the 1970s.[70]

Many of the Evangelical nonprofits have long since expanded from single-purpose to multiple-purpose operations. They combine providing food and shelter with job training, economic development or housing.[71] On the local level they often developed out of 'the common-sense ideas of foot soldiers in the war against poverty'.[72] Among crucial Evangelical organizations, Robin Garr lists The Bridge, an alliance of a dozen Phoenix-area churches providing rent for homeless families; the Lutheran Church-Missouri Synod Church Extension

Fund; the Interfaith Hunger Coalition in Houston, Texas; Citizens for Community Development in Waterloo, Iowa; Sand Mountain Parish, which operates a cannery and offers employment and low-cost housing in rural Alabama; and the well-known Habitat for Humanity, which is not specifically Evangelical, but receives strong support from Evangelicals.[73]

The renewed involvement of Evangelical churches in inner-urban relief after a long period of downtown flight has been enhanced in the 1980s by organizations geared to address systemic issues such as economic development, job training, housing and legal aid. Harvie Conn lists the Church of the Saviour in Washington DC, La Salle Street Church in Chicago and the Church of the Nazarene in New York as examples.[74] Even more apparent is the upsurge in social concern among black Evangelical churches, which have ventured far into the area of medical aid, housing corporations and credit unions.[75] In light of this, the commonplace that the religious revival of the 1970s was marked by a retreat from social activism and a concentration on personal spirituality needs to be revised.[76] Beneath the media hype and the florid conversion stories of Charles Colson, Eric Clapton, Eldridge Cleaver and Larry Flynt, a more lasting legacy of renewed social activism was established during this time.[77]

Nonprofits and Federal Funding

The growth of Evangelical charities coincided with a little-noticed but crucial development in the funding of social service nonprofits, which ultimately redefined the relationship between the government and nonprofit providers. The Great Society's dramatic increase in the amount of money funnelled into nonprofit organizations through grants, contracts, tax exemptions, donations and purchase-of-service arrangements changed the entire structure of nonprofit funding.[78] Federal grants to service agencies, which amounted to $164 million in 1963, rose to $1.688 billion by 1972 and were only temporarily capped at $2.5 billion in 1973.[79]

The close funding and programme development contacts between government and the nonprofit sector continued to grow after the demise of the Great Society. The Social Security Act of 1974 'revolutionized the funding base of the nonprofits', and by 1977 government was providing over half of all the funds for nonprofit social service programmes.[80] Although the figure had dropped to 43.9 percent by 1984 due to cuts during the Reagan administration, the precedent set by the Great Society remained a stable element of post-Sixties relations between government and the nonprofit sector. In many cases, the states picked up where the federal government had left off.[81] During the first Clinton administration, Congress passed a major initiative for the creation of Community Empowerment Zones, providing funding for selected community development projects. This programme might point the way for future government involvement in the field of social provision in the United States, once the dust stirred up by the welfare debate has settled.[82]

The question at hand is to what extent changes in public funding influenced the role and development of Evangelical charities. Here more research is needed. The nonprofit sector remains to this date one of the least studied aspects of American society. As Robert Wuthnow contends, 'research on the connections between religion and giving remains relatively underdeveloped'.[83] However, preliminary evidence indicates that three crucial and somewhat contradictory developments occurred. First, the relationship between government and nonprofit charities has blurred the traditional distinction between the public and the private sector.[84] In many cases, privatization through contracting transformed private agencies into quasi-public agencies, and promoted a coalescence of interests between both sectors. Instead of leading to market control of social services, contracting out has resulted in greater public oversight of private nonprofit agencies, and has instilled their operations with the character of the public sector.[85]

Second, the cutbacks in government funding as part of Reagan administration policies have significantly augmented the importance of the churches as funders for many nonprofit groups.[86] As many tax-exempt organizations found government financing increasingly volatile, there has been an increasing tendency to rely on church and philanthropic funds.[87]

Third, nonprofit agencies and their employees have been particularly prominent in taking actions to avert the cuts planned by the Reagan administration.[88] Federal funding since the 1960s had thus created both a network of public and private contacts and a constituency ready to defend the welfare state. Considering the significance of Evangelical social services, the large percentage of Evangelical charitable donations and the blurring of religious and secular lines in nonprofit agencies, there is sufficient reason to infer that Evangelicals played a significant role in defending the welfare state.

Religious Narratives and the Contradictions of the US Welfare State

The analysis of Evangelical political attitudes, religious social service agencies and the funding ties between the government and the nonprofit sector is only one part of the story of the impact of Evangelicalism on the development of the US welfare state. The other part is the influence of Evangelical thought, imagery, narrative styles and moral sensitivities on defining social problems, prescribing the terms of the welfare debates and devising solutions.

The welfare state in the United States traditionally embodies the moral ambiguities and contradictions of American culture. Welfare policies, Joel Handler and Yeheskel Hasenfeld insist, are contending moral systems. They are not rational responses to objective conditions of poverty, but symbolic answers to ideological constructions of poverty.[89] This explains why US debates about welfare reform, which recur with almost predictable frequency, focus more on values than on finances. Both advocates of federal social provision and proponents of retrenchment draw upon moral tales that invoke fundamental narrative traditions of US culture.[90] Many of these narrative patterns reflect moral sensitivities that developed in the context of nineteenth-century Evangelical Protestantism and social reform.[91]

Three main conflicting intellectual impulses appear to be at work in the field of social policies. First, nineteenth-century *laissez-faire* liberalism in combination with traditional Calvinist dispositions. As far as social policies are concerned, its goal is to discipline the poor, impose work requirements and regulate moral conduct, rather than economic enterprise. The modern-day expression of this outlook is the strained coalition of Fundamentalists and neo-liberals.[92] Second, twentieth-century progressive liberalism. In the field of social provision it aims to distribute the fruits of an ever-expanding economy, to build up consumer buying power and to find comprehensive bureaucratic solutions to poverty. Its heyday was in the post-war era, but its political basis collapsed in the 1970s.[93] Third, revivalist Evangelicalism. Its goal is primarily to create a moral community of converted individuals. Social reform was a defining element of Christian revivalism in the nineteenth century. It remained a significant undercurrent of the Progressive movement and there are strong indications that the welfare debate in the United States today is equally steeped in a revivalistic Evangelical mode of thinking and acting.[94] It was this setting that tempted Richard Hofstadter to comment that American reform was marked by a 'breadth of feeling' and a 'shallowness of social analysis' – a comment that many Evangelicals might not necessarily take as an insult.[95]

Evangelical Social Thought

At the centre of Evangelical social thought is the concept of conversion. In a world that is fundamentally sinful, genuine social reform, according to Evangelical teachings, cannot be effected through human reason based on rational self-interest, since the root causes of human ills are the sinful heart and mind.[96] Steeped in Augustinian thought, Evangelical social reform acknowledges the limits of human rationality and human agency. It insists on the need to awaken the conscience of the individual and to recognize the sinfulness expressed in both the cult of human rationality and the surrender to passions and desires. In Evangelical parlance, both of these keep the individual imprisoned in cyclical patterns of worldly dependency.

Evangelical reform is couched in stories of sin and salvation, repentance and reformation, despair and conversion, imprisonment and release, dependency and liberation, awakening and sanctification. Its semantic and emotional worlds are steeped in nineteenth-century revivalism and twentieth-century neo-orthodoxy. Charles Finney and Reinhold Niebuhr are the intellectual yardsticks of Evangelical social reform. While Finney provided the language of personal emotional involvement, unmediated access to God, inspiration and transformation, Niebuhr added an awareness of human limitations, a new focus on interpersonal relations and a more realistic assessment of political power.

The key distinction between Evangelical and liberal reform thought is the almost complete absence of the social rights discourse in Evangelicalism. Charity, unlike grace, is not freely given, but requires work in return. It is not an entitlement, but a gift. Receivers are supposed to turn to God, which means they are expected to be productive and responsible.[97] As one leading Fundamentalist put it, 'charity involves honest, tough love'.[98]

This type of thinking can lead to embracing contradictory approaches to social reform. It reflects the rift between Evangelicalism and Fundamentalism that Timothy Weber described as the split between the theology of the spirit and the theology of the word. On the one hand, Evangelical social service is generous and caring in trying to effect conversion. It believes in the basic dignity, freedom and moral potential of the aid recipient. On the other hand it can be merciless in its stigmatization of those seen as wayward and undeserving. It blames the poor for their fate and for bringing moral corruption upon the community, and primarily desires to discipline and punish them.

However, in Evangelical thought, conversion was never considered a one-way street. Left Evangelicalism, in particular, embraces the concept of the 'epistemological privilege of the poor'. Wealthy Christians who refuse to identify with and act on behalf of the poor are seen as incapable of truly understanding the biblical message. Thus, attending to the poor is part of the search for the spiritual gift of discernment.[99] Jane Addams, though not an Evangelical herself, eloquently expressed this sentiment: 'Nothing so deadens the sympathies and shrivels the power of enjoyment as the persistent keeping away from the great opportunities for helpfulness ... These longings for helpfulness are the physical complement of the "Intimations of Immortality", on which no ode has yet been written.'[100] In more than one way, constructing the 'other' is part of constructing oneself in social welfare.

The Social Policy Dilemma

Evangelical reform thought and imagery, it can be argued, accounts for the basic tension in the US welfare state between the goal of disciplining the poor and the aim of converting and rehabilitating them. As many excellent studies have shown, gender issues are best suited to reveal these often contradictory impulses of social legislation in the twentieth century.[101] On the one hand, welfare programmes are designed to enable poor mothers to stay at home and take care of the children. On the other hand, policies are meant to discourage welfare as an alternative to paid work. In the same vein, welfare payments are mostly geared to single-parent families headed by mothers, yet means tests, man-in-the-house rules, and suitable-home rules at various times enforced the ideal of the nuclear family. As a result, mother-headed households are both stigmatized and legitimated.[102]

The focus on character issues in the US debate on social policies; the emphasis on individual casework; the belief in rehabilitation rather than maintenance, and the constant sense of the failure of social legislation also reflect the influence of Evangelical topoi.[103] Even during the Great Society programmes, when the most fervent effort was made to part with the tradition of morally-charged categorizing, the aim remained to transform the poor, as Alice O'Connor has shown in a recent paper.[104] This goal was embedded in the liberal 'culture of poverty' argument that saw the poor as intrinsically hedonistic, improvident, unable to defer gratification and trapped in cycles of dependency.[105] This argument also anticipated the later right-wing critique of permissiveness.[106]

The closest the US welfare system ever came to a limited effort to make social provision simply a matter of economic income maintenance was the Family Assistance Plan of the Nixon administration, which was voted down in Congress.[107] The failure of Carter's plan to combine 'workfare' and guaranteed income in 1977 ended comprehensive reform efforts in this direction.[108] The next major step, the Family Support Act of 1988, construed by Daniel Patrick Moynihan, returned priority to a welfare-to-work policy which has informed welfare reform since.[109] 'Workfare' became the magic word.

If we jump to the welfare reforms of 1996, we see the continuation of this pattern. 'From the moment someone walks through the door, every signal ought to be that work is the ultimate goal and expectation,' wrote the Clinton adviser David Ellwood.[110] His admonition that welfare should not be simply about eligibility and cheque writing mirrors the Evangelical demand that assistance should be based on face-to-face giving and receiving. However, as job placements and requirements became the measure of success for welfare policies, Social Security scooped off the easy cases, leaving welfare with the hard ones and thus adding to the stigma of welfare.[111] This indicates that, the 'key purpose of the work requirement is not actually to set welfare recipients to work, but to reaffirm the work ethic, to confirm the importance of work in defining social, gender, and ethnic status, and to legitimate the morality of low-wage work.'[112] Workfare policies thus serve to perpetuate poverty as a warning to those who might be tempted to slacken off in their work habits.

The work requirement enforces discipline, without pursuing the goal of the mutual inner transformation of both giver and recipient. This appears to be the general tendency of the most recent changes in the welfare system. Important vestiges of the conversionist and protective construction of social provision are crumbling. The Clinton administration has accelerated this erosion by ending the federal AFDC programme, by including mothers and the disabled in the group of aid recipients expected to work, and by excluding many legal immigrants from receiving benefits. At the same time, Clinton has returned to Evangelical modes by using the bully pulpit for moral crusades against specific evils.[113]

Welfare policies remain a contested terrain in US society. Unlike in economics, where the fundamental axioms of the market, profit, economic growth and competition are rarely questioned, the interpretive monopoly of experts does not hold sway in the area of social policies. Moral feelings have retained legitimacy and political significance. Political Evangelicalism in all its facets constitutes one of the most important moral parameters of American society. Its study is a key to understanding the cultural, political and moral dynamics of US social reform and social policies. In the final analysis, the old nineteenth century conflict between scientific charity, which was scrupulously utilitarian in its calculation of benefits so that no pauper might find relief more rewarding than work, and religious philanthropy, which desired to relieve suffering first and ask questions later, remains one of the central features of the system of social provision in the United States.[114]

Notes

1. George Marsden, *Understanding Fundamentalism and Evangelicalism* (Grand Rapids, MI: William B. Eerdmans, 1991), 63.
2. I tend to agree with Leo Ribuffo, who notes a paranoid strain in the liberal perception of the New Right. Themes born in the polemics of the 1930s, he argues, were recycled to interpret the rise of the Protestant Right in the 1960s. Calling the Left-liberal attack on the Christian Right a 'failure of thought ... and nerve', Ribuffo warns about a 'brown scare' of secular liberals overstating the power of the Right. See Ribuffo, *The Old Christian Right. The Protestant Far Right from the Great Depression to the Cold War* (Philadelphia: Temple University Press, 1983), 261, 273.
3. Alonzo Hamby maintains that the central tenet of the New Right, 'composed of evangelical Protestants and an emergent class of policy intellectuals', is supply-side economics. See *Liberalism and Its Challengers: FDR to Reagan* (New York: Oxford University Press, 1985), 356–7; see also Ralph W. Hood and Ronald J. Morris, 'Boundary Maintenance, Social-Political Views, and the Presidential Preference among High and Low Fundamentalists', *Review of Religious Research* 27 (December 1985): 135–6. James Davison Hunter argues that the 'association between Protestant orthodoxy and political conservatism is perhaps the most reliable and enduring commonplace concerning this subject'. Cited in Michael Lienesch, *Redeeming America. Piety and Politics in the New Christian Right* (Chapel Hill: University of North Carolina Press, 1993), 19. See also Christopher Lasch, *The True and Only Heaven. Progress and Its Critics* (New York: W. W. Norton, 1991), 476–7; and Barbara Ehrenreich, 'The New Right Attack on Social Welfare', in Fred Block *et al.*, *The Mean Season. The Attack on the Welfare State* (New York: Pantheon Books, 1987), 162.
4. Frances Fox Piven and Richard A. Cloward, 'Popular Power and the Welfare State', in Michael K. Brown, ed., *Remaking the Welfare State. Retrenchment and Social Policy in America and Europe* (Philadelphia: Temple University Press, 1988), 88, 92.
5. This includes employment training funds, Aid to Families with Dependent Children (AFDC), food stamps, and medicaid. The New Federalism did not result in significant programme cutting, because many state governments maintained or even expanded them. See Piven and Cloward, 'Popular Power', 75–6. One of the main results of Reagan's policies, J. David Greenstone argues, was to preclude further advances in the social welfare area, both from a political and from a financial point of view, since the massive military build-up created a barrier to the creation of new programmes. See J. David Greenstone, 'The Decline and Revival of the American Welfare State: Moral Criteria and Instrumental Reasoning in Critical Elections', in Brown, *Remaking the Welfare State*, 167. Some scholars have concluded that the Reagan years were no more than a mid-course correction in the development of the US welfare state. They point out that Reagan continued the retrenchment started during the Carter years, and that tax reforms actually resulted in larger income for

the poor. See Barbara Gottschalk and Peter Gottschalk, 'The Reagan Retrenchment in Historical Context', in Brown, *Remaking the Welfare State*, 62, 71.
6. Cited in Hood and Morris, 'Boundary Maintenance', 136.
7. Craig Gay, *With Liberty and Justice for Whom? The Recent Evangelical Debate over Capitalism* (Grand Rapids, MI: William B. Eerdmans, 1991), 1–2.
8. The number of committed Evangelicals already drops significantly when other qualifiers are added, such as encouraging others to believe in Christ, and belief in the literal interpretation of the Bible. See George Gallup Jr and Jim Castelli, *The People's Religion. American Faith in the 90s* (New York: Macmillan, 1989), 13.
9. Donald W. Dayton and Robert K. Johnston, eds, *The Variety of American Evangelicalism* (Knoxville: The University of Tennessee Press, 1991), 2.
10. Donald W. Dayton, 'Some Doubts about the Usefulness of the Category "Evangelical",' in Dayton and Johnston, *Variety of Evangelicalism*, 245.
11. See Lienesch, *Redeeming America*, 20; Marsden, *Understanding Fundamentalism*, 116–17.
12. Robert K. Johnston, 'American Evangelicalism: An Extended Family', in Dayton and Johnston, *Variety of Evangelicalism*, 261.
13. Cited in Stuart Rothenberg and Frank Newport, *The Evangelical Voter. Religion and Politics in America* (Washington, DC: The Institute for Government and Politics, 1984), 25. George Gallup substantiates this claim with his 1988 findings that 78 percent of Americans believe Jesus was the son of God or God; that 93 percent of Evangelicals have no doubt about Christ's return; that the percentage of those who believe in the literal truth of the Bible is still at 31 percent; and that 33 percent of Americans claim to have had 'a religious experience, a particularly powerful religious insight or awakening'. See Gallup and Castelli, *People's Religion*, 60–1, 63, 66, 68–9.
14. Donald G. Bloesch, *The Future of Evangelical Christianity. A Call for Unity Amid Diversity* (Garden City, NY: Doubleday, 1983), ix.
15. Rothenberg, *Evangelical Voter*, 32. However, Rothenberg's findings might be compromised by his close ties to Paul Weyrich, the New Right, and the Free Congress Foundation.
16. Rothenberg, *Evangelical Voter*, 13.
17. In Johnston, 'Extended Family', 264–8.
18. Lienesch, *Redeeming America*, 15; Marsden, *Understanding Fundamentalism*, 67.
19. Dayton and Johnston, *Variety of Evangelicalism*, 1. See also page 246.
20. George Marsden, 'Fundamentalism and American Evangelicalism', in Dayton and Johnston, *Variety of Evangelicalism*, 25; Marsden, *Understanding Fundamentalism*, 100–1.
21. Johnston, 'Extended Family', 254; Donald Dayton, 'The Social and Political Conservatism of Modern American Evangelicalism: A Preliminary Search for the Reasons', *Union Seminary Quarterly Review* 22 (Winter 1977): 73.
22. Dayton, 'Social and Political Conservatism', 74.
23. See Marsden, 'Fundamentalism and Evangelicalism', 29–30. The emer-

gence of large-scale Fundamentalist political activism since the late 1970s (Jerry Falwell, Moral Majority, Christian Coalition) and its emphasis on coalition-building across theological and ideological lines has caused serious rifts within the Fundamentalist movement. See Marsden, *Understanding Fundamentalism*, 101.
24. Eight in ten Americans say they are Christians, but only four in ten know that Jesus delivered the Sermon on the Mount, and only 50 percent could name the four gospels. George Gallup talks about a 'cycle of biblical illiteracy' in this context. Gallup and Castelli, *People's Religion*, 20, 60.
25. For an example of the rural-urban approach see Winthrop S. Hudson, *Religion in America* (New York: Scribner's Sons, 1965). For references to research on lower-class features, see R. Stephen Warner, *New Wine in Old Wineskins. Evangelicals and Liberals in a Small-Town Church* (Berkeley: University of California Press, 1988), 59; see also Gallup and Castelli, *People's Religion*, 73–4, 94. For a critique of these interpretations, see Rothenberg, *Evangelical Voter*, 27, 31, 32, 34. Rothenberg claims that the researcher 'can create a sample of evangelical Christians in this country who are distinctly different from other Christians simply by tailoring his definition', page 35.
26. Leon McBeth, 'Baptist Fundamentalism: A Cultural Interpretation', in Martin E. Marty, ed., *Fundamentalism and Evangelicalism* (Munich: K. G. Saur, 1993), 210; Marsden, *Understanding Fundamentalism*, 108.
27. For a concise description of the enlightenment paradigm, see M. L. Bradbury and James B. Gilbert, eds, *Transforming Faith. The Sacred and Secular in Modern American History* (New York: Greenwood Press, 1989), ix–x.
28. James Davison Hunter, *Evangelicalism. The Coming Generation* (Chicago: University of Chicago Press, 1987), 47. See also Joel Carpenter, 'Revive Us Again: Alienation, Hope, and the Resurgence of Fundamentalism, 1930–1950', in Bradbury and Gilbert, *Transforming Faith*, 105.
29. Carpenter, 'Revive Us Again,' 105; see also Warner, *New Wine*, 72.
30. The Evangelical disposition to embrace total transformation can be compared to the Enlightenment belief in the ability to make the world over again.
31. Dayton, 'Some Doubts', 246–7.
32. See Marsden, *Understanding Fundamentalism*, 120–1. Marsden also discusses the contradictions involved in this. See also page 82.
33. See, for example, Timothy Weber as cited in Johnston, 'Extended Family,' 263.
34. Cited in Warner, *New Wine*, 45–6; William McLoughlin, *Revivals, Awakenings, and Reform. An Essay on Religion and Social Change in America, 1607–1977* (Chicago: University of Chicago Press, 1978), 213–14.
35. Lienesch, *Redeeming America*, 47.
36. See, for example, Gay, *Liberty and Justice*.
37. Lienesch, *Redeeming America*, 108ff.; Ribuffo, *New Christian Right*, 274; for a discussion of conservative social Evangelicalism, see also Augustus Cerillo Jr, 'A Survey of Recent Evangelical Social Thought', *Christian Scholar's Review* 5 (1976): 273.
38. Lasch, *True and Only Heaven*, 486–8.

39. *Ibid.*, 509, 512, 516, 518.
40. *Ibid.*, 532.
41. Piven and Cloward, 'Popular Power,' 80; Michael K. Brown, 'The Segmented Welfare System: Distributive Conflict and Retrenchment in the United States, 1968–1984,' in Brown, *Remaking the Welfare State*, 204.
42. Brown, 'Segmented Welfare System', 188, *passim*. Examples of federal income support programmes for the industrial workforce include social security and unemployment insurance. Non-wage benefits are mostly confined to health insurance, disability insurance and pensions. Federal and local in-kind transfer programmes consist mainly of food stamps, medicaid, and relief programmes such as the recently abolished AFDC.
43. Brown, 'Segmented Welfare System', 196. On income redistribution see also Gottschalk and Gottschalk, 'Reagan Retrenchment', 62. See also Piven and Cloward, 'Popular Power', 87.
44. Brown, 'Segmented Welfare System,' 203. Despite the growing antipathy to welfare spending, levels of support for public spending in general remained high. See page 198.
45. Cited in Lasch, *True and Only Heaven*, 505.
46. *Ibid.*; Ehrenreich, 'New Right Attack,' 181.
47. Marsden, *Understanding Fundamentalism*, 105.
48. See Lienesch, *Redeeming America*, 8; Ribuffo, *Old Christian Right*, 263. In the meantime, the Evangelicals had become hopelessly divided over theological and political issues. See Marsden, *Understanding Fundamentalism*, 76. Although in the 1980 election, Carter still had the support of Oral Roberts and Jim Bakker in the three-way race featuring himself, John Anderson, who had solid Left-liberal Evangelical credentials, and Ronald Reagan, who also claimed the now-respectable status of born-again Christian, Carter lost many of the Evangelical votes he had gained in 1976; see Leo Ribuffo, 'God and Jimmy Carter,' in Bradbury and Gilbert, *Transforming Faith*, 155; Lienesch, *Redeeming America*, 7–8; Marsden, *Understanding Fundamentalism*, 77. In the end it turned out that Reagan adopted little more than Fundamentalist rhetoric, continuing the trend toward the southernization of the political discourse, while doing almost nothing to push for Fundamentalist demands such as anti-abortion policies and school prayer. Hence, there is much controversy about the strength of political Fundamentalism in the late 1970s and early 1980s. See Rothenberg, *Evangelical Voter*, 5; Lienesch, *Redeeming America*, 2.
49. See Gallup and Castelli, *People's Religion*, 16; Rothenberg, *Evangelical Voter*, 77–8. See also Seymour Martin Lipset and Earl Raab, 'The Election and the Evangelicals', *Commentary* 71 (March 1981): 25–31.
50. Gallup and Castelli, *People's Religion*, 94, 98.
51. *Ibid.*, 215.
52. *Ibid.*, 217, 249.
53. Cited in Allen F. Davis and Harold D. Woodman, *Conflict and Consensus in Modern American History* (Lexington, MA: D. C. Heath, 1988), 539.
54. Davis and Woodman, *Conflict and Consensus*, 540.
55. *Ibid.*, 528.
56. Robin Garr, *Reinvesting in America. The Grassroots Movements That Are*

Feeding the Hungry, Housing the Homeless, and Putting Americans Back to Work (Reading, MA: Addison-Wesley Publishing Co., 1995), viii.
57. Piven and Cloward, 'Popular Power,' 90.
58. See Marsden, *Understanding Fundamentalism*, 104–5; Ronald B. Flowers, *Religion in Strange Times. The 1960s and 1970s* (n.p.: Mercer University Press, 1984), 52.
59. For an example of this distinction between liberal and conservative religion see Flowers, *Strange Times*, 53.
60. Hunter, *Coming Generation*, 256 n. 30. It would be interesting to see if the distinction between Evangelicalism and Fundamentalism I outlined earlier is mirrored in the kind and extent of social service activities. Charitable giving and belief in charity is also one of the most important differences between religious and secular conservatives. The New Christian Right is actively present in the field of social charities, though it limits its range to specific areas. See Lienesch, *Redeeming America*, 124–125.
61. Leonard Sweet states that '[i]n the second sixties and the seventies evangelicals ... restored a social dimension to the faith that had been missing in conservative Christianity for many years'. See Leonard Sweet, 'The 1960s: The Crisis of Liberal Christianity and the Public Emergence of Evangelicalism', in George Marsden, ed., *Evangelicalism and Modern America* (Grand Rapids, MI: William B. Eerdmans, 1984), 44.
62. Richard Quebedeaux, *The Worldly Evangelicals* (San Francisco: Harper and Row, 1978), xi; Flowers, *Strange Times*, 55–6. In a recent conversation with the author, Richard Pierard argued that Quebedeaux's focus on the 'young evangelicals' underestimated the role older Evangelicals played in the emergence of the Evangelical Left in the 1970s.
63. Quebedeaux, *Worldly Evangelicals*, 164.
64. For figures on views of evangelical seminarians and collegians on social ministry see Hunter, *Coming Generation*, 43; Flowers, *Strange Times*, 42–3.
65. Quebedeaux, *Worldly Evangelicals*, 84; Flowers, *Strange Times*, 56.
66. For a discussion of the various colleges, see Quebedeaux, *Worldly Evangelicals*, 84–97; Hunter, *Coming Generation*, 43ff.; and Flowers, *Strange Times*, 42–3.
67. For a more detailed discussion see Quebedeaux, *Worldly Evangelicals*, 98–100.
68. For further details on the development of the Evangelical Left see Quebedeaux, *Worldly Evangelicals*, 147ff.; Cerillo, 'Survey of Evangelical Social Thought', 276ff.; and Marsden *Understanding Fundamentalism*, 74ff.
69. Hunter, *Coming Generation*, 42.
70. *Ibid.*, 257 n. 35.
71. Garr, *Reinvesting*, xii.
72. *Ibid.*, 7.
73. *Ibid.*, 32, 43–5, 77, 89f, 169–70, 196; see also Harvie Conn, *The American City and the Evangelical Church. A Historical Overview* (Grand Rapids, MI: Baker Books, 1994), 159.
74. Conn, *American City*, 153.
75. For a discussion of the role of philanthropy in the black community, see

Emmett D. Carson, 'Patterns of Giving in Black Churches', in Robert Wuthnow, Virginia Hodgkinson and Associates, *Faith and Philanthropy in America: Exploring the Role of Religion in America's Voluntary Sector* (San Francisco: Jossey-Bass Publishers, 1990), 232–52.
76. James Davison Hunter, *American Evangelicalism. Conservative Religion and the Quandary of Modernity* (New Brunswick, NJ: Rutgers University Press, 1983), 46.
77. In the words of Leonard Sweet, therapeutic Christianity, promising success and health through faith, used Jesus as a 'kind of theological chaser, making it all go down easier'. Sweet, 'Crisis of Liberal Christianity', 34; see also Marsden, *Understanding Fundamentalism*, 78.
78. Michael O'Neill, *The Third America. The Emergence of the Nonprofit Sector in the United States* (San Francisco: Jossey-Bass Publishers, 1989), 96–7.
79. Stephen Rathgeb Smith and Deborah A. Stone, 'The Unexpected Consequences of Privatization', in Brown, *Remaking the Welfare State*, 237–8. See also Kenneth A. Wedel, Arthur J. Katz and Ann Weick, eds, *Social Service by Government Contract: A Policy Analysis* (New York: Praeger, 1979), vi–vii.
80. O'Neill, *Third America*, 97.
81. 'Even after the 1981 cutbacks ... there has been no (or relatively minor) retrenchment in terms of overall levels of spending.' Smith and Stone, 'Unexpected Consequences', 240.
82. See Garr, *Reinvesting*, ix.
83. Robert Wuthnow, 'Improving Our Understanding of Religion and Giving: Key Issues for Research,' in Wuthnow *et al.*, *Faith and Philanthropy*, 271.
84. O'Neill, *Third America*, 105. See also Wedel *et al.*, *Social Services*, vi.
85. Smith and Stone, 'Unexpected Consequences', 235, 240.
86. Alan Rabinowitz, *Social Change Philanthropy in America* (New York: Quorum Books, 1990), 123.
87. Tracy Daniel Connors, *The Nonprofit Organization Handbook* (New York: McGraw-Hill, 1980), 4–6. Of course this tendency is embraced by the New Christian Right, which wishes to create a church-centred alternative to the welfare state. See Lienesch, *Redeeming America*, 137. In general, churches and synagogues in the United States are in the vanguard of providing money for social service efforts. Their contributions often amount to more than what all foundations and corporations combined provide. O'Neill, *The Third America*, 23.
88. Piven and Cloward, 'Popular Power', 92.
89. Joel Handler and Yeheskel Hasenfeld, *The Moral Construction of Poverty. Welfare Reform in America* (Newbury Park: Sage Publications, 1991), 2.
90. Robert B. Reich identifies four basic 'myth-based morality tales that determine when we declare a fact a problem, how policy choices are characterized, how the debate is framed'. He calls them 'The Mob at the Gates', 'The Triumphant Individual', 'The Benevolent Community', and the 'Rot at the Top'. See Robert B. Reich, *Tales of a New America* (New York: Times Books, 1987), 6–7, *passim*. It should be noted that Reich, a Harvard economist, was secretary of labour in the first Clinton administration.

91. See Alan Heimert, *Religion and the American Mind from the Great Awakening to the Revolution* (Cambridge, MA: Harvard University Press, 1966); Timothy Smith, *Revivalism and Social Reform: American Protestantism on the Eve of the Civil War*, rev. ed. (Baltimore, MD: Johns Hopkins University Press, 1980); Anne C. Loveland, *Southern Evangelicals and the Social Order, 1800–1860* (Baton Rouge, Louisiana State University Press, 1980).
92. David J. Greenstone argues that Reagan embodies this combination of *laissez-faire* and Calvinist themes. See Greenstone, 'Decline and Revival,' 172. See also Lienesch, *Redeeming America*, 124–138, for an excellent discussion of Fundamentalist and Evangelical views of social welfare.
93. For an incisive critique of post-war liberalism, see Lasch, *True and Only Heaven*, esp. 476–523.
94. A *Times Mirror* study concludes that 'religion is a major factor in determining political attitudes' and that politically active Americans are more likely to be highly religious. See Gallup and Castelli, *People's Religion*, 167, 224. For a useful but limited study on the significance of Evangelicalism in the Progressive movement, see Robert M. Crunden, *Ministers of Reform. The Progressives' Achievement in American Civilization, 1889–1920* (New York: Basic Books, 1982).
95. Cited in William Lee Miller, 'American Religion and American Political Attitudes', in James Ward Smith and A. Leland Jamison, eds, *Religious Perspectives in American Culture* (Princeton, NJ: Princeton University Press, 1961), 108. See also Richard Hofstadter, *The Age of Reform. From Bryan to F.D.R.* (New York: Vintage Books, 1955).
96. George Gallup concludes that Evangelicals distinguish themselves by crediting traditional religious values (56 percent), rather than reason and intellect based on learning and experience (36 percent), with the advancement of mankind. Gallup and Castelli, *People's Religion*, 70.
97. Lienesch, *Redeeming America*, 129. R. Stephen Warner noticed with mild surprise when he attended an evangelical service in celebration of the 1976 bicentennial that the scriptural text was not the Declaration of Independence, but the Mayflower compact. The sermon emphasized responsibility, restraint and liberty through self-control, and held up self-imposed constraint as a guarantee against government control. Warner, *New Wine*, 8.
98. George Grant of the Christian Worldview Institute, cited in Lienesch, *Redeeming America*, 127.
99. Gay, *Liberty and Justice*, 60.
100. Jane Addams, 'The Subjective Necessity of Social Settlements (1892)', in David A. Hollinger and Charles Capper, eds, *The American Intellectual Tradition. A Sourcebook*, vol. 2, *1865 to the Present* (New York: Oxford University Press, 1993), 160.
101. Among the studies that address this issue are Linda Gordon, ed., *Women, the State, and Welfare* (Madison: University of Wisconsin Press, 1991); Linda Gordon, *Pitied But Not Entitled. Single Mothers and the History of Welfare* (Cambridge, MA: Harvard University Press, 1995); and Mimi Abramowitz, *Regulating the Lives of Women: Social Welfare Policy from Colonial Times to the Present* (Boston: South End Press, 1988).

102. For a detailed discussion of the gender-related contradictions, see Wendy Sarvasy, 'Reagan and Low-Income Mothers: A Feminist Recasting of the Debate,' in Brown, *Remaking the Welfare State*, 253–76. See also Handler and Hasenfeld, *Moral Construction*, 37.
103. In the nineteenth century, character talk was an expression of the close association of bourgeois social norms of self-help, productivity and competitive achievement, with the Evangelical demand for self-control, personal piety and stable community and family life. These two traditions began to diverge in the twentieth century with the advent of consumer culture and its hedonistic imperative. See Ehrenreich, 'New Right Attack', 182; see also Lasch, *True and Only Heaven*, 487.
104. Alice O'Connor, 'Neither Charity nor Relief: The War on Poverty and the Efforts to Redefine the Basis of Social Provision' (paper presented at the conference 'From Poor Law to the Modern Welfare State: Private Charity and Public Assistance in Historical Perspective', Saint Louis University, Saint Louis, MO, 1996), 21.
105. O'Connor, 'Neither Charity nor Relief', 12; Ehrenreich, 'New Right Attack', 175; for an in-depth study of the Great Society, see Allen J. Matusow, *The Unraveling of America: A History of Liberalism in the 1960s* (New York: Harper and Row, 1984).
106. For example the charge that AFDC enabled young women to scoff at parental authority and indulge in sexual promiscuity. Ehrenreich, 'New Right Attack', 175.
107. In fact, many of the arguments about the immoral results of entitlements that dominated the discussion of the 1980s and '90s emerged from the debate over the Family Assistance Plan. See O'Connor, 'Neither Charity nor Relief,' 10; see also Edward Berkowitz, *America's Welfare State* (Baltimore, MD: Johns Hopkins University Press, 1991), 122–32.
108. Berkowitz, *America's Welfare State*, 140.
109. The law established state education and training programmes, transitional childcare and medical benefits and stronger child support enforcement. While the programme was infused with rehabilitative overtones and seemingly generous provisions for childcare, it emphasized first and foremost the work requirement. See Handler and Hasenfeld, *Moral Construction*, 205.
110. David Ellwood, 'Welfare Reform As I Knew It', *The American Prospect* 26 (May–June 1996): 23.
111. Berkowitz, *America's Welfare State*, 147.
112. Handler and Hasenfeld, *Moral Construction*, 40.
113. In a front page article in the *International Herald Tribune*, R. W. Apple recently observed with barely concealed disdain that President Clinton had now appointed himself chief of the vice police. 'Not for many a day has a president tried as hard as Bill Clinton to save Americans from their bad habits, like smoking and drinking,' Apple noted. In the name of the nation's children the president had attacked the tobacco and liquor industry, regulated pornography and headed off moves to legalize marijuana. Since the electorate has trouble seeing Clinton as a beacon of moral righteousness, Apple surmises that this crusading spirit is rooted in the

president's personal history (he is the son of an alcoholic and has a brother who had a drug problem), and in political expediency, since the political appeal of the bully pulpit is infinitely enhanced by the fact that it does not cost the public a dime. The article does not mention Clinton's southern Baptism as an explanation for his actions.

114. Recent examples of this conflict include the debates in the 1970s and 1980s over bureaucratic tightening, cost efficiency and measurability of social programmes, as opposed to the renewed community-based non-profits which emphasized mission and community building. Peter Dobkin Hall, 'The History of Religious Philanthropy in America', in Robert Wuthnow *et al.*, *Faith and Philanthropy*, 56.